Deng Xiaoping and the Chinese Revolution

To the outside world Deng Xiaoping represents a contradiction – he is both China's supreme leader who must take responsibility for the events surrounding Tiananmen Square in June 1989, and the man who, more than any other, has been responsible for reform and economic growth since the late 1970s. However, Deng the politician has no such contradiction: in his view only the Chinese Communist Party can bring modernization to China. For Deng, any threat to the Communist Party is a threat to the project of China's modernization.

This book attempts to reach beyond the spectacular economic success of recent years to understand Deng's own particular role and the sources of his political power. Deng Xiaoping was involved with the communist movement before there was even a Communist Party of China, and his entire career has been shaped by both the party and the network of relationships and people within it. David Goodman explores the way in which Deng has survived being purged three times via his contacts with key politicians: Zhou Enlai from Paris in the early 1920s and Mao Zedong after 1933. His close relationship with the military, from the Sino-Japanese War of 1937 through to the present day, has also enabled him to survive difficult political periods. Indeed, Deng's wartime experience, in the Taihang Mountains, plays a central but often overlooked role in his later career, particularly as a source of political support.

David Goodman has been able to draw on the substantial documentary sources that have become available from China since 1989 as well as on the analysis of Deng's political life that has proliferated inside the People's Republic in recent years. In addition, this biography includes a catalogue and analysis of the speeches and writings of Deng Xiaoping since 1938 which will prove to be an invaluable reference aid to his years of influence and power. The result is a balanced evaluation of Deng the politician which provides fresh insights into the career of one of the twentieth century's greatest political survivors.

David S.G. Goodman is Director of the new Institute for International Studies at the University of Technology, Sydney.

Deng Xiaoping and the Chinese Revolution

A political biography

David S.G. Goodman

London and New York

First published 1994
by Routledge
11 New Fetter Lane, London EC4P 4EE

Simultaneously published in the USA and Canada
by Routledge
29 West 35th Street, New York, NY 10001

Typeset in Times by
Solidus (Bristol) Limited
Printed and bound in Great Britain by
Clays Ltd, St Ives plc

British Library Cataloguing in Publication Data
A catalogue record for this book is available from the British Library

Library of Congress Cataloging in Publication Data
Goodman, David S. G.
    Deng Xiaoping and the Chinese revolution : a political biography /
David S.G. Goodman.
        p.   cm.
    Includes bibliographical references and index.
    ISBN 0–415–11252–4 : $59.95. — ISBN 0–415–11253–2 (pbk.) : $16.95
    1. Teng, Hsiao-p'ing, 1904–   2. Heads of state—China—Biography.
I. Title.
DS778.T39G66   1995
951.05'8'092—dc20
    [B]   94–21699
                                                        CIP

ISBN 0–415–11252–4 (hbk)
ISBN 0–415–11253–2 (pbk)

Contents

Preface

In the twentieth century the term 'The Chinese Revolution' has been used to refer to three relatively distinct but overlapping ideas. One is the transformation of China from Napoleon's 'sleeping giant' to a modern state, which has been the goal of various different kinds of nationalists for most of the century. The second is more narrowly the revolution that brought the Chinese Communist Party (CCP) to power in 1949 after its foundation in 1921, its abortive revolution of 1927, war with Japan and two civil wars. The third is the revolution – often variable in trajectory – waged by the CCP in the People's Republic of China (PRC) after 1949 to establish new social, political and economic structures.

Of all China's leaders in the twentieth century, few have played such a central role in all three of those ideas of China's revolution as Deng Xiaoping. Socialized into the organizations of what later became the CCP at the early age of 16 or 17 when in France, his life has been, to quite a remarkable extent, the history of the CCP. He travelled around Europe and China with many of those who became the senior post-1949 leadership. He worked closely with many different parts of the party from a relatively early age, attended most of the key CCP meetings on the road to eventual success in 1949, and played a considerable and central role – when based in the Taihang Mountains – in the successes of the War of Resistance to Japan, and the later civil war. In the 1950s he became the General Secretary of the CCP and remained Mao Zedong's right-hand-man, in the thick of politics right through to the Cultural Revolution when he fell from grace for five years. On his return to politics he was at the centre of the ideological struggle that racked China through most of the 1970s.

Mao Zedong, it is true, can be credited with much of the responsibility for steering the CCP from its difficulties in the late 1920s through to eventual success in 1949. However, in the final analysis, as even the CCP has admitted in its 'Resolution on Certain Questions in the History of the CCP since the establishment of the PRC' passed by its Central Committee in 1981, he failed to ignite the spark of sustained modernization. According to current economic predictions around the world, some time during the second decade of the twenty-first century the PRC will boast the world's largest aggregate economy. If any one person can be held responsible for China's rapid economic growth – and the laying of the foundations for the grand transformation idea of the Chinese revolution – since the late 1970s, then that individual must be Deng Xiaoping.

As 22 August 1994 is the 90th anniversary of Deng's birth, his daughter, Deng Rong (or Maomao as she is often, and more familiarly, known) felt that she could not let the moment pass without some acknowledgement, not only to her father but also to the generation that had constructed the PRC. Although, as Deng Rong herself admitted, Deng Xiaoping had earlier said he would prefer no biographies she produced for his birthday the first volume of a projected two-part biography – *My Father Deng Xiaoping* – during 1993.

For me the 90th anniversary of Deng Xiaoping's birth has provided the opportunity to revise a biography originally published in 1990. As luck would have it, soon after the earlier biography went on sale its publishers ran into difficulties (for reasons completely unrelated to the publication of that biography), remaindered their stock, and ceased operations. An encouraging and different publisher, the realization that much more material was now available than had been the case four years earlier, and the opportunity to make revisions of fact and interpretation in a longer edition were all too inviting.

Since the late 1980s when research was undertaken for the earlier version of this book, considerable material has been made available in China on Deng Xiaoping, his life and works. Some indication of the extent to which documentary material became available in 1989 and after is indicated in the Bibliography. In addition, as a result of the changed times and the writing of the earlier biography, I have found that academics and politicians in China have been more willing and prepared to talk to me about Deng Xiaoping than was earlier the case. Interviews are now possible, and though sources must sometimes be protected and their contents must always be handled carefully, they are certainly of considerable use.[1] The new research material of all kinds that has been generated has added immeasurably to the task of biography, both in detail and interpretation, and has been included where appropriate. It ranges from relatively small differences, like knowing the exact date of Deng's appointment as Minister of Finance, revealed in an article by Rong Zihe, to a re-evaluation of the relationship between Mao Zedong and Deng Xiaoping for the period after 1957.

The date at which Deng Xiaoping started to seek different solutions to China's problems from Mao Zedong, and the ways in which this affected their relationship, is obviously important to an interpretation of Deng's place in China's politics, and was itself a matter of debate in the Cultural Revolution and after. In the earlier biography it was possible to suggest that this divergence started in a mild way towards the end of the Great Leap Forward, and increased to the Cultural Revolution. Deng's view in that earlier interpretation was not shaped by ideological or policy considerations so much as his concerns that Mao was flagrantly not maintaining the principles of CCP organization and discipline.

As the result of further reflection – in which the scholarship of Frederick Teiwes has played no small part – this biography suggests that the sense of a growing divide between Deng and Mao before the Cultural Revolution is easily exaggerated. Deng's relationship with Mao was and remains more complicated. Deng could, and often did after 1949, have different policy positions to Mao whilst remaining a supporter. Deng had been very close to Mao for a very long time (since the early 1930s) – possibly closer for longer than with anyone else in the CCP hierarchy. It seems likely that he never thought Mao would turn on him, not even during the Cultural Revolution. What happened precisely during the Cultural Revolution, particularly in terms of intra-leadership dynamics, remains undetailed. However, it is clear that even after the Cultural Revolution, and even in his retirement, Deng has a highly specific reverence for Mao Zedong that goes way beyond any obeisance to a potent symbol of political legitimacy for the party-state. It is difficult to believe that by 1975 Deng could not see a huge ideological gap opening between himself and the Chairman. At the same time it is not impossible that well into the Cultural Revolution Deng thought he was consistently and conscientiously doing what Mao wanted, or perhaps more to the point that he was not doing anything Mao definitely did not want, or that might cause friction with the Chairman.

Both at the Central Work Conference that preceded the landmark 3rd plenum of the 11th Central Committee of the CCP in November and December 1978, and later when the CCP was drafting the 'Resolution on Certain Questions in the History of our Party since the Founding of the People's Republic of China' adopted by the 6th plenum in June 1981, Deng has differentiated between Mao's role in the Cultural Revolution and that of Lin Biao and the so-called 'Gang of Four'. Where he has regarded Lin Biao and the Gang of Four as 'grabbers of power' and 'counter-revolutionaries', he has criticized Mao Zedong for his mistakes, but more in the way he did things than in his goals. In 1978, having criticized Lin Biao and the Gang of Four for their political practices, Deng went on to say: 'The Cultural Revolution should also be viewed scientifically and in historical perspective. In initiating it Comrade Mao Zedong was actuated mainly by the desire to oppose and prevent revisionism.'[2] In 1981 the 'Resolution on Party History' eventually suggested that Mao Zedong himself negated Mao Zedong Thought: Deng in 1980 in the drafting process suggested that in the 1970s Mao himself had been inconsistent and 'mutually contradictory in some of his statements' about what he wanted.[3]

Revision of the text presented here has resulted in three new chapters and several new sections, as well as a new bibliography and chronology. One new chapter deals with Deng Xiaoping's most militarized period, from 1937 to 1952, when he and Liu Bocheng developed what later became the PLA's Second Field Army, and led it via the Huai-Hai Campaign to establish communism in South-west China. A second new chapter comes from the expansion of material related to the reform era, and the development of two chapters where previously there was only one.

The third new chapter is less obviously a chapter than an appendix, resource and research tool for those wanting to take their interest in Deng Xiaoping further. Chapter 10 introduces Deng Xiaoping in his own words from 1938 to 1992. In addition to an introductory essay on Deng's speeches and writings, it includes a list of published collections of Deng Xiaoping's speeches and writings, and a detailed chronological catalogue. The chronology of the earlier volume has been completely rewritten and extended in the light of the much larger information base now available. A new Bibliography contains a brief essay on the Deng Xiaoping literature, and the bibliographic part itself is divided into two: a bibliography of China-based publications, and another of books and articles published elsewhere. A list of abbreviations and a map are provided at the beginning of the book, and notes appear at the end of the volume.

A few words of explanation of essential technicalities are perhaps necessary for those less familiar with the complexities of China's politics and the history of the Chinese Communist Party.

As the text details, Deng has gone by several names during his life, and Deng Xiaoping was not the one originally chosen for him by his family. He was born Deng Xiansheng and did not become Deng Xiaoping until the latter part of 1927. In the mean time, for some twenty years he had been known as Deng Xixian and when in the Soviet Union he had been known as Dozolev. In 1929, when travelling to and working for the CCP in Guangxi in South-west China, he adopted Deng Bin as his *nomme de guerre*. None the less, to avoid confusion he has been consistently referred to as Deng Xiaoping throughout.

Similarly, though of considerably less significance, the CCP's English translation of the term for its leading institution changed during the 1980s from 'politburo' to 'political bureau'. Again to avoid confusion, the latter term has been used consistently.

In the Sino-Japanese War, border regions, border areas and base areas were established by the CCP behind enemy lines. On the whole, border regions were larger than both border areas and base areas and in the case of the Shanxi–Hebei–Shandong–Henan Border Region – Deng's principal location during this time – contained several border areas and base areas. However, the system of nomenclature is inherently confusing. For a start, the names of the provinces involved are often rendered using single character abbreviations derived from classical Chinese and referring to regions which approximate to contemporary provinces. Thus, Shanxi is often referred to as 'Jin', Hebei as 'Ji', Shandong as 'Lu', and Henan as 'Yu'. The whole of the Shanxi–Hebei–Shandong–Henan Border Region is more usually described as JinJiLuYu, which apart from any other consideration has the advantage of brevity.

The terms for 'region' and 'area' in Chinese are often translated into English interchangeably. Moreover, the conditions of guerrilla warfare often meant that border regions, border areas and even base areas (which were supposed to be more stable) fluctuated wildly in size. To complicate matters even further, border regions and areas were so designated for two reasons: they bordered the enemy – initially the Japanese and after 1945 the Nationalist Party – and they were established on the borders of various provinces. Thus, JinJiLuYu was the border region located where the provinces of Shanxi, Hebei, Shandong and Henan meet; it did not include all of all four provinces.

During the Sino-Japanese War, and for some time after, Deng was the ranking political cadre of the JinJiLuYu Border Region which had been established on and included the Taihang base area. Not least because the border region had such a long name, both will be referred to as 'Taihang', though maintaining the distinction between border region and base area. Taihang is thus used to describe the Shanxi–Hebei–Shandong–Henan Border Region in the same way that Yan'an refers to the Shaanxi–Gansu–Ningxia Border Region. In fact, this has been fairly standard procedure for veterans of JinJiLuYu in re-examining their history,[4] even though it is strictly inaccurate. The Taihang region, though always part of JinJiLuYu (indeed its source and most important part politically and administratively), was only coterminous with the Border Region during 1942–3 – and then because the latter had shrunk under the pressures of war.

The term 'cadre' in this context refers to an official of party or state, as is usual practice in communist party states. It can be a singular as well as a plural or collective noun.

CCP Central Committees and their meetings are numbered after the CCP Congress which elected them. Thus the 3rd Plenum of the 11th Central Committee refers to the third full and formal meeting of the central committee elected by the 11th CCP Congress of 1977. Since 1977 there have been regular five-yearly party congresses, so that in 1982 the 12th CCP Congress elected the 12th Central Committee to serve until the 13th CCP Congress in 1987, followed by the 14th CCP Congress in 1992.

In the term 'Mao Zedong Thought', the 'Thought' refers to ideology (or rather a specific kind of ideology) in Chinese. Mao Zedong Thought is thus to be differentiated from Mao Zedong's thoughts, his personal ideas or actions.

The 'Gang of Four' were Jiang Qing, the wife of Mao Zedong, and three colleagues based in Shanghai and associated with her during the Cultural Revolution: Wang Hongwen, Yao Wenyuan, and Zhang Chunqiao. There seems little doubt that they acted in concert for much of the Cultural Revolution. They were arrested in October 1976 one month after the death of Mao Zedong, and tried between November 1980 and January 1981 for a series of 'counter-revolutionary' crimes.

In general, the *pinyin* system of romanization has been used for Chinese throughout this book. The exceptions are names more familiarly rendered otherwise – notably Canton and Chiang Kai-shek – and references to publications and quotations which have employed other methods of transliteration, where the original has been cited. Because this book has been written for a predominantly English-speaking audience, all quotations, citations and titles are rendered in English unless a specific linguistic point is being made. Similarly, wherever possible priority in references and citations has been given to English language sources; where no English-language source is available, translations are provided.

It would be rare for a book to be produced without the help of many others and this one is no exception. Acknowledgement is due to colleagues and staff – in particular, Richard Robison, Dellas Blakeway, and Elissa d'Alton – at the Asia Research Centre, Murdoch University, which has supported this project in a number of different ways. Gary and Valerie Steenson have been much-appreciated company and counsel, not least on frequent visits to Hong Kong. The

East Asia collection at the Australian National University and its staff, in particular Susan Prentice, have as always provided an incomparable resource; as has Sonja Lee and her news cuttings service. Gordon Smith of Routledge has my obvious gratitude, not least for being prepared to consider publishing even a revised version of a book well within four years of its first publication.

My thanks must also go to several colleagues and friends, who, though they have given generously and willingly of their various advice, encouragement and assistance, and in the process added immeasurably to the writing of this biography, bear no responsibility for the final product: John Clark, Chen Shuping, Chen Yung-fa, James Cotton, Mark Elvin, Feng Chongyi, Li Rui, Rachel Murphy, Cathy Poon, Gerry Segal, Fred Teiwes, Tian Youru, Wei Hongyun, Wu An-chia, and You Ji. Mabel Lee in particular has been a constant source of support and inspiration.

David S.G. Goodman
Sydney

Abbreviations

CCP	Chinese Communist Party
CPSU	Communist Party of the Soviet Union
DXS	*Gongfei yuanshi ziliao huibian: Deng Xiaoping yanlunji 1957–1980* [*Collection of CCP Materials: Collection of Deng Xiaoping's Words and Writings, 1957–1980*]
DXWI	*Deng Xiaoping wenxuan 1938–1965* [*Selected Writings of Deng Xiaoping 1938–1965*]
DXWII	*Deng Xiaoping wenxuan 1975–1982* [*Selected Writings of Deng Xiaoping 1975–1982*]
DXWIII	*Deng Xiaoping wenxuan Vol. III* [*Selected Writings of Deng Xiaoping, Vol. III, 1982–1992*]
DZS	*Zhongguo renmin jiefangjun dierye zhanjun shiliaoxuan 1947–1949* [*Selected Historical Materials on the PLA's 2nd Field Army 1947–1949*]
JJLY	JinJiLuYu: the Border Region of Shanxi–Hebei–Shandong–Henan, 1937–48
JJLYGS	*JinJiLuYu genjudi shiliaoxuan* [*Selected Historical Materials on the JinJiLuYu base area*]
JZTS	*Jianshe you Zhongguo tesede shehuizhuyi* [*Build Socialism with Chinese Characteristics*]
KMT	Kuomintang (*Guomindang*): the Nationalist Party of China
LDJ	*Deng Xiaoping lun dangde jianshe* [*Deng Xiaoping on Party Development*]
LGJJ	*Deng Xiaoping lun guofang he jundui jianshe* [*Deng Xiaoping on National Defence and Military Development*]
LGK	*Deng Xiaoping tongzhi lun gaige kaifang* [*Comrade Deng Xiaoping on Reform and Openness*]
LJ	*Deng Xiaoping tongzhi lun jiaoyu* [*Comrade Deng Xiaoping on Education*]
LJDRG	*Deng Xiaoping tongzhi lun jiaqiang dang tong renmin qunzhong de guanxi* [*Comrade Deng Xiaoping on Strengthening Relations between the Party and the Popular Masses*]
LJS	*Deng Xiaoping tongzhi lun jianchi sixiang jiben yuance fandui*

	zichan jieji ziyouhua [*Comrade Deng Xiaoping on Support for the Four Cardinal Principles to Oppose Bourgeois Liberalism*]
LMF	*Deng Xiaoping tongzhi lun minzhu yu fazhi* [*Comrade Deng Xiaoping on Democracy and the Legal System*]
LTZ	*Deng Xiaoping lun tongyi zhanxian* [*Deng Xiaoping on the United Front*]
LW	*Deng Xiaoping lun wenyi* [*Deng Xiaoping on Art and Literature*]
LZ	*Deng Xiaoping tongzhi lun zhexue* [*Comrade Deng Xiaoping on Philosophy*]
LZG	*Mao Zedong, Deng Xiaoping Lun Zhongguo guoqing* [*Mao Zedong and Deng Xiaoping on the State of the Chinese Nation*]
MAC	Military and Administrative Committee
NPC	National People's Congress
PLA	People's Liberation Army
PRC	People's Republic of China
RMB	Renminbi [People's Currency] 10 *yuan* (dollars) RMB=1US$
SCC	*Fundamental Issues in Present-Day China*
SEZ	Special Economic Zone
SWI	*Selected Works of Deng Xiaoping 1938–1965*
SWII	*Selected Works of Deng Xiaoping 1975–1982*
TGS	*Taiyue genjudi shiliaoxuan* [*Selected Historical Materials of the Taiyue base area*]

Deng Xiaoping

A chronological summary

1904	August	Deng Xiansheng born in Guang'an County, Sichuan Province
1909		Attends local private school, renamed Deng Xixian
1911		Attends local modern primary school
1918	late-year	Leaves Guang'an to study in Chongqing
1920	August	Leaves for France on work-study programme
	year-end	Enrols in Bayeux middle school
1921	end March	Returns to Paris and La Garenne-Colombes
	April	Employed at Schneider–Creusot Factory
1922	February	Living in Montargis, worked at Hutchinson's Rubber Factory. Joins Socialist Youth League of China
	October	Moved to Chatillon-sur-Seine
1923	February	Returned to Montargis
	June	Left Montargis to return to Paris, employed at Renault plant, Billancourt
1924	February	Starts work with Zhou Enlai on *Red Light*
	July	Elected to Secretariat of European Branch of Socialist Youth League of China at 5th European Congress; dates CCP membership from this time
1926	January	Leaves Paris for Moscow. Student at Sun Yatsen University, Moscow
1927	January	Returns to China
	March	Political Instructor at Xian Military and Political Academy under Feng Yuxiang
	July	Becomes secretary to the CCP Central Committee in Hankou. Changes name to Deng Xiaoping
	September	Moves with CCP Central Committee to Shanghai. Chief secretary to CCP Central Committee, responsible for headquarter's documents, confidential work, communications and financial affairs
1928	Spring	Marries Zhang Xiyuan
1929	September	Leaves Shanghai for Guangxi and Right River via Hong Kong, under name of Deng Bin

	December	Returns to Shanghai to report on Bose Uprising and formation of 7th Red Army
1930	January	Zhang Xiyuan dies
	February	Longzhou Uprising and formation of 8th Red Army. Returns to Guangxi
	September	8th Red Army defeated
	October	7th Red Army under Zhang Yunyi, Li Mingrui and Deng Xiaoping sets out for Jiangxi
1931	February	7th Red Army separated into two regiments. Deng leaves 7th Red Army and returns to Shanghai
	April	Reports to CCP Central Committee on 7th and 8th Red Army
	May/June	Inspection tour for CCP Central Committee in Anhui Province (Wuhu)
	August	Moves to Central Soviet Area, Jiangxi, and is appointed Secretary CCP Committee, Ruijin County
1932	March	Marries Jin Weiying (Ah Jin)
	May	Secretary CCP Committee Huichang County, responsible for Huichang, Xunwu and Anyuan Counties
	December	Director, Propaganda Department, CCP Jiangxi Province
1933	April	Disciplined for following the 'Luo Ming defeatist line' and removed from positions. Criticism led by Li Weihan. Jin Weiying divorces Deng and marries Li Weihan
	May	Sent to Le'an County, Nancun, for ten days. Returns to CCP Jiangxi Province Committee
	August	Secretary-General, General Political Department, First Front Army
1934	August	Assigned to work in Propaganda Department, General Political Department, Red Army. Editor *Red Star*
	October	Leaves Ruijin on Long March
1935	January	Appointed Secretary-General CCP Central Committee. Attends Zunyi Conference of the CCP Political Bureau
	June	Appointed Head of the Propaganda Department, General Political Department, First Army Corps
1936	February	Deputy Director, Political Department, First Army Corps, Shanxi Expedition
	December	Director, Political Department, First Army Corps
1937	July	Appointed Deputy Director, Political Department, Eighth Route Army
	September	Attends Eighth Route Army War Council in Taiyuan. Organizes 'War Mobilization Committees' in area north of the Shijiazhuang–Taiyuan railway
1938	January	Appointed Political Commissar, 129th Division, Eighth Route Army
	March	Taihang base area established

	August	Leaves Taihang base area for Yan'an
	November	Attends enlarged 6th plenum of 6th Central Committee CCP, Yan'an
	December	Leaves Yan'an for 129th Division HQ in South Hebei
1939	August	Attends enlarged meeting of CCP Political Bureau, Yan'an
	September	Marries Zhuo Lin, Yan'an. Returns to 129th Division HQ, now in Liaoxian
1940	April	Appointed Secretary, Taihang Military and Administrative Committee (for Taihang, Taiyue and South Hebei base areas)
	December	129th Division HQ settles in Shexian
1942	September	Appointed Secretary, Taihang Bureau, CCP Central Committee (to October 1943)
1943	October	Acting Secretary, North China Bureau, CCP Central Committee
1945	February	On inspection tour of JiLuYu base area
	June	Elected (in absentia) to Central Committee at 7th CCP Congress. Attends 1st plenum of 7th Central Committee, Yan'an
	August	Secretary, JinJiLuYu Bureau, CCP Central Committee; Political Commissar, JinJiLuYu Military Region
	Sept/Oct	With Liu Bocheng, directs Battles of Shangdang and Handan
	December	129th Division HQ leaves Taihang Mountains and moves to Wu'an
1946	March	129th Division HQ moves to Handan
1947	May	Appointed Secretary, Central Plains Bureau, CCP Central Committee
	July	JinJiLuYu Field Army crosses Yellow River and marches south to Dabieshan
1948	May	Appointed First Secretary, Central Plains Bureau, CCP Central Committee; Political Commissar, Central Plains Military Region
	September	Participates in discussion meeting with Mao Zedong. Attends enlarged meeting of Political Bureau in Xibaipo
	October	Chen Yi and Deng direct capture of Zhengzhou
	November	Appointed Secretary, General Frontline Committee
	November	Huai-Hai Campaign (to January 1949)
1949	February	Central Plains Field Army formally becomes 2nd Field Army, with Deng as Political Commissar. Appointed Secretary, General Frontline Committee
	March	Attends 2nd plenum of 7th Central Committee, CCP. Appointed First Secretary, East China Bureau, CCP Central Committee

	April	Yangtze Crossing and capture of Nanjing
	July	Attends meeting of CCP Central Committee in Peiping. Appointed First Secretary of South-west Bureau, CCP Central Committee
		To South-west with 2nd Field Army
	September	Appointed member, Central People's Government Council; and Revolutionary Military Council
	October	Attends proclamation of PRC, in Beijing
	November	2nd Field Army enters Chongqing
1950	July	Vice-Chairman, South-west Military and Administrative Committee. Political Commissar, South-west Military Region
1951	February	Reports to Central People's Government Council on South-west Region
	October	Attends enlarged meeting of CCP Political Bureau in Beijing
1952	July	Presides over opening ceremony for Chengdu–Chongqing railway. Appointed Vice-Premier, Government Administration Council (later State Council), to 1966. Vice-Chairman, Financial and Economic Commission
1953	January	Appointed to Constitutional Committee for PRC
	February	Appointed Vice-Chairman, South-west Administrative Committee
	September	Appointed Minister of Finance, and Director of the Office of Communications, Central Financial Commission (to September 1954)
1954	April	Secretary-General, CCP Central Committee
	September	Vice-Chairman, National Defence Council, and Director, Organization Department, CCP Central Committee
1955	March	Reports on investigation of Gao Gang and Rao Shushi to National CCP Conference
	April	Elected to CCP Political Bureau at 5th plenum of 7th Central Committee
1956	February	Visits Moscow for 20th Congress CPSU
	September	At 8th Congress CCP: reports on revision of CCP Constitution; is elected General Secretary of CCP, and to Standing Committee, CCP Political Bureau
1957	September	Reports to 3rd plenum, 8th Central Committee, on Anti-Rightist Rectification Campaign
	November	Accompanies Mao Zedong to Moscow for celebration of 40th Anniversary of the October Revolution and Moscow Summit of Communist Parties
1958	February	Inspection tour to Sichuan
	May	Attends 2nd session, 8th CCP Congress

	May–July	Attends enlarged meeting of Central Military Commission
1959	January	Attends meeting of provincial-level CCP secretaries in Beijing on economic development and difficulties in the year ahead
	July	Injures leg playing billiards at Central Work Conference, Lushan
1960	January	Attends special enlarged meeting in Guangzhou of Central Military Commission on questions of national defence convened by Mao Zedong
	February	Inspection tours to Henan, Anhui, Tianjin, Shandong
	March	Attends enlarged meeting of CCP Political Bureau in Tianjin to propagandize Mao Zedong Thought
	November	Deputy Head (under Liu Shaoqi) of delegation to Moscow Conference of Communist Parties
	December	Attends Central Work Conference in Beijing (to January 1961)
1961	September	Heads delegation to North Korea
	March	Involved in development of economic recovery programmes in industry and agriculture
1962	January	Attends and speaks at 7,000 Cadres' Conference
	May	Attends enlarged meeting of CCP Political Bureau in Beijing on economic planning
	September	Attends 10th plenum of 8th Central Committee of CCP, where Mao Zedong urges the party to 'Never forget class struggle'
1963	July	Heads delegation to Moscow (with Peng Zhen and Kang Sheng)
	December	Acting Premier, State Council (to February 1964)
1964	May–June	Attends Central Work Conference in Beijing on rural work
	December	Attends Work Conference of the Political Bureau in Beijing on the 'socialist education campaign'
1965	March–April	Acting Premier, State Council
	July	Heads delegation to Romania
	September	Attends Central Work Conference in Beijing on long-term planning
	Nov–Dec	Inspection tour to Sichuan, Guizhou and Yunnan
1966	April	Inspection tour to Yan'an
	May	Liu Shaoqi and Deng Xiaoping convene enlarged meeting of CCP Political Bureau on Beijing schools and universities
	October	Self-criticism at enlarged meeting of CCP Central Committee
	November	Participates in activities for the various Mao Zedong Red

		Guard receptions
	December	Attends enlarged meeting of CCP Political Bureau convened by Lin Biao to discuss industrial and communications work
1969	October	Moved from Beijing to do manual labour in Xinjian County, Jiangxi Province
1971	November	Writes to Mao Zedong
1972	August	Writes to Mao Zedong and the CCP Central Committee about 'his mistakes'
1973	February	Returns to Beijing
	April	Appointed Vice-Premier, State Council
	August	Elected to 10th Central Committee, CCP
	December	Appointed Chief-of-Staff, PLA
1974	January	Elected to CCP Political Bureau
	April	Heads delegation to UN Special Session on Problems of Materials and Development
	October	Appointed 1st Vice-Premier, State Council
1975	January	Appointed to Standing Committee, CCP Political Bureau, and Vice-Chairman CCP Central Committee
	May	Heads delegation to France
1976	January	Self-criticism at meeting of CCP Political Bureau
	April	Public removal from office after Tiananmen Incident
1977	March	At a Central Work Conference it is suggested that Deng be invited back to work, but the conference confirms the CCP's decision of April 1976. With Ye Jianying in Guangdong
	April	CCP Central Committee distributes two letters written to it by Deng
	July	Reappears in public. Reinstated as Vice-Chairman, CCP Central Committee; Vice-Premier, State Council; Vice-Chairman, Military Commission; and Chief-of-Staff, PLA
	August	Elected to 11th Central Committee, CCP
1978	January	Heads delegation to Burma and Nepal
	March	Chairman, Chinese People's Political Consultative Conference (to 1983)
	September	Heads delegation to North Korea
	October	Heads delegation to Japan
	November	Heads delegation to Thailand, Malaysia and Singapore
	Nov–Dec	Plays central role in Central Work Conference and 3rd plenum of 11th Central Committee, CCP, which decide to reassess the CCP's recent history, to reform politics, and to restructure the economy
1979	March	Speaks at Central Theoretical Work Conference on the importance of the 'Four cardinal principles' of political rectitude

	October	Heads delegation to USA and Japan
1980	February	Steps down as Chief-of-Staff, PLA
	March	Steps down as Vice-Premier, State Council
	July	Inspection tour to Sichuan Province
	November	Hua Guofeng steps down from leadership at enlarged meeting of CCP Political Bureau. Appointed Chairman, CCP Military Commission
1981	June	6th plenum of 11th Central Committee, CCP, and 'Resolution on Certain Questions in the History of Our Party since the Establishment of the PRC'
1982	February	Visits Guangdong
	September	12th CCP Congress. Elected to Standing Committee, CCP Political Bureau Chairman, CCP Central Advisory Commission (to 1987)
1983	June	Chairman, Central Military Commission
	July	*Selected Writings of Deng Xiaoping, 1975–1982* published
1984	February	Declaration of principle of 'One country, two systems'. Visits Guangdong
	September	Agreement with UK on the future of Hong Kong
1985	February	Visits Guangzhou
	September	Speaks at National Party Conference
1986	September	Attends 6th plenum of 12th Central Committee and speaks on the establishment of a 'socialist spiritual civilization'. Is interviewed for the USA TV programme *Sixty Minutes*
1987	January	Attends enlarged meeting of Political Bureau where Hu Yaobang stands down as General Secretary of the CCP
	October	Attends 13th CCP Congress, re-elected Chairman, CCP Military Commission (to 1989)
1988	January	*Deng Xiaoping Pictorial* published
	September	Central Work Conference in Beijing, discusses economic development and management
1989	May	Gorbachev visits Beijing. *Selected Writings of Deng Xiaoping, 1938–1965* published
	June	Beijing Massacre
	November	Retires from all formal public offices
1990	December	Votes in Beijing Municipal elections
1991	June	Deng's calligraphy used for the second edition of the 4-volume *Selected Works of Mao Zedong*
1992	January	Makes 'Southern Inspection Tour' to Shenzhen, Shunde and Zhuhai
	February	Visits Shanghai
	April & after	Publicity for 'Southern Inspection Tour' reignites pace of reform programme

	August	Reported heart attack
	December	14th CCP Congress adopts principles of 'socialist market economy'
1993	October	*Selected Writings of Deng Xiaoping, 1982–1992* published

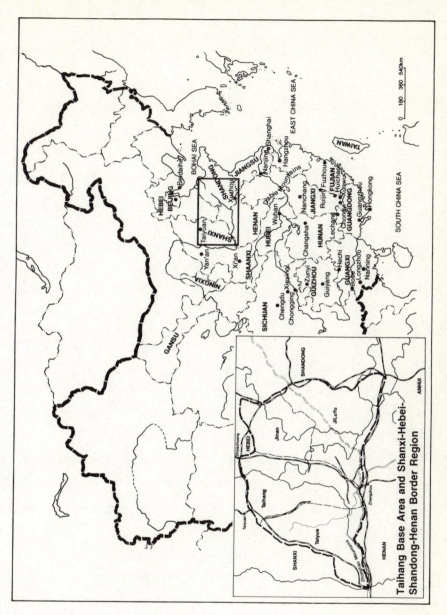

CHINA. Inset map shows the Taihang Region at the time of the Sino–Japanese War

1 Deng Xiaoping, communism and revolution

In China, the period after the 3rd plenum of the 11th Central Committee of the CCP in December 1978 is usually regarded as both the era of reform and of Deng Xiaoping. However, during that time Deng was never Chairman or General Secretary of the Chinese Communist Party (CCP), President of the People's Republic of China (PRC) or Premier. Though he had been General Secretary and (twice) Acting Premier of the State Council before the Cultural Revolution, he did not resume those positions in the 1970s or 1980s. Indeed, after 8 November 1989, when his request to retire was officially approved by the 5th plenum of the 13th Central Committee, he held no formal position at all. His leadership of the CCP, the PRC and of reform was derived from the way he was regarded as China's 'paramount leader' practically after Hua Guofeng stepped down from the Chairmanship of the CCP in 1980, but in effect after the 3rd plenum.[1]

Deng Xiaoping remained better known, both inside and outside China, than those who were more formally appointed to positions of authority and few doubt that through the late 1970s, 1980s and into the 1990s he was the single most important individual in China. Together with Mao Zedong and Zhou Enlai, Deng is usually regarded, with reason, as one of the key figures in the evolution of communism in China. Whatever else he may have achieved, more than anyone else it was he who was responsible for reversing the political and economic lunacy of Mao's later years, and for starting the process of bringing China into the twentieth century.

There are two radically different images of Deng Xiaoping in the West. One is as a communist modernizer acceptable to the capitalist world: an image that first emerged during the late 1970s and early 1980s. In the years before Gorbachev, Yeltsin, the disintegration of the Soviet Union and the collapse of communism in Eastern Europe, the CCP under his leadership abandoned the political strait-jacket Mao had imposed on the PRC during the Cultural Revolution, decided on a programme of modernization and instituted considerable political reforms. At times it even seemed that the CCP was prepared to abandon any pretence of communism. Both reform and modernization were based to a large extent on foreign economic involvement in China. There was an urgent need for China to improve its image abroad and its foreign relations. Deng Xiaoping was a key player in those efforts, speaking at the United Nations and touring the world, visiting the United States, Japan, Western Europe and South-east Asia at the head of government delegations. Appearing on television in a ten-gallon hat when in Houston did his and China's cause no harm at all. A short man with a round face, he projected a comfortable image like that of everyone's favourite uncle. For the United States government, China under Deng seemed an appropriate ally in its strategic moves against the Soviet Union, and it was fully prepared to play the China Card. In 1979 Deng was even nominated as *Time* magazine's Man of the Year, the first time a communist had been so honoured.[2]

The second image of Deng is less comfortable to the West. In 1989 the CCP under Deng's leadership suppressed popular demonstrations throughout China, often quite brutally. This confrontation, between the population on the one hand and the CCP and the government of China on the other, came to a head on 4 June with the forced clearing of Tiananmen Square (where the demonstrations had been concentrated) by armed troops of the People's Liberation Army (PLA) and the subsequent considerable loss of life. Deng Xiaoping's responsibility was not something attributed to him by an outraged Western public opinion, it was a responsibility he publicly welcomed in order to ensure, in his view, that modernization could and would continue: turmoil had been developing into a 'counter-revolutionary rebellion' which had to be brought into line. In Deng's own words, 'This was the storm that was bound to happen...it was just a matter of time and scale. It has turned out in our favour ...'[3] Once again television has undoubtedly had a role to play, for the events unfolded under the eyes of the international media whose reporters had gathered in Beijing, originally for the historic visit of President Gorbachev in May.

This political biography provides an explanation of the relationship between those two images of Deng. Both tend to over-simplification, as must necessarily be the case, and as indeed is any assumed contradiction between them. In the West there is a tendency to believe that in general the drive for economic modernization is accompanied by the emergence of liberal politics. This may eventually happen in China but it does not of course mean that those who advocated economic modernization in the post-Mao era were necessarily going to be political liberals in any meaningful sense other than preferring to emphasize economic growth rather than class conflict in the programme of the CCP.

Deng Xiaoping was a committed communist for all his adult life, and for part of his adolescence. However, this was probably as much an organizational and social commitment as one including ideological concerns. At the age of 16 in France he became involved with the people and organizations who were soon to form the Communist Party of China, and some of whom within a very short period of time were to wield considerable influence within its leadership. From then on the CCP not only organized his life, it was his life. The CCP took him to Moscow to train as a political organizer and back to China. At its direction, he travelled all over the country before the CCP came to power in 1949, working and fighting for the communist cause. Though the CCP may not have formally decided whom he was to marry, it certainly determined his marriage choices and his divorce, and there is more than a suggestion in his daughter's biography that

CCP colleagues acted as match-maker for all three of his marriages.[4]

After 1949 Deng's commitment led not only to high office – particularly membership of the CCP's Political Bureau and to be General Secretary of the party as early as the mid-1950s – but also to persecution and vilification. In 1966, at the start of the Cultural Revolution, he was dismissed and castigated as China's 'Number Two Person in Authority Taking the Capitalist Road' – the second most important 'capitalist roader' after Liu Shaoqi in opposition to Mao Zedong. In 1976 in Mao's last days when opposed by the Gang of Four, he was again criticized and removed from the leadership. Though on the second occasion he was cushioned from the worst effects of dismissal through support and assistance provided by supporters, notably Ye Jianying and the Guangdong-based military command, during the Cultural Revolution he had not been so lucky. None the less, on both occasions, as when he had been disciplined in 1933, Deng accepted the need for party discipline to be maintained through the process of criticism and self-criticism – though not necessarily the conclusions of that criticism. He accepted party discipline as stoically as possible and waited for the opportunity to re-present his case.

Deng Xiaoping was also a committed modernizer and nationalist, determined to make China both economically strong and politically powerful in international terms. In that endeavour he is often misleadingly characterized as a pragmatist. It is certainly true that he was no slave to dogma, and he clearly did not believe that all the truths of the successful road to socialist development were to be found in the works of Marx, Lenin or Mao. Though he always, including into the 1990s, urged China to follow Mao Zedong and Mao Zedong Thought,[5] he was not the communist politics equivalent of a 'black-letter lawyer': it was the spirit of what Mao said that Deng regarded as important, the direction in which Mao wanted to see China go, not the written word.

After Mao's death and the arrest of the Gang of Four, Deng's interpretation of the epistemology of Mao Zedong Thought was precisely a major obstacle delaying his otherwise inevitable recall. For some time Mao Zedong's personally selected successor, Hua Guofeng, had campaigned behind the slogan of 'The Two Whatevers' – 'We should do whatever Chairman Mao said or wrote.' Deng in his enforced political exile was quite emphatic that this was too inflexible and the wrong approach to Mao Zedong Thought, and the correct approach – at least in Deng's view – was the subject of a speech to the 3rd plenum of the 10th Central Committee soon after his recall in July 1977.[6]

Indeed, Deng repeatedly emphasized that even his own speeches and writings were time- and situation-specific. One of his more famous comments is, 'It doesn't matter whether a cat is black or white, so long as it catches mice.' Despite its immediacy and accessibility, any deeper meaning is not clear. To some this phrase has been taken as a manifestation of Deng's inherent pragmatism and it was the subject of some enquiry even within China. However, when asked by fellow senior party leader Bo Yibo what he had meant by it, Deng provided two separate explanations. The first was that he could not recall exactly what he had meant; the other was that it did not matter since it had been a statement suited to the conditions at that time (1962) and not transferable.[7]

Some commentators have suggested in consequence that Deng never had any principles or political vision at all, and by extension this was one major reason why he was unlikely to have opposed Mao before the Cultural Revolution in the ways that were claimed at that time. In this interpretation of Deng's political behaviour, he was 'organization man' who saw his duty as one of serving the party and its leader, and to implement the ideas of others within the leadership.[8] However, the case can also be made that Deng did have a relatively clear vision – if neither very structured nor particularly sophisticated – of the ways in which China's modernization should proceed, and particularly of the ways the CCP should operate in that process. It was those ideas that provided the opportunities and excuses for his opponents within the CCP to remove him from office. It was a vision of socialist development which had its origins with Mao Zedong in the early 1930s in Jiangxi, which is where Deng first came into contact with him. Later these were the policies developed and implemented by the CCP in Yan'an. It reached its first large-scale manifestation for Deng and his own leadership during the Sino-Japanese War in the Taihang region as he attempted to adapt the Yan'an experience to the conditions he found there.

In Jiangxi during the 1930s Mao had attempted to build a revolution in China from the countryside into the cities and from the bottom up. At that time Mao was not hidebound by dogma or over-impatient with the revolutionary cause. He realized it would take time to transform China and that what was required at each stage of the revolution would be maximum popular participation and support, as well as a sound economic base. Thus, for example, in the process of land reform not all the peasants should be dispossessed of land. Only the very richest should be made an example of and even then they too should be allowed to benefit from the land reform. The overwhelming majority – including middle peasants, who might be quite wealthy in relative terms – should certainly not feel threatened by CCP campaigns. In these ways Mao, and later Deng, had hoped to maximize both popular support and economic production. These principles, entailing slow but steady change, lay at the heart of Mao's later appeal to what was characterized during the 1940s as 'New Democracy' as the CCP prepared for national power under conditions of war. Indeed, they were even applied after 1949 for a while, until first Mao's impatience and then his personality became the main determinants of Chinese politics.

In short, Deng was pragmatic, rather than a pragmatist: a committed revolutionary throughout his political career, attempting to ensure that the CCP achieved power and China's modernization. For Deng Xiaoping, communism was an organizational as much as, if not more than, an intellectual response to the problems China has faced in the twentieth century. What was required was a united China, strong leadership, and the energy of the Chinese people, all of which could only be provided, in Deng's opinion, by the CCP. It may well be that this vision was, and indeed remains, fatally flawed: none the less, it remained Deng's vision.

The Chinese tradition of biography is not the same as that which has become established in the West. Rather than a measured evaluation its purpose has largely been didactic, the results may often tend to hagiography, and the methodological basis which is an essential part of Western biography is absent. Anecdotes and even rumour have traditionally been the essential staple of Chinese biographies. The Western tradition relies on personal memoirs; interviews with relatives, friends, and those involved with the subject in a professional capacity; and on documents, personal and public. Usually, too, it is considered good manners to wait until the subject is dead.

As the Bibliography in this book indicates, the publication of sources and documents within the PRC during the second half of the 1980s and into the 1990s has greatly facilitated the task of biography. Personal memoirs of Deng Xiaoping abound (though not all are reliable) and it has even proved possible to conduct a few interviews in China, though not with Deng himself. His daughter, Deng Rong, even published the first volume of a projected two-part biography – *My Father Deng Xiaoping* – in August 1993. Indeed, generally after his retirement in 1989, the Deng-publication industry began to develop in ways which those familiar with Western politicians would more usually associate with a drive for political power rather than retirement. However, as Pye amongst others points out, such an interpretation would be to misunderstand a crucial cultural difference: in China's traditional political culture, real power kept a very low profile and a high profile indicated weakness.[9]

This is a political biography for practical as well as intellectual reasons. Despite the available research on Deng Xiaoping both within and outside the PRC, very little of Deng's personality is recorded or indeed probably recordable at the moment. Indeed, the lack of political distance from the subject is a major problem even in writing a political biography. It is, for example, often difficult to identify the extent of Deng's personal input and involvement in an activity or policy initiative. Though this becomes an acute methodological problem during the reform era, when there is a tendency within China for Deng to be credited with everything, it is a general problem in tracing his entire career. As a rule of thumb, an attempt has been made to identify Deng's personal involvement in events, but to assume no particular connection if no appropriate evidence is available. In terms of personality, the documentary evidence is somewhat limited, providing what information it does on Deng's activities and speeches but almost nothing on his feelings and attitudes, most of which have to be inferred from his actions. As even his daughter acknowledged in her book – which will undoubtedly remain the major source for some time of personal anecdotes about her father – Deng himself explicitly discouraged his own biography – official or otherwise.

However, this is also a political biography because Deng's life is of interest for the light it throws on the evolution and dynamics of China's politics, particularly within the CCP. Although Deng was not a major figure in the CCP leadership until the 1940s, he was involved in the party's formative processes. After 1949 the story of his life is virtually the story of China's politics. Moreover, the dramatic rises and falls in Deng's political fortune not only require explanation, they clearly are more generally instructive about the processes of politics in the PRC.

There are few political systems – particularly those dominated by communist parties – which permit one individual found guilty of political 'crimes' on three separate occasions not only to live, but to bounce back repeatedly, and eventually to become the 'paramount leader'.

The emphasis on political biography means that most of this book is concerned with Deng's life after 1937, the period when he was a central influence in the CCP and in China's politics. It ignores almost all of his early life before the age of 16 when he was growing up and a student in Sichuan. However, it does not ignore the years between 1920, when Deng went to France, and 1937, for those were the formative years in which his later political career was grounded. During those years he was a party official and political organizer, and, like the history of the party he served, he had his ups and downs, the latter including a demotion in 1933 and the Long March. It was during these early years that he formed two of the key personal associations that were to determine the rest of his career, and indeed ensure his political survival: with Zhou Enlai first, whom he met in France; and then in and after 1931 with Mao Zedong.

A third crucial relationship, or perhaps more accurately set of relationships, was forged in the years after 1937 when Deng became an essential part of the CCP's military and political leadership in the Taihang region. There he teamed up with another Sichuanese, Liu Bocheng, to lead the 129th Division of the Eighth Route Army, one of the three key communist military forces in the Sino-Japanese War. From their base in the Taihang Mountains, they established further base areas and eventually the Shanxi–Hebei–Shandong–Henan (or JinJiLuYu) Border Region, a communist area of government during the later civil war. In the process Deng and Liu together also created one of the PLA's most successful armies – that later became the PLA's 2nd Field Army. Deng's role, as political commissar, was particularly important because this was a poor region, the recruits were physically weak, and the army as it grew was poorly equipped.

Between 1937 and 1952 Deng developed a close relationship with the CCP military which became an important and recurrent theme in his subsequent career, particularly during and after the Cultural Revolution. During the late 1940s and the civil war between the CCP and Nationalist Party, he played a leading role in two military engagements that led directly to CCP success in 1949. The first was when the army led by Liu Bocheng and Deng broke through the enemy lines which had them pinned down in the north and swept into Central China. The second was the decisive Huai-Hai Campaign when the CCP forces finally defeated the Nationalist armies protecting the Yangtze and the Nationalist capital at Nanjing. For Deng and Liu Bocheng this led on to the occupation of the South-west Region. However, the importance of Deng's Taihang and later military experience is not simply that it provided him with military credentials and status. These years also provided Deng with his first substantial and sustained experience of the party's problems in mobilizing the population and providing government, as well as a whole series of personnel networks with cadres who were to play leading roles in CCP politics well into the 1990s.

The remainder of this chapter contains the essential background to Deng's political biography. It provides an introductory overview of the politics of the CCP and the PRC, before returning to a consideration of Deng's position in CCP history. One section of the overview deals with the CCP's path to power before 1949 and another with the PRC during the era of Mao-dominated politics, while a third examines the important characteristics of inner-party conflict within the CCP and their consequences for China's politics. The final section focuses more precisely on how those characteristics have helped determine Deng's career and indeed his place in CCP history and politics.

THE CCP AND THE PATH TO POWER

At the time Deng Xiaoping left China for Europe in 1920, discussions were under way that eventually led to the foundation of the CCP. The collapse of the imperial system under the weight of foreign encroachment and internal problems rapidly led to the breakdown of central authority in China. Increasingly power came to be wielded by local warlords rather than any central government. In the intellectual ferment that was the May 4th Movement – so called because on 4 May 1919 students in Beijing staged a nationalist demonstration against the decision of the Versailles Treaty which instead of repatriating Germany's former colony in Shandong simply passed it on to Japan despite China's support for the allies in the First World War – it was inevitable that some Chinese should look for national salvation to the new communist state in Russia. Apart from anything else, quite quickly after coming to power in Russia, the Bolsheviks made encouraging noises to the 'oppressed peoples of the East' to unite against imperial aggression and colonialism. They promised to restore any Chinese lands ceded to the Tsars and to share ownership of the Trans-Siberian Railway, a branch of which ran through Mongolia to Beijing. They also offered organization, finance and advice through the Comintern, the Communist International, brought into existence by Lenin explicitly to establish communist parties worldwide.

Various Marxist discussion groups had already been established in China, though the most important was undoubtedly that based Beijing University, where the demonstrations of 4 May 1919 had been organized. With the combined forces of national salvation associations, self-help groups and study societies of various kinds, there were sufficient numbers on which to build a communist party and, with help from Comintern organizers, this was founded in July 1921. At first the CCP worked closely with the much larger Nationalist Party under Sun Yat-sen. Both were essentially nationalist parties initially motivated by events in the nineteenth and early twentieth centuries to restore China's dignity and integrity. Thus a first priority for both was national reunification and an end to warlordism. Moreover, the Comintern had also been responsible, at Sun Yat-sen's invitation, for reorganizing the Nationalist Party as a revolutionary organization during the early 1920s.

Relations between the Nationalist Party and the CCP were always a little strained, as indeed they rapidly became between the CCP and the Comintern. The sources of conflict between the Nationalist Party and the CCP were personal as well as ideological and political. While Sun Yat-sen was alive he managed to hold the alliance together. However, after his death in 1925 his successor Chiang Kai-shek increasingly saw the CCP as a threat, at the same time that he sought accommodation with most of the leading warlords. The two parties had not formed a two-party alliance, but had agreed instead that CCP members should join the Nationalist Party as individual members. This arrangement enabled the CCP not only to develop its influence and organization under the umbrella of the Nationalist Party but also effectively to subvert the cause of the Nationalist Party from within. Deng Xiaoping's return to China in 1927 was part of that strategy, for he went to work for the northern warlord, Feng Yuxiang, in Xian.[10] The Nationalist Party became increasingly polarized over the issue of co-operation with the CCP, and in 1927 Chiang and other figures in his wing of the Nationalist Party moved to attack the CCP openly.

The source of conflict between the CCP and the Comintern was that the latter, under Stalin's direction, saw its role and that of the CCP as an extension of the Soviet Union's foreign policy. Partly for that reason and partly because Stalin wanted to prove a point to Trotsky in their struggle for control of the CPSU, the Comintern directed the CCP not to breach the alliance with the Nationalist Party at any cost. When members of the CCP in Shanghai were being rounded up, they were supposed to hide their arms and disappear rather than resist. The CCP's organization of the peasantry for land reform was instructed to leave Nationalist Party members and their families alone. It was at this time that Deng Xixian became Deng Xiaoping. Having served as Deng Xixian with (Nationalist) Feng Yuxiang in Xi'an, when he travelled south to join up with the central office of the CCP, eventually to be engaged in underground work in Shanghai, a name change was necessary.[11] As 1927 wore on and first Chiang Kai-shek's wing of the Nationalist Party and then the party's left wing both turned against the CCP, Stalin's policies were to prove all but terminal.

Stalin's need for success in China led the CCP, now expelled from the Nationalist Party, to attempt a series of uprisings in China's cities. The intention was that CCP troops, often no more than poorly organized peasants drawn from the only recently organized peasant associations, should take the cities and bring about the downfall of the National Party government. In the event the most successful of these uprisings managed to seize and hold Nanchang, the capital of Jiangxi province, for just four days at the beginning of August. The remainder were abysmal failures entailing considerable loss of life. Still the Comintern pressed its views on the CCP, which staged an abortive uprising in Guangzhou (Canton) that threatened the very existence of the CCP as an urban force. Although CCP headquarters were located in Shanghai, where Deng now was, they were underground and by the end of 1927 the CCP's strength or what was left of it was gathering in rural guerrilla bases or 'soviets', as they were paradoxically termed.

The CCP almost did not recover from the defeat of 1927. From 1927 to 1935 there was a series of inner-party struggles for power, as well as repeated military offensives by the Nationalists under Chiang Kai-shek. Mao among others drew lessons about the importance of peasant-based revolution, about guerrilla and mobile warfare, and about the need to politicize the peasantry with programmes of social and economic reform. As part of the policy of fomenting rural insurrection now adopted by the CCP, Deng Xiaoping was sent to Guangxi. However, support for the rural soviets such as those established by Mao, first in the Jinggangshan and later in south Jiangxi around Ruijin, was ambivalent. Others within the CCP (as for example Zhou Enlai) continued to cling to the party's proletarian perspective and urban insurrection was attempted again in 1930. Deng, for example, was ordered to leave his rural base in Guangxi and march on a number of cities, including Guangzhou: a move which was totally impractical and rapidly abandoned after military defeat far from the appointed goal. Elsewhere the attempted seizure of the cities met with results as equally disastrous as 1927.

Leadership of the CCP now passed to the '28 Bolsheviks' or 'Returned Students Clique'. These were a group of Chinese students educated in Moscow who had been sent back under Comintern direction to lead the Chinese revolution. They recognized that the emphasis in CCP work had to shift from the cities to the countryside. However, they were not prepared to hand leadership of the CCP over to Mao and his supporters, who had developed the most successful rural base area, the Jiangxi Soviet. In 1931 they moved the headquarters of the CCP from Shanghai to Ruijin, the capital of the Jiangxi Soviet, and Deng went too. Throughout these years Mao's more orthodox opponents criticized him repeatedly for his pragmatic views. Because of his success and popularity it proved impossible for them to remove Mao's influence altogether, but they none the less tried through attacks on his supporters and those who shared his views. In 1933, in one such campaign directed primarily at Mao but unable for political reasons to attack him directly, Deng Xiaoping was one of those removed from office by the CCP and disciplined.

Chiang Kai-shek, meanwhile, also posed a threat to the CCP. When he could turn from his problems with recalcitrant warlords and the increasing threat of Japanese invasion, he launched a series of military 'annihilation campaigns' against the various CCP rural soviets. Up to 1934 the CCP was able to hold out in the Jiangxi Soviet because of its guerrilla warfare tactics and Chiang's other problems. However, in 1934 the Nationalist army adopted a new and highly successful tactic of blockade. At the same time the CCP under the direction of its Comintern advisers abandoned its guerrilla tactics for those of positional warfare. The results were catastrophic and, staring yet another major defeat in the face, the CCP opted for the strategic retreat which eventually became the Long March.

The Long March is justifiably famous for its heroism: in Edgar Snow's words it was 'one of the great triumphs of men against odds and man against nature'.[12] Some 90,000 soldiers of the Red Army set off to they knew not where to find sanctuary. After a little over a year and marching more than 10,000 kilometres, the remnant, 5,000 or so, finally arrived at what was to become their destination in North China. They had fought off the Nationalist armies and crossed some of the most inhospitable terrain in the world, including mountain ranges, deserts and marshes.

For the CCP, the Long March had three key political results. The first was that it essentially ended the internecine strife within the CCP which now became more or less united behind the policies of Mao and his supporters. A turning point actually came on the Long March at Zunyi in January 1935. The Comintern advisers were discredited and many who had previously opposed Mao (including Zhou Enlai) now changed their views. For those, like Deng, who had supported Mao the result was promotion. The second result of the Long March was that at its end in North China it presented the CCP with a secure base from which to expand, first at Bao'an, and then later at the more famous Yan'an. By 1935 Chiang Kai-shek was once again embroiled in problems caused by warlords and impending Japanese invasion. The third result was that the Long March not only created a tremendous *esprit de corps* among its survivors, it also created the legend of an invincible CCP and Red Army.

Undoubtedly another decisive turning point in the CCP's path to power was Japan's invasion of China in 1937. Under threat of invasion at the end of 1936 Chiang Kai-shek had been forced by his own generals to co-operate with the CCP once again. When the Japanese forces eventually advanced he retreated to Chongqing in the west, leaving the CCP to become entrenched in North China. From this position it was able not only to consolidate its position, but also to expand into the rural hinterland behind the Japanese lines and to become recognized by the population as an effective nationalist resistance. Following policies of rural mobilization, the CCP established base areas and border region governments, as it could. Deng, for example, spent most of this time not in Yan'an but in the border region centred on the Taihang Mountains, where Shanxi, Henan and Hebei provinces meet. By the time of Japan's defeat the CCP controlled well over a quarter of China's population.

The end of the Sino-Japanese War saw repeated attempts to avoid confrontation between the Nationalists and the CCP, but these soon failed. In the ensuing civil war the CCP was successful, not simply because it had developed a secure base and reputation during the Sino-Japanese War but also because of the weaknesses of the Nationalist regime: morale was increasingly low among its troops, inflation was high and corruption was rampant. At the end of 1948 CCP forces won two decisive victories against the Nationalist armies: one in the northeast, which challenged Nationalist control of North China and led to the surrender of Beijing; the other, in which Deng Xiaoping played a leading role, was for control of the Yangtze region and Central China. By April 1949 CCP success was guaranteed.

THE MAO-DOMINATED ERA OF CHINESE POLITICS

On 1 October 1949 Mao Zedong mounted the podium overlooking Tiananmen Square in the centre of Beijing to proclaim formally the establishment of the PRC. Deng Xiaoping, amongst others in the CCP's leadership, was by his side. Though the CCP had after twenty-eight years finally achieved national power, it faced enormous problems. The most urgent were to restore national unity, to bring inflation under control and to ensure the political control of the CCP, particularly in those areas where it had not been organized before 1949. As the communist armies gained control over the whole of China the device that was employed by the CCP to solve these immediate problems was the Military and Administrative Committee (MAC) – a body which not only brought temporary military rule but also allowed CCP cadres, most of whom like Deng had been in military service for some considerable time, to become civilian officials. Each of the six major armies of the PLA came to dominate a region of China, and six MACs were established, one in each region. Deng was appointed the leading party cadre in the South-west, a region where the CCP had had little organizational presence before 1949.

In the early years of the PRC, the CCP was more concerned with consolidating its position than with implementing programmes of radical change. It remained committed to its revolutionary goals, but given the size of China's economic and social problems its outlook was gradualist. Land reform was introduced but in the urban areas capitalist enterprises were urged to continue operations and intellectuals were encouraged to co-operate with the CCP under an appeal to nationalism. The restoration of economic stability and party expansion were the primary targets and, for the most part, they were successfully achieved.

Almost immediately after coming to power the PRC had allied itself with the USSR, though not enthusiastically due to the history of poor CCP–Comintern relations before 1949. Aid and advice were supplied by the Soviet Union, and the economic and political structures, as well as the policies adopted, were designed, as they had been in Eastern Europe, to create a mirror image of the Stalinist state. By 1954, the CCP's consolidation of its rule was complete and these new structures were largely in place. China's economy, in particular its infrastructure, was to be governed by Five-Year Plans; a new constitution and system of government had been established.

However, the Soviet model of development rested uneasily in a Chinese context and with the leaders of the CCP, for ideological, economic and political reasons. It was highly centralized, emphasized the development of heavy industry and addressed the needs of the cities rather than the countryside. The leaders of the CCP were not an urban, technocratic élite; and by the mid-1950s the command economy was beginning to result in shortages and bottlenecks around China. In addition, the Soviet model entailed an unequal growth strategy, causing economic inequalities between China's different regions to increase. Perhaps most important, after Stalin's death, the CCP was increasingly unwilling to acknowledge the superiority of Soviet experience and leadership. By 1955, much to its advisers' disgust, the CCP was beginning to look for an alternative 'Chinese road to socialism'. The Sino-Soviet split was not yet irreversible, but it was already in the making.

In the inner-party debates of the mid-1950s to determine what should replace the Soviet model, a number of different views on economic development emerged which were to underlie discussion within the CCP until well after Mao's death in 1976. One view was that of Mao Zedong who increasingly argued that growth should proceed as fast as possible on all fronts, fuelled by mass mobilization and enthusiasm. A more gradualist view, as articulated for example by Chen Yun – who worked in economic planning from 1949 through to the 1980s and was a primary economic architect of the 1978 reform programme – argued that China's economic development had to be slower, based on sound economic principles, and led by agricultural growth. At the same time, the measures which Mao took to argue his case and eventually to get his own way had a considerable impact on Chinese politics, which from about mid-1955 on became increasingly dominated by his personality.[13]

The extent of Mao's authority and centrality to the decision-making process became manifest in the evolution of policy on collectivization during 1955. At first the leadership, Mao included, had been extremely cautious. In late April he not only changed his mind and pushed for faster collectivization, but started throwing his weight around. Only one person – Deng Zihui – challenged his views, and Mao's annoyance was such that he hounded Deng Zihui and encouraged provincial leaders to implement the first stage of collectivization well ahead of the originally planned party policy, before the end of 1955. Before long Mao was arguing that the First Five-Year Plan could be completed in four years, a year ahead of time, and that the CCP should be bolder in its future plans. However, in the first three months of 1956 the economic results of Mao's over-enthusiasm became apparent, and, to the extent that his strategy had been adopted, it was abandoned.[14] Years later when reviewing these events Mao was highly critical of those who had made the decision. Those he criticized included Deng Xiaoping. Deng, having moved from the South-west to be a Vice-Premier in 1952, had by that time become a member of the CCP Political Bureau and Secretary-General of the CCP Central Committee.

At the 8th CCP Congress in September 1956 the party elected a new leadership, including Deng as General Secretary – that is, the leading secretary of the CCP and not just the Secretary-General to the CCP Central Committee as he had been before the congress. The congress, in all probability with Mao's assent, reaffirmed the principle of collective leadership. Mao Zedong Thought as the explicit guiding principle of the CCP was formally written out of the party constitution and Chen Yun's ideas for economic development became the basis of the Second Five-Year Plan scheduled to begin in 1958.

Mao remained somewhat headstrong and irrepressible, though not necessarily stubborn.[15] The Congress had agreed that a party rectification campaign was needed, not least to inform members of the change in line. Mao tried to force the pace by bringing forward the schedule for rectification, and by arguing that it should be carried out in accordance with his ideas on mass mobilization rather than in more orthodox ways. He wanted what he called 'extended democracy': the criticism of CCP cadres by everyone, regardless of their political affiliation, loudly and in public. In Mao's words: 'Let a hundred schools of thought contend, a hundred flowers bloom.' In his view, the experience would be good for the CCP, and would bind the CCP and potential intellectual critics more closely together. Mao argued that because the CCP was now so well grounded in society, its exercise of power would be criticized but the fact of CCP rule would not be challenged. After much opposition within the CCP a rectification movement of this kind was launched in the so-called 'Hundred Flowers Movement' of May 1957. It was a disaster, with public denunciation of the CCP from almost all sides, and was quickly curtailed and replaced by a more orthodox rectification campaign aimed at severely disciplining those who had spoken out.

One of the mysteries of Chinese politics between 1949 and 1976 is why the remainder of the CCP leadership allowed Mao his head on so many occasions, even against their experience and judgement, and indeed even when it led to their own demise. Though he may have appeared god-like to the ordinary people, to those in the CCP leadership he was a colleague, if often a difficult one. They were originally a collective leadership who had come together and fought together during the pre-1949 struggle. One possible explanation goes back to the late 1920s and early 1930s when Mao had repeatedly been proved right and the majority of the then CCP leadership wrong about the strategy and tactics to be adopted. As a result he stood above his colleagues, and his reputation for having often been right in the past and a belief in the essential unity of the leadership may have convinced many otherwise sceptical colleagues to go along with Mao, then and later.

At the end of 1957, Mao once again attempted to put his developmental ideas into practice. Through the offices of several provincial leaders an enormous mass mobilization campaign involving more than a quarter of China's peasant population was launched to improve irrigation. On paper at least the results were phenomenal and the Great Leap Forward in irrigation rapidly became a general economic Great Leap Forward. Mao's belief was that China could industrialize in fifteen years by substituting labour for capital in investment. New, large-scale rural production units – the People's Communes – were established all over China in two months. Backyard steel furnaces were started up everywhere. It was even claimed that communism – classless society – was literally just around the corner. Amongst all the other heresies, this was of course the one that annoyed the CPSU the most as relations worsened between the two parties, because as the first communist party state it assumed it would necessarily establish communism first.

By 1959 it became clear to some within the CCP that all was not well. However, when opposition to Mao's ideas came out into the open he responded by accusing his detractors, led by Peng Dehuai (the then Minister of Defence) of being counter-revolutionary. Partly as a result, the Great Leap Forward dragged on for another year but by the end of 1960 the economic situation was so critical that the CCP had no choice but to call a halt. Mao withdrew from the daily routine of government which he left to the head of state, Liu Shaoqi, the prime minister, Zhou Enlai, and Deng. In the aftermath, the leadership of the CCP differed between those who, like Mao, believed the strategy correct but flawed in its implementation and others, notably Liu and Deng, who now believed the strategy to have been a disaster and unrepeatable. At the same time, the full emergence of the Sino-Soviet split left China isolated internationally. None the less, in the first half of the 1960s under the gradualist strategy of Chen Yun, and with a relatively united leadership, China successfully started to overcome the problems caused by the Great Leap Forward.

Mao, however, had not abandoned his ideas. Moreover, through the early 1960s he increasingly came to be concerned about the dangers of 'revisionism': that the PRC was in danger of abandoning its commitment to revolution and likely to move, if unchecked, towards capitalism. It is even possible that he really did increasingly feel, as he later said during the Cultural Revolution, that he had been pushed out of political power. In his view, politics rather than economics should determine China's development. This, if over-simplified, was the essential background to the Cultural Revolution which Mao launched in 1966. His target was the CCP itself, and became, through a series of escalations, its leading cadres such as Liu Shaoqi and Deng, who were castigated as 'capitalist roaders'. Mao turned for his support in launching the Cultural Revolution initially to a small group within the leadership, including his wife, Jiang Qing; to the Red Guards, groups of politicized students; and to the PLA under the then Minister of Defence, Lin Biao. The Red Guards in particular were encouraged to overthrow all authority, to attack their teachers and almost all intellectuals, who were now criticized as the harbingers of counter-revolutionary values. In its first assaults the Cultural Revolution was wildly successful. Almost all officials of party and state were 'dragged out' and denounced; schools and educational institutions closed down; the more fortunate cadres and intellectuals who were not imprisoned, murdered, or who did not commit suicide, were sent down to the front line of production to learn the error of their ways among the toiling masses. This was to be Deng's fate: removed from power in 1966, he went into internal exile in 1969.

The result was near chaos, with order being maintained, where it was, by the PLA which consequently came to play a crucial political role in the unfolding of the Cultural Revolution. However, by the early 1970s the PLA's position in civilian politics was leading to further inner-party conflict which was only resolved with the death of Lin Biao and several other generals in an air crash over Mongolia. They were said to have plotted a coup against Mao, and when that failed to have fled to the USSR. It is unlikely that the outside world will ever know the true story of the Lin Biao affair, or even where and when he died.[16] None the less, the removal of Lin Biao provided the opportunity for a rethink in the progress of the Cultural Revolution. In particular, it became clear that there was a shortage of senior political and administrative ability to run China. The party and state had been purged during 1966–8; the PLA was being gradually returned to the barracks. Against the opposition of radical members of the CCP, more moderate leaders such as Zhou Enlai managed to have some of the victims of the Cultural Revolution restored to office. In 1973 one of these, and certainly the most significant, was Deng Xiaoping.

The remaining years of Mao's life were characterized by intense inner-party conflict. On the one hand, there were radicals, who emphasized political goals and wanted to maintain what they saw as the achievements of the Cultural Revolution, not least because that was their source of political power and authority. On the other, there were those, notably Zhou Enlai and Deng, who stressed the need for economic modernization as a prerequisite for reaching the political goals of the CCP. In January 1976 Zhou died and criticism of Deng came to a climax. Popular demonstrations in Zhou's honour and against the radicals in April provided an excuse for the latter to purge Deng once again. Hua Guofeng succeeded Zhou as prime minister and, when Mao too died, also succeeded him as Chairman of the CCP, having engineered a coup against the most extreme radicals in the CCP leadership, Jiang Qing and her three associates in the Gang of Four. The way was paved for Deng to return to office, for a reversal of the Cultural Revolution, and for a determined drive to economic modernization.

LEADERSHIP POLITICS IN THE CCP

Deng Xiaoping's repeated rise and fall from office have often puzzled non-Chinese observers, particularly those used to other communist party states where for the most part a purge is usually irreversible. Faced with this apparent enigma, some have tried to argue that Deng was more an administrator than a politician, able and willing to work with almost anyone. Bedeski, for example, suggests that 'he is not a great political visionary. He is a fixer, an organizer, and a reformer.'[17] It is undoubtedly true that a major part of his political strength did lie in his abilities as an organizer. On the other hand, although he might not have been a 'great political visionary', as already indicated and as will become apparent later, he did have a relatively clear political vision. The explanation for Deng's intermittent career is to be found more in the nature of leadership politics within the CCP than in Deng's adaptability.

An obvious starting point, and an important characteristic of leadership conflicts and their resolution within the CCP, is that purges in China have not necessarily carried the same connotation of blood and death that Stalin bequeathed to the Soviet Union and Eastern Europe.[18] Indeed, though particularly during the Mao-dominated era of Chinese politics leadership conflicts frequently did result in violence and death, before the 1950s the CCP's tradition had been otherwise. Though this changed somewhat under Mao, the belief was always that leaders could be re-educated to see the error of their ways.

Whether entirely for this reason or not, it is clear that in the history of the PRC it has been relatively common for former leading cadres of the CCP, the state administration, and the PLA who have fallen into disgrace to be recycled. Deng Xiaoping's case is clearly the most spectacular, but it is far from unusual. By the end of 1978 a considerable proportion of the leadership of the political hierarchy that had been in office on the eve of the Cultural Revolution and which had been purged during 1966–8 had regained at least equivalent positions of seniority. Some leaders purged at the start of the Great Leap Forward, for presumed or apparent opposition to Mao's ideas, were restored to office in the early 1960s, removed again in the Cultural Revolution and brought back again in either the early or late 1970s.[19]

The excessive instability of Chinese politics from 1949 to the late 1970s was matched by an extraordinary leadership stability, not in terms of specific individuals but in terms of the relatively small pool from which those leaders were chosen. During those years the political line adopted by the CCP changed on average every four or five-years. With each change came not only new policies, but also fresh organizational structures and personnel changes. However, the revolutionary generation which had fought together and won power in 1949 only relinquished its hold on the political system in 1985 when both biological and political factors became urgent considerations. Before that later date leadership changes incorporated few younger people, or those generally with different backgrounds and experiences. Remarkably, this was the pattern even during the Cultural Revolution when one of Mao's stated aims was to bring in fresh blood to rejuvenate the leadership.[20]

One explanation for this phenomenon lies in the age structure of the CCP leadership in 1949. When the CCP achieved power its leaders were, in international as well as in Chinese terms, relatively young to be national leaders. Mao, for example, one of the eldest, was still only 54; Deng was 45. Consequently there was no need initially for them to train successors and there was no planned layering of potential leadership generations. By the time of the Cultural Revolution, some seventeen years later, though there may have been an urgent need for successors, as Mao made plain, the issue became submerged in the wider conflict of the Cultural Revolution which, apart from anything else, delayed a solution still further.

A further explanation lies in the nature of factions and factionalism within the CCP.[21] The leadership of the CCP has always been highly factionalized. Individuals come together to provide mutual protection and assistance. Factional alignments may result from loyalty ties, career background, institutional affiliation, friendship, ideological perspective, attitudes to specific policy issues or personality. However, factions within the CCP are extremely fluid – not institutionalized or highly organized as, for example, in Japan's Liberal Democratic Party. Consensus and unity, rather than the divisions often associated with factions, are most definitely the order of the day for both traditional and contemporary reasons. The CCP has inherited a considerable portion of traditional Chinese political culture, not least that which emphasizes to a degree almost unimaginable in the West the requirement to maintain harmony. At the same time, the CCP's legacy from Marxism-Leninism is that the party is the correct interpreter of the one true ideology.

The size, number and complexity of factional alignments – some of which may be nested, others over-lapping and cross-cutting – make decision-making very difficult, even within a relatively small body such as the CCP's Political Bureau.[22] There is a need for individuals to build coalitions, but the process is almost impossible – not least because no one wants to be on the losing side. This was particularly the case during the Mao-dominated era of Chinese politics because the punishments for being on the 'wrong' side could be so severe. Politics have therefore been both extremely conservative and brittle. Within the leadership there is an in-built tendency to maintain the *status quo*. Normally change is introduced experimentally and incrementally, in ways which may subtly pressure the leadership without seeming to threaten the balance of power. However, dramatic, sudden and more wide-ranging change also occurs, not least when changes in the environment – for example, a major socio-economic problem, a perceived external threat – or changes in the leadership itself, through death or illness, force a decision on the leadership and trigger rapid factional re-alignments.

In both 1966 and 1976, Deng's dismissals from office resulted from the brittle nature of CCP politics. Both represented the rejection, at least temporarily, of his political vision. However, Deng's ideas do not provide an adequate guide to his career. Indeed, ideology has quite clearly never been the sole determinant of faction within the CCP. For individual leaders the relationship between ideology or policy, faction and career has been far from clear. Policy changes may result from leadership changes but factions are rarely solely policy-based. Indeed, members of a faction may not even share the same ideological perspectives or policy preferences. An illustrative example of the obvious confusion lies in the contrasting fates of Deng Xiaoping and Chen Yun during the Cultural Revolution. Of the two Deng had been more closely associated with Mao for some thirty years before the Cultural Revolution; Chen Yun's relationship, though good, was nothing like as close. In the debates of the 1950s, Chen was the major voice – sometimes the only voice – in opposition to Mao's ideas on development. Deng often did not agree with Mao, but was almost always prepared to give him support once a decision was taken despite any misgivings, and at times spoke enthusiastically. Moreover, his loyalty to Mao personally was near unshakeable. In the Cultural Revolution both were criticized, but it was Deng who was purged as a 'capitalist roader', whereas Chen maintained a leadership position, if at a lower level.

The careers of individual leaders would seem to be determined more by loyalty ties than by their political ideas. CCP politics are inherently personalist. Loyalty ties formed during an individual's career bind him or her to a specific leader or colleague. As the next and final section of this introductory chapter suggests, a major secret of Deng's success was the extent of his network of loyalty ties, in many ways a function of his age. Politicized at the age of 16 he came into contact with some of the very earliest leaders of the CCP. Thereafter, through his involvement in different aspects of party affairs in different locations, he formed relationships which provided a wide network of support well into his retirement. As a result, Deng, unlike some other leaders, could always find alternatives if one source of support failed him, particularly if and when he was involved in controversy of any kind. He had been old enough to be incorporated as a junior member of the leadership, and young enough to have had a longer and more varied active life in the CCP than most of the survivors of the revolutionary generation. Deng does not appear to have been overly ambitious in the way that Mao and Zhou both clearly were. None the less, he was an extremely able politician, as well as a superb political organizer, and he grasped every opportunity with both hands.

CONTROVERSY AND CONNECTIONS

It would be an unreasonable judgement on Deng Xiaoping to say that he had a controversial career, and that is not the function of this biography. None the less, he has been no stranger to controversy, within the leadership and more widely. He has been disciplined several times – his formal demotions in 1933, 1966 and 1976 are well known – as well as under criticism himself, or involved in the criticism of others, and there are episodes in his career that consequently remain somewhat obscured. The point of this final section is to identify the controversies in Deng's life and explain how personal political relationships and past associations may have assisted him to overcome the difficulties they presented. It is certainly not designed to provide any judgement – final or otherwise – on these matters; resolution is clearly very difficult whilst they remain sensitive issues for contemporary politics. Much of this section and indeed of the whole biography has to be based on conjecture and informed supposition. The intent is to highlight the more obviously debatable aspects of his career, both to indicate the lack of certainty that may occur later in the biography and to understand their wider implications.

In 1929 Deng Xiaoping was sent to Guangxi as a political organizer for the soon-to-be Right River and Left River base areas. To say the least, the venture was not successful and, by the time Deng returned to Shanghai and the CCP Central Committee, the rebellion had collapsed completely with the communist forces in retreat to Jiangxi. The CCP Central Committee held Deng Xiaoping, as the senior party cadre, to be the most responsible for defeat.[23] To make matters worse, there was and remains considerable doubt about the circumstances of Deng Xiaoping's return to Shanghai in February 1931. Controversy then and later centres around whether he returned to Shanghai of his own volition or on direction. In 1942 a report supervised by Chen Yi held that Deng's leaving of the Red Army was inappropriate. Red Guards in the Cultural Revolution, and some of Deng's external biographers, have used this report to build a substantial case that suggests he abandoned his troops.[24]

It seems reasonable to assume that Deng's support in the early part of 1931, if any were needed, came from the offices of the CCP Central Committee in Shanghai and in particular from Zhou Enlai. Zhou had recruited Deng Xiaoping to work on the Socialist Youth League journal *Red Light* in 1924, and the two appear to have had a close personal as well as professional relationship. According to Deng he 'always looked upon him as my elder brother'.[25] When Deng left Feng Yuxiang's employ in 1927 he headed south and was employed by Zhou in the CCP Central Committee offices in Hankou, where he worked under another party activist who had also been in Paris, Li Weihan. Deng went with Li and Zhou when the CCP Central Committee moved to Shanghai, and Deng Rong provides a portrait of close relations between Zhou and his wife, Deng Yingchao, and Deng and his new wife, Zhang Xiyuan, in the Shanghai underground where they shared a house.[26] In any case, in 1931 Deng was certainly not heavily censured for either the failure of the Guangxi uprisings or leaving his troops. By

May he was the representative of the CCP Central Committee on an inspection tour of Anhui.[27]

A more serious – at the time – brush with controversy came in 1933. Deng moved to the Central Soviet Area with the CCP Central Committee in 1931. Within a short time he found himself as party secretary for three counties on the borders of the Soviet Area where CCP rule was not secure, one of which – Xunwu – had been an area investigated by Mao Zedong in developing his ideas about peasant mobilization. Whether for this reason or simply because in the inner-party debate Deng saw more sense in Mao's prescriptions, Deng became identified with Mao's cause. He was accused of 'defeatism' – Xunwu and the surrounding area had been lost in the Nationalists' Fourth Encirclement Campaign – and together with three others was severely censured and disciplined by the CCP.[28] History necessarily obscures the degree of Deng's responsibility.

Support for Deng came from the obvious source: indeed, Mao Zedong's trust in Deng Xiaoping dates clearly from this time, not least because Mao Zedong was the real target of the campaign rather than those who were disciplined as followers of the so-called 'Luo Ming line'. However, in addition to the burgeoning relationship with Mao, Deng was also able to rely on others whom he had befriended during his earlier years in party activities. One in particular was Wang Jiaxiang, whom Deng had first met when both were students in Moscow. It was Wang who rescued Deng from involuntary exile in a relatively dangerous part of the Central Soviet Area and gave him a job in the General Political Department of the Red Army. He soon became editor of the Army's magazine *Red Star*, and it was in that position that he started the Long March. At the recommendation of Zhou Enlai and with Mao's support he became the record taker at the Zunyi Conference of January 1935.[29]

As already indicated, Deng's relationship with Mao Zedong is both complex and difficult to analyse at present. The revisions of history in and after the Cultural Revolution provide filters whose influence is probably unknowable for some time to come. Before the Cultural Revolution Deng was regarded as 'Mao's man'- his loyal, most trusted and able follower. This changed in 1966 when Deng became 'China's Number Two Capitalist Roader', and was accused of having ignored or avoided Mao during the 1960s, and of having plotted against him since the mid-1950s.[30] Since the 3rd plenum of 1978, and particularly since the CCP adopted a standard interpretation of the pre-Cultural Revolution years in its 'Resolution on Party History' of 1981, the attempt has been made to differentiate Deng from Mao, and particularly the worst excesses of his policies, from about 1957 on. In that year Deng Xiaoping was responsible for the Anti-Rightist rectification campaign that followed the 'Hundred Flowers' and which is generally held to have assisted the emergence of Mao's developmental ideas in the Great Leap Forward. In the 1980s Deng defended the need for a rectification campaign, but freely admitted it went too far at the time, and his final report is not included in the authorized collection of his writings.[31]

Deng's road back from the Cultural Revolution is indicative of the importance of personal relationships in China's politics. Mao's attitude to Deng was clearly important, and he is reported to have indicated on a number of occasions that he did not regard Deng in the same poor light as Liu Shaoqi, and others, whom he thought or said had opposed him. In 1972 Mao, whilst not forgiving Deng his 'serious mistakes', also pointed out that he did 'not have a historical problem'[32] and it seems likely that the closeness of their relationship for so long before 1966 facilitated Deng's recall. Deng's earlier associations with Zhou Enlai were also far from insignificant, and the two worked closely together after Deng's return to the leadership in 1973. In addition, one of the largest groups in the CCP leadership during the early 1970s consisted of Deng's colleagues and subordinates from the Taihang region during the Sino-Japanese War. At the beginning of 1973 six of the CCP Political Bureau's sixteen members were veterans of the 129th Division of the Eighth Route Army and JinJiLuYu.[33]

Deng's dismissal in 1976, and his later return in 1977, would seem to be a function of the highly polarized politics of the mid-1970s. The precise point at which Deng Xiaoping decided that Mao Zedong was either not functioning properly, under somebody else's control, or just plain wrong will probably never be known. However, it is clear that by 1975 he was advocating prescriptions for the future that negated the policies and results of the Cultural Revolution, and that he was not alone in that endeavour. Removed from all operational responsibility in January 1976, the Tiananmen Incident of April provided the excuse for his formal dismissal. Support for Deng was immediately forthcoming, and he was taken under the wing of the veteran army Marshal, Ye Jianying, and into protective custody by the Guangzhou Military Region, whose commander was Xu Shiyou, a former commander and colleague in the 129th Division of the Eighth Route Army. Deng's return to the leadership after Mao's death and the arrest of the Gang of Four was a near-formality, not least because of his activities in building support when in internal exile in Guangdong.

Even this brief overview of Deng Xiaoping's personal connections reveals the extent to which CCP politics were the preserve of a relatively small and close-knit group. At the most senior leadership level of the CCP Political Bureau there were only eighty-seven individual members between the founding of the PRC in 1949 and Deng Xiaoping's retirement. To some extent, particularly before 1966, the shared experiences of early struggle mediated the effects of any political conflicts and created general feelings of 'family togetherness'. In Deng Xiaoping's case there were more than general feelings and some genuine historical ironies. In 1933 Li Weihan was Deng's main antagonist who led the criticism of the 'Luo Ming' line. Deng's wife divorced him at the time and shortly after married Li Weihan. Their son, Li Tieying, became Deng's protégé in the 1980s and joined the CCP Political Bureau in 1985. Li Weihan's assistant in 1933 was Yang Shangkun. Deng and Yang not only worked closely together in the Taihang Region, and in the CCP Central Committee in the 1950s and 1960s, but one of Yang's sons married one of Deng's daughters. On the other hand, although Deng Xiaoping's personal and political connections were extensive, and that clearly helps explain his survival, they were not comprehensive. There were those within the CCP and its leadership with whom he had bad relations – Lin Biao and Jiang

Qing are obvious examples. There were also those with whom relations were always poor or unreliable: as for example, Peng Dehuai, with whom Deng had an uneasy relationship after 1938.

2   Childhood, youth and travel, 1904–1937

Unlike many of those who later became leaders of the CCP, the years of Deng Xiaoping's youth were years of travel. He left Sichuan in 1920 to work and study in France, and went on to Moscow before returning to China in 1927 and mainstream CCP activities until the outbreak of war with Japan in 1937. These were uncertain years, both for Deng Xiaoping and the CCP. Two of the friendships and associations he made during those years were to prove particularly important, not only at the time but later as his career developed. In France in the early 1920s and back in China again, on several occasions during the late 1920s and early 1930s, he worked with Zhou Enlai; in the Jiangxi Soviet during the early 1930s he first became closely associated with Mao Zedong. At the same time, Deng's career before 1937 did not all prove plain sailing either politically or personally. He was criticized for his handling of the 7th Red Army in 1931, and in 1933 he was severely disciplined by the CCP and demoted.

FAMILY BACKGROUND AND EARLY LIFE

Deng Xiaoping was born Deng Xiansheng on 22 August 1904 in Sichuan province, in West China. However, when at the age of 5 he attended private school his new teacher considered this name (meaning 'late sage') improper and an insult to Confucius, and promptly changed it to Xixian.[1] Like many revolutionaries, Deng adopted a *nomme de guerre* which became common usage – in his case in 1927 when civil war between the CCP and the nationalists first broke out. Later, in 1929 when he went as a political organizer to Guangxi Province, he once again changed his name, if only temporarily, to Deng Bin.

China at the time of Deng's childhood was still a traditional society unaffected by national politics and more concerned with the farming cycle and the weather. Modern schooling was just being introduced, but Deng's first school experience was in a traditional Classics-oriented private school – the usual education in the old imperial system for the sons of landowners. Tradition played such a role in everyday life that even when Deng reached France he still preferred to render his birthdate according to the Chinese agricultural calendar as 12 July (that is the 12th day of the 7th month) when he registered as an alien in Marseilles, rather than according to the Western Gregorian calendar.[2]

Deng's family lived in Paifang village of Xiexing township in Guang'an County, some 100 kilometres north of Chongqing. Chongqing, the last major city upstream from Shanghai on the Yangtze and some 2,500 kilometres from the sea, has historically been a large metropolis. However, its hinterland, unlike other parts of Sichuan province such as further west around Chengdu, has not been notably wealthy. Deng Xiaoping's father, Deng Wenming, was a relatively prosperous farmer, a landlord who rented out his land and who worked for most of his later life as a minor official in local government.

The Deng family were originally from Jiangxi but moved to Guang'an during the reign of the first Ming emperor. According to Deng Rong the family fell into poverty until Deng Xiaoping's grandfather accumulated some wealth as a master craftsman.[3] Some commentators have suggested that Deng is from a Hakka background, and in consequence have emphasized the Hakka reputation for being doughty fighters and for sticking together.[4] However, as far as can be ascertained, if the family ever were Hakka they seem long since to have lost any such identity. Certainly there is no particular evidence that links Deng Xiaoping with a Hakka background. He appears not, for example, to speak Hakka, and speaks Chinese with a pronounced Sichuanese accent.[5] Indeed, Sichuanese, rather than Hakka characteristics, are usually used to describe Deng Xiaoping. For example, the Sichuanese are often described in terms of their food which is noted for being hot and spicy. The Sichuanese temperament is regarded as peppery – it has a short fuse and inflames quickly, but bears no grudge or malice when it cools down.

Deng Wenming's relative wealth was reflected in the size of his family. Altogether he had four wives and seven children of his own who lived – four sons and three daughters.[6] His first wife, Zhang, had no children. His second wife, Dan, had one girl and three boys. The third wife, Xiao, had a son who died soon after birth; and the fourth, Xia Bogen, had a daughter from an earlier marriage, and a son and two daughters. Deng Xiaoping was the eldest son though not the eldest child – having an elder sister, Deng Xianlie – of Deng Wenming's second wife, Dan. However, she died early in her children's lives and it appears that Deng had a closer relationship with his father's fourth wife, Xia Bogen. Years later when Deng Xiaoping suffered internal exile during the Cultural Revolution, Xia Bogen accompanied Deng and his wife to Jiangxi. Deng's children referred to her as their paternal grandmother, even though she was not actually related by blood.

Deng Xiaoping lost contact to some extent with his immediate family once he left home, though it seems that later when he could he tried to do his best by them. Interestingly, a number of his siblings, including his eldest sister, were still alive in 1993. As just indicated, he attempted to look after his step-mother Xia Bogen during the Cultural Revolution and spent a large part of that time in nursing her. One of Deng Xiaoping's younger brothers, Deng Ken, who was born in 1910, became a schoolteacher in Guang'an County, and then later a newspaper editor. He joined the CCP in 1937, went to Yan'an and worked in the nascent New China News Agency. In 1949 he became deputy mayor of Chongqing and later moved to a similar post in Wuhan. Criticized as a 'capitalist roader' during the Cultural Revolution – no doubt a classic case of guilt by family association – he was later rehabilitated and able to retire in 1982 when Deputy Governor of Hubei province.

Another of Deng Xiaoping's brothers was not so lucky. Deng Shuping, born in 1912, became head of the family on his father's death and a local official in the Nationalist Party. After 1949 he read law at university, and was appointed to positions first in Guizhou Province (just south of Sichuan) and then in Chongqing. Under the pressure of criticism from Red Guards during the Cultural Revolution – presumably as much about his earlier career in the Nationalist Party as his relationship to Deng Xiaoping – he committed suicide in 1967. Deng Xiaoping's father, Deng Wenming, died in 1936.

In 1909 at the age of 5, Deng Xiaoping started out on the traditional path to imperial service by being enrolled in a private preparatory school to be educated in the Confucian classics. However, with the collapse of the imperial system and the revolution which overthrew the Qing dynasty in 1911 there was little point in continuing. Deng was enrolled instead in a primary school with a modern curriculum and later graduated to the middle school in Guang'an. From there he moved to study first in Chongqing, and then in France. The impetus came from his father, who was in Chongqing at that time and encouraged Deng, his own brother (and Deng Xiaoping's uncle) and another relative to come to Chongqing to study further at a preparatory school for young Chinese planning to continue their education in France.

The early decades of the twentieth century were a turbulent time for China's intellectuals. They recognized the challenge to China posed by the Western imperial powers and Japan, and sought solutions to its problems. Though many of these problems had been caused during the nineteenth century by colonial incursions into Chinese territory, none the less there was a kind of love–hate relationship with the West and several Chinese reformers looked to the promotion of Western ideas and systems of education as a means of modernizing China and making it strong again. One of these was Li Youying, who had himself been educated in Montargis just south of Paris. In 1912, with the active co-operation of the Mayor of Montargis and several other French notables, as well as Cai Yuanpei, Li established the Chinese Association for French Education to send Chinese students to France.

By 1919 many Chinese had gone abroad to study, and, though the original intention of educationists such as Li might have been that their parents should pay for their education, this rapidly proved impractical. Instead the Work-study Movement was started – in Chinese it was called *Qingong jianxue*, literally 'diligent work, thrifty study' – whereby Chinese students abroad engaged in part-work, part-study. With the birth of modern Chinese nationalism in the May 4th Movement many young Chinese were attracted by the opportunity to travel and be patriotic at the same time.

Necessarily if Chinese students were to live in France they would have to learn French. In 1919 Wu Yuzhang, a member of the Chinese Revolutionary Party, opened a school in Chongqing to prepare Sichuanese students for France, and it was here that Deng and his relative enrolled.[7] In 1920 some ninety of the students in Deng's class were selected to go to France through competitive examination, and Deng and his uncle were both successful. On 11 September 1920 the group left Shanghai aboard the Messageries Maritimes liner *Porthos*, bound for Marseilles. They arrived on 13 December 1920.[8] David Bonavia speculated in his biography that Deng's departure for France suggests some possible friction with his father or family on the grounds that Deng Xiaoping was the eldest son and there would have been at least an expectation that he should stay at home and prepare to take his father's place after the latter's death, rather than go on to France.[9] However, Benjamin Yang suggests almost the opposite – that Deng's father 'wanted his son to pursue something loftier and greater, something which he himself had not been able to accomplish.'[10]

CROISSANTS, LE CREUSOT AND COMMUNISM

Although Deng Xiaoping spent five years in France, from December 1920 to January 1926 – from the age of 16 to 21 – there is little evidence that he became a francophile, at least politically, during those years. On the other hand, he did acquire Western tastes in some areas. His love of soccer dates from this time, as well as of French food and especially croissants. Prince Sihanouk, the former Cambodian leader exiled in Beijing in the 1970s and 1980s, used to enjoy cooking French meals and would often send one round to Deng. Deng himself once confessed to Yang Shangkun that when he wanted to treat himself in Paris he would have a croissant with a glass of milk. Interestingly, it appears to have been Ho Chi Minh who instructed the young Deng on where to obtain the best of such delights. In 1974, on his first trip outside China since the Cultural Revolution, Deng visited New York and was intent on buying some croissants until it was suggested to him that since he was returning to China via Paris he could do better there. This he did, buying a hundred which returned to China with him, some to be duly supplied to Zhou Enlai and others who had also eaten croissants during their Paris days.[11]

As Deng's comment to Yang Shangkun appears to indicate, life was not easy for Deng or indeed the other Chinese worker-students in France. France in the early 1920s was in the middle of an economic crisis and work was hard to find. The Chinese rapidly found that their Chinese academic qualifications were not acceptable for entry to French institutions, and that their spoken French was really inadequate for study. Most tended to drift to Paris and those large industrial plants that employed large numbers of foreign workers, such as the Renault plant in Billancourt (a south-western suburb of Paris) where Deng worked for most of the last three years of his time in France. There they lived together in close proximity, and many became involved in the nascent communist movement as much for social as political reasons.

One fairly reliable source for Deng's movements in France is his police record, though even then Deng only came under their relatively close scrutiny during 1925. [12] It seems Deng spent the first half of his stay in France travelling around quite widely, taking work – including spells as a fireman on a locomotive and as a kitchen hand – almost as he could find it. From Marseilles he travelled to Bayeux where he enrolled in a secondary school for three months. Running out of money he drifted to the Chinese *émigré* community in La Garenne-Colombes, a south-western suburb of Paris, and worked in a factory. It was precisely at this time and place that Zhou Enlai and three or four other politically active Chinese *émigrés* were establishing the Socialist Youth League of China – the forerunner of the CCP in France – though there is no direct evidence that Deng was as yet immediately brought into their orbit. Later in 1921 he worked at the Le Creusot Iron and Steel Plant and by early 1922 finally arrived in Montargis, which must have been one of his goals when he had left Chongqing.

During the early 1920s Montargis – still a pretty and genteel provincial town whose inhabitants then would have been mightily surprised if they had known what was going on – played host to a series of Chinese radical worker-students. Chinese came not only from Sichuan but from other provinces too, including a significant number from Changsha in Hunan. They had been amongst the first to arrive in Montargis and had established a branch of the New People's Study Society which later became the nucleus for the formation of the Socialist Youth League of China. The New People's Study Society had been formed in 1918 in Changsha by Cai Hesen and Mao Zedong, and in 1919 had been active in recruiting students to go to France. Mao stayed in China but Cai and many others went abroad. These included Li Weihan, whom it seems reasonable to assume Deng met at this time, who was to play a less benign role for a while later in Deng's life. The Chinese attended the Montargis Institute and many, like Deng, worked at Hutchinson's Rubber Factory.

On this occasion Deng stayed in Montargis for the best part of seven months. However, towards the end of 1922 he moved on again, this time to Chatillon-sur-Seine where he attended secondary school. Early in 1923, he returned to Montargis, and for a much shorter time to Hutchinson's. His work record card notes not only that he was assigned to work in the boot and shoemaking workshop, but also that after March 1923 he was not to be re-employed.[13] There is no indication of what caused this remark though it is possible that Deng had fallen foul of tensions within the Chinese community because of his increasing involvement in political activities. Deng stayed in Montargis until June 1923, when he returned to south-west Paris and work as a fitter in the Renault factory in Billancourt, where he stayed until he left France in January 1926.

It is reasonable to assume that Deng's movements around France had some political motivation. In 1936 Deng told Edgar Snow that he had been recruited to the CCP from the French Communist Party.[14] Whilst this may or may not be the case, Deng's organizational abilities had become clear at a very early stage, and he was rapidly engaged in the work of the European Branch of the Socialist Youth League of China after 1922. One of his colleagues on the trip from China recalled how when they reached Marseilles Deng took charge of arranging the Sichuanese students' disembarkation, with their luggage, whilst others of the incoming students were left not really knowing what came next.[15] His organizational skills were soon to be engaged in political activities. In 1922, Deng joined the European

Branch of the Socialist Youth League of China, which had been formed by radical Chinese then in France (as a precursor to the establishment of the European branch of the CCP) and included Zhou Enlai and Cai Hesen. Deng himself, according to his daughter, appears to date his membership of the CCP from 15 July 1924. On that day he was elected one of the five-man leadership group of the European Branch of the Socialist Youth League, which according to party rules entailed the responsibilities of a member of the European Branch of the CCP.[16]

Zhou Enlai was the editor of first the League's and later the CCP's bi-monthly newsletter and Deng worked with him, with responsibility for publishing it. In fact the documents and newsletters were simply reproduced, most often through hand-cut stencils and hand-rolled duplication. Deng's responsibility was as much practical as administrative, for he personally duplicated most of the League's, and later the CCP branch's, materials from then until he left France. When the Paris police raided his room on 8 January 1926, after he had left for the USSR, they discovered 'two oil-based ink printing kits with plates and rollers and several packets of paper for printing'.[17] For these efforts his colleagues dubbed him, doubtless somewhat ironically, the 'Doctor of Duplication'.

When Zhou Enlai left France for China in 1924, Deng took over his editorial responsibilities for the CCP newsletter *Red Light*. However, he was soon to become one of the more senior members of the CCP in France, though still only 21 years old himself. In June 1925 a group of demonstrators organized by the CCP stormed the Chinese government's embassy in Paris in a purely symbolic gesture of solidarity with the party and workers in Shanghai. French public opinion was horrified and the action led to the deportation of some fifty CCP members and the voluntary return to China of about fifty more. Deng found himself elected as one of the new leaders of the party branch and as such came under close police scrutiny.

During the second half of 1925, Deng spoke on several occasions at meetings in the Paris area to promote the CCP cause or to discuss the current situation in China. One of these ended in a near-riot as opinions amongst the Chinese worker-students were highly polarized into pro- and anti-communist groups. It is reported that as the chairs flew across the room, Deng watched quietly from the platform. At another, five days before he left France, Deng argued strongly for a close alliance between the northern Chinese warlord Feng Yuxiang and the USSR. Strangely, within a little over a year Deng was to be appointed to work with Feng in Xi'an. The French police finally raided Deng's house in Billancourt on 8 January 1926. However, Deng and his companions had left for Moscow the day before.

STUDENT TO POLITICAL WORKER

In Moscow, Deng Xiaoping was finally able to engage in some further study, though this was largely more political than academic. The path he followed from Europe to Moscow was one that had been well trodden by young CCP members, and from the late 1920s on many Chinese were to study in Moscow at the

University of the Toilers of the East, Moscow's Sun Yat-sen University. The latter had been founded in late 1925 – at a time of maximum co-operation between the CCP and the Nationalists – in order to train personnel for the revolution in China, largely with funds donated by wealthy Nationalist Party members. It was an interesting time in the history of the CCP. Not only was there close co-operation between the CCP, the CPSU and the Nationalist Party, but the Chinese students themselves were caught up in the intra-party conflicts of the CPSU and courted by the followers of Bukharin, Stalin and Trotsky.

Amongst those Deng was likely to have encountered in Moscow would have been Chen Shaoyu, more widely known since as Wang Ming, the most high profile of the '28 Bolsheviks' who dominated the CCP from late 1930 until early 1935; and Zhang Wentian, another of the same group. Amongst his classmates at Sun Yat-sen University were three of more than passing significance. One whom there is no evidence he knew personally was Chiang Ching-kuo, the eldest son of Chiang Kai-shek, who himself was to become President of the Republic of China on his father's death, albeit when the Republic was confined to Taiwan. Another was Wang Jiaxiang, who returned to China as part of the '28 Bolsheviks', though perhaps more loosely associated than most. Wang was to prove an invaluable source of support to Mao in the latter's struggle for supremacy within the CCP in 1935, and was one of the main leaders (together with Mao and Zhang Wentian) of the Long March. In 1933 when Deng's career was under a cloud, it was Wang who provided immediate assistance.

A third classmate was Feng Funeng, eldest daughter of Feng Yuxiang. During 1926 Feng Yuxiang visited the USSR looking for aid and assistance. Feng Yuxiang was not a typical warlord: he was a Christian who maintained a highly disciplined army. Despite his fundamental anti-communism Feng was temporarily prepared to accept Soviet aid. However, Comintern assistance was made dependent on Feng's joining the Nationalist Party and his participation in Chiang Kai-shek's military attempt to reunite China – the Northern Expedition – which was also supported by the CCP. Feng returned to China and was followed by about a hundred Comintern advisers, including several Chinese, one of whom was Deng Xiaoping.[18]

Feng Yuxiang's National United Army was based in Xian in north-western China. A military academy, dominated by several communist officers – until later in 1927 CCP members were all also members of the Nationalist Party – had been established there under the army's general headquarters, and it was Deng's intention to work there as a political instructor helping to train future communist officers. However, it was April 1927 and any such plans had to be rapidly dropped. The growing conflict between the CCP and the Nationalist Party came out into the open and Feng Yuxiang sided openly in this conflict with Chiang Kai-shek, rounding on his communist officers and executing those of them who had not taken evasive action.

Deng changed his name to Deng Xiaoping and went south to Wuhan, on the Yangtze, where he once again joined up with Zhou Enlai. Whether through that connection, or simply because he was around, Deng was appointed as a secretary to the CCP's Central Committee, currently headquartered in Wuhan. The Nationalist Party had split into two wings and the left wing had established its capital in Wuhan, away from Chiang Kai-shek's influence. It was a natural place for the CCP to establish its central secretariat for it seemed to offer some political protection. Unfortunately, this calculation also went awry in July and August of 1927 when, largely as a result of Comintern interference, even the left wing of the Nationalist Party turned on the CCP, forcing it underground. The CCP Central Committee held an emergency meeting in Wuhan, which as a secretary (but not as a member with speaking or voting rights) Deng attended. The emergency meeting held General Secretary Chen Duxiu personally responsible for the party's catastrophe and removed him from office; adopted a new policy of military insurrection; and moved CCP headquarters, including Deng, secretly to Shanghai.

In Shanghai, Deng, who was still only 23, was appointed chief secretary of the Central Committee. His responsibilities included looking after the CCP's central documents, confidential work, communications and financial affairs. It was a testing time for the CCP. In Shanghai and other urban areas CCP activities were almost totally underground. In 1927 and 1928 the CCP was engaged in a series of military insurrections, the most famous of which occurred at Nanchang in August 1927, all of which were unsuccessful and expensive in terms of human life and organizational strength. To cap it all the CCP itself was bitterly divided and was to remain that way for some time, as different tendencies within the party all struggled for control.

Deng's activities during 1927 and 1928 remain obscured, even in his daughter's biography, presumably because running an underground secretariat, though at times dangerous, remains rather routine. As Deng later recalled the tension was great, but the house he and his wife shared with Zhou Enlai and Deng Yingchao (Zhou Enlai's wife) was only raided once.[19] In June 1928 the 6th CCP Congress was held in Moscow, both because of the situation in China and because the Comintern wanted to reassert its control. Most of the members of the new collective leadership of the CCP, including Zhou Enlai and Qu Qiubai, who had led the attack on Chen Duxiu, went to Moscow. However, the labour organizer Li Weihan, whom Deng had probably encountered in Montargis, stayed behind to manage CCP routine during the congress, and Deng assisted him.

On a personal note, in the Spring of 1928 Deng married for the first time. His wife was Zhang Xiyuan, a European languages expert, who also worked in the CCP secretariat. They had met in Moscow and married in Shanghai. Unfortunately, it was to be but a short-lived marriage. She died in January 1930, after a complicated pregnancy. Although the CCP Central Committee had sent Deng to Guangxi as a political organizer in September 1929 he had come back to Shanghai to report some time during the second half of December and was there at the time of his wife's death.[20]

GUANGXI AND PEASANT INSURRECTION

By the late 1920s the CCP was dominated by Li Lisan, who aimed, at first at least, to follow the political line agreed at the 6th CCP Congress in Moscow. The peasantry were to be mobilized under CCP leadership, rural soviets were to be established and peasant uprisings were to be linked to urban insurrections. In line with these policies Deng Xiaoping was sent to Guangxi Province, in South-west China, in April 1929 to assist a minor warlord, Li Mingrui, who had communist sympathies, and Wei Baqun who had launched a peasant rebellion in the early 1920s.

Here, the historical record is in conflict. According to Hu Hua, Deng travelled to Guangxi via Vietnam with the aid of Ho Chi Minh who was living in Shanghai at the time and whom Deng had met in Paris. He advised Deng how to travel, to disguise himself as a businessman, and what other precautions to take *en route*. Under the *nomme de guerre* of Deng Bin, Deng Xiaoping set off, first by boat to Hong Kong, then with the aid of the Indo-Chinese underground communist movement by boat again to Haiphong in present-day Vietnam, then overland, re-entering China through the south-west; a long way round, but at the time probably the safest way politically, and also the quickest. According to Deng Rong, though Deng Xiaoping went by boat to Hong Kong, he then travelled overland via Guangzhou to Guangxi.[21]

The situation in Guangxi was not simple, and the CCP had been trying to expand its activities there for some years.[22] Deng was neither the only nor the first CCP cadre to be sent as a political organizer at this time: Yu Shaojie and Zhang Yunyi had preceded him during the previous two years. CCP support came from two different directions, a peasant movement and local army officers.

Guangxi is an area only half of whose population is ethnically Chinese. The rest belong to one of the many minority groups that populate China's south-western border with South-east Asia. Of these, by far the largest minority nationality are the Zhuang – indeed they are the largest non-Chinese group in the whole of China, and account for about 35 per cent of Guangxi's population. During the best part of 1,000 years most of the Zhuang in Guangxi have been thoroughly sinicized, with the exception of those in the poorer and more remote areas around the Left and Right River Valleys in the province's north-west. Conflict was endemic between these remnant Zhuang and the rest of Guangxi, and in the early 1920s the collapse of government led to the emergence of a self-protection Zhuang Peasant Movement based at Donglan to the north of the Right River under the leadership of Wei Baqun. Initially defeated by local landlords, Wei trained at the CCP's Peasant Movement Training Institute in Guangzhou before returning to Guangxi. This time the Zhuang Peasant Movement was more successful, forcing the provincial Nationalist Party authorities by 1926 to recognize its control of Donglan county. The leading Nationalist who dealt with Wei was also a member of the CCP, and he took the opportunity to recruit Wei and other peasant leaders. The Zhuang Peasant Movement was so well established that by 1927 when the Nationalist Party turned on the CCP it was able to survive.

The Guangxi Clique was an important factor in national politics during the mid-1920s, not least because of Guangxi's army which was active well beyond provincial boundaries. Its leader Li Zongren was not only anti-communist but also not well-disposed towards Chiang Kai-shek. None the less, many of its officers were left-inclined or members of the CCP. One of these was Yu Zuobo who with CCP approval engineered the officers' defection from Li Zongren to Chiang Kai-shek, thereby not only enabling Chiang to defeat the Guangxi Clique but also bringing himself and another CCP sympathizer, Li Mingrui, to power in Guangxi. This was the situation Deng Xiaoping encountered in Nanning, the capital of Guangxi, when he arrived in 1929.

In Nanning Deng and Zhang Yunyi, a CCP veteran of the Nanchang Uprising in 1927, set about developing two brigades of pro-CCP soldiers, and continued Yu Zuobo's policy of sending aid and assistance to the Zhuang rebels in the Right River area. In September 1929 a CCP congress in Nanning agreed to establish a Red Army and to arm the peasantry. At the end of the month, Li Mingrui and Yu Zuobo were forced into battle against the reconstituted army of the Guangxi Clique, but without Deng and Zhang Yunyi who led their two brigades – some 1,000 men – up the Right River to Bose, not far from Wei Baqun at Donglan. Li and Yu were rapidly defeated, and Li retreated to Bose.

Bose is in the heart of one of the poorest areas of China. In the 1990s it remains economically backward and is one of only six counties in the whole country which receives special central assistance for that reason.[23] In the late 1920s it was a major market area for the local production of opium and by imposing a tax on the movement of opium through the town, but not curtailing its production, the CCP had access to an invaluable source of income. This revenue was used to pay members of the newly constituted 7th Red Army, and undoubtedly helps explain its rapid growth within a very short time to about 7,000 men.[24]

In addition, in Bose the CCP adopted a programme of organization and peasant mobilization which brought rapid results. The local people and the new soldiers of the Red Army were to be politicized; the army was to be expanded and improved in quality as well as quantity; the peasantry was to be armed under CCP leadership; landlords were to have their property confiscated; and land reform was to be introduced. By December Deng, Zhang Yunyi, and Wei Baqun came together to organize the Bose Uprising and establish the Right River Soviet Government. Quite quickly, the soviet spread to cover some twenty counties with a population of a million people. Deng, who was already the CCP's ranking secretary in Guangxi, became the political commissar of the 7th Red Army,[25] though he appears not to have been in Bose on the day fixed for rebellion (11 December 1929) having returned to Shanghai to report to the CCP Central Committee.

Emboldened by success, the rebellion spread to Longzhou on the Left River and in February 1930 a second soviet and the 8th Red Army were established. However, this enterprise was always much smaller, less well organized and lacking in local support. The Longzhou Uprising was also much more violent than that in Bose. The French Consulate and the Catholic mission were both attacked because it was claimed that they were protecting rich landlords and merchants. The French responded by bombing Longzhou, and the border between Indo-China and Guangxi was closed. Within two months the Longzhou Uprising was crushed by the Nationalist Army and the remnants of the 8th Red Army made their way to Bose.

However, even in Bose success proved to be much more illusory than at first had seemed to be the case. The Right River Soviet faced two major problems: it had failed to disarm its opponents and the local militias; and it had failed to politicize adequately. In particular, it had failed to recognize the importance of not being seen to behave as a warlord itself (which was on the whole the local perception) – not that the local Zhuang were likely to be as opposed to communist Chinese as they were to anti-communist Chinese. As the Right River Soviet tried to expand it found that when the Red Army moved on the landlords were able to reassert their authority and the *status quo ante* with little difficulty.

Deng had returned from Shanghai in February but appears to have concentrated on rural reform in Donglan, part of the Right River Soviet. By August the military situation had deteriorated, but worse was to come. Under Li Lisan's direction the CCP had adopted a renewed policy of urban insurrection and the 7th Red Army was ordered to leave its base and march on Liuzhou, Guilin (both in Guangxi) and Guangzhou (Canton). Unsurprisingly, there was a clash between the native Zhuangs under Wei Baqun, who wanted to disobey CCP orders and stay, and those like Deng, who though they must have found the orders impractical in the extreme none the less felt duty-bound to obey. In the event Deng, Zhang Yunyi and the majority of the 7th Red Army (some 20,000 men) set out for Liuzhou in September, leaving a small force behind under Wei Baqun. The soviet was attacked and collapsed almost immediately.

In October, Deng and Zhang Yunyi called a party congress of the 7th Red Army at Hechi *en route* to Liuzhou. Losses required that the army be reorganized and their goals reassessed. They decided instead to head for southern Jiangxi and the rural soviet established by Mao. It was a long and tortuous journey which took the 7th Red Army into northern Guangdong, back to Guangxi where Deng and Zhang became separated, and on to Jiangxi via Guangdong and Hunan, all the while harried by Nationalist armies. In February 1931 the 7th Red Army was reunited and took the county seat of Chongyi in Jiangxi. It had been a terrible precursor of the Long March that was to come. By the time the 7th Red Army reached Jiangxi it had been reduced to fewer than 4,000 men.

Before this, however, as discussed in the previous chapter, Deng Xiaoping had left his troops and travelled separately to Shanghai. Various accounts have tried to suggest that Deng abandoned his command perfunctorily or acted improperly in some way.[26] Others have argued, either implicitly or explicitly, that Deng was in some way acting according to either CCP orders or agreed procedures, possibly even in concert with Li Mingrui, after the two became separated at a river crossing.[27] Certainly there is real controversy here as indicated by the disproportionate number of chapters devoted to the Guangxi Uprisings and the 7th Red Army in Deng Rong's biography of her father.[28] The CCP Central Committee held Deng to be the person most responsible for the defeat of the 7th Red Army, even though in his report he had pointed out that in his view the uprisings had failed because too much emphasis had been placed on military engagement rather than mass mobilization.[29] It is an event which has resurfaced historiographically to embarrass Deng. Apparently, at the 7th CCP Congress in 1945, one of the former 7th Red Army officers, Mo Wenhua, spoke out about Deng's action in 1931. [30] In that context it is interesting to note that though the particular incident of leaving the 7th Red Army to return to Shanghai was not mentioned, the story of the Right River Soviet was given an airing in *People's Daily* immediately before the 3rd plenum of the 11th Central Committee in 1978.[31]

JIANGXI, MAO ZEDONG AND THE LONG MARCH

Having left Li Mingrui and the 7th Red Army and headed for Shanghai, Deng Xiaoping met up again with Zhou Enlai and those with whom he had worked before he had left for Guangxi. In whatever manner his report on the Guangxi Uprisings was accepted, criticism was not too great, for he soon found himself delegated to make an inspection tour of the CCP organization in Anhui for the Central Committee during May and June.[32] At this time Li Lisan had been replaced as leader of the CCP by the '28 Bolsheviks' – some of whom, such as Wang Jiaxiang, Deng would have met in Moscow. Although the new leadership was reluctant to acknowledge that Mao was pursuing a more sensible, if gradual, revolutionary path in Jiangxi, they none the less recognized that Jiangxi was now the centre of CCP activities, and in the first half of 1931 resolved to move party headquarters there. To that end Zhou Enlai, who had characteristically survived Li Lisan's purge despite his own close association, was appointed director of the Central Bureau for Soviet Affairs, one of whose tasks was to oversee the transfer of personnel to Jiangxi over the next two years.

In the middle of 1931 Deng Xiaoping was transferred to Jiangxi, and it was here that he first came into close contact with Mao Zedong, through his appointment first as party secretary of Ruijin county, and then later of the border area of Huichang, responsible for Huichang, Anyuan and Xunwu counties. Xunwu is particularly important in the development of Mao's eventually successful strategy of peasant mobilization. Mao developed this strategy through a series of rural surveys, one of which was based in Xunwu.[33] There is no contemporary record of Deng's view of Mao's peasant policy at that time. However, Deng with his practical outlook cannot have failed to be impressed by the contrast between southern Jiangxi and the events in the Right River Soviet. Certainly, later – when Deng was responsible for the Taihang region during the Sino-Japanese War and in the mid-1940s – the lessons of politicization, production and guerrilla warfare were repeatedly emphasized.

On the other hand, Deng's first contact with Mao could well have been confrontational. When Deng first arrived in Ruijin, he found many party members awaiting execution. A mutiny had broken out against Mao amongst an army group loyal to Li Lisan in southern Jiangxi at the end of 1930. Mao acted ruthlessly in putting it down and executed several thousand party members, who were castigated as belonging to a Nationalist Party secret organization designed to undermine the CCP. One consequence was a witch-hunt in which many other loyal CCP members uninvolved in any way in the dispute with Mao and certainly not engaged in anti-CCP activities came under suspicion. Deng acted promptly to end the hysteria: all cases were examined according to party rules, and those unfairly accused released. When Zhou Enlai arrived in Ruijin towards the end of the year he fully endorsed Deng's actions. [34]

Deng's appointment in Ruijin did not last long. As more personnel were transferred into the Jiangxi Soviet Deng was moved aside for senior cadres. He moved first, as already noted, to Huichang county and was given the responsibility for the three adjacent counties of Huichang, Xunwu and Anyuan, though only the first of these was genuinely under CCP control. [35] As 1932 progressed it became clear that Deng Xiaoping had become an energetic supporter of Mao's policies and that a good relationship had developed between them. He became director of the Propaganda Department of the Jiangxi CCP committee during the year, but this too was to be a short-lived appointment. However, this time the reason was political disgrace. As already indicated, there was considerable tension within the CCP between Mao and his followers on the one hand, and the '28 Bolsheviks' and their followers on the other. As the latter moved into Jiangxi they tried to oust Mao and his followers from positions of authority and to minimize his influence politically. They opposed his views on guerrilla warfare, argued that the local armed forces should be disbanded and that a single powerful united Red Army should be created, and were dogmatic that land reform should dispossess former rich and middle peasants as well as landlords.

Presumably because of his experiences in Guangxi, as well as later in Jiangxi, Deng Xiaoping found himself in opposition to the CCP leadership on almost all counts. In particular, he argued that it was necessary to pursue a lenient policy towards the relatively prosperous peasants both to ensure that the CCP had sufficient support to ensure it could implement land reform and because as a guerrilla force the CCP required a sound economic base for its own sustenance. In 1933 the CCP leader of Fujian province, Luo Ming, who had been an associate of Li Lisan's, was criticized by one of the '28 Bolsheviks' for being too negative in his attitude to mass mobilization. In fact he had simply pointed out that those living in border areas could not be mobilized endlessly with promises of future glory, however sympathetic they might be to the CCP: repeated enemy attacks were sapping morale. This was the time of Chiang Kai-shek's Fourth Encirclement Campaign against the Jiangxi Soviet. The CCP leadership took the opportunity to attack Mao and his supporters for their views, linking them to what they regarded as Luo Ming's defeatism, the so-called 'Luo Ming line.'

The attack on the 'Luo Ming line' started with an article in the party newspaper in April 1933 by Li Weihan, [36] whom Deng had known in France and worked with in the Central Committee. Mao could not be criticized by name but others were, notably Deng, Mao Zetan (Mao's third brother), Xie Weijun and Gu Bo. The attack continued with an article in the May edition of the party's journal *Struggle* when Li Weihan called for 'an attack without mercy and a struggle with brutality' against the miscreants. He certainly had his way, for Deng lost his position, was imprisoned and interrogated. He reportedly wrote two or three self-criticisms, or confessions, and when these failed to satisfy he apparently dug in his heels, saying 'I cannot write more. What I say is true.'

In addition, Deng also lost his wife, Jin Weiying, whom he had met in Shanghai in 1931 and married in Ruijin during 1932. At the time of his disgrace she divorced him, and soon after married Li Weihan, Deng's antagonist at the time. This has led some commentators to argue that a deal of some kind might have been struck.[37] Quite apart from any other more obvious explanation, if later experience, particularly during the Cultural Revolution, is any guide, it is also possible that Deng and Jin divorced in order simply to protect Jin. In those circumstances it is even possible that Deng might have taken the initiative. Whatever may have been the relationship between Mao and Deng before these incidents, afterwards it is clear that a strong political bond had been formed.

While he had been imprisoned and underfed, food had been smuggled in to Deng by Wang Jiaxiang, a friend from Moscow days, and his wife, and it was Wang who again helped Deng after the latter had been posted in disgrace to the Nancun district CCP committee in Le'an county, a poor border area. Deng spent only some ten days in Nancun district before Wang had him assigned to the General Political Department of the 1st Front Army which Wang headed. Deng was eventually appointed secretary-general to the department and worked in the Propaganda Division where his main task became that of editing the army's official journal *Red Star*. It was a task he was to maintain right through the Long March.

When the CCP's central offices left Ruijin on 10 October 1934 on what was to become the Long March, so too did Deng Xiaoping, but details of Deng's participation remain sketchy. When asked by his daughter what he did on the Long March, Deng is reported to have replied simply that he 'went along', though he does remember that he lost his horse, his overcoat and a roll of dried meat crossing the mountains.[38] According to Harrison Salisbury, when the Long March started Deng was in semi-disgrace and he later developed typhoid, from which he was seriously ill by the time the CCP reached north Shaanxi.[39]

The turning point in Deng's fortune, and indeed the CCP's, was the Zunyi Conference in January 1935 at which the leadership of the '28 Bolsheviks' was overturned and Mao's policies adopted. Deng left Ruijin on foot; a junior colleague remembers walking with him as far as Zunyi but not afterwards. Deng was nominated by Zhou Enlai, with Mao's full approval, to take minutes at the Zunyi Conference of the Political Bureau.[40] There is no record that he said a word at the meeting, simply sitting to one side, no doubt entirely satisfied by the proceedings.[41]

As for others who had supported Mao before the Long March started, promotion soon accompanied rehabilitation. Deng became secretary of the CCP Central Committee under Zhou Enlai once again, and later in the Long March when the Red Army was reorganized he was appointed to head the Propaganda

Division of the Political Department of the First Army Group.

When the Red Army arrived in northern Shaanxi in late 1935 its first task was to set about strengthening its much-weakened resources. A rural soviet had existed in the area since the late 1920s and this was now developed, later moving its capital to the more famous Yan'an in January 1937. Recovered from his illness, in the first half of 1936 Deng participated in the Red Army's expedition to Shanxi Province, and then was appointed Deputy Director and, later, Director of the Political Department of the First Army Group. It was the first of many senior military appointments that were to occupy much of his time for the next sixteen years.

3 Military service, 1937–1952

The start of the Sino-Japanese War in July 1937 drew almost all of the CCP into either the military or war-related service. Nevertheless, Deng Xiaoping became and remained engaged in military activities to a remarkable extent, not only from January 1938 when he first joined the 129th Division of the Eighth Route Army to the end of the Sino-Japanese War, but right through to the CCP occupation of South-west China in the early 1950s. At first Deng's involvement with the military was almost certainly a function of his relationship with Mao Zedong, who wanted someone he could trust in a number of key positions. However, with the passage of time, Deng's relationship with the military developed its own momentum. By the end of the Sino-Japanese War though he was political commissar to Liu Bocheng's commander, the army they led was known as the 'Liu–Deng Army'.

These fourteen years saw Liu Bocheng and Deng Xiaoping working closely together, first to consolidate the position of the 129th Division in the Taihang Mountains, and then expanding both the CCP base area and the size of the army.[1] The base areas they established eventually coalesced into four – the Taihang, Taiyue, South Hebei and Hebei–Shandong–Henan base areas – that came together to form the JinJiLuYu (Shanxi–Hebei–Shandong–Henan) Border Region, which itself eventually became an important constituent part of the North China People's Government formed in 1948 as a precursor to the PRC. The army they developed not only grew to be one of the largest CCP forces by the end of the Sino-Japanese War but went on to significant victories in the Civil War – notably in the Huai-Hai campaign – becoming the PLA's 2nd Field Army in the process. During 1949 to 1952 they established and organized CCP rule in China's South-west region. These years provided Deng Xiaoping with military credentials and status which were to prove important to him personally later, particularly after the Cultural Revolution. However, they also provided him with practical experience of mass mobilization and policy implementation which he was to draw on in the future, as well as a substantial network of colleagues and subordinates who were to become an essential part of his base of support in post-Cultural Revolution politics.[2]

THE EIGHTH ROUTE ARMY

In July 1937 the Red Army was reorganized as the Eighth Route Army, as a result of the agreement between the CCP and the Nationalist Party to co-operate to resist the Japanese. The Communist forces, the Eighth Route Army, were in three divisions of the national army: the 115th, under Lin Biao, headed for north-east Shanxi from Yan'an; the 120th, under He Long, went to north-west Shanxi; and the 129th Division, which was led by Liu Bocheng, made for south-east Shanxi. Although as far as the Nationalist government was concerned the Eighth Route Army was redesignated as the 18th Army Group in September 1937, the name stuck as a descriptor of the communist forces. One reason for this was the CCP's success in recruiting support and soldiers at a very early stage, and Deng's role in that process was far from insignificant.

At the start of the war Deng had been appointed Deputy Director of the Political Department of the Eighth Route Army under Ren Bishi as Director. His tasks, which were initially concerned with propaganda, rapidly became those of recruitment and mobilization. In early September 1937 he attended the War Council convened by Zhou Enlai in Taiyuan – the capital of Shanxi Province, which was to fall to the Japanese in two months – and was appointed to be the CCP's representative on the General Mobilization Committee of the Second Battle Front established with Yan Xishan and the Nationalists.[3] From Taiyuan, Deng moved with the headquarters of the Eighth Route Army to the area north of the Shijiazhuang–Taiyuan railway and centred on Mount Wutai, the northern part of the Taihang range. From this base, Deng travelled round setting up War Mobilization Committees and an associated organizational infrastructure to prepare for war, including peasant associations, workers' unions and training schools. The appeal was most definitely to nationalism and saving the country from Japanese invasion, even though the techniques may have been from Moscow's Sun Yat-sen University.[4] Interestingly, though he met Agnes Smedley at this time, others in the Eighth Route Army's headquarters seem to have imposed more on her consciousness. She simply records having met Ren Bishi's assistant, and missheard his name as 'Ting'.[5]

However, at the beginning of 1938 Deng was on the move again, joining Liu Bocheng – they had originally met in 1931 in the Jiangxi Soviet[6] – and the 129th Division as political commissar. In the early years of the war it seems that Mao had some concerns about his ability to control the 129th Division. There were reasonable grounds for doubt in the not so distant past. In the course of the Long March, Zhang Guotao and the Fourth Front Army had disagreed with Mao's conduct of CCP affairs and particularly the intended destination of strategic retreat. For a time they had split the CCP as well as the communist forces and marched towards the USSR, though they eventually rejoined Mao and the rest of the CCP in the North Shaanxi base area.[7] It was these troops who became the 129th Division, initially under their commander Xu Xiangqian with Chen Changhao as political commissar. In August 1937 Mao replaced the leadership of the 129th Division, bringing in Liu Bocheng, an experienced soldier, as commander and Zhang Hao as political commissar. Zhang Hao's problem, as far as Mao was concerned, was that he was somewhat old and set in his ways. Presumably because he wanted someone younger whom he could trust Mao turned to Deng.

Given Deng's relative lack of experience the extent to which he spent time away from Yan'an and, more generally, CCP headquarters during those years was quite remarkable, and almost certainly reflects the degree of trust placed upon him by Mao Zedong. Even in 1942 and 1943 when Mao and his supporters finally stamped their control on the CCP and 'sinicized' the Chinese communist movement, Deng was not required to return to Yan'an for the rectification campaign. As far as Mao was concerned he had no problem with Deng Xiaoping: he was a subordinate not a colleague, and in any case had already shown that he could be trusted. Moreover, someone had to remain in the field and provide leadership to the CCP's work, and that task fell to Deng Xiaoping.[8]

Deng Xiaoping only visited Yan'an three times after his appointment as political commissar of the 129th Division. The longest period was August to December 1938, and included attendance at the enlarged 6th plenum of the CCP Central Committee. In August 1939 he attended an enlarged meeting of the CCP Political Bureau; and in June 1945 he participated in the 1st plenum of the CCP Central Committee to which he had just been elected, though he did not attend the 7th CCP Congress, being on an inspection tour of the Hebi–Shandong–Henan base area at the time. On one of these visits to Yan'an, in September 1939, he married Zhuo Lin, whom he had met the previous month.[9]

The institution of political commissar was one that the CCP had inherited from the experience of the CPSU, which in trying to create the Red Army after the Russian Revolution recognized that many of the soldiers would not be committed communists and so required both political education and control. For the CCP the work of the political commissars and the political departments was somewhat different. It was their task not only to politicize and propagandize within the army but also amongst the civilian population. Indeed, under the conditions of guerrilla warfare this was a crucial responsibility for the CCP cause. In border regions, where the CCP was not well established and enemy attack always likely – as where Deng operated for almost twelve years – the army required the support of the local population to survive. In a very real sense there was no difference between army and party – CCP members had to be peasants by day and soldiers by night. Deng was thus responsible for political affairs within the military, and the ranking party cadre in the region. Indeed, when the CCP Central Committee established its Taihang Bureau in 1942, Deng's status was recognized by his appointment as secretary, the highest ranked position.

Liu Bocheng, like Deng and many of the original troops of the 129th Division from the Fourth Front Army, was a Sichuanese. Born in 1892 he had a distinguished military career, despite losing one eye, before joining the CCP in 1926. In the latter part of 1937 he led the 129th Division into the southern part of the Taihang Mountains from the north across the Shijiazhuang–Taiyuan railway line through Pingding County. Though there were some 6,000 troops in the division at the time, and more soldiers were allotted to the 129th Division than to the other divisions of the Eighth Route Army, it was still well below full division strength. The Taihang Mountains run to the south-west of Beijing, and the southern part has long been a strategic position for movement between North and Central China. Even before Deng's arrival Liu had carried out successful raiding parties against Japanese troops and aircraft.[10] However, that was in the early part of the Japanese advance and, as the year progressed and the Japanese occupied the cities of northern China, the Taihang base rapidly found itself a major centre of CCP activity behind enemy lines – Zhu De even moved the general headquarters of the entire Eighth Route Army there in November 1937.

Wuxiang, Licheng and Liaoxian (later renamed Zuo Quan in memory of the CCP commander killed there[11]) in the mountains to the north of the Handan–Changzhi road were the heartland of the Taihang base area. From here as the Japanese moved on into China, largely moving down the railways to ensure their lines of communication, the 129th Division spread out behind them, and established guerrilla groups, local governments and an organizational infra-structure for resistance to Japan. In 1938 and the first part of 1939 CCP expansion in the Taihang base and the area around for quite some way was both rapid and spectacular. By the end of 1939 the 129th Division's area of operations was considered to include four base areas in a large region bounded by the Yellow River (to the south), the Shijiazhuang–Jinan–Xuzhou railway to the north-east, and the Shijiazhuang–Xi'an railway to the north-west: the Taihang base itself; the Taiyue base area to the west of Changzhi; and the South Hebei and Hebei–Shandong–Henan areas, both to the east of the Beijing–Wuhan railway.

In part, the early success of the 129th Division was because of the Japanese blitzkrieg which kept the Japanese Army moving forward with less care for the moment about its rear areas. In part, success was also due to the specific relationship enjoyed by the CCP with Yan Xishan, the provincial warlord of Shanxi. In 1936 Yan Xishan had entered a patriotic alliance with the CCP against Japan and had accepted organizational assistance, and by late 1937 a large part of Shanxi's military and civilian organization was under CCP control. In the area of the 129th Division's operations this was particularly true in Changzhi and the later Taiyue base area, which thus did not require further assistance from the mainline force of the 129th Division. In this part of the province Yan's local government and units of the New Shanxi Army were under the control of provincial CCP leaders such as Bo Yibo and Rong Zihe, through the National League for Self-sacrifice and Salvation, and until the Japanese counter-attack Eighth Route Army troops were not involved.[12] By the end of 1938 the 129th Division had crossed the Beijing–Wuhan railway and was so successful in its expansion it even moved its headquarters out of the mountains on to the plains of South Hebei for a short while at the end of 1938 and beginning of 1939.

For much of the period to 1940 the 129th Division was engaged more in positional than guerrilla warfare. Its first opponents were the Nationalist Party's forces stationed locally. Despite a formal United Front between the CCP and the Nationalists after 1936, conflict between the two was not uncommon. Friction finally exploded into civil war in late 1939,[13] necessitating a negotiated agreement in March 1940 whereby CCP troops withdrew from that part of the Taihang base area to the south of the Handan–Changzhi road and the acknowledgement by the CCP that this would be an area reserved as a Nationalist base – a decision in which Deng Xiaoping seems to have participated, and which certainly fitted in well with his plans to win over Nationalist forces.[14]

At the same time that agreement was reached with the local Nationalist forces, the 129th Division was preparing to participate, along with other CCP and Nationalist forces, in the Hundred Regiments Campaign against the Japanese, a strategem devised by the Commander of the Eighth Route Army, Peng Dehuai. At first sight the campaign appeared successful and to justify Peng Dehuai's enthusiasm: the Japanese lines of communication were severely disrupted, and several counties and county towns were captured or regained.[15] However, one important result was that the Japanese now turned their military attention fully on the CCP border regions. Deng's reaction to the proposal or results of the Hundred Regiments Campaign appears not to have been recorded contemporaneously. Some later commentators have suggested that he would not have approved of its impetuousness and that he would have shared Mao's reservations.[16] In addition it appears that Deng Xiaoping had his own difficulties with and reservations about Peng Dehuai, dating from early 1938 when he joined the 129th Division only to be met by petty squabbling between the headquarters staff of the 129th Division and that of the Eighth Route Army in the Taihang base area.[17]

THE TAIHANG REGION

The 129th Division and its base areas and border region had already begun to be pushed back by the Japanese by 1940. On the eastern side of the Taihang Range the Japanese started building fortifications and blockading the CCP, using the line of the Beijing–Wuhan railway as their base. On the western side, the Japanese successfully separated the Taihang and Taiyue base areas by building a railway from Taigu (on the Shijiazhuang–Xi'an line) towards Changzhi in the second half of 1939. The extent to which the CCP was responsible for its own victory in 1945 remains a matter of some considerable debate.[18] None the less, its eventual survival in the face of repeated attacks in JinJiLuYu, and indeed the expansion of the area of control once Japanese pressure was lifted, owes much to the political and organizational skills of Deng Xiaoping.

The establishment and development of base areas was largely Deng Xiaoping's responsibility, under the Military and Administrative Committee of which he was secretary. This involved close co-operation with Yang Shangkun, the representative of the North China Bureau of the CCP Central Committee engaged in base area development in the region. Deng spent considerable time travelling around the region, encouraging here, organizing there. Touching stories are told of the dangers he faced and how Liu Bocheng, fretting for the safety of his colleague, would demand to receive regular messages when Deng was away. Even allowing for hagiography towards a 'paramount leader' in his lifetime, it would seem that he played a central role in base area development.[19]

However, base area development was not always a rising curve. The Taihang base area was the most secure of the four, but even that was sorely pressed during 1941–3.[20] In both South Hebei and the Hebei–Shandong–Henan area, geopolitics were against the CCP.[21] Once the Japanese North China Army began to strengthen its forces the CCP was forced underground, in many cases quite literally. Japanese and CCP would often share the same village, with the CCP protected by a system of tunnels and bolt-holes. In April 1942, at Deng's suggestion, direct CCP involvement was abandoned east of the Beijing–Wuhan railway.[22] The various problems were exacerbated by one of the tactics adopted to meet the challenge of the Japanese presence. The CCP appears to have been prepared to co-operate with the puppet government regimes in order to subvert them from within and retain its mobilizatory facilities. Far from maintaining a CCP presence the tactic backfired and severely dented its legitimacy, though the impact was undoubtedly worsened by the simultaneous environmental disasters of the early 1940s that affected the border region: drought, crop-failure and locust plagues.[23]

Deng's strategy for developing the border region appears to have had three parts, targeted at three different though not necessarily separate constituencies. One was the Nationalists, soldiers as well as supporters, whom he hoped to win over. Indeed this appears to have been a substantial part of his thinking in supporting a local truce in 1940.[24] A second was the traditional landowning ruling class and its supporters, who were targeted through appeals to various forms of nationalist democracy. The third was the peasants, whose support Deng hoped to gain by introducing economic stability and a rising standard of living.[25] At the same time, he took measures to ensure that special benefits came to the families of CCP guerrillas and military recruits, even after death. In none of this was Deng particularly unique in CCP North China, but he certainly appears to have been the vehicle for the carriage of these ideas both into and around JinJiLuYu.

Deng appears to have been particularly active in bringing the idea of a border region government to JinJiLuYu,[26] following the example of the Shanxi–Chahar–Hebei (JinChaJi) border region immediately to the north along the Taihang range. Co-operation amongst the base areas had been mooted in early 1940 as Japanese pressure built up in their counter-attack. Deng proposed that the new border region government should have an assembly and that neither should be dominated by the CCP, given that both were designed to maximize nationalist support:

> We Communists always oppose a one-party dictatorship, and don't approve of the Nationalists having a one-party dictatorship. The CCP certainly doesn't have a programme to monopolize political power because one party can only rule in its own interests and won't act according to the Will of the People. Moreover, it goes against democratic politics.[27]

Moreover, the assembly would only be a 'provisional' assembly according to Deng, not because it was a wartime assembly sometimes meeting under difficult conditions that required the occasional waiving of formalities, but rather because a genuine assembly would have to be directly elected.

Economically, the policies Deng advocated did not produce utopia, but particularly in the middle of war, a military and economic blockade imposed by the Japanese, and severe natural disasters the results were quite an achievement. They also provide interesting similarities with the economic policies of the post-Cultural Revolution period. By late 1942 the Taihang Region could just about produce enough food to feed its population though it needed to import salt and matches, and could itself export some simple manufactured goods. The border region government had its own tightly regulated credit and monetary system, based on the issue of banknotes through the South Hebei Bank, and raised its own taxes. In 1943 taxes fell by almost a fifth, though this was probably more the function of political expediency – given the locust plagues, famines and other difficulties facing the local population – rather than the result of fiscal efficiencies.

One interesting aspect of the taxation system, and a parallel with the reforms Deng oversaw in the 1980s, was that individuals were taxed according to their average production in previous years and allowed complete control over any surplus. Another parallel with later reforms was the 'responsibility system' Deng introduced whereby public land was rented out to individuals in return for a set contract. As in later years any surplus beyond the contract was retained by the producer.[28] In general, again as in later years, Deng was not slow to articulate his opposition to the blanket criticism of capitalist practices. According to Deng, capitalism was not *per se* opposed by the CCP: individual creativity and improved living conditions should be encouraged almost no matter what. As Deng directed senior cadres at a meeting of the Taihang Bureau of the CCP Central Committee:

> establish a system of reward and punishment ... models of individual production and labour heroes are to be given bonuses of between one hundred and two hundred *yuan*. Some comrades say this is too much, but I don't agree. If they've acquired it through their own labour and not corruption it's entirely appropriate. Those who are lazy and unenthusiastic should suffer ... units with poor production results must eat the consequences.[29]

In words which were to bring him problems during the Cultural Revolution he also argued that 'our principle is not only to improve the livelihood of the peasant but also to protect the economic position of landlords' and 'our policy towards the rich peasants is to reduce their feudalistic aspects, but encourage their capitalist aspects'.[30]

Deng's report of July 1943 on economic reconstruction in the Taihang Region is not only a model of the philosophy behind the CCP's successful guerrilla strategy – emphasizing the key relationship between economic production, politics and military victory – it is also a taut summation of Deng's later ideas on progress in general, and a paradigm of his economic pragmatism. Social transformation can only come gradually, and then by showing people that whatever policies are being implemented serve their economic, as well as their political, interests. Socialism requires organization and economic might, and can only be built on 'capitalistic production'. (This phrase was omitted from the 1989 officially published and authorized version of the report, brought out after the Tiananmen Incident of that year, doubtless so that there should be no possible confusion as to the context of Deng's remarks or his intent.) Deng finished his report by quoting a recent Mao directive that: 'Fighting, production and education are the three main responsibilities for us behind the enemy lines.' He then continued: 'We do everything for victory in the war; production directly guarantees victory and education serves both the war and production. Closely combining these three will give us invincible strength. Therefore, we should do everything in our power to strengthen leadership in economic development in the days to come.'[31]

Deng's experience in the Taihang Region may well have shaped his ideas about the politics of change. However, it certainly provided him with the connections which were to ensure that he would have the opportunity to put those ideas into practice more generally. The roll call of those who served under or alongside Deng in the Taihang region is an impressive section of the CCP's post-1949 leadership. For example, of the 87 individuals who served as members or alternate members of the Political Bureau of the CCP between 1949 and 1989, 17 spent the years 1938–45 in either the organizations of the 129th Division, the JinJiLuYu Border Region or its constituent parts. By way of comparison, 16 were based in Yan'an during 1937 to 1945.

Those who were members of the CCP Central Committee's Political Bureau after 1949 and who had spent the Sino-Japanese War years in the organizations of the Taihang Region included not only Deng Xiaoping himself and Liu Bocheng, but also Bo Yibo, Chen Xilian, Ji Dengkui, Li Desheng, Li Xuefeng, Liu Huaqing, Qin Jiwei, Song Renqiong, Su Zhenhua, Xie Fuzhi, Xu Shiyou, Xu Xiangqian, Yang Baibing, Yang Dezhi, Zhao Ziyang and Wan Li. That calculus does not include those based in the Taihang area but not organizationally part of the border region or the local base areas, such as those working in the Eighth Route Army headquarters or with the CCP North China Bureau. Apart from the more obvious figures such as Zhu De and Peng Dehuai who were for the most part little involved in the activities of the local organizations, these also included Yang Shangkun, who was closely involved in JinJiLuYu affairs, at least until 1941, through his role as a representative of the North China Bureau of the CCP.

The list of prominent post-1949 figures active in the Taihang Region during the Sino-Japanese War extends well beyond membership of the Political Bureau. Amongst members of later military establishments were Li Da (Vice Minister of National Defence and Deputy Chief of Staff of the PLA), Yang Baibing (Secretary-General of the CCP Military Affairs Commission) and Chen Zaidao (the leader of the Wuhan Rebellion in 1967). Later central civilian leaders included An Ziwen (Director of the CCP's Organization Department); Wang Renzhong and Huang Zhen (Director and Deputy Director of the CCP's Propaganda Department); Rong Zihe (Vice Minister of Finance); and several ministers including two Ministers of Railways (Duan Junyi and Teng Daiyun), as well as Yang Xiufeng (the then Chairman of the Border Region Government and later Minister of Higher Education). The group of later ranking provincial leaders included Huang Oudong (Liaoning), Li Dazhang (Sichuan), Liu Jianxun (Guangxi and Henan), Pan Fusheng (Heilongjiang), Tao Lujia (Shanxi), Yan Hongyan (Yunnan), Zhang Guohua (Tibet), and Zhao Jianmin (Shandong.)

A substantial number of those who had been with Deng in the Taihang Region were to play significant roles in implementing reform during the 1980s. One of those was Bo Yibo, the former Taiyue base area leader and then Vice-Chairman of the Border Region Government, who was less than enthusiastic about Mao's ideas on economic development when an alternate member of the CCP Political Bureau during the 1950s,[32] and who co-operated with Deng during the early 1960s to mitigate the worst effects of the Great Leap Forward. Another was Zhao Ziyang, who met Deng for the first time in 1938 when he was a party secretary in his native Hebei–Shandong–Henan border area.[33]

Some sources report that Hu Yaobang (whom Deng had already, presumably, met in Yan'an in 1937 when Hu had been a student at the Resist Japan University and Deng had lectured there) was yet another, having become a political commissar under Deng in the Taiyue base area during 1942 to 1945. This is unlikely and the confusion probably arises because Hu later joined troops who had served under Deng in the Taihang Region, and was himself part of the PLA's 2nd Field Army led by Liu and Deng, and served in Sichuan under Deng. It is more likely that Hu spent all the years of the Sino-Japanese War in Yan'an as the Director of the Organization Department of the Military Commission of the CCP Central Committee, a position which brought him into regular and close contact with the commanding officers of all the CCP's regions, including Liu and Deng. These considerations apart, the relationship between Hu and Deng certainly became close. Hu had recruited Deng's wife-to-be Zhuo Lin into the CCP in 1938; served under Deng in South-west China during and after 1949; and became the Secretary of the Young Communist League under Deng in the 1950s.[34]

CIVIL WAR

At the end of the Sino-Japanese War the CCP expanded rapidly to fill most of the JinJiLuYu Border Region, and established its capital at Handan. The 129th Division had become a substantial army, soon to be reorganized as the Central Plains and later the 2nd Field Army of the PLA. In the manoeuvrings that accompanied the false attempts at a negotiated settlement between the CCP and the Nationalist Party, Liu and Deng were able to defeat Nationalist armies at the Battles of Shangdang and Handan. None the less, were the Nationalist Army to move north and east to defeat the CCP, Liu and Deng and their troops, because they occupied a strategic position, were always going to be a first target in the coming civil war. Chiang Kai-shek did indeed move troops to both northern Shaanxi (against Mao Zedong and the CCP forces concentrated there), and to Henan and Shandong, surrounding Liu and Deng in what the latter described as a 'dumb-bell strategy'.[35] Deng and Liu had long been prepared for a move south, but this had been planned originally for late August after they had received favourable reports from investigations made during May and June.[36] Hearing from Mao Zedong of his problems, and sensing perhaps the need for some relieving or distracting action, and rather than waiting to be squeezed themselves, Liu and Deng (to the Nationalists' surprise) made a bolt for the south in July 1947. The aim was to reach the Dabie Mountains, between Nanjing and Wuhan north of the Yangtze, where some rudimentary guerrilla activity was already taking place. Such a position would be relatively easy to defend and provide the CCP both with control of the Central China plains and with a vantage point to attack the Nationalists along the Yangtze.

Despite the element of total surprise the strategy almost failed. The terrain was barely passable, because of mud and marsh, and after a 28-day battle to break through the initial encirclement the army undertook a 20-day 500-kilometre forced march to safety. For a full army this was no mean feat and something of a gamble, particularly since they could not secure a retreat. The decisive battle on the march was at the crossing of the Ru River, which was nearly a disaster as the army came under enemy artillery fire. Success here ultimately owed much to both Liu and Deng, who not only personally led the march, for much of the way on foot, but continually exhorted their tired troops to greater feats of heroism.[37]

The occupation of the Dabie Mountains had several consequences for the 2nd Field Army. It allowed it time to recuperate and rebuild in a new base area; it allowed it to occupy a sizeable proportion of the Nationalist Army that might have been fighting the communists elsewhere; and it allowed the CCP to use its superior strategic position to plan a final campaign in the south against the Nationalists. That final campaign – the Huai-Hai campaign, so called because it took place between the *Huai* River and the sea (*hai* in Chinese) – centred on Xuzhou. Once again Deng Xiaoping was chosen by Mao to be his trusted eyes and ears, this time as the secretary to the General Frontline Committee.

Activities in East China brought Deng into closer contact with Chen Yi. Indeed, for the first time in a long time Deng and Liu Bocheng were separated when Deng joined Chen Yi for the capture of Zhengzhou in October 1948. In November 1948 Chen Yi's 3rd Field Army was brought together with the forces of the 2nd Field Army for the Huai-Hai campaign. In a classic encirclement, often cited by military historians as one of the greatest land battles of the twentieth century, the CCP destroyed a Nationalist army of half a million men between November 1948 and January 1949.[38]

Together with CCP victory in the north-east and the surrender of Beijing, success led directly to national power in 1949. The 2nd and 3rd Field Armies, with Deng now leading secretary of the CCP's East China Bureau, crossed the Yangtze in April 1949 taking Nanjing, Shanghai and the surrounding provinces and directly causing the Nationalists to leave the mainland for Taiwan. Undoubtedly Deng's roles in both the Huai-Hai campaign and the drive on the Dabie Mountains have been overstated for contemporary political reasons by Chinese historians during the 1980s. Without doubt, though, his military as well as his political contributions were real enough. The role of political commissar would bring him into the orbit of commanders. However, even a summary examination of his writings for the four-year period between the end of the Sino-Japanese War and the establishment of the PRC reveals the active role he took in military planning. Where necessary and appropriate, as during the Liu–Deng Army's forced march south to the Dabie Mountains or earlier in 1947,[39] he had been heavily involved in military actions in the field.

Certainly, by late 1947 members of the Central Plains Field Army had already decided that it was now Deng, rather than Liu Bocheng, who was the senior of their two leaders. Not that there was any rivalry between the two, for right from when they first came together in 1938 it seems they liked each other immensely and formed a long-lasting friendship. However, it was not Liu's personal support alone that was to prove so important to Deng in the future, but rather the network of relationships he had developed within the CCP's military and political leadership.

RETURN TO THE SOUTH-WEST

In October 1949 both Deng and Liu attended the celebrations marking the establishment of the PRC in Beijing, after which they returned to lead the 2nd Field Army in its advance on the South-west Region – the provinces of Sichuan, Yunnan and Guizhou, as well as Tibet – from the east. Its immediate task, in co-operation with part of the 1st Field Army moving in from the north, was to complete the CCP's victory, which was duly achieved by the end of the year, meeting very little resistance. For Deng personally, it meant the first family reunion since he had left home in 1920, and he set up house in Chongqing with his brother Deng Shuping, his elder sister, Deng Xianlie, his sister-in-law (married to a younger brother) Xie Jinbi and his father's fourth wife, Xia Bogen. Professionally, he was appointed the 1st secretary of the CCP in the South-west Region and now officially outranked Liu Bocheng, who was his deputy.

During the first five-years of the PRC, and particularly until late 1952, politics and government were highly regionalized under military control in order to facilitate the reconstruction of state power. The South-west Military and Administrative Committee, like its counterparts in China's other five regions, was a temporary measure designed to start economic reconstruction, provide political stability, and consolidate the position of the CCP. Until 1952 the regional Military and Administrative Committees were responsible for all civilian and military activities in each region: a kind of military control commission. Liu and Deng headed the South-west Military and Administrative Committee until 1952 when they were both called to national service of other kinds in Beijing.

Deng's organizational skills and political perspectives were very much in evidence during those years. In his biography of Deng Xiaoping, Harrison Salisbury has suggested that during this period Deng was also instrumental in helping Mao develop his ideas for the Third Line – a series of projects to base China's economy in the interior in case of external threat.[40] Though the suggestion is possible in terms of political trust, it is unlikely – given that Deng was in the South-west well before the dates usually considered as marking the start of Mao's thinking about these matters.[41] Deng was certainly active in encouraging all kinds of major engineering projects – of which the construction of the Chengdu–Chongqing railway line was probably the most famous – and ensuring economic reconstruction.

The South-west faced three particular tasks. Because it had been the last region to be conquered as the PLA swept through China from the north, the remnants of the Nationalist armies which had been swept before it were concentrated in the region and were either forced to surrender or turned to banditry. Altogether the South-west was left with some two million government dependants, including not only former Nationalist soldiers but also former government officials who had fled from other parts of China. Deng's solution was to disperse those displaced as quickly as possible, and to ensure a steady supply of homes and jobs in order to meet their immediate needs and to make banditry less attractive. None the less, where bandits continued they were met with force.[42]

A second task facing the South-west more seriously than elsewhere was to combat the weakness of CCP organization. The CCP had almost no experience or organization in the South-west before 1949, and few members. Recruitment was a major priority, but even the speed with which that was achieved brought further problems as it adversely affected the quality of leadership, leading to a need for immediate rectification, not least to instil party discipline; something Deng was to become preoccupied with during the 1950s.[43]

A third and similar problem was that of the minority nationalities. The South-west has a higher proportion of non-Han Chinese than other regions. Relations between the minority nationalities and the Han Chinese were traditionally poor and the CCP had few native cadres. In addition, the CCP considered many aspects of their social structures to be both feudal and antagonistic to the CCP's goals. In addition to a policy of positive discrimination towards non-Han administrators and CCP recruits, Deng exempted those areas where they were concentrated from participation in national political campaigns – such as land reform – until other more fundamental social reforms – the abolition of slavery, for example – were completed.[44]

4 Party affairs and leadership, 1952–1960

With the consolidation of CCP rule, the era of regional rule almost inevitably came to an end, and Deng Xiaoping, along with every other senior regional leader, moved to Bejing and national politics. His first position, as Vice-Premier of the Government (a position then titled Vice-Chairman of the Government Administration Council) reunited him working closely with Zhou Enlai. However, it was not long before his even closer political relationship with Mao Zedong occupied his attention, first in helping to settle the untoward consequences of factionalism within the party's highest leadership, and then in running the CCP. In early 1954 he once again became the Secretary-General to the CCP Central Committee, and then, after his election to the CCP's Political Bureau in 1955, he became the General Secretary of the CCP (a much more senior position of leadership) at the 8th CCP Congress in 1956. By this stage Deng was the fourth-ranked of the party's leaders. When the Great Leap Forward was called to a halt at the end of 1960, he and Liu Shaoqi were given the prime responsibility, by the CCP and by Mao, for the future direction of the party and government.

Deng's politics during this period are most often portrayed in one of two ways. In one view he is seen as a long-time member of Mao's personal loyalty group, whom Mao Zedong brought into the leadership and could rely on, particularly when there was a specific job requiring his organizational capabilities. In the other view, much favoured by the Red Guards during the Cultural Revolution (but not totally to be discounted for that reason), particularly in and after the 8th CCP Congress in 1956, he was one of those coming into increasing conflict with Mao over the latter's vision of China's future.

Remarkably, these two interpretations are not totally contradictory. When proposing Deng's appointment as General Secretary of the CCP in September 1956, Mao had praised Deng's 'rectitude, reliability and far-sightedness in dealing with problems'. According to Mao:

Deng Xiaoping is like me – it's not that he doesn't have defects, but he is comparatively fair and just. He's comparatively able and manages things well. Do you think he can do everything well? No. He's like me. There are things he's handled poorly and there are things he's said which were wrong. But comparatively speaking he is able. He's comparatively thoughtful and considerate, fair and just, honest and kind, and doesn't frighten people. Moreover, I'll see when he says something wrong. There are of course others if he isn't acceptable, but the others aren't as acceptable to me. However, everyone says he takes a balanced and all-round view of things, that he's conscientious, and that he handles problems properly, even accepting strict discipline for himself if he makes mistakes.[1]

Even allowing for the circumstances of Mao's speech in nominating Deng to high position within the CCP, it would seem that the working relationship between the two since the early 1930s – from Jiangxi to the Taihang Region, to the march on the Dabie Mountains, to the Huai-Hai and Yangtze Campaigns – was demonstrably good, and showed Mao that he could rely on Deng to act as his eyes and ears.

Mao was the leader and Deng the subordinate, and that was mutually accepted and unquestioned. At the same time, Deng's policy prescriptions did not always tally with those of his mentor, and he reputedly was always prepared to articulate his view, particularly where he thought the norms of party unity or party discipline were at stake.[2] For Deng, as for others in the CCP leadership at that time, differences of opinion were not only possible, they were even welcomed, explicitly so on occasion, as for example at the 8th Congress of the CCP, where there was a relatively open and frank discussion of the options for China's development.[3] Negotiation and compromise would be the expected outcome, rather than conflict. Moreover, Deng Xiaoping, along with Chen Yun, had long since learnt that there were times and ways in which to challenge Chairman Mao, and circumstances when silence or absence was a better strategy.

LEADERSHIP CONFLICT

When Liu Bocheng and Deng Xiaoping left the South-west for Beijing it was as part of a national change in policy that meant the end of regional government. On the whole, regionalism was not a problem, and a regional system of government had only been adopted as a temporary measure. The leaders of the six large regions were appointed primarily because – as was the case with Liu and Deng – they had held military positions in the CCP armies at the end of the civil war with the Nationalists. If they happened to serve in their native region, as was the case with both Deng and Liu, it was a happy coincidence that may have helped make them that much more acceptable to the local population, not least because they were literally able to speak the same language. In 1952, when the CCP started the process of recentralization there was no apparent resistance. Liu became Director of the PLA Military Academy in Nanjing (he was 60 by this time) and Deng became a Vice-Premier of the Government Administrative Council (later under the 1954 State Constitution, the State Council) and for a short time a member of the Central Financial Commission and the Minister of Finance.

However, there was a regional dimension to the new regime's first major leadership crisis, which Deng found himself in the thick of within a year of his arrival in Beijing, and whose resolution was to play an important role in Deng's career. In a series of events that have been shrouded in mystery until relatively recently, Deng's regional counterparts in North-east and East China – Gao Gang and Rao Shushi respectively – were first dismissed from their posts in the leadership (in early 1954) and then expelled from the CCP altogether in 1955.[4] Deng's role in these events not only highlights the importance of his relationship with Mao Zedong, it also indicates his usefulness more generally to the leadership because of his other relationships in drawing together different parts of the CCP.

Deng's first responsibilities when moving to Beijing involved him in the preparations for the new state constitution, which was eventually promulgated in 1954. His particular area of activities appears to have been to chair the committee responsible for setting up electoral procedures, in which capacity he led the team that drafted the Electoral Law for the National People's Congress and local people's congresses.[5] However, before he could deliver his final report on the first national elections in June 1954[6] he had become embroiled in the Gao Gang and Rao Shushi episode, which amongst other things forced him into an unlikely one-year stint as Minister of Finance from September 1953 to September 1954.

This sudden and unusual – he had never previously been particularly involved in economic or financial affairs, and would not be again[7] – diversion in Deng's career was a function not simply of his relationship with Mao, but also of Deng's connections with Zhou Enlai and his acceptability to many of those in senior levels within the Ministry of Finance. Though in 1953 both Gao and Rao were regional leaders, they also held national positions. Gao was Chairman of the State Planning Commission and Rao Director of the Organization Department of the CCP. Both were in favour of recentralization, and the real source of conflict was ambition. Gao, who took the initiative, wanted to replace Liu Shaoqi (Vice-Chairman of the CCP) and Zhou Enlai (Premier) in the hierarchy, and particularly the former as Mao's deputy and presumed successor.

Emboldened by what he presumed to be Mao's favour and support, Gao Gang actively campaigned against Liu and Zhou. He portrayed them as anti-Soviet, whereas he had good relations with the USSR: a double-edged sword given the history of relations between the CCP and the CPSU. His justification for attacking Liu Shaoqi's seniority was an appeal to the most obvious fault-lines within the leadership of the CCP. His case was that it had been the Red Army (not the urban underground where Liu had operated) which had brought the CCP victory, and he attempted to recruit former rural revolutionaries and guerrillas to his conspiracy. Gao himself had been a graduate of the Xi'an Military Academy where Deng had been assigned in 1927 and had established a rural soviet in north Shaanxi which had eventually been journey's end for the Long March.

Gao's views met with some, though possibly muted, support from, amongst others, Lin Biao and Peng Dehuai, both veteran army commanders and now the party leaders of the Central–South and North-west China Regions respectively. However, it foundered badly when he approached Deng Xiaoping and Chen Yun. According to Deng in 1980, after being lobbied by Gao Gang and discussing the matter with him on a number of occasions, Deng realized the need to defend Liu

Shaoqi and that Gao's behaviour was deliberately factionalist.[8] He eventually – Teiwes suggests the delay may have been as long as two months[9] – informed Mao Zedong, as apparently had Chen Yun independently, and matters were brought out into the open at a meeting of the CCP Political Bureau in December 1953.

Apart from any personal motives, Deng and Chen were concerned about the threat to party unity and Gao's flagrant disregard for party rules. Deng in particular repeatedly attended meetings during the second half of 1953 where the various tensions that had created the environment for Gao's factionalism kept coming out into the open, and found himself having to make strong appeals for the importance of party unity. There can be little doubt that Gao and Rao had genuinely conspired – as Deng was later to report to the National Party Conference called on the affair in March 1955 – though perhaps in a less than efficient and somewhat shambolic manner, to operate outside the established norms.

The Gao–Rao attack went through several stages and was quite sustained for part of the second half of 1953. On the way they managed to ensure that Liu Shaoqi engaged in self-criticism, that Zhou Enlai accepted some blame for defects in financial work, and that Bo Yibo – the Minister of Finance – stepped aside. A crucial meeting – where as Bo Yibo later pointed out he was criticized as a surrogate for Liu Shaoqi – was the National Conference on Financial and Economic Work during the summer.[10] Since the beginning of 1953 Bo Yibo's tax reform proposals had created a furore within the leadership, not simply because they were 'soft' on former capitalists and the private sector but also because their effect would be to alter the balance of fiscal advantages away from the state sector back to the private sector, and force the former to compete more directly with the latter. At the National Conference Gao's comments were trenchant, and to some extent Bo's defence, or at least his lifeline from complete political annihilation, came from Mao. None the less, Bo was forced to step down as Minister of Finance.

A new minister was required; but one who could be trusted by Mao, would be acceptable to the senior officials of the ministry as it went through a testing time, and someone who was acceptable in the factional considerations that were uppermost at the time. Deng fitted the bill though he was clearly not the obvious choice as a Minister of Finance. As is clear from Rong Zihe's account of his time in the ministry,[11] he did not play an active role in developing policy or the 1954 Budget which he presented,[12] but allowed officials to provide drafts. His role was one of political presentation and of smoothing feathers within the ministry.

Deng was suitable because he could certainly be trusted by Mao – indeed, in the late 1980s Rong Zihe could still recall that in December 1953 Minister Deng lectured him specifically on the 'Chairman Mao approach to financial management'. However, Deng was also a suitable appointment as far as Rong Zihe and other senior cadres in the ministry were concerned. They had come predominantly from the financial and economic administration of the former JinJiLuYu Border Region Government with Bo Yibo (Rong Zihe had also, like Bo Yibo, been a Vice-Chairman of that body) and those who had not actually worked with Deng at that time had close organizational ties. In addition, Deng was acceptable to at least two of the groupings in the factional conflict that was emerging. He had been Zhou Enlai's protégé for a long time and was now able to return the compliment in a slight way by protecting Zhou's flank in the Ministry of Finance; and he was also regarded as a military representative in the leadership because of his service from 1937–52 and so was acceptable to those who were prepared to support Gao's and Rao's complaint that those in the Red Army who had made the revolution were benefiting less than those from the 'White' underground areas.

THE 8th CONGRESS OF THE CCP

The collapse of the Gao–Rao conspiracy in December 1953 led to a renewed emphasis on party unity and an exercise in damage limitation, which were not altogether immediately successful. CCP meetings early in 1954 could not obtain easy or full confessions from Gao or Rao, and had a hard time finding a way forward. In the end Deng Xiaoping through his new appointment as Secretary-General to the CCP Central Committee played a central role in the investigation work, and presented the final report to the National CCP Conference in March 1955.[13]

Lin Biao and Peng Dehuai were not, unlike Gao and Rao, disgraced, though in at least Peng's case any potential involvement in the Gao affair had repercussions after 1959 when Peng himself ran foul of Mao Zedong. Lin Biao was considered less important since at this time he was not regarded as politically involved. In order to meet at least one of the claims that had led to any base of support for Gao Gang, Lin Biao and Deng Xiaoping were both appointed to the CCP Political Bureau; both were seen as representative of the pre-1949 military interests within the CCP. In addition, Deng became Director of the CCP's Organization Department, and Vice-Chairman of the National Defence Council. Peng Dehuai, who had been Commander of the Chinese People's Volunteers (the PLA by another name) in the Korean War, became Minister of National Defence. However, Deng's usefulness as a link between the 'military' and 'civilian' wings of the CCP leadership did not end there. As the PLA moved to appoint its generals for the first time in September 1955, recognizing the years of war service, the CCP's Central Military Commission made Deng the final arbiter of promotion. The General Political Department of the PLA made a provisional assignation of ranks which was then passed on to Deng and Long Ronghuan before final approval was sought.[14]

Once again the bonds between Mao and Deng seemed to have been a central relationship in CCP politics, and at the same time Deng had been able to ensure the maintenance of unity and the CCP's organizational strength. Khrushchev, who visited Beijing later in 1954 and again in 1958, and who hosted the CCP delegation led by Mao to Moscow in 1957 that included Deng, had an interesting recollection of this relationship. He did not take to Mao, not least because the Chairman never had anything good to say about any of his colleagues in the Chinese leadership:

Mao never recognized his comrades as his equals. He treated the people around him like pieces of furniture, useful for the time being but expendable. When in his opinion, a piece of furniture – or a comrade – became worn out and lost its usefulness, he would just throw it away and replace it. . . . The only one of his comrades whom Mao seemed to approve of was Teng Hsiao-p'ing [Deng Xiaoping]. I remember Mao pointing out Deng to me and saying, 'See that little man there? He's highly intelligent and has a great future ahead of him.'[15]

Deng's promotions put him at the very heart of the CCP's organizational affairs and these were to be his major concern for the remainder of the decade. The other members of the Central Committee Secretariat appointed at this time were Liu Lantao, Song Renqiong, Tan Zhenlin and Yang Shangkun. Its composition was clearly designed to emphasize CCP unity, for these men, together with Deng, represented the various organizational and political strands within the party. Liu Lantao had even been a former associate of Gao Gang's in the North Shaanxi Soviet. Though their paths had crossed several times since 1933, notably during 1938–41 in the Taihang Region, Yang Shangkun had been one of the '28 Bolsheviks' who had been actively involved in the attack on Deng in that year. However, it is a measure of Deng's networking that he had extremely good political ties with the majority of his Secretariat. Song Renqiong had been a subordinate in the 129th Division of the Eighth Route Army; Tan Zhenlin had been, like Deng, associated with Mao since the early 1930s; and Liu Lantao was a protégé of Bo Yibo, an associate of Deng's from the Taihang Region, and as already indicated a main victim of Gao's assault in 1953.

The work of the Secretariat for the next two years was largely organizational, and it was a very different and more political Secretariat which was approved at the 8th CCP Congress in September 1956, when Deng was elected General Secretary of the CCP (as opposed to Secretary-General to the Central Committee, which was not a major leadership position despite the way Deng had filled his appointment during 1954 and 1955). Deng had been given responsibility for the revision of the CCP Constitution and this was one of the many major changes he introduced at the CCP Congress. As he explained in his speech, the party and its needs had changed considerably since the last congress in 1945. It had achieved national power and grown from just over a million members to about 11 million; it had previously been almost exclusively rural based, whereas now a disproportionate number of its members lived and worked in towns and cities. It had turned from the goals of achieving power to those of national development. To meet the changed political environment Deng proposed a complete overhaul of the CCP's organization, all of which was incorporated into the new party constitution.[16]

Interestingly, many of Deng's proposals not only presaged the political reform programme he would initiate during the early 1980s, they also continued the principles and practices he had developed during the early 1940s in the Taihang Region. One example was the need for party leadership to be strengthened by structures that clearly separated the functions and organization of the CCP and the government. Necessarily, during guerrilla war the CCP's involvement in other activities was its strength. However, during the early 1950s CCP leaders frequently criticized the party's tendency to step in and run everything as dysfunctional; government units would wait on party interference and the CCP became overloaded. Deng had outlined solutions to these similar problems in 1941, as implemented in the Taihang Region, in a speech to a meeting of the CCP's North China Bureau, later published as an article in the CCP journal *Party Life* under the title 'The Party and the Anti-Japanese Democratic Government'.[17]

However, Deng was not simply concerned with administrative matters and at the CCP Congress he also dwelt at considerable length on party procedures and norms. He emphasized the CCP's traditions after 1935 as a guide to action, particularly with respect to its maintenance of popular support and internal unity. This was the essential context for one of the most dramatic and later most misunderstood changes to the Constitution. The 1945 CCP Constitution had explicitly recognized that Marxism-Leninism-Mao Zedong Thought was the party's ideology. However, Mao Zedong Thought was written out of its 1956 version, leaving only Marxism-Leninism as the description of the CCP's guiding ideology.

Sources originating during the Cultural Revolution, particularly those written and distributed by various Red Guard groups, were highly critical of Deng's action in proposing the removal of the reference to Mao Zedong Thought from the Constitution. They regarded it as prima facie evidence of Deng's opposition to Mao's developmental programme and his, that is Deng's, subservience to the Soviet Union.[18] Deng had recently returned from Moscow (in April) where he had attended the 20th Congress of the CPSU and heard Khrushchev's denunciation of the cult of personality.[19] Some Western commentators, for example Chang and Bonavia, have dated Deng's break with Mao from this date for similar reasons.[20]

It is unlikely that following the example of the Soviet Union was the major reason for change in the CCP, not least because the Constitution of the Young Communist League had already removed its references to Mao Zedong Thought in 1953. The change of ideological descriptor was so symbolically important that it is inconceivable that the decision was not taken collectively by the CCP's leadership, all of whom after the early 1940s were fiercely nationalistic. Indeed nationalism was at the heart of the concept of Mao Zedong Thought – the codification by Mao of Marxism-Leninism as applied to Chinese conditions – which Deng had propagandized so effectively throughout the 1940s.[21] Though he did indeed criticize the cult of personality in his speech to the 8th Congress, he emphasized that unlike the CPSU the CCP had always regarded people and parties as fallible and so had never gone in for such practices. Moreover, his major concern at this time, and indeed for a number of years before and after, had been and was with party discipline and its impact on unity. It seems likely that he was worried in this particular case that the status of Mao Zedong Thought was leading to a growing personalization of China's politics, and not just on Mao's side, which in turn was posing a threat to party leadership. Though he disagreed with many of Mao's ideas for China's future, he still at this time believed disagreement was possible, legitimate and desirable as long as party unity was not threatened and decision-making was collective. Indeed, whilst understanding completely Mao's unique role in CCP politics, Deng none the less saw the party leadership's collective unity as an additional strength – hence his desire to maintain the propagandization of Mao Zedong Thought, even if the phrase itself had been formally withdrawn from the CCP's Constitution.

In his major speech on the revision of the Constitution to the 8th CCP Congress, Deng dwelt at some length on the correct procedures for inner-party debate, the requirements of collective leadership and the importance of democratic centralism. According to Deng, open debate within the CCP was necessary if correct solutions were to be found to problems. In those debates individuals should be free to articulate their views. Minority views should be respected even when wrong and inner-party struggle should not lead to 'a policy of excessively harsh struggle and wanton punishment' (the so-called 'ruthless struggle' and 'merciless blows' which Deng himself had experienced in 1933). On the other hand, mistakes should not be treated with over-tolerance or over-indulgence. However, once a decision had been taken then every party member was duty-bound to carry it out. Criticism and collective leadership were necessary supports for intra-party debate. Without criticism, individuals, including leaders, could not improve their work-style and ideas. Without collective leadership politics would become personalized. Party rules were to apply impartially, there should be no 'deification of the individual' and individual leaders should not abuse their positions in dealing with either their subordinates or each other.

With the exception of Gao Gang and Rao Shushi, Deng did not name names, but his comments were none the less pointed, as for example when he said, 'Some responsible comrades are still prone to exercise exclusive personal control'; 'Love for the leader is essentially an expression of love for the interests of the Party, the class and the people, and not the deification of an individual'; and 'Even now not a few responsible comrades ... do not encourage and support criticism from below ... [they] use the shameful method of making personal attacks and carrying out reprisals against their critics'.[22]

Necessarily, those remarks might have been interpreted as being directed at Mao, particularly later. The debate on collectivization that took place in 1955 and that led to the 'High Tide of Agricultural Co-operativization' was a roller-coaster of rapidly changing policy directions, and often highly charged.[23] It used to be thought that the Chairman had occasioned the High Tide by appealing to provincial leaders over the heads of his colleagues once some central decisions he did not like had been taken. Though that interpretation of the High Tide's genesis now appears somewhat extreme, from the second half of 1955 onwards he did come to rely increasingly on provincial leaders in the formulation of policy, as in the attempt to force the leadership's hand on the pace of development in early 1956, and the development of the 'Twelve Year National Agricultural Development Outline'.[24] However, the behaviour which characterized Mao in his later years and which is foreshadowed in Deng's speech had not yet fully emerged. Equally, at this time others were also guilty of not observing party norms, and they too were the target of Deng's criticisms. Gao Gang's conspiracy had been built on more than two individuals and the aftermath had badly shaken party unity. Peng Dehuai, in particular, may well have been someone Deng had in mind. Not only had he been implicated with Gao Gang, but he was currently engaged in an intense, long-running and highly personalized disagreement with Deng's former comrade-in-arms, Liu Bocheng.[25]

RECTIFICATION

One extremely important aspect of Deng Xiaoping's speech to the 8th CCP Congress, which came to dominate politics for the next year, was the question of party rectification. On this point it seems likely that he was more than hesitant about Mao's plans and interpretation of the need for a party rectification movement, including the kind of rectification that should occur. In this he was not alone, for Mao's views were not immediately shared by many in the leadership, including Liu Shaoqi and Peng Zhen (the Mayor of Beijing).

To some extent the spectre hanging over the party debate on rectification was the challenge to communism in the USSR and Eastern Europe during 1956. The CCP delegation to the 20th Congress of the CPSU had left Moscow perturbed at Khrushchev's apparent belief that there would be a peaceful transition to socialism within the capitalist world, not least since that view undermined the basis of the support, both military and economic, they hoped to receive from the USSR.[26] The CCP had also been concerned at the impact of liberalization in Hungary and Poland, and the threat to party rule.

Deng, in his speech to the 8th CCP Congress, and later, had argued that the problems of Eastern Europe could be avoided and the future of socialism in China ensured if three conditions were met: democracy within the party, party leadership and a good working relationship between the people and the party. He had been generally optimistic about the CCP's achievements and prospects, arguing that class struggle was fundamentally over in China: 'The working class has become the leading class of the state; the peasantry has changed from individual farming to co-operative farming; and the bourgeoisie as a class is on its way to extinction.'

However, Deng was characteristically hard-hitting about the CCP's mistakes and he criticized what he described as a 'drift away from reality and from the masses'. Party leadership meant listening to people as well as telling them what to do – the tried and tested principles of the 'mass line' as practised before 1949 – yet since 1949 he felt that cadres had tended to rest on their laurels. Moreover, the expansion of the CCP since 1945 meant that the quality of political education was necessarily diluted.[27]

Deng's solution to the problems of the CCP's work-style, inner-party democracy and its relationship to the population was to launch a rectification campaign within the CCP and to establish structures for popular supervision of CCP activities. Criticism and self-criticism within the CCP would, as in the past, 'maintain Party solidarity and unity on the basis of Marxism-Leninism, and help comrades overcome their shortcomings and correct mistakes'. Supervision from outside the CCP would come largely through workers' congresses, people's congresses, local councils and from the non-communist parties.[28]

Mao's view of rectification was radically different and tied to his vision of a developmental model based almost totally on mass mobilization. Politics not economics was to be the key to future success and the solution to China's problems. In particular, he appears to have believed during 1956 and the first half of 1957 that development depended on politicizing the intellectuals and professional groups in society – of whom he was almost obsessively suspicious for much of his life – not least to create a close working relationship with the CCP. This was the essential context of his exhortation to 'Let a hundred schools of thought contend, a hundred flowers bloom'. Unlike Deng, he believed that class struggle was far from over. In a famous speech of February 1957, 'On the correct handling of contradictions amongst the people', he outlined the nature of antagonisms that would remain even after the establishment of socialism. Some of these antagonisms would have to be dealt with forcefully, but others, the majority, required education, propaganda and mobilization to be resolved. Criticism and self-criticism needed to be extended to the whole of society otherwise the revolution would simply become bureaucratized.[29] This wider notion of 'extended democracy' was still being explicitly denounced by Deng in early April 1957 in a report to party cadres in Xi'an, 'The Communist Party Must Accept Supervision'. Here he attributed the blame for what he described as the 'disturbances' in Eastern Europe on 'extended democracy'.[30]

Not for the last time, at the end of April 1957, Deng and others in the leadership, including Peng Zhen but excluding Liu, allowed themselves to be persuaded to agree with Mao. There followed five weeks of almost unfettered criticism of the CCP in the 'Hundred Flowers Movement' of May and June and the leadership was quickly forced to call a halt. Far greater than the threat to party unity was the threat to party rule.[31] An 'Anti-Rightist Campaign' was launched, under Deng's direction, against all those who had spoken out as they had been encouraged to. A large proportion of those who had criticized the CCP and who were later attacked were indeed intellectuals and the professional classes. As later, in the Cultural Revolution, they were characterized as 'counter-revolutionaries' and punished severely. As Deng, amongst others, pointed out after the Cultural Revolution, the long-term damage to their participation in China's development was considerable. Though he still believed a rectification campaign to have been necessary, he came to regard its methods and results as excessive and counter-productive.[32]

After the campaign ended, Deng reported on its results to the 3rd plenum of the 8th Central Committee, in September 1957. Unlike his pronouncements before April, his comments on the need for rectification, though not of course the form it should take, were more in accord with Mao's views on the subject. He now regarded intellectuals with some suspicion, held out the prospect of a bourgeois revival and condemned the emergence of capitalist tendencies (largely free markets) amongst the peasantry.[33] Of all Deng's speeches this is probably the one which departed the most from his earlier and later ideas. It clearly proved problematic for Deng, particularly during the 1980s. Even after the Tiananmen Incident of 1989, when Deng might be assumed to have been prepared to take a harder line against intellectuals once again, he appeared reluctant to recognize the 'Report on the Rectification Campaign' of September 1957 as his own, even though it has always been an 'open' statement, having been published in *People's Daily* at the time. It is not included in the volume of his writings published in August 1989 as a political primer in the wake of the disturbances of May and June, and dealing with the years 1938–65. On the other hand, even in this report Deng continued to urge caution and gradualism. He emphasized that the vast majority of most social groups, including the intellectuals, were still prepared to support the CCP. Rectification and inner-party democracy as he had outlined them in September 1956 were still necessary, and he stressed, as always, the need to find economic solutions to political and social problems.

THE GREAT LEAP FORWARD

Undoubtedly Deng's later reluctance to acknowledge the 1957 'Report on the Rectification Campaign', quite apart from its rhetoric and content, is that the 3rd plenum of the 8th Central Committee where it was delivered was the occasion on which the leadership effectively agreed to the development strategy since better known as the Great Leap Forward.[34] The Great Leap Forward in question was initially a movement of popular mobilization to engage in water conservation work during the winter of 1957–8 which was so successful, in terms of the number of people it mobilized, that in the following year it led to a number of policies based on the principle of mobilization. Those policies taken together formed a broader programme for development which is now also referred to as the Great Leap Forward, and included the attempt for China to catch up and surpass the West's 150 years of industrialization in only fifteen.

The experience of the 'Hundred Flowers' was clearly a major shock for the leaders of the CCP. Within the leadership it raised questions about Mao's judgement and lent force to arguments for collective leadership. It demonstrated both the need for sustained party rectification and that prolonged periods of disunity within the leadership had considerable costs. The dispute between Liu Shaoqi and Mao over rectification had continued for the best part of the whole year after the 8th CCP Congress, right through the 'Hundred Flowers' of May and June 1957, and its recriminatory aftermath – despite repeated attempts by Deng during June and July to bridge the gap between them. Ironically, it also made eventual adoption of Mao's mobilization-based model of development more likely. Chen Yun's strategy for development, which had been the basis of the 2nd Five-Year Plan drafted at the 8th CCP Congress, had assumed the creation and encouragement of a technocratic élite. This was one reason why the intellectuals had been courted since the beginning of 1956 and encouraged to 'supervise' the CCP in May and June 1957. Now, however, their political loyalty was in doubt.

In the autumn of 1957 the CCP leadership seemed obsessed by party unity. This obsession was to last for over a year and led to the launching of the broader programme of the Great Leap Forward during 1958. It was helped by Mao's announcement to his close colleagues, though not yet in public, that he would be stepping down from his position as Head of State in 1959 and replaced by Liu Shaoqi, in order to retreat to the second line of politics, a move which he had foreshadowed and prepared for at the 8th Party Congress. Throughout most of that year the leadership stayed united, with only Zhou Enlai and Chen Yun opposing the strategy, though in effect they and the central planning bureaucracy were shunted aside from September 1957 to mid-1959.

The strategy of the Great Leap Forward called for the substitution of capital in investment by labour; the substitution of technology and economics by politics; and the substitution of expertise and skilled labour by enthusiasm. It reflected Mao's belief in the benefits to be derived from economies of scale – as summed up in his slogan of 'more, faster, better and more economical' – with no consideration of diminishing marginal utility. Its most enduring symbols were the backyard steel furnaces, which produced considerable amounts of largely useless pig iron; and the people's communes, the new and extremely large rural collectives combining economic, political and social functions for over 80 per cent of China's population. The results during 1958 appeared spectacular, as output figures reported record levels, no doubt because the State Statistical Bureau had also been taken over by enthusiasts who believed that even statistical work had to serve politics rather than reliable reporting.[35] By November the people's communes were being hailed not simply as a successful experiment in rural living but also as the 'sprouts of communism' – the final goal of classless society – much to the consternation of the CPSU.

However, the winter of 1958–9 saw many of the leaders of the CCP setting out on inspection tours of the provinces to see the achievements of the Great Leap Forward for themselves. The experience was clearly a cruel shock for those, such as Deng and Peng Dehuai, who might have harboured any doubts. Peng's inspection tour of his native Hunan, after he had been to Gansu, and followed by visits to Jiangxi, Anhui and Hebei, are probably the most famous because they led to his confrontation with Mao at the Lushan conference of the CCP later in 1959. However, it was by no means a unique experience. Peng found the peasants starving and local party cadres complaining in private about the excesses of the Great Leap.

Deng, for his part, visited several provinces, including Guizhou where on a celebratory return visit to Zunyi in January 1959 he found conditions to be unbelievably wretched given the advances of the early 1950s. There was a serious shortage of food, not least because earlier in the enthusiasm of the Great Leap the reported record high production figures for grain had led to the peasants' being directed by local cadres to 'eat until your bellies are full' and little had been kept back for seed or future supply. Deng suggested that one way to alleviate this problem was to establish communal mess halls in the people's communes, rather than everyone attempting to fend for themselves. Local leaders accepted the idea, which they appeared not to have thought of before, with some enthusiasm.[36] It was not only a practical solution to their problem but it also met the emphasis on collectivism inherent in Mao's vision and the current political rhetoric.

By February and March 1959 Deng, like many of the other more pragmatic members of the leadership, was urging caution, though by no means outright opposition to the strategy of the Great Leap. For example, at one meeting of the CCP Secretariat to discuss the importance of including productive labour in educational curricula – a favourite initiative of Mao's – he argued that whilst there were obvious benefits, such developments should not go too far or too fast lest they have an adverse effect on the quality of education.[37] At another, held to discuss the people's communes, he suggested that they were perhaps not such an unqualified success, as they were continuing to have problems in production and management.[38]

Peng Dehuai was less temperate than Deng and, bolstered by an erratic relationship with Mao over the years, became somewhat critical of both the Great Leap Forward and Mao more widely.[39] Years later, Ye Jianying, one of the more important post-Mao leaders of the PLA, was to claim that originally Deng, Liu Shaoqi, Zhou Enlai and himself all sympathized with Peng Dehuai's position.[40] On the other hand they did not promise him support. Unlike Mao, Peng was not a particularly skilful political manipulator, and he seems to have gone for a simple policy of surprise and confrontation at the annual summer work conference of the CCP leadership held during July 1959 in Lushan.[41] Though he had gathered some support and written an ingeniously barbed 'Letter of Opinion' to Mao *qua* Chairman of the CCP, he had not confined his criticisms to the strategy of the Great Leap Forward but extended them to blame Mao for the excesses of the past year. In particular, he accused Mao of 'leftist' errors and 'petty-bourgeois fanaticism': almost identical wording to the criticisms made by Mao's enemies during the late 1920s and the early 1930s, and not epithets that Mao was likely to accept readily.[42]

Mao counter-attacked brilliantly, not least by using his position as Chairman of the CCP to control the agenda of the Lushan conference. His speech in answer to Peng's attack was measured, obscured the real issues, characterized Peng as a 'right opportunist' seeking power, and gave him no right of reply (or defence.) He also bullied, reminding his colleagues of their collective past and offering them a clear choice. Since Peng was also Minister of Defence he warned: ' If the Chinese People's Liberation Army should follow Peng Dehuai, I will go to fight guerrilla war.'[43] Had one or two participants spoken out in Peng's defence or even commented modifyingly about the Great Leap Forward, the outcome might have been different. However, Mao was not the only one taken by surprise. It seems even Peng's supporters before Lushan had not known that he was going to write a letter to Mao. In the event Mao's escalation of the conflict carried the day. The designation of Peng Dehuai and his supporters as 'right opportunists' meant that the opposition to the Great Leap was temporarily stilled.

Deng attended neither the formal plenum of the Central Committee in August when Peng and his associates were denounced as an 'Anti-Party Clique' nor the month-long central work conference which had preceded it and where the confrontation had occurred. (Another notable absentee was Chen Yun.) There is an element of intrigue here, which is probably unnecessary. Later during the Cultural Revolution he was to write in his 'Self-criticism' that he had not gone to the work conference because of trouble with his leg and had written excusing himself at the time.[44] It sounds like a political illness, but Deng had indeed broken his leg playing billiards some time before Lushan, though what is not clear is that someone else had apparently accidentally hit him with a cue.[45] MacFarquhar suggests he broke it right at the beginning of the Lushan work conference, thus necessitating his withdrawal.[46]

On balance it seems reasonable to assume that there was no political motive for his absence, but that there had been complications with his leg for some time. Certainly that would appear consistent with the photographic evidence. Neither he nor anyone else had known that a crisis of the kind that occurred was coming at the Lushan conference, and it is conceivable that he took the opportunity of the Central Committee's summer break to seek medical treatment. From December 1958 until April 1961 he was usually photographed carrying a walking stick, though that was not his normal practice either before or after. If that inference is correct, then it may well be that Deng's visit to Moscow in late 1960 was also the opportunity to obtain medical treatment as well as to deal with Sino-Soviet relations. At this time the CCP's top leadership were taking it in turns to visit the USSR. Deng had visited in 1956 and 1957, and was not entrusted with prime responsibility in the handling of relations with the CPSU until later. Throughout the 1950s it had been the practice for Chinese leaders to seek medical treatment in the USSR.

Deng's contemporary attitude to the events at the Lushan work conference are not recorded, but it is unlikely to have been one of joy. Peng had to some extent personalized politics himself and infringed what Deng, at least, would have regarded as the norms of inner-party discipline through his clumsy attempt at conspiracy during the first half of 1959. In that context, as well as for other more straightforward reasons, as in the past, Mao could certainly rely on Deng for support. Moreover, there was something of a history of bad relations between Deng and Peng that went back to at least the late 1930s. Liu Bocheng and Peng had apparently always disliked each other, and they had recently been at loggerheads over the modernization of the PLA. On the other hand, it was clear that after Lushan CCP norms were never going to be applied to Mao again and that the conduct of Chinese politics had changed, perhaps irrevocably. Although the Great Leap Forward was wound down in 1960 after a short burst of renewed enthusiasm and Mao withdrew to the 'second line' of politics, Deng is likely to have been well aware by the end of the 1950s of the further difficulties he now faced.

5 Reconstruction and Mao, 1960–1966

The period from the end of the Great Leap Forward to the start of the Cultural Revolution remains probably the most obscured in the history of the PRC. One reason for this is that, with the failure of the Great Leap, the Chinese authorities imposed tighter restrictions on information of all kinds, but particularly the printed media, leaving the country. Another is that at the time China was becoming increasingly isolated internationally. Relations with the West had been excessively low-key since the establishment of the PRC, and in the middle of 1960 Soviet advisers and technicians were withdrawn.

Partly as a result the history of these years tends to be shaped disproportionately by subsequent events in the Cultural Revolution. Then the Red Guards and those supporting Chairman Mao characterized almost all CCP leaders, but particularly Liu Shaoqi and Deng Xiaoping, as having shunted Mao aside and thereby followed the 'Capitalist Road' throughout the first half of the 1960s. Moreover, many sources of information on this period were published during the Cultural Revolution, notably by Red Guard groups competing to be loyal Maoists by denigrating 'capitalist roaders', and consequently creating conflict out of the earlier differences between Mao and those of his colleagues later under attack. Such sources necessarily reinforced their own 'two-line' perspective – Chairman Mao's 'completely revolutionary line' versus that of 'the capitalist revisionist counter-revolutionaries' – and are notoriously unreliable, though not of course uninformative.[1]

Deng almost certainly did disagree with Mao, and their differences probably increased towards the Cultural Revolution as Mao became more concerned with the problems he associated with 'revisionism'. However, Deng had often disagreed with Mao in the past, and would not have considered any such differences to be a new development in their relationship. Indeed, for much of the leadership before the Lushan plenum – Peng Dehuai included – there had never been much doubt that conflict and co-operation amongst Mao and other leaders could and did co-exist.

As already indicated, the relationship between Mao Zedong and Deng Xiaoping was never regarded by either of them as an equal relationship, which perhaps explains both why it lasted so long and why it retained its influence even after Mao's death. Mao was the leader and Deng the loyal subordinate. They both would probably have believed that they could continue to work together, as indeed they did very successfully in foreign affairs. Moreover, given the nature of their relationship, if Mao were to criticize Deng for not informing, disregarding or avoiding Mao, as he apparently did in 1964,[2] then Deng would expect to respond by attempting to correct his ways, which is what he appears to have done. In his October 1966 'Self-criticism' Deng acknowledged the earlier rebuke, and not only took full responsibility for its causes but also indicated that he had adjusted his behaviour accordingly at the time: a statement which even allowing for the circumstances of its genesis carries the ring of authenticity given the contemporary evidence.[3]

Immediately after the Lushan plenum relations between Mao and Deng were extremely good. The Political Bureau of the CCP had an enlarged meeting in Shanghai in January 1960 at which Mao is said to have even described Deng as his deputy in public.[4] This somewhat cavalier attitude to the hierarchy of the CCP, which then had official rankings in which Deng was only fourth, would not have been unusual behaviour for Mao,[5] even though he already had a formal deputy in Liu Shaoqi. He was well known for testing out both situations and people in this way, as well as for kite-flying. Indeed, some similar kind of encouragement is usually regarded as having provided a necessary stimulus to Gao Gang's ambition in 1953.

The evidence that this relationship started to change, and even then not dramatically for some time, dates only from 1962. Moreover, the cause of change was organizational rather than ideological differences or discussions over policy. Mao's withdrawal to the 'second line' left routine matters to the leadership of Zhou Enlai for state affairs, and Liu Shaoqi for party affairs. This put Deng Xiaoping in a difficult position. To meet protocol any leadership communication with Mao Zedong would now have to be routed through Liu Shaoqi – and Deng was always a stickler for status as witness his extreme deference to both Mao Zedong and Zhou Enlai. However, in the past Mao Zedong had become used to approaching Deng Xiaoping directly, particularly where party and inner-leadership work were concerned. Deng had an obvious dilemma: to respond directly to Mao would cause friction with Liu Shaoqi, but not to deal directly with Mao when requested would run the risk of incurring the Chairman's wrath. Feeling cross-pressured, Deng under-played his hand and tried to step back a bit from everyday politics. Though he clearly did not opt out completely he spent more time engaged in his hobbies, such as playing bridge, a habit he had developed in his army days, or in watching soccer. Necessarily, his bridge-playing was to bring down the scorn of the puritanical Red Guards during the Cultural Revolution, but their criticisms were correct in one sense: those he played with – notably Hu Yaobang and Wan Li – on the whole had been and were to remain his long-time political allies.

Even as the Cultural Revolution rolled in and the differences of opinion between Mao and Deng were probably more real than most, they remained differences of opinion and were never highly personalized. For example, Deng was never criticized by name in the official media during the Cultural Revolution but simply referred to as 'The Number Two Person in Authority Taking the Capitalist Road', after Liu Shaoqi, the 'Number One'.[6] Even in the Cultural Revolution Mao was prepared to differentiate between Deng and others in the CCP leadership, and he insisted that Deng be allowed to retain his membership of the CCP even after Deng's removal from the leadership at the end of 1966.[7]

On the other hand, this was in retrospect to prove an important period in Deng's own separate political development independent of Mao Zedong. The changing relationships within the CCP leadership saw Deng come into closer contact with those who would eventually be responsible with him for launching the reform era in 1978. Many of the policies discussed and implemented, particularly during the early 1960s in order to overcome the consequences of the era of the Great Leap Forward, were to prove the basis for those at the heart of later reform. Despite the rhetoric of the Cultural Revolution, Deng's closest working relationship at this time appears not to have been with Liu Shaoqi, to whom he had never been particularly close, nor Zhou Enlai, whom he looked up to as (in his own words of 1980) an 'elder brother' rather than an equal,[8] but with Peng Zhen. Peng was the pre-Cultural Revolution Mayor of Beijing, and its first major victim. Throughout the early 1960s, they worked together to develop policy in a number of areas.

RECONSTRUCTION

The year 1960 was a truly appalling one in China. The leadership became entangled in the massive failure of the Great Leap Forward and obsessed by the widening rift with the USSR. Agricultural output fell to about three-quarters of its 1958 level. There was widespread drought and famine, and during 1959 to 1961 China's population actually fell by 13.5 million. Looking back from the 1980s, Deng was to regard the period immediately after the Lushan plenum as 'the most difficult of times'.[9]

The disastrous economic aftermath of the Great Leap Forward during the early 1960s would be hard to overstate. Agricultural output continued to decline and food was in short supply. Industry, which relied on agriculture for either its raw materials or capital, also went into decline. Light industry fell by 10 per cent in 1960 over the (reported) figures for the previous year, 22 per cent in 1961 and 8 per cent in 1962. Heavy industry was even harder hit, dropping by 47 per cent in 1961 over 1960 and 22 per cent in 1962 over 1961.[10] Even contemporary newspapers, particularly at the local level, bear the scars. CCP leaders are referred to in headlines by their personal name, rather than their family name, to instil a feeling of solidarity under crisis. Moreover, the quality of newsprint declined so much that very often the newspapers are impossible to read: thin blotting paper soaked in runny ink.

The immediate task for the CCP leadership in the wake of such massive failure had to be economic reconstruction. Emergency meetings in the second half of 1960 brought the Great Leap Forward to an end at the turn of the year and adopted a series of measures effectively targeted at restoring production by any measures possible in the immediate term. The economy was to be 'readjusted,' gradualism was to replace speed, and agriculture was to be regarded as the key economic sector. In most cases this led to the reorganization of the people's communes so that they now became reasonably manageable units. However, in some places it appears the economic situation was so serious that there was even complete decollectivization and the restoration of individual farming.

Though there was still a fundamentally united leadership, it could not agree on what to do next; or, of equal importance, what had gone wrong and why. The CCP held a series of meetings during 1961 to discuss these matters and from the first Mao's attitude, understandably given his responsibility, was that though there had been mistakes the party should view the whole experience as a learning process. Others, though still not inclined to confront the Chairman, remained determined that nothing like the Great Leap should ever happen again and that the economy should be restored to a basic functioning strength as quickly as possible.

Deng's first attempt to construct a new consensus and develop new policies was successful as far as it went, not least because it gained Mao's approval. In March 1961 the CCP held a Central Work Conference in Canton to discuss rural policy, particularly with respect to people's communes. Deng and Peng Zhen had previously carried out an on-the-spot investigation of the situation in a number of communes to the north of Beijing by way of preparation. They came to the conference armed with data, analysis and proposals resulting from their research. In particular, Deng suggested that the communes had been established too quickly and without adequate preparation, discussion or investigation of specific circumstances. Mao apparently accepted both their research and their conclusions on the grounds that 'without investigation, there is no right to speak', though still maintaining that their research was part of the necessary learning experience for the CCP. [11]

One result was that the CCP agreed, as a result of Mao's imprimatur, to prepare a series of investigative reports on different aspects of government work. Several committees were established, each under the leadership of a major CCP figure and with a remit to draft a policy paper. For example, Mao was given responsibility for communes, Bo Yibo for industry, Li Xiannian for finance, Zhou Yang and Lu Dingyi for culture, and Peng Zhen for education. The whole process was co-ordinated by Deng through the Secretariat, which established another three broad co-ordinating committees – one each for economics, culture, and political and legal work – chaired by, respectively, Chen Yun, Peng Zhen and Deng himself. [12]

Even allowing for the glosses of revisionist history – those of Red Guards in the Cultural Revolution and of post-Mao reformers – the resulting policy papers appeared to contain recommendations that worked completely against the strategy of the Great Leap Forward: economics not politics was emphasized as the motor of development. Modern technology, if necessary from abroad, was to be a new driving force; and gradual, capital-led investment was to replace mass mobilization. Communes were to be made smaller, with the basic accounting unit reverting to the production team – the equivalent of the small co-operatives established (for the most part) in the second half of 1955. Education was to re-emphasize quality, and expertise was to be valued once again. The ideas proposed at this time were to become the initial intellectual foundations for the reforms of the late 1970s and the early 1980s.[13] Moreover, Bo Yibo, Li Xiannian, Zhou Yang, Lu Dingyi, Peng Zhen, Chen Yun and Deng were all to play a leading role in the later reform era, as they did in this earlier period of economic reconstruction.

It may not have been general practice at the time but it appears that Deng and Peng Zhen established a 'think-tank' of intellectuals and officials to assist them. Later, in the 1980s, such organizations were to be more formally organized and to play a significant political role. The group took the name of the building in which it met in Beijing's western suburbs – the Changguanlou – and through a review of all central documents for the period of the Great Leap, and a series of more detailed investigations, prepared reports for the two CCP leaders on a whole range of issues. Its conclusions favoured policies based on planning rather than mobilization.[14]

Mobilization and the 'mass line' were key issues for Deng, as they had been throughout the 1950s and indeed earlier. He was presumably concerned that the concept of the 'mass line' should not be defined only in terms of mass political campaigns. During 1961 and 1962 in particular he reflected on a number of occasions on the nature of the 'mass line', arguing that there was more than one technique of mass mobilization and that mass campaigns might often be both inappropriate and counter-productive. As he had stressed in his speech at the 8th CCP Congress, the 'mass line' also entailed other more sophisticated techniques, and indeed if a close relationship between party and people was to be maintained then these too must be employed, not least so that campaign weariness did not result.

Deng pursued this theme in both of his speeches to the Central Work Conference of January and February 1962. This meeting of some 7,000 party officials had been convened to come to a judgement on the Great Leap Forward and to decide on a plan for future action. Deng once again stressed the importance of party discipline, democracy within the CCP and party leadership. In particular, he argued strongly that those, as for example Peng Dehuai, who had been attacked as 'rightists' during the Great Leap Forward should have their cases re-examined and, where appropriate, they should be rehabilitated. Though the support for Peng Dehuai might have upset Mao, the way Deng put the case was designed not to antagonize the Chairman. In Yan'an, as Deng pointed out, Mao had urged the CCP to 'seek truth from facts'. Moreover, the remainder of this proposal was not put confrontationally but as part of a general examination of the CCP's achievements and shortcomings. It was an injunction that was to play an important political role in launching the reform era in 1978, but in the interim became submerged in Mao's concerns with political rectification.[15]

Unfortunately, the Central Work Conference could not resolve the related problems of agreeing on the cause of problems in the Great Leap Forward and a development strategy for the future. Much was said about the need for self-criticism – for example, Mao apparently confirmed that he had made a formal self-criticism in the middle of the previous year and Deng presented a self-criticism of the CCP Secretariat – but there remained a basic uncertainty. Though the leadership's views were probably at this time not particularly polarized, they did tend in two irreconcilable directions. One view was that the Great Leap Forward had been an economic disaster which should not be repeated, with future policies based on economic solutions. The other view was that extraneous factors (the weather, the withdrawal of Soviet assistance) and inadequate politicization were important to an understanding of the failures of the recent past. Future success would then depend on a party rectification campaign and mass political education. These were to be the issues that would dominate the political agenda for the next four years and lead eventually to the Cultural Revolution.

RECTIFICATION AND 'CLASS STRUGGLE'

The failure of the Central Work Conference of February 1962 to agree policies for the future was exacerbated soon afterwards by the discovery that the economic crisis was worse than the most pessimistic had predicted. The government faced an even bigger than imagined budgetary deficit and increasing inflation. Deng's response, for one, was straightforward. He argued that production was the first priority and that,'As long as we can bring about a rapid restoration, it doesn't matter how we do it,'[16] or, in the words of a speech to the Communist Youth League in July 1962 for which he is probably most famous, 'It doesn't matter whether a cat is black or white, so long as it catches mice.'[17] Deng's speech to the League was almost certainly not delivered accidentally. He seems to have taken no regular or particular interest in youth work previously. On the other hand, the League's Secretary at the time was Hu Yaobang, one of Deng's protégés since the 1940s, who was later to become the CCP General Secretary himself during the 1980s.[18]

Deng's speech directly confronted the problems of mobilizational politics, which – exactly as he had over the years, from his February 1943 speech to party cadres in the Taihang Region, to his September 1956 speech at the 8th CCP Congress[19] – he criticized as leading too easily to over-zealous enthusiasm and 'leftist' excess. He cited examples from both industry and agriculture but saved his most trenchant criticisms for the people's communes and collectivization. Both, he said, had come about too quickly without adequate preparation, at a cost to economic production which could not be sustained. He discussed various solutions, including the redivision of collectivized landholdings, but appears not to have advocated total decollectivization at this time, as had experiments in Anhui province which presaged the individual household responsibility system introduced in the late 1970s. Instead, Deng favoured smaller collectives with production guaranteed at fixed prices on a household basis. Necessarily, though at the time all these proposals and preferences were intended as practical solutions to immediate problems, in the heat of the Cultural Revolution they became hard evidence of Deng's ideological opposition to Mao Zedong.

Mao reacted differently to the problems facing the leadership of the CCP. In the ringing tones of his injunction to 'Never forget class struggle' – announced at the CCP's summer work conference in 1962 and accepted by the 10th plenum of the Central Committee immediately following – he launched rectification campaigns aimed at cadres and the party's organization in the rural areas. The Socialist Education Movement was designed to re-orientate the CCP towards Mao's vision of China's future by stressing its revolutionary past. As envisaged by Mao, the Socialist Education Movement would mobilize the peasantry to supervise their local party cadres, much as he had imagined the intellectuals would 'rectify' the CCP in the urban areas during the 'Hundred Flowers' of 1957. He called for the study of past injustices and class struggle as a precursor to the establishment of Poor and Lower Middle Peasants' Associations. However, it was a campaign which met with considerable resistance, not only from party cadres but also from the peasantry who in the wake of the Great Leap Forward were somewhat disillusioned with and alienated from the CCP.[20]

In the summer of 1963, Deng and Peng Zhen engaged in another of their investigative endeavours which later, in the Cultural Revolution, was to lead to considerable criticism.[21] This time they moved further afield to the South-west, Deng's area of operations during the early 1950s and where he was still well connected, in order to research the problems of the Socialist Education Movement and to experiment with new developments. In the process they found that in the South-west at least the peasants' associations were poorly organized. As an alternative they suggested instead that in future the peasants' associations be led by work-teams sent out from the cities to carry out the rectification campaign. They also suggested that the first targets in the campaign should be the middle levels of the bureaucracy rather than the most local cadres. The results were, of course, that the whole campaign moved away from the countryside to focus on the towns and cities where the bureaucracy was located, leaving the peasants' associations with even less to do, and effectively returned rectification to an internal party matter. In the Cultural Revolution it was, of course, suggested that this had been a deliberate act of defiance against Mao's original intentions.

During 1963 and 1964 the rectification campaign developed in a number of different directions, with Liu Shaoqi, for example, emphasizing economic corruption, rather than political revisionism, as the main target. In some cases there can have been no thought from the proposers of new initiatives within the Socialist Education Movement that they were opposing Mao's intentions as opposed to assisting in the development of a campaign he had favoured. At the same time, more radical differences of opinion within the leadership on the future trajectory for China's development were beginning to surface, as in discussion of the form and content of the Socialist Education Movement.

In early 1965 Mao Zedong attempted to regain the initiative and to reformulate the focus of the Socialist Education Movement, which he re-launched as a campaign of political education throughout the CCP and for the whole population. The work teams were withdrawn and their responsibilities handed back to the peasants' associations. The target was now revisionism – the movement away from the path of communism – in all its manifestations, and it was at this time that Mao first raised the possibility that the CCP had been hijacked by 'those in authority taking the capitalist road'. However, it is unlikely that at this stage he had anyone specific in mind, and indeed possibly no notion that it might apply to the senior leadership at all: rather it seems likely that he was referring to local cadres, who had incidentally and not purposively become revisionist. Within two years it was to carry more sinister connotations. However, in the 1980s Deng Xiaoping was still prepared to concede that Mao at that time was genuinely concerned with revisionism.[22]

Mao's concern with rectification after 1962 was, however, not confined to the Socialist Education Campaign. As he developed his critique of revisionism within the CCP during the 1960s he increasingly emphasized the need for politicization in a variety of activities, including education and culture. These were particularly crucial areas for Mao as he became almost obsessed with the importance of value change – hence the usage of the term 'culture' in the naming of the Cultural Revolution. In Mao's view all cultural and educational activities served specific political ends, and whoever controlled their implicit values also controlled society.

Lacking support for the most part within the CCP establishment, Mao had to look elsewhere for those who would help him re-politicize China. One person he turned to was Lin Biao, the Minister of National Defence, who launched a political education campaign – first within the PLA, and then later, when Mao launched a 'Learn from the PLA' Movement in 1963, for the whole country. The political primer for this campaign was a selection of Mao's writings in a little red book – *Quotations from the Thought of Mao Zedong*. During the Cultural Revolution Deng was criticized for his dislike of the 'little red book'. There is no contemporary evidence, but such a view would have been consistent with Deng's previous attitudes, and was certainly consistent with his later articulated views. His objections were twofold. In the first place, as he was often at pains to stress, he regarded Mao Zedong Thought as a product of the CCP's collective leadership and not Mao's personal property as it effectively became during the Cultural Revolution. In the second place, his objections were those of the non-dogmatist: Mao's writings were no infallible guide to anything, not even Mao Zedong Thought. As he pointed out in 1980, even Mao negated Mao Zedong Thought: 'Comrade Mao Zedong's mistakes consisted in violations of his own correct ideas.'[23] Certainly, when offered a copy of the 'little red book' as a study guide in 1970 he reportedly rejected it unceremoniously.[24]

Another person Mao turned to for support was his wife, Jiang Qing, a former actress to whom he entrusted the task of rectifying art and literature. Starting in 1963 during the Cultural Revolution she successfully re-shaped Chinese culture. In her own words she 'revolutionized' and 'modernized' China's traditional art forms. Culture was to reflect class struggle and serve the politics of mobilization as defined by Mao: heroic workers, peasants and soldiers were to do battle with evil landlords, capitalists and the old society. In particular, she was largely responsible for promoting the eight modern revolutionary ballets and operas which came to dominate the Chinese performing arts from 1966 to 1976. As her rectification of Chinese culture proceeded her political importance also increased, until she became part of the CCP leadership in her own right during the Cultural Revolution.[25] Deng, apparently, was unimpressed by her efforts, and said so in public on at least one occasion too many, thereby ensuring a lifelong enemy, if their antagonism had not already developed beforehand. On the eve of the Cultural Revolution, all CCP leaders were obliged to attend the performance of these new modern revolutionary operas and ballets. A common rumour, even at the time, was that Deng had managed to avoid most, but at last could procrastinate no further. He attended but made his point by falling asleep during the performance.[26]

THE SINO-SOVIET SPLIT

One area where Mao and Deng were able to continue their close working partnership right up to the Cultural Revolution – and indeed in which they seem to have co-operated remarkably successfully, or at least to their mutual satisfaction – was in the handling of Sino-Soviet relations. Mao Zedong apparently had nothing but praise for Deng's handling of repeated negotiations with the USSR and CPSU.[27] Deng for his part, particularly during the early 1980s when Mao's role in the politics of the PRC was being reassessed, has been at great pains to stress that Mao Zedong's policy in foreign affairs had been correct and highly successful.[28]

An essential part of the background against which the decision to launch the Great Leap Forward had been taken, and which was to play an important role in the economic crisis of the early 1960s, was China's deteriorating relationship with the USSR. The search for a 'Chinese road to socialism' in and after the mid-1950s undoubtedly resulted from the CCP's inherent nationalism, but it was also a consequence of worsening Sino-Soviet relations. Though the detail is far from clear, Deng Xiaoping appears to have played a central role in the politics of the Sino-Soviet split, and indeed in the management of PRC relations with the USSR from the early 1950s on.

Once again this role appears to have come his way because of his special relationship with Mao Zedong. It may have helped that he had been in Moscow as a trainee political organizer, but a number of senior CCP figures have also confirmed over the years that Mao simply admired the way he dealt with the Russians.[29] Certainly and unusually, given its constancy, a somewhat hostile attitude towards the USSR seems to have been a feature of Deng's politics well into the late 1980s, though this may have simply been a reflection of Mao Zedong's attitudes.[30] Between 1956 and 1963 he visited Moscow four times for discussions and often hard-headed negotiations. He even reported to the CCP on the results of negotiations on occasions when he was not the formal head of the Chinese delegation, as in 1958.[31] During the 1960s, when the polemic between the CPSU and the CCP came out into the open, Deng was the formal head of the group within the CCP Central Committee – the Anti-Revisionist Writing Group

– that drafted the Chinese party's replies.[32]

The Sino-Soviet Alliance had always been somewhat uneasy, often more a function of Sino-American relations than of a genuine desire for co-operation on the part of the CCP. Relations between the CCP and CPSU had been difficult since the mid-1920s. A prime aim of the early 1940s rectification campaign had been the removal of Soviet influence and the nationalization of the Chinese communist movement. Their paths to power had been radically different and had resulted in competing ideological perspectives. Under the impact of conflicting mutual expectations and developments in the wider international community, co-operation rapidly turned to rancour. From the start both sides probably had unreasonable expectations. China sought military and economic aid to a staggering degree. For most of the 1950s it was almost totally dependent on Soviet aid. When this was suddenly withdrawn in mid-1960, as a result of growing tensions, it made a disastrous economic situation in the wake of the Great Leap Forward even worse. The cost to the USSR was high at a time when, in the aftermath of the Second World War and the establishment of communist regimes in Eastern Europe, it could barely afford such support. None the less, China's expectation was that the USSR would supply more economic aid, be prepared to share its nuclear technology and come to China's assistance with military force in the event of local conflicts.

In return the CCP was not willing to meet the expectations of the CPSU for military bases and co-operation, as well as for support within the world communist movement, even when this might meet its own ends. In 1958, for example, having asked the USSR for assistance in developing a navy, both Mao and Deng reacted aggressively to the Soviet Union's suggestion that this could occur as a joint venture.[33] On the contrary, the CCP seems rather to have resented the CPSU's arrogation of seniority. Partly this was personal, for after Stalin's death Mao seems to have believed that he rather than Khrushchev was the next most senior communist leader. However, there was also an institutional and historical dimension to this belief since the CCP had come to power largely without, if not actually despite, the involvement of the CPSU.

In September 1954 Khrushchev came to Beijing for the first of many negotiations during the mid-1950s between the leaders of the CCP and the CPSU. The Chinese side was led by Zhou Enlai, and Deng was one of the other five negotiators. Agreement was reached across a wide range of issues including the final withdrawal of Soviet troops and economic interests in China and the granting of substantial economic aid. It was the last occasion on which solid and lasting agreement was to prove possible.

February 1956 saw a Chinese delegation under Zhu De, including Deng, attend the landmark 20th Congress of the CPSU, at which Khrushchev criticized the cult of personality. Despite Mao's later ascribed reaction to this event, with its attack on the personality cult, that aspect was probably less shocking to the CCP delegation than Khrushchev's acceptance of peaceful coexistence between capitalism and socialism for this impinged on the amount of aid China could expect from the USSR. There was still very definitely a hope amongst the delegation that the USSR would provide China with yet more assistance, including the nuclear technology it requested.[34] When Mao Zedong, accompanied by Deng, attended the 40th Anniversary celebrations for the Russian revolution in 1957, agreement appears to have been reached to that effect, although the promise was never fulfilled.

However, in 1958 the Sino-Soviet alliance started to run into problems from which it never recovered. The CCP's insistence on a nuclear capacity was coming into increasing conflict with Khrushchev's attempts at *détente* and his global political strategy. The launch of the Great Leap Forward represented a significant ideological challenge to the USSR's claim to be furthest along the road to communism. Personal relations between Khrushchev and Mao were deteriorating and the CCP was becoming involved in European communist politics against Moscow.

By 1960 the Sino-Soviet split had become irreversible. CCP delegates at various meetings of international communists attacked the CPSU, and the two parties started publishing scarcely veiled critiques of each other's rapidly solidifying positions. Following the Bucharest Conference of the Romanian Workers' Party in June 1960, at which Peng Zhen and Khrushchev had a stand-up slanging match, Soviet aid to China was totally withdrawn. Under Liu Shaoqi's nominal leadership, a Chinese delegation including Deng attended two meetings in Moscow designed to heal the rifts in world communism. Both saw a series of heated exchanges between Khrushchev and Deng, which, but for the intervention of Ho Chi Minh, who personally brought the two together, would have ended with no communiqué agreed. In the event the compromise was little more than a vague commitment to unity and to meet again.

The final act precipitating an open rift, which had so far been averted, came in 1963. From 1960 until that date, various communist parties, but particularly the North Vietnamese, had tried to bring the CCP and the CPSU to the negotiating table. In July 1963 Deng headed a small delegation, which included Peng Zhen, to Moscow. The failure to shore up Sino-Soviet relations was greeted as a victory over revisionism by the CCP leadership who turned out in force to welcome Deng back from Moscow.[35] Thereafter the dispute went public through a series of highly confrontational open letters between the CCP and the CPSU. As already indicated, Deng was responsible on the Chinese side for the group that drafted the CCP's letters.

THE CULTURAL REVOLUTION

It is not clear when, if ever, Mao took a decision to launch an attack of the scale of the Cultural Revolution on the CCP leadership. Deng, at the time the CCP formally reassessed its history and Mao Zedong's role in it during 1980–1, on one occasion reflected that Mao had in fact never intended to attack veteran cadres to such an extent.[36] A theory that once Mao had set certain wheels in motion conflict emerged and developed a dynamic of its own is easy enough to sustain. In Deng's view the wheels that Mao set in motion included Lin Biao, the Gang of Four,

Kang Sheng, and those associated with them, for it would appear he holds them particularly responsible for the way the Cultural Revolution developed, including his own fate after the end of 1966.

It would also seem reasonable to argue that Deng even now considers himself to have been a loyal supporter of Mao, in all the ways he had grown used to operating, right up to and beyond his dismissal in the Cultural Revolution. Whatever reservations Deng may have had about the cult of personality in general, in terms of his political life these do not seem to have been applied to the specific case of Chairman Mao. Throughout the 1960s he stressed not only the importance of studying Mao Zedong Thought but also its personal relationship to Mao himself. For example, at the Enlarged Central Work Conference of February 1962 he emphasized the need for cadres to 'truly understand . . . [the] Chairman's exhortations'.[37] Few of Deng's speeches during these years are available, but those that are as, for example, his July 1964 speech to the Communist Youth League – 'The red flag of Mao Zedong Thought Advances the Revolutionization of China's Youth' – all place the study of Mao Zedong Thought in the forefront of political considerations.[38]

Deng's confidence in his relationship with Mao would also seem to be the most plausible explanation for his actions during 1965 and 1966 when he accepted criticism, responded with self-criticism (at least twice) and joined in other emerging Cultural Revolution activities. Despite his disbelief in the accusations made about Lo Ruiqing, the Chief of the General Staff of the PLA whom Mao had insisted should be dismissed at the end of 1965, Deng accepted Mao's ruling and participated accordingly in the meetings called to deal with disciplinary action. Similarly, he not only participated in Peng Zhen's dismissal in Mao's absence in May 1966, but took on the mantle, with Liu Shaoqi, of heading a new Cultural Revolution Group. Even after his own self-criticisms, in August and October, he continued to attend Red Guard receptions.

It is obviously hard to assess the extent to which there was conspiracy in the emergence of the Cultural Revolution. At the very least, though the details are hard to trace, it does seem that those new forces in CCP politics brought into being by Mao Zedong did rapidly move to use different parts of the central political system to set their own agenda and to attempt to implement their own policies. In the ensuing chaos, and under the various pressures of the Red Guards from outside the decision-making bodies, politics became widely unpredictable. However, it also seems likely that at some time during 1965 Mao himself came to the conclusion that part of the leadership – notably Lo Ruiqing, dismissed as Chief of Staff of the PLA at the end of 1965, and Liu Shaoqi – might have to be removed.[39]

Peng Zhen was to be the first major public victim of the Cultural Revolution. Apparently under consideration by Mao as his potential successor during the 1960s, Peng had been given the task in 1965 of extending rectification and politicization into the educational sector. A Cultural Revolution Group was established under Peng's leadership, but when it reported in February 1966 it ran into opposition and led to Peng's removal at an enlarged meeting of the CCP

Political Bureau in May, along with several others in the leadership including the later President of the PRC, Yang Shangkun.

Although Mao was absent, the enlarged meeting of the CCP Political Bureau brought direction of the campaign directly under its control and established a new Cultural Revolution Group led by Liu Shaoqi and Deng. Deng once again was acting to minimize damage, not least by ensuring Peng Zhen's replacement as Mayor of Beijing: the appointment went to Li Xuefeng, a former subordinate and the leading CCP secretary for the Taihang Region during the mid-1940s after Deng. However, the situation was basically uncontrollable, not least because the new Cultural Revolution Group also included those such as Kang Sheng, Jiang Qing and Zhang Chunqiao, who were now advocating the power of mobilizational politics.

By August and the 11th plenum of the CCP Central Committee, Deng found himself, along with Liu Shaoqi, repeatedly under criticism both at party meetings and less formally from groups of Red Guards when he attended mass meetings. When attacked, he responded, as usual, by admitting his 'mistakes' and pointing out that his intentions had been correct.[40] At a meeting of the Cultural Revolution Group he is reported to have been characterized by Chen Boda as 'the spearhead of the erroneous line', though Mao is said to have given both him and Liu another chance to 'correct their mistakes'.[41] However, by October Deng was in even more serious trouble and forced to present a formal self-criticism detailing how he had opposed Mao Zedong and Mao Zedong Thought for some time.[42]

Even then Deng apparently had reason to believe that his career might not be anything other than temporarily halted. He continued to attend Red Guard receptions, as well as struggle meetings, and was at an enlarged meeting of the CCP Political Bureau at the beginning of December convened by Lin Biao to discuss industrial and communications work.[43] Information is scarce on precisely what happened in and after 1967. In February there was apparently an attempt by other surviving CCP leaders, and particularly those with links to Liu and Deng, to call a halt to the internecine strife within the CCP's leadership. However, it failed spectacularly, leading to criticism as the 'February Adverse Current' and the removal of more senior figures in the leadership. A reading of Deng's views on the Cultural Revolution would seem to suggest not simply that he differentiated between Mao Zedong's behaviour and that of Lin Biao, Jiang Qing, Kang Sheng and their supporters, but also that he focuses on February 1967 as the point of no return in the development of the Cultural Revolution.[44]

In the Cultural Revolution, Deng, along with all the other CCP leaders who had been purged, was reviled as part of a 'revisionist' clique which had wormed its way into the CCP in order to subvert the Chinese revolution. Though officially he was not named directly but only indirectly, most notably as the 'Number two person in authority taking the capitalist road', his 'crimes' were dissected at length by wall posters and in Red Guard publications. According to some of these accounts he continued to protest his innocence stubbornly throughout as he had done in 1933.[45] Mao's criticism of Deng, also disseminated unofficially during the Cultural Revolution, dwelt at length on Deng's personal conduct as well as his espousal of 'revisionist' policy preferences. One of Mao's major complaints was that Deng had sidelined him in various ways after the Great Leap Forward. Deng and Liu, said Mao, 'had treated me like I was their dead parent at a funeral', forgetting perhaps that it had been at his suggestion not theirs that he had retired to the second line of governance. In addition, according to Mao, at the meetings Deng had used to position himself as far away as possible so that he did not have to hear what the Chairman was saying – although Deng is profoundly deaf in his right ear.[46]

6 Modernization and conflict, 1969–1978

Almost nothing is known about what happened to Deng Xiaoping between the end of 1966 and October 1969. It appears he was struggled against for about a year and then kept in solitary confinement for almost another two. For example, he and Zhuo Lin were the focus of a 'struggle meeting' together with Liu Shaoqi and Wang Guangmei (Liu's wife) in July 1967.[1] However, the decade after Deng was released from imprisonment in 1969 was extremely eventful. In the course of that decade he twice spent periods in internal exile, only to return on each occasion to the centre of the political stage and the highest levels of party leadership. Unlike the 1950s, when a spirit of unity could be relied upon within the CCP's leadership, the 1970s was a period of intense factionalism. The CCP leadership was increasingly divided over the results of the Cultural Revolution; the efficacy, or otherwise, of Mao's mobilizational approach to development; and the question of the succession to Mao. In this uncertain political environment Deng was helped by his past relationships, not only with Mao Zedong and Zhou Enlai but also with those who had been his colleagues and subordinates during the Sino-Japanese War and the War of Liberation.

JIANGXI DAYS

During 1967 and 1968 the Cultural Revolution severely disrupted the work of the CCP and the state administration. Even the direct intervention of the PLA in civilian politics from the beginning of 1967 was not an immediate check on the political chaos. The PLA was no more united in political terms than the CCP, and though under Lin Biao's direction (and in support of Mao) it was directed to 'restore order' it often ended up becoming embroiled in local factionalism.

Order was eventually restored by early 1969, shortly before the CCP's 9th Congress was convened in April, but it was a very new political order. In particular, by 1969 civilian politics were heavily dominated by PLA officers. Of course, the relationship between the CCP and the PLA had always been very close, not least because of the communist path to power before 1949. Thus, most of those who held positions of leadership within the CCP between 1949 and the Cultural Revolution, and beyond to about 1985 – essentially the first revolution generation of the PRC's leadership – had some army background in addition to their CCP experience.[2] However, the extent to which actively serving PLA officers had come to dominate the CCP during the Cultural Revolution was a new development. Almost half (some 46 per cent) of the new CCP Central Committee elected in 1969 were concurrently in the PLA. If not exactly identical to a South American military junta, this was still an inordinately high involvement of military personnel in government.

The restoration of administrative order and the worsening Sino-Soviet relations across China's northern borders led in late 1969 to the decision to disperse all the CCP's purged leaders being held in Beijing to other parts of the country; allegedly the decision was taken on Lin Biao's specific orders. Despite its presentation in the Red Guard press, Deng's case had been differentiated from that of Liu Shaoqi and other pre-Cultural Revolution leaders, not least by Mao Zedong who is rumoured to have said something to that effect at the 9th CCP Congress. Certainly, Zhou Enlai seems to have gone considerably out of his way to ensure a suitable reception for Deng when he was sent out of Beijing in October 1969.[3]

Deng was sent to Xinjian County in Jiangxi Province where for three and a quarter years he was theoretically under house arrest in a former infantry academy whilst working part-time in a nearby tractor repair plant. With him went his wife, Zhuo Lin, and his step-mother, Xia Bogen. Of the three, Deng, at the age of 65, was undoubtedly the fittest and part of the mythology of this episode in Deng's life which was promoted during the 1980s is the picture of Deng cleaning, cutting wood and breaking up coal.[4]

Life was undoubtedly very hard for Deng and his family, particularly before the end of 1971. However, a remarkable feature of the time they spent in Xinjian is the extent to which local conditions were adapted by Deng's 'minders' to make life more comfortable within the parameters established by Beijing. Partly this may have been the result of Zhou Enlai's influence, or the genuine respect of the local people for Deng. The situation was almost certainly helped by the fact that the party secretary of the factory where Deng worked in Xinjian County had served under him during the Sino-Japanese War.

When Deng and his immediate family had arrived in Xinjian it had been under strict guard and instructions that limited their activities. Yet within a short while, a special path had been laid for Deng and his wife to cover the two kilometres from where they lived to the factory where they worked so that they would not have to walk on the public highway; it was whimsically dubbed the 'Deng Xiaoping trail' by the locals, alluding to the then Vietnam War and the Ho Chi Minh Trail. Deng was allowed to keep chickens and he and Zhuo Lin started a vegetable garden. Deng was even instructed in how to make his own wine and spirits by a local woman.

Eventually he was even allowed to have his children move in with the rest of the family in Jiangxi. For Deng Pufang, the eldest son, this was rather important. During the Cultural Revolution Deng Pufang, who had been a physics student, had been expelled from the CCP and either thrown from an upper floor, or pushed down a flight of stairs according to another account, by Red Guards because his father was a 'capitalist roader'. The attack had left him paralysed, confined to a wheelchair, and living for a while in a welfare centre in Xi'an. In 1972 he was allowed to travel to Beijing, with his sister, Deng Rong, to receive proper medical treatment. However, by then it was too late for remedial action. By the time Deng returned to Beijing in 1973 a total of ten members of his family had been reunited in Jiangxi.

In September 1971 Lin Biao died, probably but by no means certainly in an air crash over Mongolia after having unsuccessfully tried to hang on to power within the CCP. The news reached Xinjian and Deng Xiaoping on 5 November, when for the first time since the end of 1966 Deng and Zhuo Lin were invited to hear a political report. It appears that within a very short time the attitude of Deng's jailers changed dramatically for the better, not least because local party officials up to the provincial level started coming to call.

In early 1972 Mao Zedong attended the memorial meeting for Chen Yi who had just died. Chen had been a former military leader and foreign minister, as well as a close associate of Deng Xiaoping during the War of Liberation. They had fought together at the Battle of Zhengzhou, and during the Huai-hai Campaign and its aftermath. Mao apparently praised Chen Yi to his widow, and then went on to talk about the frailty of the leadership. He concluded by passing an apparently unprovoked favourable comment on Deng to the effect that his case belonged to 'the category of contradictions among the People' and therefore capable of peaceful resolution. Zhou Enlai, who was there at the time, relayed this message to Chen Yi's children and to Deng, and is reported to have publicized the incident as part of the lobby to have Deng reinstated as quickly as possible.[5]

In August 1972 Deng wrote to Mao Zedong and the CCP Central Committee, through Wang Dongxing, asking to be allowed to return to work. In Beijing it appears that Wang Zhen and Wang Jiaxiang both lobbied Mao on Deng's behalf, and at the beginning of March 1973 the CCP Central Committee passed a resolution which recalled Deng from Jiangxi. His first post-Cultural Revolution official public engagement was at an official banquet for Prince Sihanouk of Cambodia, when he passed almost unnoticed at first by the Western press corps. This was in marked contrast to his first post-Cultural Revolution unofficial public activity. Finding himself back in Beijing at the end of March with some free time it appears he decided to attend a soccer match between a local team and a visiting foreign team. When he was spotted in the crowd an ovation broke out that lasted for some time and could not be stopped until he acknowledged the applause.[6]

THE 'FOUR MODERNIZATIONS'

Several explanations have been provided for Deng's reinstatement and rehabilitation in 1973. The generational structure of the CCP leadership before the Cultural Revolution meant that it would be difficult to replace the large number of those who had been purged during 1967 to 1968 with enough administratively competent cadres within a reasonable period of time. Indeed, one remarkable aspect of the Cultural Revolution was its inability to bring about generational change in the ranks of leading cadres.[7]

Significantly, at approximately the same time that Deng was rehabilitated other leaders who had also been in disgrace or criticized during the Cultural Revolution were rehabilitated or brought back into active service, including two others who also might be thought of, like Deng, as members of Mao's personal loyalty group from before 1949: Chen Yun and Tan Zhenlin. Lin Biao's death and the subsequent removal of his supporters from the CCP and the PLA may have left Mao feeling that the new leadership was not balanced in the way he would prefer between the more radical forces of Jiang Qing and the more moderating influences of Zhou Enlai. Zhou Enlai, for his part, may have felt, not without considerable reason, that Deng would be an ally against dogma and radicalism within the leadership.

All these explanations probably contain an element of truth. In addition, it seems reasonable to assume that there was considerable goodwill extended towards Deng generally within the leadership. Although Deng and his civilian associates had been purged during the Cultural Revolution, one irony of the leadership changes of 1966–8 was that they had resulted in a disproportionately large number of Deng's former military colleagues and subordinates – from the Taihang Region, the 129th Division of the 8th Route Army and the 2nd Field Army of the PLA which grew out of it – being promoted to leadership posts, particularly those which had a military connection, as many even civilian posts did by the early 1970s. In part this was because the changes wrought by Lin Biao (of the 4th Field Army) had come as the result of attacks on the Field Army groupings associated with Peng Dehuai, and He Long, one of Lin Biao's bitterest enemies.[8] Simply because 2nd Field Army officers were relatively numerous, and there were far fewer 4th Field Army officers, the former were often appointed to fill the vacuum caused by the ravages of the Cultural Revolution.[9] With the removal from the leadership of Lin Biao and his supporters after 1971 that disproportion was magnified still further.

Of course, loyalty ties of this kind are not an exclusive or particularly precise predictor of political or factional activity. Deng Xiaoping's former subordinates in the Taihang Region of the late 1930s and early 1940s included Li Xuefeng, Xie Fuzhi and Ji Dengkui, all of whom were members of the CCP Political Bureau and all of whom were at different times regarded as Cultural Revolutionary radicals, as well as many who later supported his reform programme.[10] However, by the beginning of 1973, when the Political Bureau had only sixteen active members, six – Liu Bocheng, Chen Xilian, Xu Shiyou, Su Zhenhua, Ji Dengkui and Li Desheng – had served with or under Deng in Taihang during the Sino-Japanese War. A seventh, Chen Yonggui, the peasant leader from Dazhai, had also been there at the same time but there is no evidence of particular personal or organizational contact with Deng.

Deng's appointment as Vice-Premier brought him into immediate conflict with the more radical elements of the CCP leadership. Jiang Qing, and her associates Zhang Chunqiao, Yao Wenyuan and Wang Hongwen – later to be characterized as the 'Gang of Four' – derived the legitimacy of their position in the leadership from their close relationship to Mao and their emergence during the Cultural

Revolution. As a result, throughout the 1970s until their arrest in October 1976 they campaigned strongly to protect what they regarded as the 'new-born experiences' of the Cultural Revolution: for example, the replacement of party committees and people's governments by revolutionary committees; the encouragement of 'open door schooling' (learning on the job) rather than any technical training; and positive discrimination in social, educational and economic activities for those classified as soldiers, workers or peasants. Deng not only had a wider and more independent legitimacy in the history of the CCP, he also remained opposed to the excesses of the politics of mobilization.[11]

On the eve of the 10th CCP Congress, shortly after Deng's recall, the Gang of Four, undoubtedly concerned by the prospect of Deng and Zhou Enlai working together again, launched oblique attacks on them both, disguised as criticism of the now-departed Lin Biao. This opposition intensified when Deng was reappointed to the CCP's Political Bureau and Military Affairs Commission at the end of 1973 (he had been elected to the 10th Central Committee along with a number of other prominent victims of the Cultural Revolution in August) and was to continue for the next three years. In the context of the coming succession to Mao, for the latter was increasingly ill and frail for the remainder of his life after the 10th CCP Congress, Deng, despite his own advanced years, was seen as the main rival. Thus, when Deng led a delegation to the United Nations in 1974, where he spoke on Mao's 'Theory of the three worlds', he was criticized, together with Zhou, by Jiang Qing on his return for their handling of foreign affairs.[12]

At the end of 1974 relations between Deng and the Gang of Four worsened, not least as a result of Zhou Enlai's deteriorating health: he was seriously ill and hospitalised much of the time. Deng replaced Zhou as the person responsible for overseeing the routine work of the CCP and the government, and was appointed 1st Vice-Premier, Vice-Chairman of the CCP, and Chief-of-Staff of the PLA. From this position he was able, under Zhou's guidance, to do much to set what he saw as the necessary new policy agendas. Although his activities were necessarily constrained, he was able to have a few of his pre-Cultural Revolution associates, notably Hu Yaobang, brought back into active service. In a particularly astute move he also engineered the return of cadres, such as Hu Qiaomu who had previously been a subordinate in the CCP Secretariat before the Cultural Revolution, thereby presumably hoping to rapidly develop a new coalition for the future. The Hu Qiaomu case is particularly instructive because Hu Qiaomu had been an early and vociferous critic of Deng Xiaoping at the beginning of the Cultural Revolution. Under Deng's co-ordination and with the assistance of other leaders, as well as the support of the State Planning Commission, as in the early 1960s a series of policy reports were commissioned.[13]

Deng and Zhou's new policy agenda was referred to as the 'Four Modernizations' and took its cue from Zhou Enlai's 'Report on the work of the government' presented to the National People's Congress in January 1975. Here Zhou referred to the very general idea he had articulated in 1964, with Mao's support, that China should ensure the 'comprehensive modernization of agriculture, industry, national defence, and science and technology before the end of the century'.[14] Deng organized a series of meetings and conferences during 1975 at which the goals and methods of achieving the Four Modernizations were discussed. A series of documents were drafted – three of which, dealing with the general problem of economic modernization, industrialization, and the development of science and technology, were later criticized by the Gang of Four as 'Three poisonous weeds'.[15]

Deng himself spoke out on the need to modernize the PLA, railway transport, and the iron and steel industry. The essence of his vision was the almost complete negation of Mao's politics of mobilization and the Cultural Revolution. Deng and his supporters emphasized the importance of classroom education, and of providing workers and peasants with material incentives to encourage them to produce more rather than relying largely on ideology and exhortation. It was argued that China should abandon its policy of economic self-reliance and expand its foreign trade. In particular, it was suggested that the PRC should export raw materials such as coal and oil, as well as manufactured chemical products (mainly coal by-products), in order to import 'high-grade, high precision, advanced technology and equipment to speed up the technical transformation of our industries and to raise the productivity of labour'. The PLA was criticized, and not just from outside its ranks – Deng was currently Chief-of-Staff – for its 'bloating, laxity, conceit, extravagance, and inertia' which, given the role of the PLA in the CCP's tradition, and especially in Mao's vision, was sailing very close to the wind indeed. Even closer perhaps was Deng's stated desire to see quality and gradualism replace quantity and speed in economic production.[16]

THE TIANANMEN INCIDENT, 1976

Deng's critique of the Cultural Revolution was by no means confined to economic development. Once again, he returned to his constant preoccupations with party leadership and party discipline, which he described as having been threatened and destroyed by the Cultural Revolution. Under cover of attacking Lin Biao, he in effect criticized the dependence on the power of Mao Zedong's words that the Cultural Revolution had created. His argument was essentially that Mao Zedong Thought could not be reduced to just a few quotations, and that he disapproved of 'Lin Biao's vulgarization of Mao Zedong Thought'. This was simply the 'fragmentation of Mao Zedong Thought' which resulted in the CCP's becoming 'divorced from reality and the masses'.[17] In his view Mao Zedong Thought had to be constantly tested in practice, though he did not yet, as he was to do in 1978, refer back to Mao's much earlier comment on the need to 'seek truth from facts'.

As at the 8th CCP Congress in 1956, Deng advocated a rectification of the CCP according to the principles originally articulated by the party during the early 1940s. Indeed, on a number of occasions he made specific reference to the party's heritage from the Sino-Japanese War. According to Deng, the CCP had more recently omitted 'to integrate theory with practice, maintain close ties with the masses, and practise self-criticism'. The results were that the CCP had become characterized by factionalism, and there was a shortage of suitable party officials, particularly at the basic level.

These comments were clearly not intended to appeal to Deng's opponents within the CCP leadership. However, as 1975 progressed he went further and called for a re-examination of the cases of those, like himself, who had been purged at the start of the Cultural Revolution. This was a direct threat to the position of those who owed their position in the leadership to those events and it eventually provided the opportunity, or at least one excuse, for his criticism in November 1975 and his later dismissal in 1976.[18]

Throughout 1975 the radical elements within the CCP leadership had tried to keep Deng in check. In March and April, Yao Wenyuan and Zhang Chunqiao launched an attack on Deng's policies by claiming that, if followed, they would lead to the restoration of capitalism in China. In particular, Deng's proposal that there should be an incentive scheme to improve production was characterized as the thin edge of the wedge as far as the dilution of socialism and its replacement by capitalism were concerned.[19] Though unnamed, Deng and Zhou were characterized as revisionists and 'rightists' who opposed Mao Zedong's vision.

Later in the year Deng was more specifically targeted in a trial by allegory that became front-page news. The lack of open and institutionalized politics, particularly during the Mao-dominated era of Chinese politics, meant that contemporary political debate was often presented as reinterpretations of history or classical literature. In this case, the focus was on the famous *Water Margin* story and one of its heroes, Song Jiang. Song Jiang is immensely popular in Chinese culture, China's equivalent in many ways of Robin Hood, an outlaw who eventually takes service with the Emperor. The debate, which started during late 1975, was about whether Song Jiang should be viewed more critically than was usually the case for having capitulated to the establishment. For 'Song Jiang' the Chinese public was to read 'Deng Xiaoping', under attack for capitulating to capitalism.

For most of 1975 it appears that Deng was able to call on Mao's approval for his actions. Mao was ill and dying at this time, and it is possible that he may not have had a clear grasp of what was going on in the wider politics around him. However, as Deng's proposals to reverse the Cultural Revolution gathered pace, so did Mao's concerns, particularly when Deng argued that the cases of those criticized at that time should be re-examined – or at least when this was brought specifically to Mao's attention. At a meeting of the CCP Political Bureau in early November, Deng was suspended from all his responsibilities except in foreign affairs – where he had taken responsibility for negotiations on the establishment of diplomatic relations with the USA and led a delegation to France. There followed a political campaign with a highly specific target against the 'Right deviation of reversing correct verdicts': in short being Deng Xiaoping and wanting the CCP to revise its recent history and current policies.

Deng's particular problems came to a head quickly as his long-term protector, Zhou Enlai, died on 8 January 1976. Sensibly Deng realized that his political existence was extremely precarious, at least in the immediate future, and his speech in Zhou's memory was not, as it easily might have been, concerned with the present. Instead Deng stuck almost stolidly to recounting Zhou's revolutionary achievements. For the post-1949 period he mentioned only two aspects of Zhou's work in particular: his work in foreign affairs, and his support for Chairman Mao.[20]

At the end of January Deng Xiaoping tried to present a report on the work of the government and economic planning to a Central Work Conference. The meeting was scheduled for a lengthy discussion, but rapidly disintegrated into an attack on Deng himself. Deng was forced once again to examine his past career and sign yet another 'self-criticism'. However, unlike his 'self-criticisms' of 1966, this time confession was designed to portray a long-time 'counter-revolutionary'. Most of these charges had been raised during the Cultural Revolution, but this time the thrust of the 'self-criticism' was historical. Deng's problems of 1931 involving the 7th Red Army were raised once again, as were accusations that he had supported Wang Ming and the 'rightist' line after 1937, that he had consorted with the Nationalist Party in the 1940s, that he had launched the 'Hundred Regiments Campaign' against Mao's wishes in 1940, had favoured rich peasants during land reform, had developed an 'Independent Kingdom' in the South-west when he was that region's CCP First Secretary, had taken Mao's name out of the CCP Constitution in 1956, and transgressed in various ways in the 1960s and during the Cultural Revolution.[21]

Mao Zedong had apparently at some stage approved not only Deng's dismissal but also his criticism by name.[22] Deng's position as the successor to both Mao and Zhou was formally taken by Hua Guofeng, a provincial party secretary who had risen to national prominence during the Cultural Revolution. In January 1976, when Zhou Enlai died, he was appointed Acting Premier and placed in charge of the CCP Central Committee's daily routine. He attempted to cement his new position at the end of February with the first explicit criticism of Deng Xiaoping by name since his recall after the Cultural Revolution.[23] That the move to shunt Deng aside met with considerable confusion and resistance was to become clear very shortly. None the less, radical attacks on Deng and his policies, and the memory of Zhou Enlai, continued. On 28 March, the Shanghai newspaper *Wenhui Bao* carried a lead article which criticized Zhou Enlai and Deng respectively as 'that capitalist-roader within the party who had wanted to reinstate in power the capitalist-roader who had been overthrown and is unrepentant to this day'.

Reaction to the *Wenhui Bao* article in Nanjing, capital of Jiangsu Province, was intense. There were mass demonstrations against the dishonouring of Zhou Enlai's memory, and for Deng and the Four Modernizations.[24] A few days later, as news of the Nanjing Incident (as it became known) spread to Beijing, the same was to happen there. The 4th of April 1976 was *Qing Ming*, or the Festival of Sweeping the Graves, when Chinese traditionally pay homage to the dead. It provided an excellent opportunity to organize demonstrations in memory of Zhou Enlai, and by extension in support of Deng Xiaoping, and against the largely unpopular Gang of Four. Crowds flocked to Tiananmen Square in the middle of

Beijing on 4 April with floral wreaths to Zhou Enlai, and poems making political points about Zhou and Jiang Qing, all of which were placed round the Revolutionary Martyrs Memorial in the centre of the square.

On the evening of 4 April, the area was cleared of the wreaths and poems by local security forces. Popular reaction on 5 April was extremely hostile, and it was not long before the fast-gathering crowd turned violent. Its targets were those associated with the Gang of Four and the repressive power of the state. Thus, at least one student from Qinghua University in Beijing, where the Cultural Revolution radicals had established a 'think-tank', was strung up and hanged from a lamp-post. A police station on the south of the square was set on fire. Towards evening there were several ugly scenes and the crowd was only dispersed by the use of force. Public security forces were called in by the Mayor of Beijing, Wu De, with the assistance of the Minister of Public Security (as well as acting Premier) Hua Guofeng, and the commander of the guard unit attached to the CCP Political Bureau, Wang Dongxing, all of whom were members of the Political Bureau.

Meeting on 6 and 7 April 1976, the CCP Political Bureau denounced the demonstrations as a 'counter-revolutionary incident' for which Deng was held responsible, dismissed Deng from all his posts in the CCP and government, and appointed Hua Guofeng as First Vice-Chairman of the CCP and Premier of the State Council.[25] Carefully stage-managed demonstrations followed in which Deng's supporters from organizations all over Beijing, but from the central economic planning institutions in particular, were forced to march round Tiananmen Square denouncing him. Though the Tiananmen Square demonstrations only lasted a few days, for several months Deng was characterized in the media in almost identical terms to those used during the Cultural Revolution as 'the bourgeoisie within the communist party', and the three major reports prepared in 1975 continued to be denounced as the 'Three poisonous weeds'. At the same time, other veteran cadres who had long been associated with Deng, notably two of his erstwhile bridge partners, Hu Yaobang and Wan Li, were forced out of office as they had been in the Cultural Revolution.

THE 3rd PLENUM OF THE 11th CCP CENTRAL COMMITTEE

Though the official media may have treated Deng as it had during the Cultural Revolution, Deng did not otherwise suffer as he had earlier. One of those who immediately offered protection, judging that a Mao-engineered situation was once again likely to get out of hand, was Ye Jianying. Ye was a Marshall of the PLA, a senior member of the CCP Political Bureau, and the Minister of National Defence, who shortly after Deng's recall in 1973 had made clear to Deng his support for change and his opposition to the Gang of Four. Deng went south where Ye, through his and Deng's personal connections, could offer protection. Ye was a Guangdong native and maintained good relations in his home province even during all the years he worked in Beijing.[26] The commander of the Guangzhou (Canton) Military Region was Xu Shiyou, also a member of the CCP

Political Bureau, and a former subordinate of Deng's from the Sino-Japanese War.

China's politics were clearly extremely unstable and unreal at the time. Everyone seemed to know Mao was dying, and that the Gang of Four would be looking to consolidate their position against considerable opposition, yet on the surface nothing was happening. On 9 September 1976 Mao Zedong died, and the question of the succession – both in terms of people and of policies – finally had to be settled. Despite their aspirations, the Gang of Four had for the most part during the 1970s successfully alienated both their own social constituency and any other potential support within the party leadership. The result was that their relationship with Mao Zedong had become almost their only base of support. Within a month of his death, the other members of the CCP Political Bureau had met separately and decided to act. They moved to arrest the Gang of Four and elected Hua Guofeng Chairman of the CCP.[27]

Deng's position, despite being formally outside the leadership, was almost impregnable. From the moment Mao died Deng Xiaoping was considered the leader in exile, and from the moment the Gang of Four were arrested, Deng was the leader in waiting. A major source of his political power was paradoxically precisely the kind of legitimacy the Gang of Four had attempted to claim – and Hua Guofeng was soon to attempt to claim – through their closeness to Mao and particularly their self-appointed positions as 'guardians of Mao Zedong Thought'. However, Deng Xiaoping had been closer to Mao Zedong and those who supported him in the leadership – and particularly those who had supported him well before the Cultural Revolution – for considerably longer than any of those in the Gang of Four, or even the group that supported Hua Guofeng. His claim to leadership was firmly grounded in his relationship to Mao.[28] Those who had been Mao's victims and wanted change turned to him for leadership; others regarded Deng as the almost 'natural' post-Mao leader because the long-term relationship between Deng and Mao, and Deng's intense loyalty, were tangible manifestations of the revolution in which they had all participated. At the same time, Deng had decades worth of organizational and political associations which he could, and did, mobilize for political support, as for example from his time in the CCP Secretariat before the Cultural Revolution and his work as a Vice-Premier since his return in 1973. In addition, and in particular, these included not only the former supporters and protégés of Zhou Enlai but also his own not inconsiderable connections through the experience of the former Taihang Region and the 2nd Field Army.

In exile in Guangzhou Deng had reportedly outlined three conditions which he insisted should be met before he was prepared to be rehabilitated once again. He insisted that the Tiananmen Incident of April, and his role in it, should be reconsidered; that he should be reinstated in the positions he held before the end of 1975; and that his reinstatement should be approved by both a National People's Congress and a CCP Congress. Though he was to reappear in public before all three conditions were met in full, by the end of 1978 they had all been fulfilled.[29]

The delay, and indeed the source of most of the problems generally at this time, was that Chinese politics could not be readily freed from the influence of ten years of Cultural Revolution. One immediate problem was that Deng's return was necessarily related to Hua Guofeng's future, since the latter had only become First Vice-Chairman of the CCP because of Deng's dismissal at the end of 1975. Another was that the CCP leadership had to decide how much of the Cultural Revolution it was going to reject. At the same time many of those in the leadership owed their position to the Cultural Revolution in some way. Even if they had been prepared to move against the Gang of Four it did not necessarily follow that they would also be prepared to reject all or even most of the Cultural Revolution.

Deng wrote to Hua Guofeng almost immediately after the latter's confirmation as Chairman of the CCP on 10 October 1976, requesting permission to go back to work.[30] Chen Yun, Li Xiannan, Ye Jianying and Wang Zhen (who had lobbied Mao on Deng's behalf in 1972 and was now Vice-Premier) were loud in their calls for his return. Hua Guofeng stalled on the holding of a CCP Central Committee meeting where these pressures would undoubtedly lead to a resolution for Deng's return. Whilst one obvious explanation of this political behaviour was the desire to reinforce his own extremely vulnerable political position, another more charitable interpretation might argue that Hua was also acting to preserve maximum unity within the leadership of the CCP at a difficult period in its evolution.[31]

An attempt to build a 'personality cult' around Hua was launched through the official media. Considerable publicity was afforded Hua's quasi-official appointment by Mao as the latter's successor on 30 April when Mao was reported to have told Hua, 'With you in charge, I am at ease'. In January 1977, building on this relationship with Mao, Hua suggested that 'We must resolutely uphold whatever policy decisions Chairman Mao made and unswervingly carry out whatever Chairman Mao instructed' in order to strengthen his legitimacy. Wang Dongxing wrote a joint editorial for *People's Daily*, *Red Flag* and *Liberation Army Daily* which appeared on 7 February extolling the virtues of this position, now known as the 'Two whatevers'. Hua's position was supported by several other members of the leadership, who though they had not been followers of the Gang of Four none the less owed their positions for the most part to promotion during the Cultural Revolution.

However, the tide was running too fast against Hua – not least because after Mao's death and the arrest of the Gang of Four those who had been the victims of the Cultural Revolution were being rehabilitated in increasing numbers. In addition, Hua needed to call a CCP Central Committee meeting in order to legitimize the arrest of the Gang of Four and to confirm his own position. Moreover, Deng, who probably knew more about Mao's policy decisions and instructions than anyone else then in the CCP's Political Bureau, started campaigning, albeit obliquely, both on his own behalf and against the concept of the 'Two whatevers'. According to the authorized history of the CCP, Deng started 'canvassing' his 'comrades' views' only to find that they, like he, did not believe that this was the correct approach to Mao Zedong Thought.[32]

In March, a Central Work Conference was enthusiastic in calling for Deng's recall, agreed to his reinstatement to all the positions he had held at the end of 1975, but left the time of his recall to Hua Guofeng. An exchange of correspondence followed from Deng to Hua and Ye Jianying in April, in which Deng once again pushed home the point about the importance of not 'vulgarizing Mao Zedong Thought' and treating it as 'doctrine' but regarding it as a more flexible and ideological system.[33] The stage was then set for a meeting of the CCP Central Committee and both Deng's return to active politics and Hua's confirmation as Chairman of the CCP. It was to be a hollow victory for Hua.

Deng's reinstatement was timed for the 3rd plenum of the 10th Central Committee of the CCP in July 1977 where he immediately attacked the basic epistemological point about Mao Zedong Thought. On the whole he ignored Hua Guofeng's 'Two whatevers' but was scathing about the Gang of Four and Lin Biao. He differentiated between their behaviour and politics and those of Mao Zedong, and moreover drew the legitimacy for his position from Mao's inscription for the Central Party School in Yan'an – 'Seek truth from facts'.[34]

It was a debate that was followed up rapidly at the 11th Congress of the CCP in August. Hua's speech to the conference brought this particular Cultural Revolution to an end by promising that 'in line with Mao Zedong Thought' it would not be the only one and there would be more in the future. Moreover, in defending the principle of Cultural Revolution he emphasized Mao's correctness in targeting 'capitalist-roaders'. Deng, in contrast, by stressing the need to revive the CCP's traditions and work-style, promised the opposite.[35] Indeed, by the end of the year Deng had already started to implement the plans that had been on the drawing board since at least 1975, with the introduction of a scheme for the modernization of the PLA.

In March 1978 the second of Deng's conditions for his recall was fulfilled when the 5th National People's Congress met in Beijing. By that time a 'Counter Cultural Revolution' was already well under way. Following Mao's death there had been a dramatic turnover in the leadership, as great as that which had occurred at the height of the Cultural Revolution. However, this time it was those who had been dismissed or removed from office during 1967–8 who were returned to power, and unsurprisingly their support went to Deng and those campaigning for a full rejection of the Cultural Revolution.[36]

Deng's position during 1978 was so secure that he was able to visit a number of countries in East and South-east Asia; to finalize arrangements for the establishment of diplomatic relations with the USA (which he had been responsible for negotiating during 1974–5); and to announce new policies on intellectuals and education which in effect reversed those of the Cultural Revolution. At the same time he continued to build his coalition for change, and Hu Yaobang played a central role. He organized a writing group at the Central Party School to rewrite an essay by Hu Fuming of Nanjing University as 'Practice is the sole criterion of truth' which came to provide the ideological basis for the changes to come.[37] It took its cue from Mao's Yan'an injunction to 'seek truth from facts' which Deng had already been emphasizing for some time. Essentially it argued that the importance of Mao Zedong Thought was in the perspectives and general principles it provided, not in the letter of its quotations, and that 'only the test of social practice can show whether a theory actually works'.[38] In this case the test of theory rapidly gathered the necessary support from senior and influential figures in the CCP's leadership, including Lo Ruiqing (shortly before his death in August) and Li Xiannian.[39]

In 1977 it had been necessary for Deng to admit that he had committed mistakes. By the end of 1978 the criticisms of CCP leaders were increasingly focusing on the 'mistakes' of those who had supported the 'Two whatevers'. The immediate climax came at the landmark 3rd plenum of the 11th Central Committee and the Central Work Conference which preceded it. Together they lasted for most of November and December in an atmosphere of high excitement. In addition to the work conference, border tensions with Vietnam were increasing; it was announced that diplomatic relations were to be established with the USA; and a 'Democracy Movement', no doubt inspired by events at the Central Work Conference, developed on Beijing's streets.

The Central Work Conference must have been one of the most remarkable in the history of the CCP and has certainly been presented that way since, as it signalled the final rejection of the Cultural Revolution and the start of the reform era. It decided to make economic modernization the most important priority; to introduce political, administrative and legal reforms designed to support economic modernization; to reverse the verdicts on a number of key pre-Cultural Revolution leaders of the CCP who had not yet been rehabilitated, including Deng's former close associates Bo Yibo, Peng Zhen and Yang Shangkun, as well as Tao Zhu and Peng Dehuai; to restore party democracy; to decollectivize agriculture; and, after a preliminary assessment, to carry out a more thorough-going reassessment of Mao Zedong and the Cultural Revolution.[40] It also met the third of Deng's conditions for his recall and declared that the Tiananmen Incident, far from being 'counter-revolutionary', was 'a completely revolutionary event' by ratifying a decision taken in the middle of November by the Beijing CCP Committee.[41]

Though all the outcomes of the 3rd plenum were not immediately apparent at the time, in effect Hua Guofeng had lost the battle to maintain his leadership of the CCP to Deng, whatever formal position the latter held. The policies on economic modernization he had supported in the early 1960s and again in the mid-1970s could now be implemented, and the team that had co-operated in their design was now together again in command of the CCP and the economy. The policies on party leadership and party discipline that Deng had tirelessly advocated since the 1950s could now be given their first real chance since the 1940s to be put into practice. For Deng the 3rd plenum was undoubtedly a great success, but the real challenge – of putting his vision into practice – still lay ahead.

7 The foundations of reform, 1979–1984

Particularly within the PRC it has been fashionable to regard the 3rd plenum of December 1978 as the third great turning point in China's twentieth-century history, after the revolutions of 1911 and 1949.[1] The force of this interpretation is relatively obvious: by the mid-1990s the reform era that started with the 3rd plenum had resulted in substantial economic transformation and political change. The economy has grown at an annual average of something over 9 per cent of GNP since 1978 to become the world's fourth largest aggregate economy by 1993. More spectacular, however, than the gross statistics of growth have been the structural changes in an economy that has moved from government management through direct involvement towards the exercise of macro-economic control. By 1994 the state sector of the economy only produced a little over half of the output value of industrial production, compared to close on 80 per cent in 1978. In the state sector by 1994 it was reported that some 30 per cent of state employees worked under contract rather than in tenured positions, as would previously have been the case.[2] An even more remarkable measure of change in the structure of state socialism was provided in early 1994 by the action of the People's Bank of China – China's central bank – in prohibiting the Ministry of Finance from borrowing bank funds to finance state debt.[3]

The 3rd plenum was undoubtedly important, and not only symbolically. However, it was only one of a series of major meetings – though perhaps the most important – at the end of 1978 and the beginning of 1979 that set the agenda for the reform. These meetings laid the foundations for economic growth and modernization both immediately and in the longer term. The period through to the end of 1984, though not without its difficulties, was one of considerable achievement for both the leadership of the CCP in general and Deng Xiaoping in particular. This was not only the period of Deng Xiaoping's ascendancy – he retired to the 'second line' from the daily routine of government at the National Party Conference in September 1985 – but also of his most productive participation in policy formulation. In addition it was a period of unprecedented political stability for the PRC.

The economic reform programme which started with an immediate policy of consolidation and readjustment was spectacularly successful through to 1984, though up to that time reform largely concentrated on rural China. By 1983 the targets of the 1981–5 Five-Year Plan had been met two years ahead of schedule and it began to look as if the longer-term goal of quadrupling per capita income by the year 2000 might be achieved. Rural industry began to grow rapidly as a result of reform and increased economic wealth in the countryside, and the standard of living of most Chinese improved.

Politically, the leadership of the CCP experienced its longest period of unity and stability for some considerable time. Intra-party disputes, though perhaps not meeting Deng's ideal description of such processes, were kept within bounds and resolved without the dogmatism and violence of the Cultural Revolution. Though the Cultural Revolution's legacy in terms of factionalism took longer to disappear than was officially recognized, it no longer remained an important determinant of politics. A legal system, albeit one working within the confines of a communist party state, was re-established and a start was made on overhauling the system of government.

Particularly in the late 1980s and early 1990s there has been a tendency within China to regard Deng Xiaoping as a metaphor for the whole of the reform era since 1978, or at least for its achievements. Large numbers of books have been published on different aspects of the reform process and Deng Xiaoping's life and work.[4] Deng is justifiably regarded as the architect of the reform era, but that is not quite the same as being the architect of reform. It is probably an inappropriate time to attempt to make such a distinction, not least because of weak or non-existent evidence; none the less a biography of Deng requires that the attempt be made.

Deng led a collective leadership, and his contribution in many areas of the reform programme was to create the conditions for others to act rather than being directly responsible himself: a leadership style which has been usefully described in traditional terms as 'leading from behind the scenes'.[5] In particular, though he clearly did not ignore economic reform – and could and has claimed personal responsibility for a number of significant economic initiatives and actions by the leadership – he left its precise direction to others,[6] particularly those who had previously come together to draft the proposals for China's economic recovery and development during the early 1960s – Chen Yun, Bo Yibo, Peng Zhen and Li Xiannian – as well as a new generation of front-rank leaders including Zhao Ziyang, Hu Yaobang and Wan Li.

Deng for his part, particularly during the first half of the 1980s, appears to have concentrated on the two major policy areas where he had some depth of experience and expertise: political reform and foreign affairs. An early concern was to ensure the final rejection of the Cultural Revolution, necessarily related to Deng's longer-term attempts to establish party democracy and a more open – though still limited – political system. That last goal proved particularly elusive, not least because of its inherent ambiguity. The tension between a more open political system and the principle of party leadership was a recurrent theme throughout the 1980s, even before attempts at compromise broke down in May 1989.

In foreign affairs, Deng met with greater success in gradually mapping out for

China a genuinely independent foreign policy, while embracing at the same time international interdependence. The 'Open door' policy has ensured not only rapid economic growth, but also China's economic integration with large parts of East and South-east Asia – albeit in ways that were probably unforeseen, and whose final impact is yet to be determined.[7] Increasing *détente* between the CCP and the CPSU during the decade led eventually to the restoration of party-to-party relationships and Gorbachev's visit, under the most difficult of circumstances, to Beijing in May 1989. In 1984, tough negotiations with the UK led to an agreement for procedures whereby Hong Kong might pass to PRC jurisdiction in 1997.

LAUNCHING REFORM

Though by all accounts the Central Work Conference that preceded the 3rd plenum was one of intense debate, none the less the plenum's final communiqué was quite decisive in providing the CCP with a change of direction. However, the process of restructuring and reform still could not proceed smoothly. There were ideological, economic and political problems facing the change of direction, and these continued to preoccupy the leadership at a series of high-level meetings during the first half of 1979, culminating in the 2nd session of the Fifth National People's Congress.

The ideological problems were discussed at a party conference that started in January and rolled on, through different stages, to early April. Chaired by Hu Yaobang, who had been appointed Secretary-General to the Central Committee of the CCP shortly after the 3rd plenum, it basically carried on the discussion of the relationship between theory and practice he had developed on Deng's behalf in 1978. In its earlier stages its participants were predominantly those working at the centre, whereas in its later stages it incorporated cadres, officials and theorists from the provinces. It was in the course of this meeting's deliberations that limits were set to the movement for greater democracy.[8]

During 1976 to 1978 the economy had overheated, in ways which were to become cyclically familiar throughout the 1980s. Indeed in 1992, in retrospect, Deng Xiaoping was to indicate not only that the repeated pattern of periods of rapid growth followed by the need for retrenchment was apparent to the CCP leadership but that it was also a matter of some dispute, both as to the cause and the solutions to be adopted.[9] In this case, a period of rapid growth had been associated with excessive capital construction, the use of foreign investment to un-productive ends, severe economic imbalances and the spectre of runaway inflation.

Throughout the first few months of 1979 Chen Yun, who had been the architect of the 2nd Five-Year Plan rejected by Mao in favour of the strategy of the Great Leap Forward, had been active in mobilizing support behind his ideas on the introduction of market forces and proportionate development into the economy. In March, with the economic planners of the early 1960s almost totally back in control, Chen Yun put a revised short-term economic strategy to a meeting of the

CCP Political Bureau which after laying out the options called for a policy of readjustment – essentially one of extreme fiscal conservatism and restructuring – for the next three years.[10] Deng Xiaoping spoke at the meeting and put his full support behind Chen Yun's position.[11]

However, this decision did not mean that all attempt at reform ceased, and even at this early stage the general direction to be set for the economic reforms was clearly visible. A key principle in both Chen Yun's and Deng's thinking was that the over-bureaucratized state machinery was simply not up to running the production process in a modernizing economy in a flexible way. Instead, they proposed that production units should be given more autonomy in management, not only from the CCP interference – which during the Cultural Revolution had meant that political work often replaced production as the main activity – but also from government. With the exception of a few sizeable enterprises in strategic industries, local and central government was to be drawn back from what had been one of its main activities. The radical dimension in this reform was not simply that enterprises were to be given greater autonomy from government – that had been advocated before – but that the role of the CCP in enterprises and factories was for the first time challenged by the prospect of complete withdrawal.[12]

Support for Deng Xiaoping in experimenting with different kinds of decentralization in economic management came from two long-term associates – Wan Li and Zhao Ziyang – both of whom had served under Deng in the Taihang Region during the 1940s and who had worked quite closely with him at various stages since. Wan was also a frequent bridge partner from before the Cultural Revolution and he had been removed from office precisely as one of Deng's supporters in both the Cultural Revolution and again in 1976. In the late 1970s he was the leading party secretary in Anhui Province where he oversaw the decollectivization of agriculture and the introduction of a 'responsibility system'; similar initiatives had been implemented there experimentally during the early 1960s, and Deng had discussed their impact in a speech during 1962.[13] It was an experience which was to become a model for the rest of China. Essentially the responsibility system meant that each peasant household would farm its own land and undertake responsibility to produce a given output, on a contractual basis, which the state guaranteed to purchase. Any surplus produced by the peasant household could then be disposed of as it chose. Though the context of the late 1970s and early 1980s was very different to the wartime conditions of 1943, these principles – of dual responsibility, and freely disposable surpluses – were those that Deng had advocated to meet the economic problems of the Taihang Region at that time.[14]

In the late 1970s Zhao Ziyang was the leading party secretary in Sichuan Province, where he not only implemented similar rural reforms to those under way in Anhui but was also responsible for the introduction of the urban equivalent of the rural responsibility system – often referred to as the 'Sichuan experiment' – into industrial enterprises under which enterprises acquired considerably more operational autonomy. Interestingly, in this case too it was not the first time such economic reforms had been suggested. Sichuan had proposed similar ideas in

1955 and 1956.[15] On the other hand, despite Deng's service in Sichuan during the early 1950s there is less evidence of long-term personal attachment to the principles or practices of the urban reform programme.[16]

A further feature of the new economic order, and one which is now credited firmly to Deng Xiaoping, was the Special Economic Zones (SEZs). The SEZs were originally proposed at the major Central Work Conference called to discuss economic reforms in April 1979, and designed as areas with an economic and fiscal environment that would be advantageous to foreign entrepreneurs and that would attract foreign technology as well as investment. Deng proposed that these should be established in southern China's Guangdong and Fujian provinces, not specifically because they were adjacent to Hong Kong and Taiwan respectively (though that obviously became increasingly important during the 1980s) but because these were the provinces which had historically acted as China's gateways to the rest of the world.[17] Later in the 1990s, when in part claiming credit for the establishment of SEZs generally, Deng suggested he had been in error in not having established an SEZ in Shanghai.[18]

Much is now claimed for and by the SEZs, in particular Shenzhen. However, it is easy to forget that their existence was politically sensitive within the leadership for some time. Indeed, one of the reasons for their establishment, though not necessarily a view held by Deng, was that it was hoped that any potentially harmful influences which might be imported along with the foreign technology might be restricted in their impact to the Special Economic Zones. It is unlikely though that at this time the CCP leadership had any thought that developing the SEZs would assist the political incorporation of Hong Kong into the PRC in and after 1997. In the first place, growing friction with Vietnam was higher on the agenda than relations with either; and second, in any case the leadership seemed to be considerably more interested in its relations with Taiwan than those with Hong Kong at this stage.[19]

Despite changes in and, as they later developed, away from the centralized, planned economy, Deng in 1979, and indeed throughout the 1980s and into the 1990s, never abandoned a commitment to socialism, though necessarily his understanding of socialism was somewhat broader than had previously been the case. In economics, Deng, though considerably less forceful than Chen Yun, always regarded the public sector as the leading sector in the economy. In politics he went much further to make it clear that he did not believe the central role of the CCP could or should be questioned at all.[20] For Deng, democracy was a matter of making the communist party state more efficient, not of making it possible for the communist party state to disappear through the ballot box.[21]

The challenge to Deng's central belief in party rule was one of the first items to be of concern immediately after the 3rd plenum. Undoubtedly aware of the politics that were running their course out behind closed doors at the end of 1978 during the Central Work Conference and the 11th Central Committee's 3rd plenum, a 'Democracy Movement' had come alive on the streets of Beijing and other cities. One of the key issues of the Central Work Conference and the 3rd plenum, as already indicated, was Deng Xiaoping's insistence that the 1976 political verdict on the Tiananmen Incident of that year should be reversed. The editorial in *People's Daily* greeting the decision of the Beijing CCP Committee to reverse the verdict on those events (and indeed the publicity generally afforded that decision) was almost extreme in its avowal of mass popular action:

> this movement, unprecedented in scale declared to the whole world that China did not belong to the 'Gang of Four'. The people and the people alone decide the destiny of China and determine the advance of history ... Who organised the April events in Tiananmen Square? The people. Who directed these events? The people ...[22]

This editorial acted as a signal for further demonstrations requesting yet more democracy, however that concept was conceived, and the establishment of meeting places on the streets for the discussion of democracy and indeed politics generally in Beijing and a number of cities. To some extent this emergent Democracy Movement had even been encouraged by Deng himself. In his speech to the Central Work Conference he had been quite explicit about the articulation of very different views: 'One thing a revolutionary party does not need to worry about is its inability to hear the voice of the people. The thing to be feared most is silence.'[23] For the most part those who joined in Democracy Movement activities considered themselves part of the loyal opposition who thought they had approval to call for democracy, since that was indeed a key word at the 3rd plenum. There were, however, one or two demonstrators and wall-posters that challenged the CCP's monopoly of political power, and even Deng Xiaoping himself.

Deng's reaction was swift in defining the new 'socialist democracy'. At the party's conference on theoretical work at the end of March 1979 Deng outlined the 'Four cardinal principles' (sometimes also referred to as the 'Four basic principles') by which acceptable political behaviour could be judged: 'Keep to the socialist road ... uphold the dictatorship of the proletariat ... uphold the leadership of the Communist Party ... uphold Marxism-Leninism and Mao Zedong Thought.'[24] Anything which challenged any of these four would immediately be regarded as beyond the boundaries of the permissible.

'PROBLEMS INHERITED FROM HISTORY'

Apart from basic questions of economic and political reform, the CCP leadership after the 3rd plenum still had to face what Deng described as the 'problems inherited from history' that required resolution sooner rather than later.[25] The CCP had to decide what to do with the Gang of Four now under arrest; and how, as it had indicated at the 3rd plenum, it was going to reassess the Cultural Revolution, Mao Zedong's role in Chinese politics and the nature of Mao Zedong Thought. Necessarily, such questions were also related to the future of Hua Guofeng and his supporters. Though they were at least partially responsible for the arrest of the Gang of Four, they had none the less entered the leadership and gained politically as a direct result of the Cultural Revolution.

The reassessment of the CCP's history, agreed at the 3rd plenum, was less easily implemented. One or two 'problems', such as Liu Shaoqi's position in CCP history, could rapidly be agreed in principle even if the detail still had to be determined – Liu's widow reappeared in public for the first time since the Cultural Revolution at Spring Festival Celebrations in February 1979. However, reassessment also had implications for Hua Guofeng and his supporters, and would be related to the eventual treatment of the Gang of Four. Deng's emphasis on the need for democracy and legality in order to support modernization virtually ensured that they would be put on trial, if only for educational purposes. A trial would propagandize the rejection of the Cultural Revolution, as well as the wider importance of legal processes.

The trial of the Gang of Four and Lin Biao and their followers was delayed while the wider issues were discussed. As always in the post-Cultural Revolution period, Deng wanted the CCP to make a clear distinction between Mao Zedong personally and Mao Zedong Thought as the codification of the collective wisdom of the CCP before 1949. He also wanted a clear distinction to be made between Mao Zedong Thought and Mao's actions after 1958. If these distinctions were not made, and the Gang of Four were held solely responsible for the Cultural Revolution, rather than some responsibility also being assigned to Mao, then Hua Guofeng and his supporters who had come to power towards the end of the Cultural Revolution had some grounds on which to build a case in their own defence. If, on the other hand, Mao was held responsible for the Cultural Revolution and could be said to have negated Mao Zedong Thought himself after 1958, then all his subsequent actions were suspect and Hua Guofeng was out on a limb.

In the event, the Cultural Revolution was rejected according to Deng's interpretation. The 'Resolution on certain questions in the history of our party since the founding of the People's Republic of China' was drafted by a small group led by Hu Qiaomu, under the supervision of Deng and Hu Yaobang during 1980, and was circulated for discussion several times before it was finally adopted by the 6th plenum of the 11th Central Committee of the CCP in June 1981.[26] By then Hua Guofeng and the others in the leadership associated with him – notably Wang Dongxing, Wu De, Ji Dengkui, Chen Yonggui and Saifudin – had bowed to the inevitable and either stepped down from office voluntarily or been demoted.

From the first Deng Xiaoping had insisted that an essential part of the rejection of the Cultural Revolution should be that its victims, like Deng himself, be fully reinstated. This process continued in 1979 with a whole stream of Deng's former associates – including Bo Yibo, Peng Zhen and Yang Shangkun – and several others being restored to membership of the Central Committee. At the same time Peng Zhen was reappointed, and Zhao Ziyang was appointed for the first time, to the CCP Political Bureau. In February 1980, Liu Shaoqi was posthumously rehabilitated, and four members of the Political Bureau who had supported Hua Guofeng's 'Two whatevers' were removed from the leadership. However, these were not purges. In line with Deng's renewed emphasis on inner-party democracy, these were demotions: neither life nor livelihood was threatened. In the middle of 1980 Zhao Ziyang replaced Hua as Premier; and at the end of 1980 the trials of both the Gang of Four and those co-conspirators of Lin Biao's who were still alive began, with predictable results.[27] By then Hua had offered to resign as Chairman of the CCP, to be replaced by Hu Yaobang after Deng had refused the post on grounds of old age (he was by then 76), though he did agree to become Chairman of the Central Military Commission.[28]

Deng's intention quite clearly was to create a new style of politics, though presumably he would not have seen it as new but rather a return to the CCP's earlier political style. In January 1980 he proposed the removal from the Constitution of Article 45, long associated with Mao's notions of democracy and previously regarded as one of the Cultural Revolution's 'new born things' – the right 'to speak out freely, air one's view fully, write big character posters, and hold great debates'.[29] In the spirit of the renewed style of politics, Deng even offered Hua Guofeng the Vice-Chairmanship of the CCP when the latter stepped down as Chairman, though he in turn declined. Even to a wider audience Deng was determined to establish a new style of leadership. For example, on a visit to Sichuan in 1980 he refused his assistants' requests to close Mt Emei to the public whilst he was at the scenic and sacred site; and similarly turned down the offer of a private performance of a Sichuan Opera, saying that he was perfectly capable of attending just like anyone else.[30] In the same spirit, at the 12th CCP Congress, the position of CCP Chairman, created specifically for Mao Zedong, was abolished and replaced by the post of General Secretary of the CCP.

AN AGENDA FOR POLITICAL REFORM

The 'Resolution on CCP history' played an important role in Deng's plans for political reform, as well as in resolving some of the immediate political problems facing the new leadership. Whilst it criticized Hua Guofeng for 'left' errors during the two years after Mao's death, and decisively rejected the Cultural Revolution for which it held Mao himself primarily responsible, it was its reinterpretation of Mao Zedong Thought and the CCP's traditions that specifically supported Deng's vision.[31] Mao Zedong Thought was essentially redefined and codified in terms of Deng's view of those traditions – the integration of theory with practice ('seek truth from facts'), inner-party democracy and a close relationship between party and people – and the purpose of political reform was to restore those traditions.

Though the reinterpretation of Mao Zedong Thought was only formally accepted by the CCP in June 1981, Deng had been consistently arguing the case for some time. In particular, his speech to the CCP Political Bureau in August 1980 – 'On the reform of the system of party and state leadership' – was the most thorough statement of his views on political reform.[32] Indeed, thereafter throughout the 1980s, whenever the topic of political reform was being particularly emphasized, discussion invariably proceeded from analysis of this speech.[33] He stressed the need for the routinization of government, for the rejuvenation of the leadership, for the re-establishment of party democracy and the maintenance of party-led democracy. These became common themes in Deng's politics throughout the 1980s and indeed have strong resonances back to the early 1940s.

In Deng's view the routinization of government was necessary in order to encourage both economic modernization and good relations between party and people. There had to be an efficient separation of the functions of party and government, individuals had to be more restricted in their spheres of influence and an administrative order had to be created. These requirements arose from his criticisms of three tendencies which had become particularly acute during the Cultural Revolution, but which had been long-term problems faced by the CCP. One was the tendency for the party to step in and replace government, which he had first addressed in the early 1940s in the Taihang Region, albeit in radically different wartime conditions.[34] According to Deng the CCP should guide not govern: if it replaced government then neither performed efficiently. Government waited on CCP interference and the latter became overloaded. A second tendency was the over-concentration of authority, not only in the CCP's hands but in the hands of specific individuals who had come to monopolize positions of leadership in the CCP, PLA and government, thereby personalizing politics as well as leading to inefficiency. A third and associated tendency was that within the bureaucracy, systems of responsibility and administrative regulations were frequently absent.[35]

Deng's call for the rejuvenation of the CCP pulled no punches, either in 1980 or later, and remarkably, for the most part Deng appeared prepared to some considerable extent to accept the same advice he handed out to others. He did not become Chairman of the CCP when offered the position in 1980; retired from the front line of administration in 1985; stepped down from membership of the CCP Political Bureau in 1987; and resigned from his Chairmanship of the Central Military Commission in 1989. In his speech of 1980 he pointed out that too many of the leaders of the CCP were either too old, too ill or too inexperienced to carry out the new tasks of economic modernization facing the PRC. He recommended retirement as soon as possible for those of the revolutionary generation who had been purged in the Cultural Revolution and only recently reinstated. To this end, and to allow these veterans to continue to play a role in contemporary politics, Deng suggested in 1982 the temporary creation of a Central Advisory Commission, in effect a second chamber to the CCP Central Committee. In 1989 it was to play a crucial role in the unfolding political crisis. However, at this stage Deng was also concerned with the longer-term prospects of succession. He wanted to ensure that in future there would be more orderly generational change. To this end he proposed that the CCP should have training programmes in which it identified likely leaders for the future and that it abolish the system of life-long tenure for cadres.

These suggestions were all linked to Deng Xiaoping's vision of party discipline and the re-establishment of inner-party democracy.[36] The personalized and dogmatic politics of the Cultural Revolution were to be replaced by a system based on collective leadership, discussion and debate. According to Deng, the

CCP should accept that mistakes would inevitably happen and attempt to mitigate their consequences. In retrospect Deng claimed as 'his invention' the lack of bitter controversy within the leadership in the period after the 3rd plenum, and stressed that the correct policy could only come through trial and error, with some risk involved because 'No one can be sure at the beginning that their ideas are a hundred percent correct'.[37]

In Deng's view disciplinary problems should be handled within the CCP and to this end at the 3rd plenum a Central Discipline Inspection Commission had been established, which at the 12th CCP Congress in 1982 became the Central Discipline and Control Commission under Chen Yun's leadership. The rules for individual party members and for political behaviour within the CCP were set out in the 'Guiding Principles for Inner-Party Life' adopted in 1980.[38] Of the greatest importance, Deng insisted that party affairs had to be kept within the CCP and he had no time for Mao's 1950s' notion of 'extended democracy'.

The final plank in Deng's programme of political reform was the encouragement of party-led democracy. Both sides of that imperative were central to Deng's vision. He emphasized the need to stimulate individual and group initiative within society. In particular, Deng went out of his way to re-enlist the intellectuals – the 'stinking ninth' category of counter-revolutionaries, as they had been castigated during the Cultural Revolution – to the cause of economic modernization. However, as the 1979 announcement of the Four Basic Principles had made clear, there were limits to that vision. The resulting more open society could not challenge the leadership of the CCP.

'SOCIALISM WITH CHINESE CHARACTERISTICS'

Deng's programme for political reform was part of his much wider vision for China's future. At the 12th CCP Congress of September 1982 he described this as the attempt to 'build socialism with Chinese characteristics'. In addition to political and economic reform, that vision rested on a more active foreign policy. Deng's 'open-door policy' was designed, within limits, to bring the PRC more into the world and the world into the PRC in order to assist economic modernization.

One tangible sign of the 'open-door policy' was the Special Economic Zones. Originally established in Guangdong Province (Shenzhen, Zhuhai and Shantou) and then later in Fujian Province (Xiamen), another was created on Hainan Island (in 1988). At the start of 1984, the existence of the SEZs was questioned, largely because they were seen as importers of 'spiritual pollution'. However, Deng's intervention proved crucial: following a visit, similar economic rights to encourage foreign investment and trade were granted to some fourteen more coastal cities.[39]

The other side of Deng's desire for China to be part of the international economic order was a fierce nationalism and a drive for a truly independent foreign policy. Deng told almost every foreign visitor he met during the 1980s, but particularly those from communist Eastern Europe, often in no uncertain terms – Kissinger reportedly regarded Deng as 'a nasty little man'[40] – that no one was entitled to tell China what to do, because the conditions in every country are unique. That perspective led Deng from a near alliance with the USA at the end of the 1970s to the establishment of better relations between the CCP and the CPSU at the end of the 1980s.

There is no suggestion that the USA had tried to dictate terms to the PRC. It even seems likely that Deng, mindful of the experience of Sino-Soviet relations in the 1950s and 1960s with which he had been intimately involved, and its lesson regarding over-dependence on any one ally, had always intended the PRC's close relations with the USA during the late 1970s to be temporary.[41] However, after his famous visit to the USA in 1979 – when amongst other things he appeared on television at a barbecue and wearing a ten-gallon hat – Deng acted decisively to ensure that over-dependence on either superpower was avoided. Throughout the 1980s, and not always in response to Soviet overtures, he spent considerable time and energy indicating his conditions for the restoration of CCP–CPSU relations, largely the mutual recognition of equality and independence. Perhaps with an ageing politician's sense of history he seemed proud to welcome Gorbachev to Beijing in May 1989.[42] It was a long way from his statement at the 3rd plenum of the 10th Central Committee in 1977: 'In almost no likelihood will my generation or the generation of Comrade Hua Guofeng and Wang Dongxing or even the following generation ever re-establish close contact with the CPSU.'[43]

Deng's nationalism was also evident closer to home. It is not known to what extent Deng initiated the decision to invade Vietnam in early 1979, after conflict along the border, though it would appear he was at the meeting which took the final decision.[44] He was certainly responsible for the decision to withdraw troops once the PLA's action started to meet unexpected difficulties.[45]

Deng was closely involved in the negotiations over the future of Hong Kong, and the policy of 'One country, two systems' is widely attributed to him. Under this rubric, in 1984 the PRC agreed that Hong Kong's social and political system, clearly different from that in the PRC, could continue to exist even after Hong Kong passes from British to PRC jurisdiction in 1997. The agreement on Hong Kong was, of course, a sufficient economic and political goal in itself, though at the time the bigger prize Deng was chasing was Taiwan.

Until the end of 1984 the notion of 'Socialism with Chinese characteristics' remained somewhat limited, not least because reform had barely touched the urban economy. This changed with the 3rd plenum of the 12th Central Committee of the CCP in October 1984 which decided to turn the focus of reform on the urban and necessarily more complex part of the economy.[46] Even more so than earlier in the reform era, the initiative for this development in economic policy lay with Chen Yun rather than Deng Xiaoping. Chen Yun delivered the key report on further economic restructuring to the plenum, which essentially set out an economic future in which the government's economic management would change from direct involvement to the exercise of macro-economic control. At the same time that Chen Yun was encouraging dramatic and far-reaching reform in the economy, he was considerably more cautious about the political and social consequences, and stressed the need to check the potential excesses of modernization.[47]

Deng was similarly concerned with the wider consequences of modernization, and echoed Chen Yun's call in October 1984 for a 'material and spiritual civilization'. His notion of a more open 'Socialism with Chinese characteristics' was based on a highly specific notion of social order. When he later met with Stefan Korosec (of the Yugoslav League of Communists) he provided a crisp summation of his vision of technocratic democracy:

> The greatest advantage of the socialist system [over liberal democracy] is that when the central leadership makes a decision it is promptly implemented without interference from any other quarters ... we don't have to go through a lot of repetitive discussion and consultation, with one branch of the government holding up another and decisions being made but not carried out. From this point of view our system is very efficient.[48]

The corollary of that position was Deng's emphasis on the need to combat what he had earlier described as the 'spiritual pollution' of Western or bourgeois influences. In 1982 he had called for the creation of a 'socialist spiritual civilization' to support the CCP's drive for economic modernization. As he pointed out when meeting the Spanish Vice-Premier, Alfonso Guerra: 'Some of our young people ... are not clear about what capitalism is and what socialism is. So we have to educate them about all these things.'[49] On four occasions during the 1980s – in 1981, 1983, 1986 and 1989 – Deng took the lead in launching political campaigns against 'spiritual pollution' or 'bourgeois liberalization'. In January 1986, at a meeting of the CCP Political Bureau, he even singled out an individual Chinese writer, Zhou Erfu, for attack (and consequent expulsion from the CCP) because the latter had reportedly visited a Japanese war shrine, and had also visited a red light district when in Japan,[50] both of which were considered examples of precisely the kind of 'spiritual pollution' which were of concern to Deng Xiaoping and others within the leadership of the CCP.

8 Reaction, readjustment and retirement, 1985 and after

Retirement – his own and other people's – and rejuvenating the leadership appear to have been the matters of most concern to Deng Xiaoping in and after 1985. He had already in 1980 when refusing the Chairmanship of the CCP indicated that he considered himself too old to take on new responsibilities, and in general he was concerned to ensure generational change amongst the leadership. Deng himself retired from daily administration in September 1985, from the CCP Political Bureau at the 13th Congress of the CCP, and from his last formal position as Chairman of the Central Military Commission in November 1989. Though his position as 'paramount leader' – from which it appeared there was no retirement – still meant that he had a role to play as a final political and military authority, none the less his retirement to a position to a certain extent above politics was real.

In ensuring the generational change he desired, Deng was less successful. When looking back at the reform era from the vantage point of 1992, Deng Xiaoping was more than somewhat rueful about the slow pace of generational change:

> As long as we, the older generation are still around ... the hostile forces know that change cannot happen. But who can guarantee this once we old people pass away?[1]

In retrospect, for Deng the problem had been both general and specific. The leadership as a whole had remained too old in his view, and it was still imperative, as through the 1980s, to recruit younger and more able leadership cadres. However, his comments were also more pointed and critical of Hu Yaobang and Zhao Ziyang, the two General Secretaries of the CCP in the 1980s. According to Deng, both had failed to take on the mantle of the successor generation, not least because in his view they had not been able to rise to the challenge that 'bourgeois liberalization' posed to the CCP.

THE NATIONAL PARTY CONFERENCE OF 1985

Before September 1985, and the special National Conference of the CCP, economic and political reforms were put into effect – on the whole with considerable success. However, after that date the reform agenda began to lose its momentum in the face of several major economic and political problems. Political stability, based on the party democracy Deng had long advocated, had characterized the early 1980s. Although factionalism as in the Cultural Revolution did not re-emerge during the late 1980s, none the less political differences within the leadership became more acute, especially in and after 1988.

There were problems ahead as the principles of 'Socialism with Chinese characteristics' were introduced more fully into the urban economy after October 1984. Although the leadership of the CCP after the 3rd plenum had been extremely united in knowing what it did not want, its unity was considerably more fragile when it came to deciding how to proceed further. There was general broad agreement that China needed to import foreign technology, to be part of the international economic order, to introduce market forces into the economy, to plan according to economic rather than political criteria, to regularize politics and to relax controls. However, there was considerable disagreement on the extent to which, the means by which, and the speed at which these goals should be achieved, and this disagreement created difficulties which could not in the long term be ignored.

A more immediate set of problems came with a minor economic crisis. The October 1984 decision to extend the principles of economic reform, particularly the extent of enterprise autonomy, to the urban areas, led in the final quarter of 1984 to a massive inflationary boost to the economy as enterprises took advantage of their new-found freedoms. As in the recent past, Deng had not been involved in the detail of economic policy development. Management of the economy had been left to others, notably Chen Yun and Zhao Ziyang, who from August 1980 had been Premier. However, as 1985 progressed – and with it the drafting of the Seventh Five-Year Plan (to be introduced in 1986) – it became clearer that there was sharp disagreement between these two.

Deng for his part had already run into problems with his attempts to rejuvenate and reform both the PLA and the leadership of the CCP. Deng's decision to reform the PLA during the mid-1980s is politically hard to plot. During the mid- and late 1970s the PLA had been solid under its commanders, particularly Ye Jianying, in its support for Deng and the policy of modernization. Though it had not wanted to abandon its political roles completely, it had clearly wanted advanced weaponry and to become more of a professional army.[2] It is possible that Deng decided that the PLA required reform after the disastrous results of the invasion of Vietnam in early 1979 when the PLA did not live up to its own propaganda and was forced to withdraw before it became bogged down. Certainly he had proposed reforms in both March 1980[3] and November 1984.[4]

It is also possible that Deng decided to take the lead in reorganizing the PLA because he realized that he had a better chance than anyone else of carrying through a programme of reform. He had a distinguished war record and a long association with the army, and his two recalls to duty during the 1970s had both involved service as Chief-of-Staff of the PLA. Indeed, during his exile in 1977 he had greeted Ye Jianying by his title of Marshal, only to be told by Ye: 'You are also a veteran marshal. Actually you are the leader of our marshals.'[5] He had ceased to be Chief-of-Staff in 1980, but shortly thereafter – the precise date at which Deng ceased to be Chief-of-staff of the PLA remains unknown – had been appointed Chairman of the Central Military Commission. Moreover, he had used that latter position to ensure considerable support by promoting former sub-ordinates, particularly from the Taihang Region in the Sino-Japanese War. One such promotee was Yang Dezhi, who had replaced him as Chief-of-Staff.

None the less, Deng ran into trouble and the opposition of at least part of the military establishment – Ye Jianying was reportedly apoplectic – with his planned reform in 1985.[6] The essence of Deng's proposals was the attempt to bring PLA spending under control, to increase its efficiency, to rejuvenate its officer corps and generally to create a more professional army. He argued that its troop strength be reduced by about one million; that most of its veteran officers and cadres retire; that the eleven military regions be reduced to seven which were more related to China's geo-strategic situation; and that each of the PLA's constituent armies be reorganized so that they no longer reflected the infantry-based requirements of the 1940s, which had remained the PLA's order of battle.

Deng eventually overcame any resistance from within the ranks of the PLA, but only by relying almost totally on support from his former subordinates – those who had served with him in the Taihang Region, the 129th Division, and later the 2nd Field Army. As a result of the reorganization, by the end of 1985, of the seventeen most senior generals in the PLA, ten were former subordinates of Deng Xiaoping.[7] Both of the Central Military Commissions – one for the state administration, the other for the party – whose membership at this time was in any case identical, were also almost totally dominated by Deng's former colleagues and associates. Apart from Deng, five out of the other eight members of the two Central Military Commissions had this connection back to the Sino-Japanese War in common.[8]

Military politics apart, Deng's rejuvenation of the CCP leadership had progressed relatively smoothly after the 12th CCP Congress in 1982. However, there remained a substantial number of veteran cadres, including some who were PLA officers, resisting retirement. The rejuvenation of the leadership as well as discussion of economic reform were on the agenda of a special National Party Conference scheduled since the previous October for September 1985. In the event the Conference displayed a unity not to be repeated again during the 1980s, though not without some disagreement at the time.[9]

The compromise that was stitched together on the economy was inherently unstable. Whilst all speakers pledged themselves to the Seventh Five-Year Plan, to be introduced in 1986, they clearly disagreed on the emphases they favoured. Chen Yun, for example, issued dire warnings about the importance of market regulation remaining subordinate to planning. In particular, he argued that the CCP should intervene to ensure that grain production (which had reached record levels in 1984) remained high, even though it had dropped as a result of the rural reforms which directed the peasants into cash crops and other activities. He also expressed concern that party members had lost their communist ideals.[10] Deng could easily agree with that last point, but was more reticent on the first, affirming that both the predominance of the public sector and common prosperity were the fundamental principles in the process of economic reform.[11]

Leadership rejuvenation was also agreed at the Conference, but at a cost.[12] A substantial number of the more elderly members of the CCP leadership, including several veteran PLA officers such as Ye Jianying, were persuaded to stand down, and they were replaced by younger, better educated and generally more technocratically oriented leaders. The best examples are three of those who were added to the CCP Political Bureau at that time: Li Peng, Qiao Shi and Hu Qili, all of whom were then in their late 50s or early 60s. Li Peng was an engineering graduate, educated in the USSR, with considerable experience in the energy industry. Qiao Shi, though more recently a specialist in the international relations field of government, had worked in the iron and steel industry sector for a considerable period of time beforehand. Hu Qili was another engineering graduate, with leadership experience in the Communist Youth League, who had been involved in the recent reform of education. However, the veterans' resistance had only been overcome on the understanding that, as in the early 1960s, the CCP leadership was to be divided into two lines, with Deng and the older remaining members of the Political Bureau withdrawing from the daily political routine to the second line. As in the early 1960s, that division was to make the position of those supposed to be responsible for the CCP's and the PRC's routine administration – notably Hu Yaobang as CCP General Secretary and Zhao Ziyang as Premier – largely untenable.

HU YAOBANG AND ZHAO ZIYANG

After 1985 the CCP leadership increasingly began to polarize around two different visions of reform. One was of a market-determined economy with a routinized and relatively open political system, though still supporting a ruling communist party. The other was of a planned economy, modified by market-oriented policies, with considerably less political liberalization where the CCP and the state continued to dominate the economy and society. The former more liberal attitude was characterized as emphasizing an immediate need for both economic and political reform; the latter more conservative view as stressing a more gradualist approach to economic reform, and marked by extreme reluctance with regard to any political reform. At first the key issues of debate were the timing and nature of the introduction of price reform to meet the new pressures imposed on the economy by the extension of reform to the urban sector; and the separation of party and government.

The more liberal vision of reform appears to have been promoted by Zhao Ziyang and Hu Yaobang, generally at least at first with the support of Deng Xiaoping. In the mid-1980s and until late 1986 they seem to have seized the initiative. Plans for the introduction of price reforms were discussed and drafted, and in April 1986 experiments with further political reforms, and particularly the separation of party and government, were started in Taiyuan. At that point relations between Deng and Hu Yaobang appear to have gone awry.

Like Mao, Deng had frequently mentioned the possibility of his retirement, though possibly with more genuine intent given his eventual phased withdrawal through the 1980s. Indeed, he raised the question for public discussion at least as early as August 1980.[13] However, he appears to have taken offence at others raising the subject, as increasingly became the case during 1986. At the beginning of August 1986 he told a Japanese guest that he was not to be allowed to retire.[14] In early September one of the more liberal newspapers carried an article urging Deng's retirement on two counts: it would help pull the rug from under the feet of those who argued against the abolition of the system of lifelong tenure for cadres; and it would enable a more democratic system to be established.[15] Deng seems to have been extremely concerned by the extent to which this article and some of the political reforms being implemented were leading to suggestions of a wider political democracy. At the 6th plenum of the 12th Central Committee in late September he spoke determinedly against the possibility.[16] However, over the next two months Hu Yaobang reportedly fanned speculation of Deng's retirement in that context. At a meeting of the CCP Secretariat in late November there was apparently an angry showdown between Hu and Deng, with the former suggesting he should replace Deng as the Chairman of the Central Military Commission and the latter declaring that Hu had forfeited Deng's trust.[17]

The row between Deng Xiaoping and Hu Yaobang not only spelt the latter's political demotion, it also weakened the cause of greater reform, and delayed Deng Xiaoping's retirement. In January, in an interview with the visiting Secretary-General of the Japanese Liberal Democratic Party, Deng confirmed in a public way that he would not be retiring in the immediate future.[18] The November meeting of the Secretariat had decided that Zhao Ziyang would replace Hu Yaobang as General Secretary of the CCP at the 13th CCP Congress, scheduled for October 1987. However, in the event student street demonstrations for greater democracy erupted at the end of 1986 and provided the opportunity and the excuse for the opponents of all further reform to demand Hu Yaobang's removal in January 1987. Deng Xiaoping is regarded by some commentators not only to have acquiesced in this move against Hu Yaobang, but to have led the charge.[19] Whilst that may indeed have been the case, Deng none the less also moved to ensure that Hu's removal was political and not personal; and, moreover, that Hu retained his membership of the leadership. Hu Yaobang was re-elected as a member of the Political Bureau at the 13th Congress of the CCP and Chairman of the Central Commission for Guiding Party Consolidation, positions he held until his death in April 1989.

With Hu Yaobang's dismissal, Zhao Ziyang was appointed acting General Secretary of the CCP immediately, and Wan Li became acting Premier in his place. For the third time during the 1980s, Deng sanctioned a political campaign against 'bourgeois liberalization'. However, by the time the 13th Congress of the CCP met in October that same year (1987), with Deng's influence the balance once more seems to have swung back in favour of more liberal reform. In part this was also due to Deng's intervention: having seen the effects of the campaign against 'bourgeois liberalization' for a few months, he decided to reignite the drive for political reform. In May Deng's 1980 speech – 'On the reform of the system of Party and state leadership' – was reissued as a study document, signalling that the coming 13th Party Congress would probably lean in that direction. When the congress met, Zhao Ziyang's report argued that China was in the 'primary stage of socialism' when the development of productive forces had to be the CCP's priority, rather than any immediate concerns with formalistic definitions of socialism.[20]

In elections to the Central Committee, which for the very first time involved an element of genuine choice, party delegates rejected a number of those most closely associated with opposition to reform. Although Deng Xiaoping retired formally from membership of the CCP Political Bureau, so too did Chen Yun and Peng Zhen, the two most notable advocates of the now more conservative vision of reform. On the other hand, it appears that at the congress the new CCP leadership semi-formally recognized Deng as the 'paramount' leader.[21]

In late 1987 and early 1988, Zhao was ready to press ahead with economic reforms, particularly of the pricing system. The introduction of market structures alongside the institutions of the command economy had led to economic difficulties, not least because of price differentials between the two sectors. Zhao sought the introduction of a full market system for the determination of prices. However, his opponents highlighted the political dangers, which included the CCP's decreased ability to direct the economy, and also their concerns about the possible effects on the CCP's natural constituencies of support should, as they feared, price reform prove inflationary.

Experiments with price reform were implemented during the first half of 1988, but in late July the CCP's leadership postponed any such initiatives indefinitely. At that time it became clear that the leadership's worst fears might be about to be realized and that China was heading for an inflationary crisis. Prices soared, goods were stockpiled and there was a run on the banks. Zhao's position, and indeed that of the more liberal vision of reform, became extremely exposed. At a meeting to discuss the crisis he is reported to have lost his temper with Li Peng, who had succeeded him as Premier, and threatened resignation. He need not have bothered, for the CCP Political Bureau removed him from the economic policy-making process when it met in August during its regular summer session in Beidaihe. Once again, as in the case of Hu Yaobang, the support or otherwise of Deng Xiaoping was the crucial factor in ensuring his subordinate's position and indeed future career. Although Deng had supported price reform in the first half of 1988, and indeed is reported to have urged Zhao to go further and faster, by July he indicated that he had an open mind on the subject and saw no need to stand unreservedly behind Zhao.[22] Though the CCP at this stage did not ask for Zhao's resignation, he was sidelined and a more conservative economic policy introduced, discouraging both credit and so rapid capital investment.

TIANANMEN 1989

The combination of first an inflationary crisis followed by an economic squeeze, and then the frustrated democratic aspirations of student demonstrators was to prove explosive. Together with disagreement amongst the leaders of the CCP these factors were to present the regime with a major crisis for much of 1989. The difficulties started with student demonstrations in Tiananmen Square in April, and built to a crisis at the end of May. It was a crisis Deng was in retrospect to regard as 'inevitable' but one which none the less had results from which he appeared to wish to distance himself.

Tiananmen Square in the centre of Beijing is of considerable symbolic importance for China and in the history of the CCP.[23] Traditionally it was the point at which the two cultures of China – the high culture of the court and the ruling class, and the ordinary culture of the people – met. Chinese seeking justice or redress for a specific grievance would come to the Gate of Heavenly Peace ('Tiananmen' in Chinese) at the front entrance of the Imperial City to petition the Emperor. In 1919 it was the scene of nationalist demonstrations on 4 May that eventually led to the development of the May 4th Movement, and contributed to the establishment of the CCP.

Mao Zedong formally proclaimed the establishment of the PRC from the podium of the Gate of Heavenly Peace, with the leadership of the CCP in attendance – including Deng Xiaoping, who took time out from military activities in the south. During the Great Leap Forward the square in front of Tiananmen was widened, with the Great Hall of the People being added on one side and the Museum of Revolutionary History being added on the other. During the Cultural Revolution, Mao Zedong received the massed ranks of Red Guards in the square from the podium of the Gate of Heavenly Peace itself. In 1976 when Zhou Enlai died and there was considerable uncertainty about China's future trajectory, those who demonstrated in his memory and against the Gang of Four gathered in the square. Moreover, it was the description of this Tiananmen Incident as 'counter-revolutionary' that not only provided the excuse for Deng's removal from office in April 1976, but that Deng insisted had to be formally revised before he would take up the reins of office again.

In April 1989 student demonstrations once again centred on Tiananmen Square in the form of memorial marches for Hu Yaobang who had died on 15 April – a martyr in the students' eyes to the democratic cause they had championed at the end of 1986.[24] Though the demonstrators took some time to establish themselves in the popular consciousness, when they decided to camp in Tiananmen Square they began to attract the support of the urban workforce, largely for economic reasons, to the cause of change. Moreover, the longer the demonstrations continued without state intervention, the more other people became convinced that their participation was at least officially sanctioned.

If that were the case, then such equanimity would have been rudely awakened by the editorial in the *People's Daily* on 26 April which was heavily critical of the demonstrations and described them as 'a planned conspiracy to plunge the whole country into chaos'. From the available evidence, it would appear that Deng played a central role in the decision to take a hard line against the demonstrators.[25] On 25 April he had met with Li Peng (the then Premier) and Yang Shangkun (the then President of the PRC) to consider a report by the Beijing Municipal Government on the demonstrations in the square. The local government had requested permission from the Central Committee to act and Deng's response was to order both the denunciation of the demonstrations in the *People's Daily* and a crackdown on the students in the square.

Deng clearly saw the demonstrations as the manifestation of something more sinister – 'hostile forces' who were manipulating the students from behind the scenes. He blamed Hu Yaobang for not having campaigned adequately against 'spiritual pollution' and 'bourgeois liberalism'. His speech was exceptionally tough and unyielding about what should and what should not be done to deal with the situation:

> This turmoil is entirely a planned conspiracy to transform a China with a bright future into a China without hope. The major harm is to negate the leadership of the Communist Party and to negate the socialist system. A dialogue can be held, but we cannot tolerate incorrect behaviour. Pretending to overlook the problem will ... only fan the flames.... We must do our best to avoid bloodshed, but we should foresee that it might not be possible ... this is just like the rebellion faction during the Cultural Revolution.... There are 60,000 students boycotting classes but there are 100,000 who are not. We must protect and support the 100,000.... What are we afraid of? Of the 60,000 many have been forced.... We need to strengthen the Public Security Ministry's work to maintain social order.... Concessions in Poland led to further concessions. The more they conceded, the more chaos.... We should not simply administer the economic environment, we should also administer the political environment. We may have more struggles like this in future.[26]

This speech has led some commentators at the time and since to argue that Deng had, in contrast to his earlier views and practices, simply become an old man impatient with change, who had given up listening.[27] Whatever the merits of that interpretation might be, it misses an essential point in Deng's political outlook. He was prepared to encourage the young and the talented, but still wanted them to defer to both his and the CCP's age, experience and leadership. In Deng's vision of 'Socialism with Chinese characteristics', the one principle that could not be challenged was that of party rule.

The reaction the following day to the *People's Daily* editorial was to ensure that Tiananmen Square saw the biggest and most carefully organized anti-government demonstration in the history of the PRC. It also, in effect, spelt the end to an immediate crackdown: faced by the numbers involved in Tiananmen Square the use of force was judged too dangerous, physically and politically, by those more in the front line than Deng Xiaoping. Zhao Ziyang, who was then General Secretary of the CCP, had not participated in the discussions in Beijing leading to the 26 April editorial because at the time he was on a long-scheduled visit to Korea.

When Zhao Ziyang did return to Beijing on 30 April he is reported to have gone to see Deng, then in Beidaihe, to suggest a more conciliatory approach to the students.[28] Presumably with Deng's approval, Zhao legalized the publications being publicized by the students (one of the student 'demands') and on 6 May directed the CCP's Propaganda Department to 'support the freedom of the press'[29] (which was another.) Here the historical record begins to become completely unreliable. At some point Deng must have decided either that Zhao was no longer reliable or that he could simply no longer be supported. However, the sequence and timing of events remain confused.

In one account Deng is reported to have been furious with Zhao's breach of CCP discipline. According to party reference materials, Deng made it abundantly clear that Zhao's attempts at reconciliation with the demonstrators on 3 and 4 May 'represented only his personal point of view and not that of his position [as General Secretary] or of the CCP'.[30] A meeting of the leadership on 9 May, attended not only by members of the Political Bureau but also by former senior party leaders now members of the Central Advisory Commission or simply retired (notable amongst whom were Chen Yun, Peng Zhen, Bo Yibo and Li Xiannian), discussed what to do next and, it seems likely, eventually decided on the imposition of martial law. In other accounts, Zhao's attempts at reconciliation with the demonstrators simply antagonized the more conservative elements in the leadership who counter-attacked and gained Deng's support.[31]

Nothing could happen immediately for on 11 May Gorbachev was scheduled to arrive in Beijing. To the outside world, the summit meeting in Beijing was not quite the media event that had been promised – attention was directed elsewhere to the events in Tiananmen Square. It is impossible to know whether Deng felt humiliated by receiving Gorbachev under such circumstances, or whether he continued in his belief that the demonstrations were the conspiracy of a small minority. It seems likely that shortly after Gorbachev's departure an enlarged meeting of the CCP Political Bureau, with the party's senior retired leaders in attendance, met and decided on the imposition of martial law from 20 May.

Deng's role in what happened next is even less clear. Martial law proved as difficult to implement as had the 'crackdown' ordered to follow the *People's Daily* editorial of 26 April. Troops called in to Beijing were either surrounded, persuaded to go somewhere else, or left in a Mexican stand-off. At some point, and the unfolding of events remains almost completely obscured, decisions were taken both to bring in large numbers of troops and to arm them with live ammunition, which they would be prepared to use. In the event, by the evening of 3 June authorization was given to the incoming troops, who had to 'clear out and occupy' Tiananmen Square, to open fire on anyone who resisted. Though it appears no one was actually killed in Tiananmen Square itself, some 2,500 people appear to have died in the approaches to and surrounds of the square as a result.[32] Deng himself apparently left Beijing on 20 May and did not return until 5 or 6 June, and is reported not to have been told of the extent of the death toll until on or shortly before 9 June. Whatever Deng's involvement in these events, in retrospect he seems to have attempted both to take credit for dealing with the crisis, but also to distance himself from some of its processes and consequences.

On 9 June in reviewing the events surrounding what he now described as a 'counter-revolutionary rebellion' Deng was remarkably calm about what had happened. In an obvious effort to downplay the lasting significance of both demonstrations for democracy and the use of troops to suppress those demonstrations, he argued that 'this was a storm that was bound to happen' largely because political work and education had been inadequate. According to Deng, the strategy of reform and the 'Four cardinal principles' were correct but they had not been 'thoroughly implemented. They had not been used as the basic concepts to educate the people, to educate the students, and to educate all the cadres and communist party members.'

Deng went on to praise the PLA, its loyalty to the CCP and the sacrifices its members had made, including laying down their lives, in putting down the rebellion: 'they did not forget the people, the teachings of the party, or the interests of the nation ... this army retains the traditions of the old Red Army ... this army of ours is forever an army under the leadership of the party, forever the defender of the public interest'.[33] It was a message repeated in all the printed and electronic media at the time. Deng, for example, was seen on television personally congratulating troops who had been involved in the suppression of the 'counter-revolutionary incident'.

Later, there were signs of perhaps a more complex explanation of Deng's specific participation in the 1989 Tiananmen Incident. In September, Deng discussed the events of earlier in the year with Chinese-American academic Li Zhengdao. Whilst stressing once again the need for China to adhere to the 'Four cardinal principles', Deng mentioned that: 'In the suppression of the turmoil, we were at pains to avoid hurting the people, especially the students, that was our guiding principle.' Moreover, he went on to criticize Zhao Ziyang in particular, whom Deng said 'was clearly exposed as siding with the agitators and attempting to split the party. It was lucky I was there to help handle the situation. Of course, I was not the only one to play a role'.[34] Some months later, Deng is reported to have gone further in criticizing Zhao Ziyang and even exonerating the students to some extent. He is said to have told former West German Chancellor Helmut Schmidt in confidential talks that 'the students should not be blamed too much – the roots of the problem lay within the leadership of the party'.[35] Later still he appears to have indicated – in reference materials circulating within China during 1990 – that although he sanctioned the imposition of martial law, and the transfer of troops to Beijing, he had not given any orders for lethal weapons to be used.[36]

RETIREMENT AND HISTORY

The events of early June 1989 left the CCP leadership with several problems. Quite apart from the obvious political need to restore any damage to its legitimacy, the tight economic policies that had been in place since autumn 1988 – and which had contributed to popular protest – had to be maintained. At the same time, international reaction to the reported violence of the Tiananmen

Incident threatened to isolate China, not simply in terms of international politics but also (and possibly of greater importance) from its earlier sources of foreign capital and technology. There was a need for what Deng later described as a policy of readjustment, which he endorsed without hesitation.[37]

In economics and politics, this policy of readjustment was clearly in the hands of the CCP to determine. Political education was stepped up, first around the need to explain the events of June 1989 to the rest of China, and then more generally. More conservative economic measures were adopted, entailing slower more gradual growth and change, and leaving China less dependent on foreign economic involvement. In particular, the 5th plenum of the 13th Central Committee of the CCP adopted a 'Decision on Further Improving the Economic Environment, Straightening out the Economic Order, and Deepening the Reforms'.[38]

Though in the international arena policy was not the CCP's alone to determine, readjustment after June 1989 significantly increased China's rate of growth by altering its pattern of economic interaction. Whilst before the second half of 1989 China had been looking to the more advanced Western and OECD countries for trade and investment, this came to a more or less abrupt halt. Partly because of changes in the economies of East and South-east Asia, and partly through encouragement from Beijing, China's economic relations with its neighbours and near-neighbours developed at an increasing rate from the second half of 1989 on. In some cases – Hong Kong and Taiwan being the most obvious – a high degree of economic integration was achieved in a very short period of time, and provided a massive boost to China's economy as well as to the economies of the region in and after 1990.[39]

Doubtless associated with the need for political education and the reinforcement of the CCP's legitimacy, throughout the remainder of 1989 Deng was to have a higher profile in the official media than he had had for some considerable time. He was reported meeting various visitors to China, including Kim Il-sung from North Korea who paid an 'unofficial' visit in November doubtless to discuss developments in the communist world.[40] Three books of Deng Xiaoping's writings, including one covering the years 1938–65, and a two-volume collection on literature and the arts were published in as many months. In September a new film about Deng's time in Guanxi as a political organizer during the late 1920s and early 1930s – *The Bose Uprising* – was released.[41]

At the 5th plenum of the 13th CCP Central Committee, held in November, Deng finally was allowed his formal retirement, or at least resignation from his last formal office. On 8 November 1989 the Central Committee of the CCP accepted his resignation as Chairman of the Central Military Commission. Certainly he celebrated the occasion as his retirement, and said as much in a farewell speech to the plenum.[42] On 13 November he entertained his last official visitors – a Japanese business delegation – at the Great Hall of the People of Beijing, and said, 'I will take this opportunity to bid farewell to my political life and political career'.[43] It was a grand gesture: by the end of the month he was once again hitting the headlines when he called on Julius Nyerere of Tanzania, only this time in an unofficial capacity, during the latter's visit to China.[44]

In any case, neither then nor later could Deng retire from being 'paramount leader'. It has never been clear whether during the 1980s the rest of the CCP leadership felt that they would always need some final arbiter in the decision-making process, or whether Deng's position as 'paramount leader' was entirely personal. Deng as 'paramount leader' after his formal retirement was more or less the final arbiter in the decision-making process, though clearly not in a routine way. Though he no longer sat in on meetings of the Political Bureau, as he had after he had stepped down from its membership in 1987, it appears all major policy documents and reports went to him as a matter of course for approval or suggestion.[45] Deng's personal approval was apparently still needed if PLA troops were to be moved or even access gained to the PLA's Command and Control headquarters in Beijing.[46]

Moreover, as might be imagined, Deng was the one others turned to if leaders proved recalcitrant on specific points, or if particularly hard compromises had to be reached. For example, in the reform era the subject of centre–province financial relationships was a perennial problem for a number of reasons, not the least of which were the centre's shrinking revenue base and the differential rates of remittance paid by different provincial-level units. Shanghai in particular felt that it consistently lost out through the 1980s as the economies of other provinces, notably Guangdong and Fujian, with more favourable fiscal relationships with the centre grew rapidly. None the less, despite the changes of the 1980s Shanghai remained the richest provincial-level unit and the centre's single major source of revenue. Accordingly, in 1990 when the centre needed to raise additional revenue, it turned to Shanghai. Naturally there was resistance from Shanghai's leaders, so Deng was asked to intervene, and he managed to persuade Zhu Rongji (then Mayor and First Secretary of the CCP) to comply with the centre's request.[47]

This position, slightly to the side and above politics but certainly not totally divorced, allowed Deng as 'paramount leader' in retirement to play more effectively the radicalizing role he had started to develop in retreating to the second line of administration after the National Party Conference of 1985. When he had tried to act as a radicalizing element in the decision-making process when Hu Yaobang was General Secretary of the CCP in 1986 other politics had come inbetween, and the same was probably the case with Zhao Ziyang as General Secretary in 1988.

However, in 1992 he appeared to act more decisively and with no immediate side-effects to reignite the pace of reform. Apparently Deng felt by the end of 1991 that the conservative-minded readjustment of 1989 had lasted too long. With the 14th Congress of the CCP scheduled for later in 1992 there was a need for some immediate action. Though clearly not in perfect health and variable in both his strength and clarity of speech – he was 88 at this stage – Deng took a much publicized 'Journey of inspection' to the South of China and the areas of rapid economic development and close foreign economic relations: notably Shanghai, Wuhan, Zhuhai and Shenzhen.[48]

This 'Journey South' eventually received considerable publicity, after some initial opposition, and ensured both that economic policy became more expansionist and that a continued but faster reform programme was the keynote of the 14th Congress of the CCP when it met in December. Interestingly, by this stage economic development in many of the southern regions Deng visited had proceeded so far and so steadily that his visit tended to provide local leaders with legitimation for what they had already done in the last few years, often without official permission, and in an economy which was increasingly in any case not capable of immediate or direct control by government or the CCP.[49] Clearly the message of the Journey South was probably more to the rest of China.[50]

Quite apart from his role as 'paramount leader' one of Deng's major concerns in retirement, and one where his personal involvement is largely documented, was with history, in particular the history of the CCP and the Chinese revolution.[51] His personal attitude to history is unrecorded, but his political concerns were real enough. He encouraged the writing and publishing of party history in a number of different ways, presumably both in order, from his perspective, to set the record straight and to provide lessons for the present and the future. He wrote inscriptions, provided the calligraphy for titles, and otherwise encouraged a large range of party histories, biographies, and collections of documents, memoirs and reminiscences. For example, in one month alone – June 1991 – he wrote in his own calligraphy the titles of four major publications: *The Biography of Chen Yi*; *The Revolutionary History of the Hebei–Shandong–Henan Border Region*; the *Taihang Revolutionary Base Area Historical Collection*; and the newly re-edited four-volume *Selected Works of Mao Zedong*.[52]

As already indicated, Deng's sense of and struggle for history was by no means a new concern and had been a major part of his appeal to the CCP's leadership in the mid and late 1970s. However, the same concerns can also be found in Deng's speeches and writings even in the 1950s and 1960s.[53] The urgency for setting the record straight then may have been less, but not the CCP's legitimacy in its origins. Interestingly, shortly after his formal retirement on 8 November 1989, Deng attended a celebratory meeting with the historians of the 2nd Field Army, the army he and Liu Bocheng had developed.

Rumoured to have had a heart attack in August 1992 which left him weak and not always clear in his speech, Deng rapidly started to look frail.[54] His public appearances were limited, and, unlike in the 1980s when he had refused to have special treatment, now it was provided as a matter of course to allow Deng to move about discreetly. Wintering in Shanghai at the beginning of 1994, for example, as he had also done in previous years, when he returned to Beijing by train the schedules at the Shanghai Railway Station were rearranged to let him pass more easily.[55]

9 Comrade Deng
A preliminary assessment[1]

Undoubtedly for some time to come in the public consciousness worldwide Deng Xiaoping will be associated not only with China's rapid economic growth and transformation but also with the events in Beijing during June 1989. The images associated with first the demonstrations, and then the use of military force in Tiananmen Square and its surroundings, were extremely powerful. The precise detail of Deng's role in the events of 1989 may remain in doubt, but not his general attitude as demonstrated by his praise for the PLA units involved. Had he died or even retired before June 1989, history's judgement would probably have been very different. However, a picture of Deng Xiaoping as a liberal reformer would always have been a mistake. Redefining and extending rights were never Deng's major concerns, which focused instead on party rule, party discipline and economic production, in that order of priority. Indeed, even his desire after 1976 to liberalize the worst excesses of the system created by Mao Zedong and the Cultural Revolution was derived from his vision of the CCP as the panacea for all China's ills, and his desire to restore its traditions.

Any assessment of Deng Xiaoping is likely to be difficult, particularly so close to the events in which he played a key role. Moreover, the presentation of Deng in the Chinese media remains a very potent political symbol for the leadership of the CCP, as it did throughout the 1980s. Indeed, one of the paradoxes of the reform era was that while Deng attempted to depersonalize politics and emphasized collective leadership, such changes were driven to a large extent by his own personal authority. Thus the first collection of his writings to be published (the volume covering the years 1975–82) was produced to act as a primer for the rectification campaign of 1983. In that volume Deng was quite definitely portrayed as the guardian of the CCP. In other volumes and in the media generally throughout the 1980s Deng was also portrayed as a family man, a soldier, a statesman and a reformer. Those different images provide a useful framework for this preliminary assessment.

THE FAMILY MAN

Deng Xiaoping clearly revelled in his portrayal as a family man. Newspapers, magazines and books in China during the 1980s and 1990s carried plenty of photographs of him with his children and grandchildren. A cynic might argue that this portrayal was largely political. Powerful politicians often like to have their photographs taken holding young children or with their families; it is supposed to soften their public image and make them seem more like the rest of the world. This may even have been so for Deng Xiaoping, but if so he surely went to extreme lengths for the sake of an image.

It seems reasonable to assume that like many Chinese Deng had a strong emotional attachment to his family. Unlike many revolutionaries – and Mao Zedong was a notable case in point – he managed to retain that orientation. In 1949, despite having been away from home for twenty-nine years, when he returned to Chongqing he was reunited with his elder sister, step-mother and other members of his family. Except for a short break during the Cultural Revolution, he managed to look after his step-mother, and in and after 1969, when exiled to Jiangxi, he did his best to bring all the family together again, even in adversity. In the 1980s whenever he went on an inspection tour of the provinces, however distant from Beijing, he seems to have taken one of his several grandchildren along.

There are very few reliable records of any aspect of Deng's personality. In his daughter's biography he is depicted as laconic but good hearted, a lover of food and football. In the biography and elsewhere she has described him as a very private man: 'an introvert' and 'someone who has few words.... He is rather philosophical on the question of personal fate ... optimistic in the face of adversity'.[2] Mao clearly recognized some of the same qualities: 'Deng is a rare and talented man. Deng has ideas. He does not assault problems head on without thought. He finds solutions. He deals with difficult problems responsibly.' However, Mao also recognized an element of stubbornness and a propensity for direct action, for he commented: 'Deng's mind is round and actions are square.'[3] These were not inconsequential personal qualities in a career which included amongst other hardships three forced military marches and three purges.

It would seem that Deng's appearance was in itself somewhat disarming. This was not so much a function of his height – Deng was only a little over five feet tall – as his face. Photographs of Deng from the 1930s and 1940s, and well into the 1980s, show a lively and open expression. Deng clearly did have a keen sense of fun. From his army days in the South-west he had become an enthusiastic and capable bridge player – Hu Yaobang and Wan Li were both long-term partners. However, he never apparently played for money: rather the losers had to crawl on all fours under the table. On the other hand, there was also a steely side to Deng's nature, as his actions in the political in-fighting of the early 1960s and again between 1973 and 1978 bear witness. In Mao's description, Deng was 'a needle wrapped in cotton'.[4] On the whole, and unlike many of those with whom he worked, his relations with his colleagues normally appeared at least professionally cordial. The exception was an apparently profound dislike for the radicals of the Cultural Revolution. One, Chen Boda, once complained that: 'Discussing with Deng Xiaoping as equals is more difficult than putting a ladder against heaven.'[5] In return, Deng seems to have done little to hide his animosity towards either Jiang Qing or Lin Biao.

Remarkably, Deng's willingness to abide by the norms of inner-party democracy seems to have been extended even to those against whom he might well have been thought to have a justified grudge. Hua Guofeng had replaced him as successor to both Zhou Enlai and Mao Zedong in 1976, yet when Deng was in control again after 1978 he was prepared to reach an accommodation with Hua. Hu Qiaomu, who had been one of the first to criticize Deng in 1966 as the Cultural Revolution started, was none the less one of the first people Deng helped back to power in the early 1970s when he was able. In 1933 when Deng was severely criticized, imprisoned and probably tortured by the CCP, the attack had been led by Li Weihan. Deng's wife at the time, Jin Weiying, even divorced him to marry Li Weihan. Yet Deng not only worked amicably with Li Weihan later, but the son of Li and Jin became one of Deng's protégés and a member of the Political Bureau under him.

At the same time, Deng appeared not to forget his old friends and colleagues, even posthumously. One of those who bore the brunt of the attack against Mao Zedong and the 'Luo Ming line' in 1933 along with Deng was Mao Zetan, Mao Zedong's youngest brother. Left behind when the Long March retreated from Jiangxi, he was immediately captured and executed by the Nationalists in 1934. Like most of Mao's family from before he married Jiang Qing, Mao Zetan was largely unremembered publicly until after the Cultural Revolution. In 1986 Deng went to Jiangxi and opened a memorial to Mao Zetan, which he had personally inscribed.[6]

THE SOLDIER

During the 1980s and 1990s the CCP promoted Deng's image as a soldier. This was not based on his activities as Vice-Chairman of the National Defence Council before the Cultural Revolution, nor as Chief-of-Staff of the PLA during the second half of the 1970s, nor as Chairman of the Central Military Commission for most of the 1980s, but rather on his military service during the years 1938 to 1952. At that time Deng had been the political commissar of first the 129th Division of the 8th Route Army and then, after the Sino-Japanese War and during the War of Liberation against the Nationalists, the Shanxi–Hebei–Henan–Shandong Army which became the 2nd Field Army of the PLA. During the late 1980s plays, books and films appeared which dealt in particular with the 2nd Field Army's march south to the Dabie Mountains in 1947 and the Huai-Hai Campaign of 1948–9.[7]

The popularization during the mid-1980s of Deng's role as a soldier probably resulted from his and the CCP leadership's desire to reorganize the PLA and to rejuvenate its leadership. Deng was much better placed than anyone else in the leadership to bring that about and if necessary to bridge any division that might arise between the CCP and the PLA. Unlike many of those he had come into contact with between 1929, when he went to Guangxi, and the victory of 1949, Deng was not a career soldier. For example, Zhang Yunyi, whom he worked with in Guangxi; Liu Bocheng; and Chen Yi, who commanded the 3rd Field Army during the Huai-Hai Campaign, were all originally professional soldiers rather than party cadres. None the less, through his organizational and political skills, Deng managed to gain their confidence and acceptance.

The publicity afforded Deng as a soldier, in particular during the second half of 1989, was presumably also the result of contemporary politics. The message of the CCP was of the essential unity between the CCP and PLA, as had existed in the Sino-Japanese War and the War of Liberation. It was a message directed not only at the population as a whole but also towards the PLA, some of whose soldiers were concerned at the use of force against unarmed civilians in the middle of 1989.

The portrayal of Deng Xiaoping as a soldier of any military background or skill at all may seem a little odd at first sight. His military experience before he joined Liu Bocheng in the Taihang Region had been somewhat limited and not particularly successful. In Guangxi as a political organizer he had not been initially engaged in military affairs, and the Bose and Longzhou Uprisings in 1929 and 1930 initially met with almost no resistance. When they did – from the Nationalists and the French – Deng and his forces retreated. The 7th Red Army was eventually forced to retreat well across country to Jiangxi, with its commanders being separated on the way and its numbers extremely depleted. On the Long March, Deng's role appears to have been totally political.

Deng Xiaoping's appointment as political commissar of the 129th Division at the beginning of 1938 was political rather than military. The 129th Division was formed from troops who had been commanded by one of Mao's challengers for the leadership of the CCP on the Long March. Mao had already once reorganized the leadership of the 129th Division soon after its formation in order to try and ensure control. Deng was an inspired choice for Mao, who both trusted Deng – not least because of what had happened in the Jiangxi Soviet – and knew that Deng was young and able enough to do the job.

However, during the Sino-Japanese War Deng's political and organizational abilities became military skills and he rapidly developed a reputation which lasted within the PLA for being a good soldier and leader. In 1937 when the 129th Division, at that time without Deng, entered the Taihang Region it had 6,000 men; by 1940 the 129th Division had grown to 200,000. Deng's first military achievement was the creation of a substantial armed force, which later went on to become the 2nd Field Army, from a very unpromising resource base.

Considerable emphasis is usually placed on the extent to which communist forces during the Sino-Japanese War mobilized the peasantry behind appeals to either social reform, nationalism or both. These undoubtedly formed part of Deng's strategy. However, his new recruits were for the most part not tenant farmers or even landowning peasants, but rather landless labourers and displaced persons (from both the urban and rural workforce) from other parts of China. Deng, with his reputation for being tough, just and strong, offered them a comradeship and a measure of security their lives otherwise lacked.

In the 1940s the forces under Liu Bocheng and Deng Xiaoping – first the 129th

Division and then the 2nd Field Army – gained a reputation within the CCP that was very different to that of the other communist armies. They were considered the weakest of the communist troops in a number of respects: they were physically weak, had almost no equipment and were the smallest in number. However, Liu and Deng's army was always the most united, largely because of the relationship between the two, and this and its solidarity were its strengths.

Deng's role in creating the army he and Liu led rapidly gave him an equal leadership status in the field. Together they led the march south to the Dabie Mountains in 1947 on foot. It was a manoeuvre which by all accounts should not have worked. They did not secure their positions as they went and relied almost totally on the element of surprise for their progress. However, it did open up the central plains of China as a battleground for the ensuing civil war. The portrayal of Deng's participation in the leadership of the Huai-Hai campaign during that civil war was obviously exaggerated during the 1980s and 1990s. None the less, it was real enough. The front committee directing the campaign was given autonomy to act by the CCP, on the understanding that all commands had to go through and be approved by Deng, Mao's trustee and appointee in that position.

Deng's role as a soldier after 1938 became very important to his career after 1949. In between the military and civilian wings of the CCP he rapidly became the soldiers' party cadre, and the party cadres' soldier. The Gao Gang affair thrust him firmly into that kind of role, but in the aftermath of the Cultural Revolution it was a role he continued.

Of course, the majority of party cadres in the years before 1949 had been part of the military offensive. However, Deng's involvement with the military had been and was to remain more than the norm. He developed a substantial base of support within the PLA which was to come to his aid on more than one occasion when he was in political trouble. This was partly because he seemed genuinely to take to military life and related well to the military leaders he met during his military service. However, it was also because he ensured that many of his former subordinates from either the 129th Division, the Taihang Region, or the 2nd Field Army were placed in positions of importance within the PLA. In that connection, his role in the allocation of military ranks during the mid-1950s was obviously important. Moreover, Deng's continued relationship with his former subordinates from the Taihang Region and the 2nd Field Army was by no means confined to military affairs, and came to play an important role in civilian politics.

In his discussion of Deng's political style, Lucien Pye highlights the traditional elements in Deng's political behaviour.[8] In addition it is worth remembering the possible impact of the military culture, in which he worked for so long, on Deng's later approach to authority. Like a well-trained soldier, he obeyed his superiors and led his subordinates. When he became the 'paramount leader' he expected to be treated as such by everyone, whether it was Hu Yaobang, Zhao Ziyang or the students in Tiananmen Square.

THE POLITICIAN

Deng's portrayal as a statesman on the international stage was justified, particularly by comparison with his predecessors, even if somewhat exaggerated in a global perspective. From the mid-1970s into the 1990s Deng Xiaoping did more than any other PRC leader to promote relations between China and the rest of the world, particularly through the 'open-door policy'. He visited the USA, Japan, France, East and South-east Asia, and demonstrated in a number of ways – cultural and personal, as well as political and economic – an openness towards the world outside China. Particularly during the early 1980s he made skilful use of the international media in furthering China's ends.

In domestic politics, Deng was promoted as the guardian of the CCP and the epitome of its values after 1976. Of course, that was precisely the role that a 'paramount leader' was required to play, and that was certainly how Mao had seen himself, especially during the Cultural Revolution. However, there was considerable ambiguity in that role, and the relationship between party and leader was almost certain to be unstable, as it had been in Mao's case. Deng's treatment of the CCP's values, structures and mission was clearly different to Mao's, or at least it became so when he became 'paramount leader', possibly drawing some conclusions from his own analysis of the Cultural Revolution.

Even so, in the final analysis Deng allowed himself, if to a lesser degree, to fall into the same trap of personalizing the CCP for which he had criticized Mao. During the late 1980s Deng's support, or its withdrawal, appears to have determined the fates of Hu Yaobang and Zhao Ziyang. Certainly it seems that Deng's personal attitude to the demonstrations of 1989 was a crucial factor in their suppression. Certainly too, his use of the 'paramount leader's' authority proved decisive in resurrecting the drive for greater and faster reform in the period leading to the 14th Congress of the CCP after he had made his tour of inspection in the south of China.

Deng's interpretation of the CCP's role in Chinese society was not newly constructed during the 1980s and appears remarkably consistent after the early 1940s. He placed a considerably greater emphasis than Mao on the importance of organization and bureaucracy, as well as on the drive for economic modernization. Indeed, where Mao saw mass mobilization as the engine of change, Deng had a more technocratic vision of China's future, and frequently criticized the 'leftist excesses' (in his view) that came with the politics of mobilization. Only the CCP could modernize China because only the CCP had the ability to mobilize its human and material resources. Interestingly, given his views on the needs for a strong state and highly structured socialization for the young, in 1992 he expressed his admiration for Singapore's 'social order' which he compared favourably to his notion of 'Socialism with Chinese characteristics'.[9]

Deng believed that the principle of the party's monopoly of power was inviolate, hence his opposition to the Cultural Revolution – once he understood its trajectory – not simply because it involved an attack on the CCP but also because it undermined the CCP's authority. As he said to a meeting of the Young Communist League in July 1958, in a statement that could have been made at any time in his career, 'The key issue is that there is only one party. If you hold firm on this point, then whatever mistakes you make you will remain basically correct'.[10]

For Deng the CCP had a duty to lead society, and in order to exercise that leadership function it needed to be a distinct organization. Organizational confusion between party and government would only weaken its ability to lead, as would the CCP's not being responsible for its own discipline. In Deng's view the strength of the CCP depended on its solidarity and its good relations with the general population. Both depended upon education within the party and the maintenance of organizational norms. There should be discussion and debate within the party until a decision was taken, but once a decision had been taken then everyone should fall into line behind the collective leadership to enable the party to exercise leadership over the rest of society.

Education within the CCP based on Mao Zedong Thought – not Mao's personal ideas but the distilled wisdom of the CCP's collective leadership from before 1949 – could help ensure the party's feeling of solidarity and unity of purpose. However, Deng argued clearly and consistently that in order to ensure the CCP's leadership of society it was necessary to demonstrate the material advantages. During the Sino-Japanese War this was defence and the maintenance of a productive economy in the areas under CCP control. During and after 1949 it was economic modernization. As he said in 1987, when talking to the premier of Czechoslovakia, but as he might have said at any time during the previous 50 years, 'To build socialism it is necessary to develop the productive forces. Poverty is not socialism'.[11]

Because of his emphasis on material development and the need to develop China's intellectual and organizational infrastructure to that end, Deng has sometimes been portrayed outside the PRC solely as an economic modernizer. Whilst that interpretation is not self-evidently incorrect it is not the whole story for, as the quotation just cited from 1987 indicates, what Deng sought was socialism. Whatever else that meant it certainly entailed a central role for the CCP. In comparing socialism and capitalism in 1992, Deng described socialism as 'leading to the growth of the socialist state', as well as 'assisting in the development of productive forces' and 'improving the people's living standards'.[12] In Deng's cosmology economic modernization was a major concern, but the principle of party rule was an even higher priority. Indeed, as the purge of Zhao Ziyang in 1989 indicates to some extent, even the importance of party discipline and party democracy would be sacrificed if necessary to the principle of party rule.

The obvious contrasts with Mao Zedong's views and work-style raise the question of Deng's relationship with Mao, which was clearly central to Deng's political career, even after the Cultural Revolution. Before the Cultural Revolution Deng had been Mao's lieutenant for over thirty years, and Mao trusted him to be personally loyal. After the Cultural Revolution, even when Mao still lived, and even though their relationship had changed in practice, that earlier relationship between them remained a tangible manifestation of the CCP's success in revolution to many others in the party's leadership. Under such circumstances it is easy to see how Deng would have come to believe that his former mentor had come under the undue influence of less politically desirable elements – Lin Biao and the Gang of Four – and consequently gone against his own real intentions during the Cultural Revolution. It is also easy to see why Deng would remain loyal to Mao into the 1990s. As he told Oriana Fallaci in 1980, 'we will adhere to Mao Zedong Thought. We will not do to Chairman Mao what Khrushchev did to Stalin',[13] and as he pointed out in May 1989 he was still proud to have been part of 'Mao's group' in the CCP.[14]

The political relationship between Mao and Deng dated back to the attacks on the 'Luo Ming line' in 1933 when Deng had essentially been a substitute for Mao in an intra-party conflict. Thereafter Mao appears uncharacteristically to have trusted Deng to an extent which he withheld from others. Deng was sent to the Taihang Region in 1938 at least partially in order to keep an eye on the 129th Division for Mao and the Yan'an leadership of the CCP. Alone of all the CCP's leaders in the field he was not required to return to Yan'an for the party's major rectification campaign in 1942–3 which finally removed CPSU influence and ensured Mao's control. Deng became General Secretary of the CCP with Mao's support, and despite increasing differences on policy there was little evidence of friction between the two until late in 1966. Even during the Cultural Revolution, Deng was not criticized openly by name in the official media.

Deng's relationships with not only Mao Zedong but also Zhou Enlai, and indeed the extent to which he developed a vast network of associates within the CCP, are clearly important aspects of his political biography. In addition to those two more obvious relationships, this biography has also highlighted the importance of Deng's experience in the Taihang Region during the Sino-Japanese War to his later politics. Deng's vision of the politics of change was crystallized largely at that time, and the people he met and worked closely with in the Taihang Region were to form an important network of power and influence.

Deng's experience in the Taihang Region gained much of its impetus from the deliberately created 'model' border region centred on Yan'an, and from the CCP's experience elsewhere in North China, particularly JinChaJi (the Shanxi–Chahar–Hebei border region) immediately to the north. It would be reading too much into the temporary and wartime conditions of the early 1940s to suggest that all Deng's detailed post-1949 policies had their origins there. None the less, the situation in the Taihang Region posed different problems to those encountered in Yan'an, and sometimes required different solutions. The Taihang Region was bigger, more varied and more influenced by the conduct of war; it was also economically somewhat more developed. Deng's concerns with economic construction and production, democratic centralism and the rights of the minority within the CCP, the separation of party and government, and the widest possible popular support mobilized through a variety of techniques were formulated in response to conditions during the Sino-Japanese War.

Certainly, there can be little doubt about the impact of the Taihang Region on Deng's relations with others within the CCP leadership. The results of his efforts in developing the 129th Division have already been discussed. In terms of his relationships with military leaders, it is also probably significant that the headquarters of the entire 8th Route Army were located in the Taihang base area for most of the Sino-Japanese War. This brought him into close contact with those who were to lead the PLA for at least the first seventeen years of the PRC, until the Cultural Revolution.

Military affairs apart, the extent to which Deng's former subordinates and associates from the border region centred on the Taihang Region came to occupy positions of importance, not only within the CCP Political Bureau but throughout the party, is quite remarkable. Particularly after 1966 they provided Deng with a network of support within the CCP's leadership that was second to none. During June 1989 in the aftermath of military intervention in Tiananmen Square much was made in the Western media of the military relationship between the PLA's 27th Army, commonly held to have led the suppression in Beijing, its former Political Commissar Yang Baibing, and his brother Yang Shangkun, the then President of the PRC. Equally important was the relationship which went back fifty years between Deng and Yang Baibing, a former soldier in the 129th Division.

THE REFORMER

The final portrayal of Deng Xiaoping was as the CCP leader most responsible for the introduction of reform. Here too the image was justified, though with reservations. Certainly Deng led the assault on the policies and institutions of the Cultural Revolution during the mid-1970s. Certainly too his treatment in 1976 when he was once again purged from the CCP leadership ensured that he became an extremely popular figurehead to lead the drive for economic modernization and the rejection of the Cultural Revolution.

However, the policies which were implemented in and after 1978 were the product of a collective leadership who had worked together for some time within the CCP before the Cultural Revolution. Their general ideas on China's development had first been raised in the mid-1950s, notably as articulated at the 8th CCP Congress by Chen Yun. They had been resurrected in the early 1960s as part of the attempted reformulation of economic policy which followed the catastrophe of the Great Leap Forward. In the late 1970s and after the Cultural Revolution, those who had been involved in that process almost twenty years earlier were brought together again by Deng Xiaoping, and the 3rd plenum of the 11th Central Committee in December 1978 was as much their collective victory as Deng's alone.

The historical origins of the policies and practices of the reform era provide the essential clue to Deng's role as a reformer. On the whole he was not an innovator, but rather a traditionalist. Unlike a Gorbachev, he did not proceed from a radical critique of his country's problems to detail a new blueprint. On the contrary, the essence of the reforms launched at the 3rd plenum was a return to the traditions of the CCP as they had been defined during the early 1950s. The political reforms Deng was responsible for introducing can to some considerable extent be seen in his speech to the 8th CCP Congress in 1956, which in turn had drawn heavily on an interpretation of the party's experiences during the 1940s. Deng's emphasis was on the maintenance of party democracy and on making the political system as efficient as possible, in order to assist economic modernization.

For the most part Deng's innovations during the 1980s were confined to the field of foreign policy. Given the initiative of the 'open door' which followed years of, to some extent, self-imposed isolation it might seem that this signalled a rather more radical change with the past. However, even here the differences were not as great as might have seemed at first sight, for an approximation of the same policy had been suggested by Chen Yun in and around 1956. On the other hand, one very definitely innovative foreign policy initiative was that which saw Gorbachev visit Beijing in May 1989. It had not been so long since Deng himself had suggested that such a development was impossible.

Deng was essentially a conservative reformer, a traditionalist who wanted to restore what he considered had been the CCP's traditions, set aside during the Cultural Revolution. As he stressed in January 1980 (in a speech to party cadres), support for the CCP had to be renewed through economic growth and a return to what he considered as the more conventional ways of doing things.[15] His definition of Mao Zedong Thought, which he ensured was codified through the 'Resolution on Party History' of 1981, was in terms of three principles he had long championed: 'seek truth from facts', the mass line, and the independence of the Chinese revolution. He repeatedly looked back to the 1940s and resurrected its issues and rhetoric in a contemporary context.

The extent to which Deng sought legitimacy for his reforms in the CCP's traditions may be judged by his adjustment to the history of the 8th CCP Congress of 1956. During the 1980s the 8th CCP Congress was presented as a model congress and its documents were republished in both hard and soft covers. Deng and others pointed to the congress as having upheld the CCP's traditions and in particular Mao Zedong Thought. Of course, such an interpretation was not completely inconsistent with Mao Zedong Thought as defined by Deng during the 1980s. Somewhat paradoxically, it had been Deng who had formally proposed the revision of the CCP Constitution to the 8th Congress that had deleted the reference to Mao Zedong Thought.

Deng's need to create tradition in that way highlighted the major contradiction in his vision of social and political change. His traditionalism led him to concentrate on the identification of a golden age in the CCP's past – sometimes 1956, sometimes the early 1940s – in order to legitimize contemporary politics. However, that golden age had not necessarily ever existed – or if it had, only under certain highly specific and inevitably temporary conditions such as in the revolutionary base areas during the Sino-Japanese War. A vision determined to such an extent by history or tradition is inherently less flexible when faced by radically different circumstances, and the new social and political demands generated by economic growth during the 1980s and 1990s required accommodation rather than Deng's formulaic response. In that context it will be interesting to see whether in time Deng passes into the mythology of the Chinese revolution as probably its most successful economic modernizer, or as a less successful political reformer.

10 Deng Xiaoping in his own words

Speeches and writings

The collation of Deng Xiaoping's speeches and writings would seem to suggest fairly obviously that he – unlike many of his colleagues in the leadership of the CCP – had few if any pretensions to be an essayist, philosopher or even for the most part an ideologist. His work as a political organizer dominated his life and career, and his speeches and writings were overwhelmingly concerned with matters of political organization. From these works he appears as an organizer *par excellence*, though by no means an *éminence grise* sheltering behind the scenes of bureaucracy. On the contrary, he quite often appears as the 'name' on a report, speech or document, which, though he may have read and adjusted it, has presumably been drafted by others, as for example in his presentation of the Draft Budget for 1954.[1] At other times, he was the one to present a report on behalf of a group, as, for example, most spectacularly in both 1954 and 1955 through the internal party investigations of Gao Gang and Rao Shushi.

For the most part Deng's language was plain and relatively down-to-earth, leaving the impact of what he had to say to the organizational ideas he wished to propose or provide as commentary. He avoided the hyperbole and earthy language that characterized at least one of his predecessors,[2] and his speeches contained few passages that carried meaning beyond their immediate context or that were truly quotable. There are some notable exceptions. Perhaps the most famous is his comment that: 'It doesn't matter whether a cat is black or white so long as it catches mice'. Often regarded in the West as a justification for what is seen as Deng's pragmatism, he was criticized heavily for the remark during the Cultural Revolution, and again in 1975–6.[3] Another exception was his speech in June 1989, shortly after the Beijing Massacre, to the commanders of the martial law enforcement troops. When referring back to the events of May and early June he said, 'This is the storm that was bound to happen sooner or later.'

On the whole, Deng is best known in aphoristic terms, for example, for expounding 'One country, two systems' with respect to Hong Kong and Taiwan; for his 'Four cardinal principles' of political rectitude, enunciated in 1979; for the exhortation to 'Emancipate the mind' at the 3rd plenum of 1978; advocating 'Reform and openness'; the principle of 'Socialism with Chinese characteristics'; and the revival (in a different context) of Mao's imperative to 'seek truth from facts'. As Deng Rong suggests, though not exactly in this context, 'Father is a man of few words.'[4]

The starting point for any analysis of Deng Xiaoping's writings and speeches has to be the three volumes of openly published CCP-sanctioned *Selected Works* for 1938–65, 1975–82 and 1982–92. However, the selections presented in those pages are by no means exhaustive even for the period after 1938. As the Hong Kong press was not slow to point out when Volume III (for 1982–92) appeared in late 1993, selections of this kind are made and edited within the political context, and to the ends prevalent, at the time of publication.[5] The result is sometimes that relatively well-known and easily available texts are not included. For example, Deng's report on the rectification campaign of 1957, which was openly published in *People's Daily* in September 1957, was not included in the first volume of his *Selected Works* presumably because of the political sensitivities during the 1980s about the role of the rectification campaign in Mao's launching of the Great Leap Forward, and associated developments for which Mao is now considered to have been a 'leftist'.[6] The process of editing is a political censorship – things are excluded, not, for the most part and as far as can be ascertained, included after the event.

Deng Xiaoping's openly published speeches and writings after 1949, even when they have not been included in the *Selected Works*, are relatively available. However, access to openly published material from before 1949 is sometimes more limited, though there are substantial series of CCP and border region publications available, even outside China. Since 1978, as the CCP has rediscovered its own history, access has been greatly facilitated through the subsequent republication of earlier documents. Deng Xiaoping's 1941 defence of democracy and competitive elections is one such republished document.[7]

The availability of restricted circulation and internal party publications containing speeches and writings by Deng Xiaoping is much more variable for the periods both before and after the establishment of the PRC. Within China, there are of course different levels of confidentiality and restricted circulation. However, on the whole, wider dissemination is usually to specific political ends rather than serving any dispassionate idea of preserving history. This is not to say that documents are not extant: there are considerable archives, but access is limited. Once again the CCP's rediscovery of its own history – whatever the political implications – has provided some documentation, though sometimes even republication may only be for a restricted audience. In Deng Xiaoping's case his report of 1931 on the 7th Red Army in Guangxi is precisely one such example. Necessarily, the availability of sources outside China is dependent on release and access inside the PRC.

The following pages provide a catalogue of, and guide to, those of Deng Xiaoping's speeches, writings, directives and comments which are currently available generally from January 1938 (when Deng became political commissar of the 129th Division of the 8th Route Army) to the end of 1992. The catalogue is divided in two. The first part lists the various collections devoted entirely to Deng's published speeches and writings in both Chinese and English, as well as a number of significant other sources for relevant material. The second and larger part lists his individual speeches, writings, instructions and comments chronologically. The second part uses standard abbreviations, where appropriate, of the major sources identified in the first part.

In all cases, reference has only been made where a document has been obtained in the form described. It is reasonable to believe that there are more not currently available. In the first place, some of the sources listed in the Bibliography to this volume make reference to documents that could not be cited here. In any case, past experience with the CCP seems to indicate that archives, though not inexhaustible, take a while to publish their holdings.

In the catalogue, the first (and sometimes the only) reference to a speech or writing on a given date is to the Chinese version. If there is also an English version available, that is cited next. If there is no English version available, a translation is provided [in square brackets] of the title of the document in question immediately following the transliteration of the Chinese in *Hanyu pinyin*.

Not every source for each of Deng's speeches and writings is provided, even for those authorized by the CCP and openly published. The three volumes of *Selected Writings* have been treated as the most authoritative, and hence given priority in citation. Elsewhere, where more than one source is available, a judgement has been made about which source is likely to be most easily accessible to most people outside the PRC.

In most cases, there is reference to only one document for any specific date. However, in those cases where there are two or more documents with the same date, the details of each different speech or writing are provided separately. Where there are different versions of the same document available, details of all versions are provided, but within the same reference.

COLLECTIONS

Department for Research on Party Literature, Central Committee of the Communist Party of China, *Fundamental Issues in Present-Day China*, Beijing, Foreign Languages Press, 1987 [SCC]

Editorial Committee on Party Literature, Central Committee of the Communist Party of China, *Selected Works of Deng Xiaoping 1938–1965*, Beijing, Foreign Languages Press, 1992 [SWI]

Editorial Committee on Party Literature, Central Committee of the Communist Party of China, *Selected Works of Deng Xiaoping 1975–1982*, Beijing, Foreign Languages Press, 1984 [SWII]

Guofangbu zongzhengzhi zuozhanwei (ed.) *Gongfei yuanshi ziliao huibian: Deng Xiaoping yanlunji 1957–1980* [*Collection of CCP Materials: Deng Xiaoping's Speeches 1957–1980*] Taipei, Guofangbu, 1983 [DXS]

JinJiLuYu genjudi shiliaoxuan bianzhe, *JinJiLuYu genjudi shiliaoxuan* [*Collection of Historical Materials on JinJiLuYu Base Area*] 4 volumes: 1937–40 ; 1941–2; 1943–5; 1945–7, Beijing, Renmin chubanshe, 1989 [JJLYGS]

Taiyue genjudi shiliaoxuan bianzhe, *Taiyue genjudi shiliaoxuan* (3 vols) [*Collection of historical material on the Taiyue base area*] Beijing, Renmin chubanshe, 1990

Zhonggong zhongyang bangongting mishuju ziliaoshi, *Deng Xiaoping lun dangde jianshe* [*Deng Xiaoping on party development*] Beijing, Renmin chubanshe, 1990 [LDJ]

Zhonggong zhongyang wenxian bianji weiyuanhui, *Deng Xiaoping wenxuan 1938–1965* [*Selected writings of Deng Xiaoping 1938–1965*] Beijing, Renmin chubanshe, 1989 [DXWI]

Zhonggong zhongyang wenxian bianji weiyuanhui, *Deng Xiaoping wenxuan 1975–1982* [*Selected writings of Deng Xiaoping 1975–1982*] Beijing, Renmin chubanshe, 1983 [DXWII]

Zhonggong zhongyang wenxian bianji weiyuanhui, *Deng Xiaoping wenxuan Vol. III* [*Selected writings of Deng Xiaoping Vol. III*] Beijing, Renmin chubanshe, 1993 [DXWIII]

Zhonggong zhongyang wenxian yanjiushi (ed.) *Deng Xiaoping tongzhi zhongyao tanhua (eryue dao qiyue 1987)* [*Comrade Deng Xiaoping's most important talks (February to July 1987)*] Beijing, Renmin chubanshe, 1987

Zhonggong zhongyang wenxian yanjiushi (ed.) *Jianshe you Zhongguo tesede shehuizhuyi* [*Build socialism with Chinese characteristics*] Beijing, Renmin chubanshe, (2nd edition) 1987 [JZTS]

Zhonggong zhongyang wenxian yanjiushi (ed.) *Deng Xiaoping tongzhi lun jianchi sixiang jiben yuance fandui zichan jieji ziyouhua* [*Comrade Deng Xiaoping on adherence to the Four Cardinal Principles and opposition to bourgeois liberalization*] Beijing, Renmin chubanshe, 1989 [LJS]

Zhonggong zhongyang wenxian yanjiushi (ed.) *Deng Xiaoping tongzhi lun gaige kaifang* [*Comrade Deng Xiaoping on reform and openness*] Beijing, Renmin chubanshe, 1989 [LGK]

Zhonggong zhongyang wenxian yanjiushi (ed.) *Deng Xiaoping tongzhi lun jiaqiang dang tong renmin qunzhong de guanxi* [*Comrade Deng Xiaoping on strengthening the relationship between the party and the masses*] Beijing, Zhongguo gongren chubanshe, 1990 [LJDRG]

Zhonggong zhongyang wenxian yanjiushi (ed.) *Deng Xiaoping tongzhi lun minzhu yu fazhi* [*Comrade Deng Xiaoping on democracy and the legal system*] Beijing, Falu chubanshe, 1990 [LMF]

Zhonggong zhongyang wenxian yanjiushi (ed.) *Deng Xiaoping tongzhi lun jiaoyu* [*Comrade Deng Xiaoping discusses education*] Beijing, Renmin jiaoyu chubanshe, 1990 [LJ]

Zhonggong zhongyang wenxian yanjiushi and Zhonggong zhongyang tongyi zhanxian gongzuobu (eds) *Deng Xiaoping lun tongyi zhanxian* [*Deng Xiaoping on the United Front*] Beijing, Zhongyang wenxian chubanshe, 1991 [LTZ]

Zhonggong zhongyang xuanchuanbu, Zhonggong zhongyang wenxian yanjiushi (eds) *Deng Xiaoping tongzhi lun zhexue* [*Comrade Deng Xiaoping on philosophy*] Beijing, Xueyuan chubanshe, 1990 [LZ]

Zhonggong zhongyang xuanchuanbu wenyiju bianji, *Deng Xiaoping lun wenyi* [*Deng Xiaoping discusses art and literature*] Beijing, Renmin wenxue chubanshe, 1989 [LW]

Zhonggong zhongyang zhengce yanjiushi dang jianzu (ed.) *Mao Zedong, Deng Xiaoping lun Zhongguo guoqing* [*Mao Zedong and Deng Xiaoping on the state of the nation*] Beijing, Zhonggong zhongyang dangxiao chubanshe, 1992 [LZG]

Zhongguo renmin jiefangjun dierye zhanjun shiliaoxuan bianzhe, *Zhongguo renmin jiefangjun dierye zhanjun shiliaoxuan 1947–1949* [*Collection of historical material on the Second Field Army of the PLA*] Beijing, Renmin chubanshe, 1989 [DZS]

Zhongguo renmin jiefangjun junshi kexuanyuan, Zhonggong zhongyang wenxian yanjiushi (eds) *Deng Xiaoping lun guofang he jundui jianshe* [*Deng Xiaoping discusses national defence and the development of the military*] Beijing, Junshi kexue chubanshe, 1992 [LGJJ]

Zhongyang jiwei yanjiushi (ed.) *Deng Xiaoping lun xinshiqi dangfeng lianzheng jianshe* [*Deng Xiaoping discusses the development of an upright work-style in the party*] Beijing, Zhongguo fangzheng chubanshe, 1993 [LXDLJ]

SPEECHES, WRITINGS, INSTRUCTIONS AND COMMENTS

12 January 1938, 'Dongyuan xinbing ji xinbing zhengzhi gongzuo', DXWI p. 1–7. 'Mobilize new recruits and conduct political work among them', SWI pp. 9–14

10 March 1939, 'Deng zhengwei guanyu zai xin de huanjing xia women de gongzuo de zongjie baogao' ['Summary report by Political Commissar Deng on work under the new conditions'] JJLYGS 1937–1940 pp. 245–249

25 March 1939, 'Jianku fendou zhongde Jinan' ['South Hebei in Harsh Struggle'] in Zhongguo renmin daxue Zhonggong dangshixi ziliaoshi [China People's University, Department of Party History, Materials Section] (ed.) *Zhonggong dangshi jiaoxue cankao ziliao* [*Teaching and Reference Materials on CCP History*] KangRi zhanzheng shiqi [Period of the Sino-Japanese War] Volume II, Beijing, Renmindaxue, 1979, pp. 303–322

3 November 1939, 'Deng Xiaoping tongzhi zai Taibei junzheng weiyuanhui kuodahui shang de baogao' ['Report by Comrade Deng Xiaoping at enlarged meeting of the North Taihang Military and Administrative Committee'] in Taihang gefenqu dang de wenjian xuanji bianzhe, *Taihang gefenqu dang de wenjian xuanji* [*Selection of Documents on the Party in Each District of the Taihang Region (4 vols)*] 1944, Vol. I, 1939, pp. 114–120

15 November 1939, 'Liu Deng guanyu duifu Jinan mocha wenti gei Jinan junqu de zhishi' ['Liu and Deng directive to the South Hebei Military District on problems of friction'] JJLYGS 1937–1940 p. 300

28 November 1939, 'Liu Deng dui sansisi lu renwu de zhishi' ['Liu and Deng directive on the tasks of the 344th Brigade'] JJLYGS 1937–1940 p. 302

27 December 1939, 'Liu Deng guanyu zhengqu wan jun xiaceng guli qi shangceng de fangzhen gei gebu de zhishi' ['Liu and Deng directive to all departments on the policy of winning over the subordinate classes and isolating the upper classes'] JJLYGS 1937–1940 p. 303

23 January 1940, 'Liu Deng guanyu dui Zhu Shi de fenxi panduan ji wo zhi douzheng fangzhen gei Song Wang Chen Liu Li Xiao de zhishi' ['Liu and Deng directive to Song, Wang, Chen, Liu, Li and Xiao on Zhu and Shi, and our policy of struggle'] JJLYGS 1937–1940 pp. 305–306

31 January 1940, 'Liu Deng guanyu Jinan fan wan zuozhan gei Song Wang de zhishi' ['Liu and Deng directive to Song and Wang on fighting the diehards in South Hebei'] JJLYGS 1937–1940 pp. 308–309

3 February 1940, 'Liu Deng Li guanyu wajie Shi jun de zhishi' ['Liu, Deng and Li directive on the disintegration of Shi's troops'] JJLYGS 1937–1940 p. 310

6 February 1940, 'Liu Deng Li guanyu zai bushu zhong zhuyi de wenti gei Cheng Song de zhishi' ['Liu, Deng and Li directive to Cheng and Song on important military affairs'] JJLYGS 1937–1940 pp. 310–311

6 February 1940, 'Liu Deng Li guanyu Jinan fan wan zhanyi zhongxin gei Cheng Song de zhishi' ['Liu, Deng and Li directive to Cheng and Song on the central battlegrounds in South Hebei'] JJLYGS 1937–1940 p. 311

12 February 1940, 'Liu Deng guanyu Gao jun qingkuang ji Yang Yong bu xingdong gei Song Wang de zhishi' ['Liu and Deng directive to Wang and Song on the situation of Gao's army and the activities of Yang Yong's troops'] JJLYGS 1937–1940 p. 312

13 February 1940, 'Liu Deng guanyu weidong budui renwu gei Cheng Song Li Xiao de zhishi' ['Liu and Deng directive to Cheng, Song, Li and Xiao on the tasks of the eastern defence army'] JJLYGS 1937–1940 p. 312

14 February 1940, 'Liu Deng guanyu shi duhe shi weidong budui renwu gei Cheng Song Li Xiao de zhishi' ['Liu and Deng directive to Cheng, Song, Li and Xiao on the tasks of the eastern defence army as Shi's troops cross the river'] JJLYGS 1937–1940 p. 315

16 February 1940, 'Liu Deng guanyu jianjue xiaomie Shi jun yu weihe yi xi gei Cheng Song Li Xiao de zhishi' ['Liu and Deng directive to Cheng, Song, Li and Xiao on firmly annihilating Shi's troops on the Western side of the Wei river'] JJLYGS 1937–1940 p. 315

19 February 1940, 'Liu Deng guanyu zhuiji wanjun gei Cheng Song Chen Liu Xu Kun de zhishi' ['Liu and Deng directive to Cheng, Song, Chen, Liu, Xu and Kun on attacking the enemy'] JJLYGS 1937–1940 p. 316

29 February 1940, 'Liu Deng guanyu weidong zuozhan gei Cheng Song de zhishi' ['Liu and Deng directive to Cheng and Song on Eastern Defence'] JJLYGS 1937–1940 p. 332

7 March 1940, 'Liu Deng guanyu weidong zhanyi zhong liuri zhankuang xiang junwei, jizong de baogao' ['Liu and Deng report to the Military Committee and Army Headquarters on 6 March Eastern Defence Battle'] JJLYGS 1937–1940 p. 332

10 March 1940, 'Ci Wu She Lin zhanyi hou Deng Cai Li bao wojun ge bu zhudi' ['Deng, Cai and Li notice to troops after fighting in Cixian, Wuan, Shexian and Linxian'] JJLYGS 1937–1940 p. 359

December 1940, 'Yingjie yijiusiyi nian' ['Welcome to 1941'] JJLYGS 1941–1942 Vol. I, pp. 1–7

March 1941, 'Shiju he jige zhengce wenti: zai beiju taolun Jinan gongzuo shi de fayan' ['The current situation and questions of policy: talks at the symposium organized by the North China Bureau (of the CCP Central Committee) to discuss work in South Hebei'] JJLYGS 1941–1942 Vol. I, pp. 13–24

16 March 1941, 'Guanyu chengli JinJiYu bianqu linshi canyihui de tiyi' ['Proposal to Establish the Shanxi–Hebei–Henan Border Region Provisional Assembly'] in *Xinhua ribao* (Northern Edition) [*New China Daily*] 21 March 1941

15 April 1941, 'Dang yu KangRi minzhu zhengquan', DXWI pp. 8–21. 'The party and the anti-Japanese democratic government', SWI pp. 15–28

28 April 1941, 'Fandui mamu dakai Taihangqu de yanzhong jumian' ['Oppose carelessly opening up the Taihang Region'] JJLYGS 1941–1942 Vol. I, pp. 24–29

May 1941, 'Yierjiushi wenhua gongzuo de fangzhen renwu ji qi nuli fangxiang', DXWI pp. 22–29. 'The principles, tasks and orientation for cultural work in the 129th Division', SWI pp. 29–35

May 1941, 'Liu Deng guanyu fandui di qiulong zhengce gei Jinan de zhishi' ['Liu and Deng directive to South Hebei on combatting the enemy's "prisoner's cage" policy'] JJLYGS 1941–1942 Vol. I, pp. 66–67

June 1941, 'Liu Deng guanyu junqu ji difang wuzhuang jianshe qingxing xiang zhongyang junwei de baogao' ['Liu and Deng report to the CCP Central Military Committee on the strengthening of military districts and local armed forces'] JJLYGS 1941–1942 Vol. II, pp. 568–569

22 January 1942, 'Liu, Deng, Li, Cai, Huang dui Jinan xinsilu ji yifenqu zao di heji de zhishi' ['Liu, Deng, Li, Cai and Huang directive to South Hebei New 4th Brigade and 1st Sub-district'] JJLYGS 1941–1942 Vol. I, pp. 384–387

27 January 1942, 'Liu, Deng zhishi Jinan jieshou xinbalu buduan shouxi de jiaoxun' ['Liu and Deng directive to South Hebei on the lessons of attacks on the New 8th Brigade'] JJLYGS 1941–1942 Vol. I, p. 387

14 March 1942, 'Liu, Deng, Song zhi Chen, Wang, Liu dui Jinan sanyue sanri bushu de yijian' ['Liu, Deng and Song suggestions to Chen, Wang and Liu on the 3 March battle order in South Hebei'] JJLYGS 1941–1942 Vol. I, pp. 387–388

30 March 1942, 'Dui Taiyuequ gongzuo de jidian yijian' ['Suggestions on work in the Taiyue area'] TGS Vol. II, pp. 1–9

May 1942, 'Zai Zhongtiaoqu gaogan huiyishang de fayan' ['Talk at meeting of senior cadres in the Zhongtiao area'] TGS Vol. II, pp. 11–16

7 May 1942, 'Liu, Deng, Cai, Li, Song dui Jinan junshi zhishi' ['Liu, Deng, Cai, Li and Song directive on South Hebei Military Affairs'] JJLYGS 1941–1942 Vol. I, pp. 389–390

8 May 1942, 'Liu, Deng, Cai, Li, Huang, Song dui Jinan gaibian zuzhi de zhishi (jielu)' ['Liu, Deng, Cai, Li, Huang and Song directive to South Hebei on organizational changes'] JJLYGS 1941–1942 Vol. I, p. 390

17 June 1942, 'Deng Xiaoping zhengwei jiancha Zhongtiao gongzuo houzhi zhishi (huiyi jilu)' ['Political Commissar Deng Xiaoping directive after

investigation of work in the Zhongtiao area (Record of meeting)'] JJLYGS 1941–1942 Vol. I, pp. 155–157. 'Jiancha Zhongtiao gongzuo hou de zhishi' ['Directive after the investigation of work in the Zhongtiao area'] TGS Vol. II, pp. 17–22

4 July 1942, Liu Bocheng and Deng Xiaoping, 'Jinian women de zhanyou Zuo Quan tongzhi' ['Remember our Comrade-in-arms Comrade Zuo Quan'] in *Jiefang ribao [Liberation Daily]* 4 July 1942

20 August 1942, 'Zhengzhi gongshi yu dizhanqu tongbao de guanxi' ['The relationship between the political offensive and followers in enemy-occupied regions'] JJLYGS 1941–1942 Vol. I, pp. 215–216

23 August 1942, 'Taihangqu guomindang wenti' ['The Nationalist Party in the Taihang Area'] in Taihangdang liunianlai wenjian xuanji bubian bianzhe, *Taihangdang liunianlai wenjian xuanji bubian [Supplement to Collection of Documents on the Taihang Party during the last Six Years]* 1944, pp. 93–97

15 December 1942, 'Qingzhu Liu Bocheng tongzhi wushi shouchen', DXWI pp. 30–32. 'In celebration of the fiftieth birthday of Comrade Liu Bocheng', SWI pp. 36–38

26 January 1943, 'Wunianlai duidi douzheng de gailue zongjie yu jinhou duidi douzheng de fangzhen: Deng Xiaoping tongzhi zai Taihang fenju gaogan huiyishang de baogao' ['Summary of conflict with the enemy during the last five years and the consequent policy for struggle: Comrade Deng Xiaoping's report at Taihang Sub-bureau meeting of senior cadres'] JJLYGS 1943–1945 pp. 1–31 in *Zhandou [Combat]* No. 15, 15 March 1943, pp. 1–50

26 January 1943, 'Wunianlai duidi douzheng de gailue zongjie', DXWI pp. 33–44. 'A general account of the struggle against the enemy over the last five years', SWI pp. 39–50

26 January 1943, 'Dizhanqu de zuzhi gongzuo yu zhengce yunyong', DXWI pp. 45–64. 'Organizational work and application of policy in enemy-occupied areas', SWI pp. 51–68

20 February 1943 , 'Deng Xiaoping tongzhi zai Taihang fenju gaogan huiyi shang de jielun' ['Comrade Deng Xiaoping's conclusions at Taihang Sub-bureau meeting of senior cadres'] in *Zhandou [Combat]* No. 19, 25 March 1993, pp. 1–92

20 February 1943, 'Deng Xiaoping tongzhi zai Taihang fenju gaogan huiyishang de jielun diyierbufen' ['Parts 1 and 2 of the conclusions by Comrade Deng Xiaoping at the Taihang Sub-bureau meeting of senior cadres'] in Taihang dang de wenjian xuanji bianzhe, *Yijiusisannian Taihang dangde wenjian xuanji [Collection of Documents on the Taihang Party in 1943]* 1944, pp. 107–120

20 February 1943, 'Zhailu dier bufen: Zai xin xingshi xia de gongzuo fangzhen' ['Extracts from Part 2: Policies to be implemented in the new circumstances'] JJLYGS 1943–1945 pp. 31–35

20 February 1943, 'Genjudi jianshe yu qunzhong yundong', DXWI pp. 65–77. 'The establishment of base areas and the mass movement', SWI pp. 69–80

22 February 1943, 'Deng Xiaoping tongzhi eryue ershierri zai Taihang fenju gaogan huiyishang de jielun' ['Conclusions given by Comrade Deng Xiaoping

at Taihang Sub-bureau meeting of senior cadres on 22 February'] in *Kangzhan yilai xuanji* Vol. II, Part 2 [*Selected Documents in the War of Resistance*] 1944, pp. 103–157

2 July 1943, 'Taihangqude jingji jianshe', DXWI pp. 78–86. 'Economic development in the Taihang area', SWI pp. 81–89. 'Economic reconstruction in the Taihang region' in S. Gelder, *The Chinese Communists*, London, Gollancz, 1946, pp. 200–204

21 July 1943, 'Deng Xiaoping tongzhi zai fenju dangxiao xuefeng xuexi de zongjie baogao (xuexiao jilu wei jing benren jiaoyue)' ['Summary report on training and study style by Comrade Deng Xiaoping at sub-bureau party school (Party school record; unrevised by the speaker)'] in Taihangqu dangwei, *Zhengfeng wenjian huiji* [*Collection of Documents on Rectification*] Taihangqu dangweiyin, 1947, pp. 12–30

21 September 1943, 'Nuli shengchan, duguo kunnan, yingjie shengli: Deng zhengzhi weiyuan zai shengchan huiyi shang de baogao jilu' ['Work hard, overcome difficulties and prepare to greet victory: record of a report by Political Commissar Deng at a meeting on production'] JJLYGS 1943–1945 pp. 639–641

10 November 1943, 'Zai beifangju dangxiao zhengfeng dongyuanhui shangde jianghua', DXWI pp. 87–94. 'Speech at the mobilization meeting on rectification in the party school of the Northern Bureau', SWI pp. 90–96

January 1944, 'Dui jige wenti de yijian' ['Opinions on several matters'] JJLY 1941–1942 pp. 41–43

28 August 1944, 'Taihangqu guanyu shige wenti de dafu: Deng Xiaoping tongzhi gei dang zhongyang de baogao' ['Taihang Region's response to ten questions: Comrade Deng Xiaoping's report to the CCP Central Committee'] JJLYGS 1941–1942 pp. 43–46

23 December 1944, 'Deng Xiaoping tongzhi zai shadi yingxiong laodong yingxiong dahui shang de jianghua' ['Speech by Comrade Deng Xiaoping at a meeting of battle heroes from both the armed and production campaigns'] in Taihang dangde wenjian xuanji bianzhe, *1945nian Taihang dangde wenjian xuanji* [*Collection of Documents on the Taihang Party in 1945*] 1946, pp. 66–72

10 August 1945, 'Liu, Deng, Teng guanyu xunsu zhunbei duoqu dizhan chengshi ji jiaotong yaodao, bing zhunbei daji beifan zhi guomindang jun gei JinJiLuYu qu ge dangwei, junqu de zhishi' ['Liu, Deng and Teng directive to every party committee and military district in the JinJiLuYu region on immediately preparing to seize cities and vital communication lines, and to attack Nationalist Party troop advance in the North'] JJLYGS 1943–1945 p. 64

10 August 1945, 'Liu Deng Teng guanyu xunsu zhunbei duoqu chengshi he jiaotong yaodao, bing zhunbei daji beifan zhi Jiang Yan jun gei gequ dangwei, junqu de zhishi' ['Liu, Deng and Teng directive to every party committee and military district on immediately preparing to seize cities and vital communication lines and preparing to attack the advances by the armies of Chiang Kaishek and Yan Xishan in the North'] JJLYGS 1945–1947 p. 1

14 August 1945, 'Liu, Deng, Teng guanyu liji kuochong yezhanjun zhunbei daji beifan zhi Jiang Yan jun gei gequ dangwei, junqu de zhishi' ['Liu, Deng and Teng directive to every party committee and military district on immediately expanding the Field Army and preparing to attack the advance of troops led by Chiang Kai-shek and Yan Xishan in the North'] JJLYGS 1943–1945 p. 64, JJLYGS 1945–1947 pp. 1–2

26 August 1945, 'Liu, Deng, Teng, Bo guanyu Jinan budui zuozhan zhongdian he zhanshu de zhishi' ['Liu, Deng, Teng and Bo directive to troops in South Hebei on tactics and battle order'] JJLYGS 1943–1945 p. 65

28 August 1945, 'Liu, Deng, Teng, Bo dui JiLuYuqu zuozhan bushu de zhishi' ['Liu, Deng, Teng and Bo directive to troops in JiLuYu Area on the order of battle'] JJLYGS 1943–1945 p. 65

29 August 1945, 'Liu, Deng, Teng, Bo, Zhang guanyu junshi bushu wenti xiang dang zhongyang de baogao' ['Report from Liu, Deng, Teng, Bo and Zhang to the Party Central Committee on military affairs'] JJLYGS 1943–1945 p. 66

29 August 1945, 'Liu, Deng, Teng, Bo, Zhang guanyu zhunbei jinxing Shangdang zhanyi xiang zhongyangde baogao' ['Report of Liu, Deng, Teng, Bo and Zhang to the Party Central Committee on preparations for the Shangdang Battle'] JJLYGS 1945–1947 p. 21

3 September 1945, 'Liu, Deng zhishi JiLuYuqu zhuajin shijian, jixu xiang zhong, xiao chengshi jinjun, pohuai tielu kongzhi pinghan xian yiduan, wei pinghan zhanyi zuo zhunbei' ['Liu and Deng directive to the JiLuYu on best using time and preparing for battle by occupying small and intermediate cities, destroying railways, and controlling the railway between Beijing and Wuhan'] JJLYGS 1943–1945 p. 66

8 September 1945, 'Liu Deng wei que zhang Huanghe yanxian gexian ji saochu Yubei Jinnan wan wei gei taiyue junqu ji jingbei lu de zhishi' ['Liu and Deng directive to tighten control of the counties along the Yellow River and annihilate remnant enemy units in North Henan and South Shanxi'] JJLYGS 1945–1947 p. 50

29 September 1945, 'Liu Deng Zhang Li guanyu jianji Yan yuanjun ji quan qu zhan kuang xiang junwei de baogao' ['Report of Liu, Deng, Zhang and Li to the Military Committee on Annihilation of Yan's Relief Troops and the Frontier Situation'] JJLYGS 1945–1947 pp. 26–27

10 October 1945, 'Liu Deng guanyu PingHanlu zuozhan bushu gei yi, er zongdui shouzhang de zhishi' ['Liu and Deng directive to the leaders of the First and Second Columns on the order of battle for the action to take the Ping-Han Railway'] JJLYGS 1945–1947 p. 30

26 October 1945, 'Liu Deng wei dai ji zonggong gei yi, er, san zong shouzhang de zhishi' ['Liu and Deng directive to the leaders of the First, Second and Third Columns on waiting for the general offensive'] JJLYGS 1945–1947 p. 36

20 December 1945, 'Liu Deng Teng Bo Chen (Geng) dei juxing TongPu zuozhan xiang junwei de baogao' ['Liu, Deng, Teng, Bo and Chen (Geng) report to the Centre Military Committee on the Battle for the Tong-Pu Railway'] JJLYGS 1945–1947 p. 50

26 December 1945, 'Liu Deng Li guanyu lunxun ganbu ji xunlian wenti gei ge zongdui, ge junqu de zhishi' ['Liu, Deng and Li directive to all Columns and Military Districts on questions of the rotation of cadres and training'] JJLYGS 1945–1947 p. 73

3 January 1946, 'Liu Deng Li biaoyang qi zong JiLuYu junqu budui lian sanke cheng' ['Liu, Deng and Li praise the 7th column and JiLuYu troops for successively capturing three cities'] JJLYGS 1945–1947 p. 51

6 January 1946, 'Liu Deng Li wei suqing genjudi nei bai dian gei sizong ji Taiyue junqu shouzhang de zhishi' ['Liu, Deng and Li directive to the leaders of the Fourth Column and Taiyue Military District to annihilate enemy occupied sites inside the base area'] JJLYGS 1945–1947 p. 51

6 January 1946, 'Liu Deng Li wei suqing genjudi nei bai dian gei liuzong shouzhang de zhishi' ['Liu, Deng and Li directive to the leaders of the Sixth Column to annihilate enemy occupied sites inside the base area'] JJLYGS 1945–1947 pp. 51–52

6 January 1946, 'Liu Deng Li wei suqing genjudi nei bai dian gei er, qi zong Jinan, JiLuYu junqu shouzhang de zhishi' ['Liu, Deng and Li directive to the leaders of the Second and Seventh Columns and the South Hebei and JiLuYu Military Districts to annihilate enemy occupied sites inside the base areas'] JJLYGS 1945–1947 p. 52

7 January 1946, 'Liu Deng Li wei suqing genjudi nei bai dian gei Taihang junqu shouzhang de zhishi' ['Liu, Deng and Li directive to leaders of the Taihang Military District on annihilating enemy occupied sites inside the base area'] JJLYGS 1945–1947 p. 52

9 January 1946, 'Liu Deng wei kuozhan jiefangqu gei junqu, zongdui shouzhang de zhishi' ['Liu and Deng directive to all leaders of Military Districts and Columns to expand the liberated area'] JJLYGS 1945–1947 p. 52

10 January 1946, 'Liu Deng Li wei suqing genjudi nei bai dian gei Taihang junqu ji sanzongdui shouzhang de zhishi' ['Liu, Deng and Li directive to leaders of the Taihang Military District and the Third Column to annihilate the enemy occupied sites inside the base area'] JJLYGS 1945–1947 p. 53

10 January 1946, 'Liu Deng Li wei kuozhan jiefangqu gei sizong ji Taiyue junqu shouzhang de zhishi' ['Liu, Deng and Li directive to leaders of the Fourth Column and Taiyue Military District to expand the liberated area'] JJLYGS 1945–1947 p. 53

12 January 1946, 'Liu Deng Li wei anshi tingzhan gei ge zongdui, ge junqu shouzhang de zhishi' ['Liu, Deng and Li directive to leaders of all columns and military districts to schedule armistices'] JJLYGS 1945–1947 p. 53

22 January 1946, 'Liu Deng wei fanji Yanjun jingong gei sizong ji Taiyue junqu shouzhang de zhishi' ['Liu and Deng directive to leaders of the Fourth Column and the Taiyue Military District to counter the offensive of Yan's army'] JJLYGS 1945–1947 p. 54

24 January 1946, 'Liu Deng Li wei jianchi dui Yuanshi, Qinzhou, Liaocheng deng riwei de shouxiang bao junwei bing zhuan jianying dian' ['Telegraph to the Central Military Committee and Ye Jianying from Liu, Deng and Li insisting

on accepting surrender of the Japanese and puppet army in the region of Yuanshi, Qinzhou and Liaocheng'] JJLYGS 1945–1947 p. 55

February 1946, 'Liu Deng Bo Zhang Li guanyu Xinxiang, Linfen tanpan wenti bao zhongyang bing zhi Ye, Teng dian' ['Telegraph from Liu, Deng, Bo, Zhang and Li to the CCP Central Committee and Ye and Teng on problems in the Xinxiang and Linfen armistice negotiations'] JJLYGS 1945–1947 pp. 57–58

2 February 1946, 'Deng Bo Zhang Wang guanyu yijiusiliu nian budui zhengzhi gongzuo zhongxin de zhishi' ['Deng, Bo, Zhang and Wang directive on the focus of the army's political work in 1946'] JJLYGS 1945–1947 pp. 10–11

8 February 1946, 'Liu Deng Zhang Li wei fanji Yanjun xiang Houma jingong bao junwei bing zhuan jianying dian' ['Telegram to Central Military Committee and Ye Jianying from Liu, Deng, Zhang and Li on resistance to advances into the Houma by Yan's army'] JJLYGS 1945–1947 pp. 12–13

17 February 1946, 'Deng Xiaoping zhengwei wei *Renmin de jundui* bao chuangkan hao tici' ['Political Commissar Deng Xiaoping's dedication for the first issue of the magazine *The People's Troops*'] JJLYGS 1945–1947 p. 67

8 May 1946, 'Liu Deng guanyu jiaqiang da zhan zhunbei de zhishi' ['Liu and Deng directive on strengthening preparations for battle'] JJLYGS 1945–1947 p. 15

1 June 1946, 'Liu Deng Bo guanyu yi baofu zuozhan gongqu Quwo, Jiangxian, Wenxi gei sizong ji Taiyue junqu shouzhang de zhishi' ['Liu, Deng and Bo directive to leaders of the Fourth Column and Taiyue Military District to capture Quwo, Jiang County and Wenxi'] JJLYGS 1945–1947 p. 60

2 June 1946, 'Liu Deng Bo guanyu zuzhi baofu zuozhan gei san, qi zongdui ji Taihang, Ji Lu Yu junqu de zhishi' ['Liu, Deng and Bo directive to the Third and Seventh Columns as well as the Taihang and JiLuYu Military District to organize revenge military actions'] JJLYGS 1945–1947 p. 20

10 June 1946, 'Liu Deng Bo guanyu jianjue gongqu Qu, Jiang, Wen gei sizong ji Taiyue junqu shouzhang de zhishi' ['Liu, Deng and Bo directive to leaders of the Fourth Column and Taiyue Military District to resolutely capture Quwo, Jiang county and Wenxi'] JJLYGS 1945–1947 p. 61

27 June 1946, 'Liu Deng Bo guanyu quanqu zuozhan bushu xiang zhongyang junwei de baogao' ['Report from Liu, Deng and Bo to the Central Military Committee on arrangements for military action throughout the region'] JJLYGS 1945–1947 p. 99

20 July 1946, 'Liu Deng Bo guanyu Longhai zhanyi de zhunbei xiang junwei de baogao' ['Report from Liu, Deng and Bo to the Central Military Committee on preparations for the Longhai Battle'] JJLYGS 1945–1947 p. 139

6 August 1946, 'Liu Deng guanyu Longhai zhanyi faqi shijian xiang junwei de baogao' ['Report from Liu and Deng to the Central Military Committee on the start of the Longhai Battle'] JJLYGS 1945–1947 p. 139

25 August 1946, 'Deng Xiaoping zhengwei haozhao fadong zhixing jilu de qunzhong yundong' ['Political Commissar Deng Xiaoping calls for a mass movement to obey regulations'] JJLYGS 1945–1947 p. 255

25 August 1946, 'Liu silingyuan, Deng zhengzhi weiyuan qinzi zhengdun zhishu

dui qunzhong jilu' ['Commander Liu and Political Commissar Deng personally ensure codification of army rules and regulations'] JJLYGS 1945–1947 p. 256

10 September 1946, 'Liu Deng Teng Zhang guanyu Dingtao zhanyi zuozhan jingguo xiang junwei de baogao' ['Report from Liu, Deng, Teng and Zhang to the Central Military Committee on the experiences of the Dingtao battle'] JJLYGS 1945–1947 pp. 148–149

15 September 1946, 'Liu Deng Teng Zhang bao junwei zhuan Lin Biao tongzhi guanyu yejian zuozhan jingyan' ['Report from Liu, Deng, Teng and Zhang to the Central Military Committee and Comrade Lin Biao on experiences in night fighting'] JJLYGS 1945–1947 pp. 150–151

20 September 1946, 'Liu Deng Teng Zhang Li guanyu JinJiLuYu zhanchang di wo qingkuang xiang junwei de baogao' ['Report from Liu, Deng, Teng, Zhang and Li to the Central Military Committee on comparisons in strength between ourselves and the enemy on the JinJiLuYu battlefields'] JJLYGS 1945–1947 p. 151

9 October 1946, 'Liu Deng guanyu longguji yundong fangyu zhan xiang junwei de baogao' ['Report from Liu and Deng to the Central Military Committee on mobile defensive action in the Longguji area'] JJLYGS 1945–1947 p. 153

28 October 1946, 'Liu Deng guanyu jiuyuefen yilai zhandou qingkuang ji jingyan jiaoxun xiang junwei de baogao' ['Report from Liu and Deng to the Central Military Committee on battle situations and experiences since September'] JJLYGS 1945–1947 pp. 153–155

1 November 1946, 'Liu Deng Teng Zhang guanyu JiLuYu zhanchang jiben xingshi ji wo jun jinhou zuozhan qitu xiang zhongyang de baogao' ['Report from Liu, Deng, Teng and Zhang to the CCP Central Committee on the situation on the JiLuYu battlefield and on later campaign aims'] JJLYGS 1945–1947 pp. 159–164

10 November 1946, 'Liu Deng Zhang Li guanyu Juannan zhanyi jingguo yu jingyan xiang junwei de baogao' ['Report from Liu, Deng, Zhang and Li to the Central Military Committee on the processes and experiences of the Juannan battle'] JJLYGS 1945–1947 pp. 157–158

23 November 1946, 'Liu Deng guanyu Huaxian zhanyi jiankuang xiang junwei de baogao' ['Report from Liu and Deng to the Central Military Committee on the circumstances of the Hua County battle'] JJLYGS 1945–1947 pp. 164–165

18 December 1946, 'Liu Deng wei peihe Subei zuozhan zhi Shandong, Huazhong bing bao junwei dian' ['Telegram from Liu and Deng to Shandong, Central China and to the Central Military Committee on co-operation in the battle for North Jiangsu'] JJLYGS 1945–1947 p. 167

28 December 1946, 'Liu Deng Zhang guanyu peihe Huadong zuozhan xiang junwei de baogao' ['Report from Liu, Deng and Zhang to the Central Military Committee on co-operation in East China military action'] JJLYGS 1945–1947 pp. 167–168

1 January 1947, 'Wei *JiLuYu ribao* he *Zhanyoubao* xinnian tici' ['New Year's

inscription for *JiLuYu Daily* and *The Comrade*']

2 January 1947, 'Liu Deng guanyu xunji jianmie Wang Jingjiu bu xiang junwei de baogao' ['Report from Liu and Deng to the Central Military Committee on the opportunity to annihilate Wang Jingjiu's army'] JJLYGS 1945–1947 p. 168

21 January 1947, 'Liu Deng guanyu banyue zuozhan qingkuang xiang junwei de baogao' ['Report from Liu and Deng to the Central Military Committee on the battle situation during the last half month'] JJLYGS 1945–1947 pp. 168–169

28 January 1947, 'Liu Deng guanyu liu, qi zongdui chuji yu wanbian zhi Huaye bing bao junwei dian' ['Telegram from Liu and Deng to the East China Field Army and the Military Committee on sending the Sixth and Seventh columns to the boundary of Henan and Anhui'] JJLYGS 1945–1947 p. 171

30 January 1947, 'Liu Deng Zhang Li guanyu Jujinyu zhanyi jingyan xiang junwei de baogao' ['Report from Liu, Deng, Zhang and Li to the Central Military Committee on experiences in the battle for Jujinyu'] JJLYGS 1945–1947 pp. 170–171

1 February 1947, 'Liu Deng Zhang Li guanyu xiyin yiliu Wang Jingjiu bu xiang junwei de baogao' ['Report from Liu, Deng, Zhang and Li to the Central Military Committee on catching and destroying Wang Jingjiu's troops'] JJLYGS 1945–1947 p. 171

1 February 1947, 'Deng Xiaoping zhengwei guanyu YuWanbian zuozhan fangzhen xiang junwei de baogao' ['Report from Political Commissar Deng Xiaoping to the Central Military Committee on military action on the Henan and Anhui border'] JJLYGS 1945–1947 p. 172

7 February 1947, 'Liu Deng guanyu peihe Huadong zuozhan xiang junwei de qingshi' ['Report from Liu and Deng to the Central Military Committee on military activities in East China'] JJLYGS 1945–1947 p. 173

13 April 1947, 'Liu Deng guanyu An Qi jian zhankuang xiang junwei de baogao' ['Report from Liu and Deng to the Central Military Committee on the fighting between Anyang and Qixian'] JJLYGS 1945–1947 p. 197

19 April 1947, 'Liu Deng guanyu jian di kuaisu dier zongdui (sishijiu lu) deng bu jingguo xiang junwei de baogao' ['Report from Liu and Deng to the Central Military Committee on the annihilation of the enemy's Second Column (49th Brigade)'] JJLYGS 1945–1947 p. 198

11 June 1947, 'Liu Deng guanyu yuanlai jianchi Dabieshan douzheng youjidui de qingkuang xiang junwei de baogao' ['Report from Liu and Deng to the Central Military Committee on the condition of the original guerrilla troops in the Dabie Mountains'] DZS p. 62

21 June 1947, 'Deng zhengwei jieda shiju yu renwu zhong ji ge wenti de baogao (xi jilu gao wei jing benren shencha)' ['Political Commissar Deng Xiaoping's report provides some answers to questions about situations and tasks (unchecked by the reporter)'] JJLYGS 1945–1947 pp. 132–138

2 July 1947, 'Liu Deng guanyu yezhan jun chuzheng shi renyuan qingkuang' ['Liu and Deng on the conditions for organizing a Field Army'] DZS p. 182

17 August 1947, 'Liu Deng guanyu budui guo Shahe hou de bushu gei ge zongdui

shouzhang de zhishi' ['Liu and Deng directive to all leaders of columns on the battle order after crossing the Sha River'] DZS p. 61

25 August 1947, 'Liu Deng guanyu nanxia jingguo xiang junwei de baogao' ['Report from Liu and Deng to Central Military Committee on the process of moving south'] DZS p. 61

27 August 1947, 'Qiangjian gongge de Dabieshan genjudi', DXWI pp. 95–96. 'Build stable base areas in the Dabie Mountains', SWI pp. 97–98

27 August 1947, 'Liu Deng guanyu budui jinru Dabieshan hou de zhishi' ['Liu and Deng directive to leaders of all columns after having entered the Dabie Mountains'] DZS p. 63

29 August 1947, 'Liu Deng guanyu budui xiangnan zhankai de bushu' ['Liu and Deng directive on battle orders for troops moving South'] DZS pp. 63–64

30 August 1947, 'Liu Deng guanyu chuangjian gonggu de Dabieshan genjudi de zhishi' ['Liu and Deng directive on establishing a Dabie Mountains base area'] DZS p. 1

19 September 1947, 'Liu Deng guanyu suojian ling shuai jiguan banfa de zhishi' ['Liu and Deng directive on the method of reducing the size of leadership organizations'] DZS pp. 182–183

29 September 1947, 'Liu Deng guanyu budui xiang nan jidong de bushu' ['Liu and Deng's battle plan for troops moving South'] DZS pp. 63–64

6 October 1947, 'Liu Deng guanyu jinru Dabieshan hou de qingkuang he jinhou de xingdong xiang junwei de baogao' ['Report from Liu and Deng to the Central Military Committee on conditions after entering the Dabie Mountains and later activities'] DZS p. 65

20 October 1947, 'Liu Deng guanyu jiejue mianyi xunji jiandi de bushu' ['Liu and Deng make preparations for winter clothing and wait to eliminate the enemy'] DZS p. 66

12 November 1947, 'Liu Deng shouzhang haozhao shuli jianku pusu de zuofeng he fengqi' ['Liu and Deng call for leaders to establish the habits of hard work and plain living'] DZS pp. 120–121

7 December 1947, 'Liu Deng guanyu fensui diren weigong gei ge budui de zhishi' ['Liu and Deng directive to all troops to combat the enemy's encirclement'] DZS p. 70

8 December 1947, 'Liu Deng guanyu fensui diren weigong de jiben bushu xiang junwei de baogao' ['Report from Liu and Deng to the Central Military Committee on arrangements to combat seige'] DZS p. 70

17 December 1947, 'Liu Deng Li Li guanyu yezhanjun fenqian xingdong fensui diren weigong de bushu' ['Liu, Deng, Li (Xiannian) and Li (Xuefeng) order the Field Army to move against the enemy and raise the seige'] DZS p. 71

22 December 1947, 'Liu Deng guanyu he Huaye, Chen Xie bingtuan xietong fensui diren weigong de zuozhan yijian xiang junwei de baogao' ['Report from Liu and Deng to the Central Military Committee on co-operation with the East China Field Army and the Chen-Xie troops in order to raise the siege'] DZS pp. 71–72

26 December 1947, 'Liu Deng Li guanyu zai nei wai xian xun jian ruo di shenru

tugai de zhishi' ['Liu, Deng and Li directive on watching for an opportunity to eliminate the enemy from both sides of the border, and on deepening land reform'] DZS p. 72

January 1948, 'Deng Xiaoping tongzhi zai E Yu erdiwei huiyi shang de baogao' ['Comrade Deng Xiaoping reports to local party committee meeting in Hubei–Henan'] DZS pp. 11–17

1 January 1948, 'Liu Deng guanyu budui zuozhan xingdong de zhishi' ['Liu and Deng directive on military activities'] DZS p. 79

4 January 1948, 'Liu Deng guanyu diren dui Dabieshan weigong de tedian he women duice gei ge zongdui de zhishi' ['Liu and Deng directive on the characteristics of the enemy's siege of the Dabie Mountains, and on counter-measures'] DZS p. 80

25 January 1948, 'Liu Deng guanyu jiang budui zai zuo fenqian xingdong xiang junwei de baogao' ['Report from Liu and Deng to the Central Military Committee with request for further troops'] DZS p. 80

26 January 1948, 'Liu Deng guanyu he Huaye, Chen Xie bingtuan xietong zuozhan zhi yijian xiang junwei de baogao' ['Report from Liu and Deng to the Central Military Committee on co-operation with the East China Field Army and Chen-Xie army in battle'] DZS p. 81

30 January 1948, 'Deng Xiaoping tongzhi guanyu Dabieshan de jieji qingkuang yu jige zhengce wenti xiang Mao zhuxi de baogao' ['Report from Comrade Deng Xiaoping to Chairman Mao on the policies and class conditions in the Dabie Mountains'] DZS pp. 9–10

9 February 1948, 'Deng Xiaoping zhengwei guanyu budui qingkuang xiang junwei de baogao' ['Political Commissar Deng Xiaoping reports to the Central Military Committee on the conditions of the troops'] DZS p. 81

12 February 1948, 'Liu Deng guanyu budui zhuan chu Dabieshan he Huaye, Chen Xie bingtuan de xietong yijian gei Su Yu bing bao junwei dian' ['Telegram from Liu and Deng to Su Yu and the Central Military Committee on withdrawal from the Dabie Mountains and co-operation with the East China Field Army and the Chen-Xie army'] DZS p. 82

6 March 1948, 'Deng Xiaoping zhengwei zai ye zhi ganbu hui shang guanyu fangong xingshi yu zhengdang wenti de baogao (xi jilu gao wei jing benren shenyue)' ['Political Commissar Deng Xiaoping reports on conditions for warfare and consolidating the party's organization at a meeting of Field Army cadres (unrevised by the speaker)'] DZS pp. 123–128

8 March 1948, 'Deng Xiaoping tongzhi guanyu jinru Dabieshan hou ji ge celue wenti xiang Mao zhuxi de baogao' ['Comrade Deng Xiaoping reports to Chairman Mao on policies after entering the Dabie Mountains'] DZS pp. 17–18

21 March 1948, 'Liu Deng guanyu xia yi bu zuozhan xingdong yijian xiang junwei de baogao' ['Report from Liu and Deng to the Central Military Committee on the next military actions'] DZS p. 83

23 March 1948, 'Deng zhengwei guanyu budui gongzuo wenti de baogao (xi jilu gao wei jing benren shenyue)' ['Political Commissar Deng reports on the

army's work matters (unrevised by the speaker)'] DZS pp. 129–131

April 1948, 'Jiaqiang dui dang de zhengce, celue de xuexi' ['Strengthen the learning of the party's policies and strategies'] DZS pp. 133–134

6 April 1948, 'Liu Deng guanyu fensui di hewei Linquan, Shenqiu diqu de zuozhan bushu' ['Liu and Deng battle orders for resisting seige in Linquan and Shenqiu'] DZS p. 88

13 April 1948, 'Liu Deng guanyu Fuyang zuozhan hou zhongyuan qingkuang xiang junwei de baogao' ['Report from Liu and Deng to the Central Military Committee on conditions in the Central Plains after activities in Fuyang'] DZS pp. 88–89

20 April 1948, 'Liu Deng guanyu Wanxi zhanyi de bushu' ['Liu and Deng battle orders for the Battle of Wanxi'] DZS p. 89

25 April 1948, 'Yuejin Zhongyuan de shengli xingshi yu jinhou de zhengce celue', DXWI pp. 97–108. 'The situation following our triumphant advance to the Central Plains and our future policies and strategy', SWI pp. 99–109

30 April 1948, 'Liu Deng da Lin Biao, Luo Ronghuan tongzhi suo wen zhu shi dian' ['Telegram from Liu and Deng to Comrades Lin Biao and Luo Ronghuan'] DZS pp. 30–31

1 May 1948, 'Liu Deng dui jiuzong de zuozhan zhishi' ['Liu and Deng directive to the Ninth Column on military action'] DZS p. 89

9 May 1948, 'Deng Xiaoping tongzhi guanyu zhongyuanqu de zhengzhi xingshi yu dangqian renwu xiang Mao zhuxi de baogao' ['Comrade Deng Xiaoping reports to Chairman Mao on political conditions in the Central Plains Area and the current tasks'] DZS p. 33

10 May 1948, 'Liu Deng guanyu kuozhang Wanxi zhanyi zhanguo de bushu' ['Liu and Deng battle orders for enlarging the victory of the Battle of Wanxi'] DZS p. 92

13 May 1948, 'Liu Deng guanyu Wanxi zhanyi zhong kaizhan zhengzhi gongshi de zhishi' ['Liu and Deng directive on carrying out the political offensive in the Battle of Wanxi'] DZS p. 89

15 May 1948, 'Liu Chen Deng dui peihe Su bingtuan nandu zuozhan de bushu' ['Liu, Chen and Deng battle orders to Su Yu's army group as it heads South'] DZS p. 92

27 May 1948, 'Liu Deng guanyu Wandong zhanyi de jiben bushu' ['Basic arrangements by Liu and Deng for Battle of Wandong'] DZS p. 93

30 May 1948, 'Liu Chen Deng guanyu Wandong zhanyi de bushu' ['Liu, Chen and Deng battle orders for Battle of Wandong'] DZS p. 93

6 June 1948, 'Guanche shixing zhonggong zhongyang guanyu tugai yu zhengdang gongzuo de zhishi', DXWI pp. 109–124. 'Carry out the Party Central Committee's directive on the work of land reform and of party consolidation', SWI pp. 110–126

13 June 1948, 'Liu Deng guanyu Xiangfan zuozhan de bushu' ['Liu and Deng's battle orders for Xiangfan fighting'] DZS pp. 103–104

15 June 1948, 'Liu Chen Deng guanyu zuji di shiba jun baozhang Huaye zuozhan de bushu' ['Liu, Chen and Deng's battle orders to intercept the enemy's 18th

Army and protect the East China Field Army'] DZS p. 104

2 July 1948, 'Liu Chen Deng guanyu di shiba jun yi bei xiyin fanhui Xiping hou wo jun de bushu' ['Liu, Chen and Deng's battle orders after the enemy's 18th Army was turned back at Xiping'] DZS p. 104

5 July 1948, 'Liu Chen Deng guanyu zuji Hulian bingtuan de bushu xiang junwei de baogao' ['Report from Liu, Chen and Deng to the Central Military Committee on arrangements for intercepting the Hulian army group'] DZS p. 105

6 July 1948, 'Liu Chen Deng guanyu budui qingkuang he zuozhan xingdong xiang junwei de baogao' ['Report from Liu, Chen and Deng to the Central Military Committee on troop conditions and military actions'] DZS p. 105

7 July 1948, 'Liu Chen Deng guanyu Xiangfan zuozhan qingkuang xiang junwei de baogao' ['Report from Liu, Chen and Deng to the Central Military Committee on military activities at Xianfan'] DZS p. 106

8 July 1948, 'Liu Chen Deng guanyu budui zhuanyi zhi PingHanlu xi xiuzheng xiang junwei de baogao' ['Report from Liu, Chen and Deng to the Central Military Committee on troop movements to the west side of the Ping-Han railway'] DZS p. 106

15 July 1948, 'Liu Chen Deng guanyu zuji di Hulian, Wu Shaozhou bingtuan zuozhan qingkuang xiang junwei de baogao' ['Report from Liu, Chen and Deng to the Central Military Committee on intercepting Hulian and Wu Shaozhou armies'] DZS pp. 106–107

13 August 1948, 'Liu Chen Deng guanyu qiuji zuozhan fangan xiang zhongyang junwei de baogao' ['Report from Liu, Chen and Deng to the Central Military Committee on autumn manoeuvres'] DZS pp. 214–215

24 August 1948, 'Deng Xiaoping tongzhi guanyu jinhou jinru xinqu de jidian yijian xiang Mao zhuxi de baogao' ['Comrade Deng Xiaoping reports to Chairman Mao after entering new areas'] DZS pp. 43–46. 'Guanyu jinhou jinru xinqu de jidian yijian', DXWI pp. 125–130. 'Some suggestions concerning our entry into new areas in the future', SWI pp. 127–132

31 August 1948, 'Deng Xiaoping zhengwei guanyu muqian xingshi yu renwu de baogao (xi jilu gao wei jing benren shenyue)' ['Political Commissar Deng Xiaoping's report on the current situation and tasks (unrevised record)'] DZS p. 2

6 September 1948, 'Deng Xiaoping tongzhi guanyu kefu wu zhengfu wu jilu gei Zhongyuanju de laixin' ['Comrade Deng Xiaoping's letter to Central Plains Bureau on overcoming anarchy and lawlessness'] DZS pp. 202–203

6 September 1948, 'Liu Chen Deng Zhang guanyu Wanque zhanyi jihua xiang junwei de baogao' ['Report from Liu, Chen, Deng and Zhang to the Central Military Committee on plans for the Wanque Campaign'] DZS p. 215

14 October 1948, 'Liu Chen Deng Deng Li guanyu gong Zhengzhou de shijian ji bushu xiang junwei de qingshi' ['Liu, Chen, Deng, Deng (Zihui) and Li report to the Central Military Committee on the battle order for the attack on Zhengzhou'] DZS pp. 216–217

22 October 1948, 'Chen Deng guanyu zhanling zhengzhou hou zhuli dongjin

jihua xiang junwei de baogao' ['Chen and Deng report to the Central Military Committee on plans to move east of main forces after occupying Zhengzhou'] DZS p. 218

24 October 1948, 'Chen Deng guanyu zhuli dongjin hou sange zuozhan fangan xiang junwei de qingshi' ['Chen and Deng report to the Central Military Committee on conditions at the front after the main forces moved east'] DZS p. 219

2 November 1948, 'Chen Deng guanyu qianzhi di Qiu Qingquan, Sun Yuanliang bingtuan xin de zuozhan fangan xiang junwei de qingshi' ['Chen and Deng report to the Central Military Committee on a new plan to combat Qiu Qingquan and Sun Yuanliang's forces'] DZS pp. 219–220

5 November 1948, 'Chen Deng guanyu qiri faqi dui di Liu Ruming de zhandou xiang junwei de qingshi' ['Chen and Deng inform the Central Military Committee about launching an attack on Liu Ruming's troops on 7 November'] DZS p. 221

14 November 1948, 'Liu Chen Deng guanyu jianji Huang Wei bingtuan zhi fangan xiang junwei de baogao' ['Liu, Chen and Deng report to the Central Military Committee on plans to erradicate Huang Wei's Army'] DZS pp. 224–225

5 December 1948, 'Liu Chen Deng dui Huang Wei zuozhan zong gongji de mingling' ['Liu, Chen and Deng order attack on Huang Wei's troops'] DZS p. 230

22 December 1948, 'Deng Xiaoping zhengwei guanyu Zhongye xiuzheng ban yue he zhunbei da Li Yannian bingtuan xiang junwei de baogao' ['Political Commissar Deng Xiaoping reports to the Central Military Committee on the intention of the Central Plains Field Army to rest for half a month and prepare for attack on Li Yannian's troops'] DZS p. 231

25 December 1948, 'Deng Zhang guanyu zhongye zhunbei jiaru dui Du Yiming jituan zuozhan huo zuji Bengbu bei yuan zhi di de bushu xiang junwei de baogao' ['Deng and Zhang report to the Central Military Committee on preparations by the Central Plains Field Army to attack either Du Yiming's troops or the Northward reinforcements from Bengbu'] DZS p. 232

3 January 1949, 'Deng Zhang guanyu jianmie Huang Wei bingtuan zuozhan chubu zongjie xiang junwei de baogao' ['Deng and Zhang report to the Central Military Committee on the military action to annihilate Huang Wei's troops'] DZS pp. 233–236

3 January 1949, 'Zhongyuan junqu gei Huai Hai zhanyi guangrong fushang tongzhi de yi feng xin Liu Bocheng, Chen Yi, Deng Xiaoping, Deng Zihui, Zhang Jichun, Li Da' ['Letter from the Central Plains Army Region to glorious comrades wounded in the Huai-Hai battle: Liu Bocheng, Chen Yi, Deng Xiaoping, Deng Zihui, Zhang Jichun, Li Da'] DZS pp. 308–309

11 January 1949, 'Deng Xiaoping tongzhi guanyu jundui wenti xiang Mao zhuxi de zonghe baogao' ['Comrade Deng Xiaoping reports to Chairman Mao on army matters'] DZS pp. 212–213

31 March 1949, 'JingHuHang zhanyi shishi gangyao', DXWI pp. 131–134.

'Outline Plan for the Nanjing–Shanghai–Hangzhou Campaign', SWI pp. 133–135

19 July 1949, 'Dapo diguo zhuyi fengsuo zhidao', DXWI p. 135. 'Break the blockade imposed by the imperialists', SWI p. 137

4 August 1949, 'Cong dujiang dao zhanling Shanghai', DXWI pp. 136–141. 'From the crossing of the Yangtze to the capture of Shanghai', SWI pp. 138–142

12 November 1949, 'Guizhou xinqu gongzuo de zhenglue', DXWI pp. 142–144. 'Tactics for working in the new area of Guizhou', SWI pp. 143–145

11 April 1950, 'Guanyu Xinan gongzuo qingkuang de baogao' ['Report on work conditions in the South-west'] in *Zhengfu gongzuo baogao huibian 1950* [*Collection of Government Work Reports for 1950*] pp. 989–991

16 May 1950, 'Zai xinanqu xinwen gongzuo huiyi shangde baogao', DXWI pp. 145–150. 'Report delivered at a conference on the press in South-west China', SWI pp. 146–151

6 June 1950, 'Kefu muqian xinan dangnei de buliang qingxiang', DXWI pp. 151–160. 'Overcome the current unhealthy tendencies in the party organizations of South-west China', SWI pp. 152–161

21 July 1950, 'Guanyu xinan shaoshu minzu wenti', DXWI pp. 161–171. 'The question of minority nationalities in the South-west', SWI pp. 162–171

18 January 1951, 'Dang yao guowen xuexiao jiaoyu gongzuo' ['The Party must concern itself with schools and education'] LJ pp. 1–2

26 March 1951, 'Quandang zhongshi zuo tongyi zhanxian gongzuo', DXWI pp. 172–176. 'The entire Party should attach more importance to united front work', SWI pp. 172–176

9 May 1951, 'Guanyu xinan diqu de tugai qingkuang he jingyan', DXWI pp. 177–180. 'Agrarian reform in South-west China and our experience', SWI pp. 177–181

11 February 1953, 'Guanyu "Zhonghuo renmin gongheguo quanguo renmin daibiao dahui ji difang geji renmin daibiao dahui xuanjufa" caoan de shuoming' ['Explanation of the Draft Electoral Law for the PRC National People's Congress and Local People's Congress'] in *Renmin ribao* [*People's Daily*] 3 March 1953

13 January 1954, 'Caizheng gongzuo de liutiao fangzhen', DXWI pp. 181–185. 'Six Principles for financial work', SWI pp. 182–186

25 January 1954, 'Difang caizheng gongzuo yao you quanju guannian', DXWI pp. 186–188. 'The overall situation should be taken into consideration in local financial work', SWI pp. 187–189

6 February 1954, 'Jiao'ao ziman shi tuanjie de dadi', DXWI pp. 189–196. 'Conceit and complacency are the arch-enemy of unity', SWI pp. 190–196

1 March 1954, 'Deng Xiaoping, Chen Yi, Tan Zhenlin guanyu Rao Shushi wenti zuotanhui de baogao' in *Zhonggong dangshi jiaoxue cankao ziliao* [*Reference Materials for Teaching the History of the CCP*] Vol. 20, pp. 272–276. 'Report of Deng Xiaoping, Chen Yi and Tan Zhenlin concerning the discussion meeting on the Rao Shushi question' in Frederick C. Teiwes, *Politics at Mao's*

Court, New York, M. E. Sharpe, 1990, pp. 245–252

8 April 1954, 'Zhuyi zhongxuede jilu jiaoyu' ['Pay attention to discipline and education in middle schools'] LJ p. 3

17 June 1954, 'Guanyu Yijiuwusinian guojia yusuan caoan de baogao' ['Report on Draft National Budget for 1954'] in *Xinhua yuebao* [*New China Monthly*] No. 6, 1954, pp. 117–120

19 June 1954, 'Quanguo jiceng xuanju shengli wancheng' ['The whole country victoriously completes elections'] in *Renmin ribao* [*People's Daily*] 20 June 1954. 'Guanyu jiceng xuanju gongzuo wancheng qingkuang debaogao' in *Zhonggong dangshi jiaoxue cankao ziliao* [*Reference Materials for Teaching the History of the CCP*] Vol. 20, pp. 329–330

9 July 1954, 'Banhao xuexiao, peiyang ganbu', DXWI pp. 197–199. 'Run our Schools well and train cadres', SWI pp. 197–199

21 March 1955, 'Guanyu Gao Gang, Rao Shushi fandang lianmeng de baogao' in *Zhonggong dangshi jiaoxue cankao ziliao* [*Reference Materials for Teaching the History of the CCP*] Vol. 20, pp. 512–525. 'Report on the Gao Gang, Rao Shushi Anti-party Alliance' in Frederick C. Teiwes, *Politics at Mao's Court*, New York, M. E. Sharpe, 1990, pp. 254–276

28 September 1955, 'Zai Zhongguo qingnian shehui zhuyi jianshi jiji fenzi dahui shangde jianghua' ['Speech at a national youth conference of activists in the construction of socialism'] in *Xinhua yuebao* No. 10, 1955, p. 7

16 September 1956, 'Guanyu xiugai dangde zhangcheng de baogao', DXWI pp. 200–244. 'Report on the revision of the constitution of the Communist Party of China', SWI pp. 200–238

17 November 1956, 'Malie zhuyi yao yu Zhongguo de shiji qingkuang xiangjiehe', DXWI pp. 245–248. 'Integrate Marxism-Leninism with the concrete conditions of China', SWI pp. 239–241

8 April 1957, 'Jinhou de zhuyao renwu shi gao jianshe', DXWI pp. 249–257. 'Our chief task ahead is building up the country', SWI pp. 242–249

8 April 1957, 'Gongchandang yao jieshou jiancha', DXWI pp. 258–262. 'The Communist Party must accept supervision', SWI pp. 250–254

15 May 1957, 'Zai Zhongguo xinminzhu zhuyi qingniantuan disanci quanguo daibiao dahui shangde zhuci', DXWI pp. 263–267. 'Congratulatory speech delivered at the Third National Congress of the New Democratic Youth League of China', SWI pp. 255–258

23 September 1957, 'Guanyu zhengfeng yundong de baogao' ['Report on the rectification movement'] in *Renmin ribao* [*People's Daily*] 19 October 1957. 'Report on the rectification campaign by Teng Hsiao-p'ing, General Secretary of the Party's Central Committee, September 23, 1957, to the Third Plenary Session (enlarged) of the Eighth Central Committee' in R. R. Bowie and J. K. Fairbank (eds) *Communist China, 1955–1959: Policy documents with analysis*, Harvard University Press, 1965, pp. 341–363

9 October 1957, 'Zai baju sanzhongquanhui shangde zongjie fayan yaodian (jielu)' ['Major points of Summary Speech at 3rd plenum of 8th Central Committee'] in *Zhonggong dangshi jiaoxue cankao ziliao* [*Reference Materi-*

als for Teaching the History of the CCP] Vol. 22, pp. 312–313

7 April 1958, 'Ban jiaoyu yi yao puji er yao tigao' ['Develop education first through popularization then by raising standards'] LJ pp. 16–19

1 October 1959, 'Zhongguo renmin datuanjie he shijie renmin datuanjie' ['The Great Unity of the Chinese People and the Great Unity of the People of the World'] in *Hongqi [Red Flag]* No. 19, 1959, pp. 26–32 (written for *Pravda* to Greet the Tenth Anniversary of the Establishment of the PRC) in *Ten Glorious Years*, pp. 90–104

20 May 1960, 'Zhichi Sulian zhengyi liyang fandui Meiguo pohuai shounao huiyi' ['Support the USSR's Righteous Stand in Opposing US Destruction of the Summit Meeting'] in *Hongqi [Red Flag]* No. 11, 1960, pp. 1–3

25 March 1960, 'Zhengquedi xuanchuan Mao Zedong sixiang', DXWI pp. 268–270. 'Correctly disseminate Mao Zedong Thought', SWI pp. 259–260

2 June 1960, 'Deng Xiaoping tongzhi daibiao Zhonggong zhongyang zai gongji huishangde daoci' ['Comrade Deng Xiaoping represents the CCP Central Committee in speech at memorial meeting'] in *Renmin ribao [People's Daily]* 3 June 1960

23 October 1961, 'Tichang shenru xizhi de gongzuo', DXWI pp. 271–276. 'Encourage thorough and meticulous work', SWI pp. 261–266

23 November 1961, 'Dapi tifa nianqing de jishu ganbu', DXWI pp. 277–278. 'Promote large numbers of young technicians', SWI pp. 267–268

6 February 1962, 'Zai kuodade zhongyang gongzuo huiyi shangde jianghua', DXWI pp. 279–299. 'Speech delivered at an enlarged working conference of the Party Central Committee', SWI pp. 269–286

11 May 1962, 'Kefu dangqian kunnan de banfa', DXWI pp. 300–303. 'Measures for overcoming our present difficulties', SWI pp. 287–291

7 July 1962, 'Zenyang huifu nongye shengchan', DXWI pp. 304–309. 'Restore agricultural production', SWI pp. 292–296

29 November 1962, 'Shizhengdang de ganbu wenti', DXWI pp. 310–315. 'Questions concerning cadres of the Party in power', SWI pp. 297–302

March 1963, 'Wei *Guangxi geming huiyilu* tici' ['Dedication for Memoirs of the Revolution in Guangxi'] LJ p. 22

March 1963, 'Wei xuexi Lei Feng tongzhi tici' ['Inscription to Learn from Comrade Lei Feng'] LJ p. 23

24 January 1964, 'Deng Xiaoping daizongli baogao guoji shiwu wenti' ['Acting Premier Deng Xiaoping Reports on World Affairs'] in *Renmin ribao [People's Daily]* 25 January 1964

6 July 1964, 'Mao Zedong sixiang hongqi zujin woguo qingnian geminghua' ['The red flag of Mao Zedong Thought Advances the Revolutionization of China's Youth] in *Renmin ribao [People's Daily]* 7 July 1964

June and December 1965, 'Jianshe yige chengshu de you zhandouli de dang', DXWI pp. 316–326. 'Build a mature and combat-effective Party', SWI pp. 303–312

20 July 1965, 'Zhongguo gongchandang daibiao tuanzhang Deng Xiaoping

tongzhide heci' ['Congratulatory speech by Comrade Deng Xiaoping as head of CCP delegation (to the Conference of the Romanian Communist Party)' in *Renmin ribao* [*People's Daily*] 22 July 1965

6 May 1966, 'Women jianjue fandui Meidiguozhuyi he Sulian xiandai xiuzhengzhuyi ba guoji wuchan jieji he shijie renmin de geming shiye tuixiang qianjin' ['We must resolutely oppose American imperialism and Soviet modern revisionism, and carry forward the revolution of the people of the world'] DXS pp. 63–71

2 August 1966, 'Zai Beijing da hongweibing huiyi shangde ziwo jianshi' ['Self-examination at Large Red Guard Meeting'] DXS pp. 72–75

23 October 1966, in *Zhonggong yanjiu* [*Research on Chinese Communism*] Vol. 3, No. 11, November 1969, pp. 91–94. 'Self-criticism at Work Conference of the Central Committee' in *Chinese Law and Government*, Vol. 3, No. 4, pp. 278–290

10 April 1974, 'Zai lianda diliuju tebie huiyi shangde fayan' ['Speech at the Sixth Special Session of the UN'] in *Zhonggong dangshi jiaoxue cankao ziliao* [*Reference Materials for Teaching the History of the CCP*] Vol. 27, pp. 135–139 in Chi Hsin, *Teng Hsiao-ping*, Hong Kong, Cosmos Books, 1978, pp. 163–175

2 October 1974, 'Zhongguo jingji wenti' ['China's Economic Problems'] DXS pp. 96–101

25 January 1975, 'Jundui yao zhengdun', DXWII pp. 1–3. 'The Army needs to be consolidated', SWII pp. 11–13

5 March 1975, 'Quandang jiangdaju, ba guomin jingji gaoshangqu', DXWII pp. 4–7. 'The whole Party should take the overall interest into account and push the economy forward', SWII pp. 14–17

29 May 1975, 'Dangqian gangtie gongye bixu jiejuede jige wenti', DXWII pp. 8–11. 'Some problems outstanding in the iron and steel industry', SWII pp. 18–22

4 July 1975, 'Jiaqiang dangde lingdao, zhengdun dangde zuofeng', DXWII pp. 12–14. 'Strengthen party leadership and rectify the party's style of work', SWII pp. 23–26

14 July 1975, 'Jundui zhengdun de renwu', DXWII pp. 15–24. 'The task of consolidating the Army', SWII pp. 27–38

3 August 1975, 'Guanyu guofang gongye qiye de zhengdun', DXWII pp. 25–27. 'On consolidating national defence enterprises', SWII pp. 39–42

18 August 1975, 'Guanyu fazhan gongye de jidian yijian', DXWII pp. 28–31. 'Some comments on industrial development', SWII pp. 43–46

27 September/4 October 1975, 'Gefangmian dou yao zhengdun', DXWII pp. 32–34. 'Things must be put in order in all fields', SWII pp. 47–50

15 January 1976, 'Zai Zhou zongli zhuidaohui shangde daoci' ['Speech at Memorial Meeting for Premier Zhou'] DXS pp. 102–106

January 1976, 'Deng Xiaoping Zibaishu' ['Deng Xiaoping's Self-Criticism'] in Guofangbu zongzhengzhi zuozhanwei (ed) *Gongfei yuanshi ziliao huibian: Pipan Deng Xiaoping ziliao* [*Collection of CCP Materials: Materials Criticiz-*

ing Deng Xiaoping] Taipei, Guofangbu, 1983, pp. 163–171

10 October 1976, 'Gei Wang Dongxing tongzhi chuan Hua Guofeng tongzhi de xin' ['A letter for Comrade Wang Dongxing to pass on to Comrade Hua Guofeng'] DXS p. 108

10 April 1977, 'Gei Hua Guofeng tongzhi Ye Jianying tongzhi de xin' ['A letter to Comrade Hua Guofeng and Comrade Ye Jianying'] DXS pp. 109–110

24 May 1977, '"Liangge fanshi" bufuhe Makesizhuyi', DXWII pp. 35–36. 'The "Two Whatevers" do not accord with Marxism', SWII pp. 51–52

24 May 1977, 'Zunzhong zhishi, zunzhong rencai', DXWII pp. 37–38. 'Respect knowledge, respect trained personnel', SWII pp. 53–54

20 July 1977, 'Zai Zhonggong zhongyang shiju sanzhong quanhuide jianghua', DXS pp. 111–122. 'Speech at 3rd plenum of 10th Central Committee' in *Issues and Studies*, July 1978, pp. 103–108

20 July 1977, 'Zai Beijing zhaoji Ge sheng, shi, zizhiqu dangwei zeren ren zuotanhui shangde jianghua' ['Speech at a Beijing Discussion Meeting of Responsible People from Every Province, Municipality and Autonomous Region'] DXS pp. 123–127

21 July 1977, 'Wanzhengde zhunquede lijie Mao Zedong sixiang', DXWII pp. 39–44. 'Mao Zedong Thought must be correctly understood as an integral whole', SWII pp. 55–60

8 August 1977, 'Guanyu kexue he jiaoyu gongzuo de jidian yijian', DXWII pp. 45–55. 'Some comments on work in science and education', SWII pp. 61–72

18 August 1977, 'Fayang dangde youliang chuantong he zuofeng' ['Develop the party's excellent traditions and workstyle'] in Zhonggong zhongyang dangxiao dangjian jiaoyanshi (ed.) *Dangfeng wenti* [*Questions of Party Work-style*] Beijing, Zhonggong zhongyang dangxiao chubanshe, 1981, pp. 2–3

18 August 1977, 'Zai Zhonggong shiyi dahui shangde bimoci' ['Closing Address to the CCP 11th Congress'] in *New China News Agency*, 24 August 1977

23 August 1977, 'Jundui yao ba jiaoyu xunlian tigao dao zhanlue diwei', DXWII pp. 56–62. 'The Army should attach strategic importance to education and training', SWII pp. 73–79

19 September 1977, 'Jiaoyu zhanxian de faluan fanzheng wenti', DXWII pp. 63–68. 'Setting things right in education', SWII pp. 80–86

28 December 1977, 'Zai Zhongyangjunwei quantihuiyi shangde jianghua', DXWII pp. 69–81. 'Speech at a plenary meeting of the Military Commission of the Central Committee of the CPC', SWII pp. 87–100

2 March 1978, 'Zai wujie renda yici huiyi jiefangjun daibiaotuan xiaozuhui shangde jianghua' ['Speech at meeting with small group from the PLA delegation to the first session of the 5th National People's Congress'] LGJJ pp. 137–147

18 March 1978, 'Zai quanguo kexue dahui kaimoshi shangde jianghua', DXWII pp. 82–97. 'Speech at the opening ceremony of the National Conference on Science', SWII pp. 101–116

28 March 1978, 'Jianchi anlao fenpei yuance', DXWII pp. 98–99. 'Adhere to the

Principle "To Each According to His Work"', SWII pp. 117–118

28 March 1978, 'Yao zhuyi tigao xiaoxue jiaoyuande gongze' ['Attend to raising the salaries of primary school teachers'] LJ p. 57

22 April 1978, 'Zai quanguo jiaoyu gongzuo huiyi shangde jianghua', DXWII pp. 100–107. 'Speech at the National Conference on Education', SWII pp. 119–126

13 May 1978, 'Yao zhibu shixian zhihui xitong de xiandaihua' ['Phase in the modernization of the command structure'] LGJJ pp. 149–157

2 June 1978, 'Zai quanjun zhengzhi gongzuo huiyi shangde jianghua', DXWII pp. 108–120. 'Speech at the All-Army Conference on political work', SWII pp. 127–140

11 July 1978, 'Zhongshi xiandai tiaojianxiade minbing gongzuo' ['Pay attention to militia work under contemporary conditions'] LGJJ pp. 251–262

17 July 1978, 'Gao renmin zhanzheng bushi buyao jundui xiandaihua' ['People's War does not exclude military modernization'] LGJJ p. 263

16 September 1978, 'Gaoju Mao Zedong sixiang qizhi, jianchi shishi qiushi de yuance', DXWII pp. 121–123. 'Hold high the banner of Mao Zedong Thought and adhere to the principle of seeking truth from facts', SWII pp. 141–144

11 October 1978, 'Gongren jieji yao wei shixian sige xiandaihua zuochu youyi gongxian', DXWII pp. 124–129. 'The working class should make outstanding contributions to the four modernizations', SWII pp. 145–150

13 December 1978, 'Jiefang sixiang, shishi qiushi, tuanjie yizhi xiangqiankan', DXWII pp. 130–143. 'Emancipate the mind, seek truth from facts and unite as one in looking to the future', SWII pp. 151–165

18–22 December 1978, 'Bu dazhang jiu yao zuoxia laitan' ['If there's no armed conflict we can sit down and talk'] DXS pp. 157–164

1 January 1979, 'Taiwan guihui zuguo tishang juti richeng' ['Let's put forward a specific programme for the return of Taiwan to the homeland'] LTZ pp. 92–101

17 January 1979, 'Gao jianshe yao liyong waizi he fahui yuan gongshengyezhe de zuoyong' ['Development requires the use of foreign capital and entrepreneurs'] LTZ pp. 102–104

18 January 1979, 'Xiandai zhanzheng yao qude zhikongquan' ['Modern warfare has domination in the air'] LGJJ p. 263

26 February 1979, 'Zhongguo dui Yuenam de jiaoxunzhe wenti' ['The Question of China Teaching Vietnam a Lesson'] DXS pp. 165–166

15 March 1979, 'Dui dangqian sange wenti de jianshi' ['Examination of Three Questions that Face the Party'] DXS pp. 167–170

30 March 1979, 'Jianchi sixiang jiben yuance', DXWII pp. 144–170. 'Uphold the four cardinal principles', SWII pp. 166–191

6 April 1979, 'Sixiang fenqi yu jingjian bili shidiao de wenti' ['Ideological differences and the Question of Balance in Economic Construction'] DXS pp. 171–177

15 June 1979, 'Xinshiqi de tongyi zhanxian he renmin zhengxie de renwu', DXWII pp. 171–174. 'The united front and the tasks of the Chinese people's

political consultative Conference in the new period', SWII pp. 192–195

13 July 1979, 'Renzhen xuexi zhenli biaozhun wenti' ['The Question of Seriously Studying the Truth Criterion'] DXS pp. 178–181

29 July 1979, 'Sixiang luxian zhengzhi luxian de shixian yao kao zuzhi luxian lai baozheng', DXWII pp. 175–178. 'The organizational line guarantees the implementation of the ideological and political lines', SWII pp. 196–199

29 July 1979, 'Haijun jianshe yao jiang zhenzhengde zhandouli' ['The development of the navy must address its real combat effectiveness'] LGJJ pp. 264–266

1 September 1979, 'Xin shiqi tongyi zhanxian shi shehui zhuyi laodongzhe yu aiguozhe de lianmeng' ['The United Front in the new era is the alliance of the socialist workers and patriots'] LTZ pp. 105–119

6 September 1979, 'Chuli "Laodanan" wenti de jiben fangzhen' ['Basic Policy for Handling the Difficult Problem of Older Cadres'] DXS pp. 182–188

16 September 1979, 'Guanyu Liu Shaoqi tongzhi "pingfan" wenti de jianghua' ['Speech on Reversing the Verdict on Comrade Liu Shaoqi'] DXS pp. 189–195

19 October 1979, 'Ge minzhu dangpai he gongshenglian shi wei shehui zhuyi fuwu de zhengzhi liliang' ['Every democratic party and association of industry and commerce has the ability to serve socialism'] LTZ pp. 120–23

30 October 1979, 'Zai Zhongguo wenxue yishu gongzuozhe disici daibiao dahui shangde zhuci', DXWII pp. 179–186. 'Speech greeting the Fourth Congress of Chinese writers and artists', SWII pp. 200–207

2 November 1979, 'Gaoji ganbu yao daitou fayang dangde youliang chuantong', DXWII pp. 187–202. 'Senior cadres should take the lead in maintaining and enriching the Party's fine traditions', SWII pp. 208–223

26 November 1979, 'Zhongguode xiandaihua – wenti he qianjing' ['China's modernization – problems and prospects'] in *Baike zhishi* [*Encyclopedaic Knowledge*] No. 3, 1980, reprinted in Zhonggong yanjiu zazhi shebian, *Gongfei yuanshi ziliao xuanji* [*Materials from Communist China*] No. 2, 1980, Taipei, 1981, pp. 1–9

2 December 1979, 'Zai xuanba youxiu zhongqingnian ganbu huibao huishangde jianghua' ['Speech at report meeting on the selection of excellent middle-aged and young cadres'] in *Zugong tongxun 1980* [*Bulletin of the Organization Department of the CCP*] pp. 3–4

26 December 1979, 'Zai Zhonggong zhongyang zhengzhiju huiyi shangde jianghua' ['Speech at Meeting of the Political Bureau of the CCP'] DXS pp. 196–204

1 January 1980, 'Bashiniandai shi shifen zhongyao de niandai' ['The 1980s are a most important decade'] in *Renmin ribao* [*People's Daily*] 1 January 1980

16 January 1980, 'Muqian de xingshi he renwu', DXWII pp. 203–237. 'The present situation and the tasks before us', SWII pp. 224–258

29 February 1980, 'Jianchi dangde luxian, gaijin gongzuo fangfa', DXWII pp. 238–247. 'Adhere to the Party line and improve methods of work', SWII pp. 259–268

12 March 1980, 'Jingjian jundui, tigao zhandouli', DXWII pp. 248–254. 'Stream-line the Army and raise its combat effectiveness', SWII pp. 269–275

March 1980–June 1981, 'Dui qi cao "Guanyu jianguo yilai dangde ruogan lishi wenti de jueyi" de yijian', DXWII pp. 255–274. 'Remarks on successive drafts of the "Resolution on certain questions in the history of our Party since the founding of the People's Republic of China"', SWII pp. 276–296

26 May 1980, 'Shuzeng *Zhongguo shaonianbao* he *Fudaoyuan* zazhi' ['Present-ing *China's Children's News* and *The Trainer*'] LJ p. 111

31 May 1980, 'Guanyu nongcun zhengce wenti', DXWII pp. 275–277. 'On questions of rural policy', SWII pp. 297–299

31 May 1980, 'Chuli xiongdidang guanxi de yi tiao zhongyao yuance', DXWII pp. 278–279. 'An important principle for handling relations between fraternal parties', SWII pp. 300–301

12 and 30 July 1980, 'Zailun shixian shi jianyan zhenli de weiyi biaozhun' ['More on Ensuring that Experience is the Only Test of Truth'] DXS pp. 239–249

18 August 1980, 'Dang he guojia lingdao zhidu de gaige', DXWII pp. 280–302. 'On the reform of the system of Party and state leadership', SWII pp. 302–325

21/23 August 1980, 'Da Yidali jizhe Oriana Fallaci wen', DXWII pp. 303–312. 'Answers to the Italian journalist Oriana Fallaci', SWII pp. 326–334

28 August 1980, 'Di wujie zhengxie quanweuhui di sanci huiyi kaimoci' ['Opening address at the 3rd meeting of the 5th Chinese People's Political Consultative Conference'] in *Renmin ribao* [*People's Daily*] 29 August 1980

28 August 1980, 'Tongyi zhanxian he renmin zhengxie yao wei fahui shehuizhuyi youyuexing zuochu gongxian' ['The United Front and the Chinese People's Political Consultative Conference will contribute to ensure the superiority of socialism'] LTZ pp. 129–134

31 August 1980, 'Zai Zhongyang zhengzhiju kuoda huiyi shangde jianghua' ['Speech at enlarged meeting of the Political Bureau of the CCP Central Committee'] *Central Circular No. 66 (1980)* in Zhonggong yanjiu zazhi shebian, *Gongfei yuanshi ziliao xuanji* [*Materials from Communist China*] No. 3, 1980, Taipei, 1981, pp. 146–166

29 September 1980, 'Chongfen fahui renmin zhengxie de zhongyao zuoyong' ['Make full use of the important functions of the Chinese People's Political Consultative Conference'] LTZ pp. 135–36

15 October 1980, 'Womende zhanlue fangzhen shi jiji fangyu' ['Our strategic policy is one of active defence'] (Part of speech at a discussion meeting) LGJJ pp. 267–279

15 October 1980, 'Gao guofang jianshe yao jingda xisuan' ['The development of national defence requires careful planning and strict budgeting'] (Part of speech at a discussion meeting) LGJJ pp. 280–285

15 October 1980, 'Deng Xiaoping da Meiguo jizhe' ['Deng Xiaoping answers a reporter from the USA'] in *Renmin ribao* [*People's Daily*] 24 November 1980

25 October 1980, 'Tong liangwei zhongyang fuze gongzuo renyuan de tanhua' ['Talks with two responsible members of staff from the Central Committee offices'] in *Shiyiju sanzhong quanhui yilai Deng Xiaoping tongzhi guanyu*

dangde jianshe de bufen lunshu [*Deng Xiaoping's discussions on party development since the 3rd plenum of the 11th Central Committee*] pp. 34–35

25 December 1980, 'Guanche diaozheng fangzhen, baozheng anding tuanjie', DXWII pp. 313–333. 'Implement the policy of readjustment, ensure stability and unity', SWII pp. 335–355

December 1980, 'Da Nansilafu jizhe Mideweiqi wen' ['Answers to a Yugoslav Journalist'] DXS pp. 300–306

4 January 1981, 'Fazhan ZhongMei guanxi de yuance lichang' ['Develop a principled relationship between China and America'] in Zhonggong zhongyang wenxian yanjiushi (ed.) *San zhong quanhui yilai: zhongyao wenxian xuanbian* [*Since the 3rd plenum: collection of important documents*] Beijing, Renmin chubanshe, 1982, Vol. 2, pp. 649–653

14 February 1981, '*Deng Xiaoping fuzhuxi wenji* xuyan' ['Preface to *Selected Works of Vice-Premier Deng Xiaoping*'] in *Dangshi tongxun* [*Bulletin of Party History*] No. 3, 1981, pp. 5–6

27 March 1981, 'Guanyu fandui cuowu sixiang qingxiang wenti', DXWII pp. 334–337. 'On opposing wrong ideological tendencies', SWII pp. 356–359

29 June 1981, 'Zai dangde shiyiju liuzhong quanhui caimo huishangde jianghua', DXWII pp. 338. 'Closing speech at the Sixth Plenary Session of the Eleventh Central Committee of the CPC', SWII pp. 360

2 July 1981, 'Laoganbu diyiweide renwu shi xuanfa zhongqingnian ganbu', DXWII pp. 339–343. 'The primary task of veteran cadres is to select young and middle-aged cadres for promotion', SWII pp. 361–366

17 July 1981, 'Guanyu sixiang zhanxian shangde wenti de tanhua', DXWII pp. 344–348. 'Concerning problems on the ideological front', SWII pp. 367–371

18 July 1981, 'Huijian Xiang Gang *Mingbao* shechang Cha Liangkang shi de tanhua' ['Discussions when meeting the director of *Ming Bao*'] in *Shiyiju sanzhong quanhui yilai Deng Xiaoping tongzhi guanyu dangde jianshe de bufen lunshu* [*Deng Xiaoping's discussions on party development since the 3rd plenum of the 11th Central Committee*] p. 4

19 September 1981, 'Jianshe qiangda de xiandaihua zhengguihua de geming jundui', DXWII pp. 349–350. 'Build powerful, modern and regularized revolutionary armed forces', SWII pp. 372–373

13 January 1982, 'Jingjian jigou shi yichang geming', DXWII pp. 351–356. 'Streamlining organizations constitutes a revolution', SWII pp. 374–379

10 April 1982, 'Jianjue daji jingji fanfei huodong', DXWII pp. 357–359. 'Combat economic crime', SWII pp. 380–382

6 May 1982, 'Woguo jingji jianshe de lishi jingyan', DXWII pp. 360–362. 'China's historical experience in economic construction', SWII pp. 383–385

4 July 1982, 'Zai junwei zuo tanhui shangde jianghua', DXWII pp. 363–367. 'Speech at a forum of the Military Commission of the Central Committee of the CPC', SWII pp. 386–390

30 July 1982, 'She guwenweiyuanhui shi feichu lingdao zhiwu zhongshen zhide guodu banfa', DXWII pp. 368–369. 'Advisory Commissions will be a

transitional measure for the abolition of life tenure in leading posts', SWII pp. 391–393

1 September 1982, 'Zhongguo gongchandang dishierci quanguo daibaio dahui kaimuci', DXWIII pp. 1–4 and DXWII pp. 370–373. 'Opening speech at the Twelfth National Congress of the CPC', SWII pp. 394–397

13 September 1982, 'Zai Zhongyang guwen weiyuanhui diyici quanti huiyishangde jianghua' ['Speech at 1st plenum of the Central Advisory Commission'] DXWIII pp. 5–8

18 September 1982, 'Yixin yiyi gao jianshe' ['One heart, one mind for reconstruction'] DXWIII pp. 9–11

24 September 1982, 'Women dui Xiang Gang wenti de jiben lichang' ['Our basic position on the Hong Kong question'] DXWIII pp. 12–15

14 October 1982, 'Qianshinian wei houshinian zuohao zhunbei' ['Use the first ten years to prepare for the second ten years'] DXWIII pp. 16–18. 'Luoshi zhongda jianshe gongmu, heli shiyong keji renyuan', JZTS pp. 5–7. 'Decide on major construction projects, make proper use of the talents of scientists and technicians', SCC pp. 6–9

22 October 1982, 'Zengjin ZhongYin youyi, jiaqiong nannan hezuo' ['Increase Sino-Indian friendship, South–South co-operation'] DXWIII pp. 19–20

24 November 1982, 'Aiguo tongyi zhanxian qian chengyuan dada youkewei' ['The patriotic united front has a great future'] LTZ pp. 158–159

November/December 1982, 'Zhishu zaolin' ['Plant trees, create forests'] DXWIII p. 21

12 January 1983, 'Gexiang gongzuo dou yaoyou zhuyu jianshe you Zhongguo tese de shehui zhuyi', DXWIII pp. 22–23. 'Our work in all fields should contribute to the building of socialism with Chinese characteristics', SCC pp. 10–13

2 March 1983, 'Shicha Jiangsu dengdi hui Beijing hou de tanhua' ['Talks on return to Beijing from Jiangsu and other places'] DXWIII pp. 24–26. 'Zhongshi zhili kaifa', JZTS pp. 11–12. 'Tap intellectual resources', SCC pp. 14–16

29 April 1983, 'Jianshe shehui zhuyi de wuzhi wenming he jingshen wenming', DXWIII pp. 27–28. 'Build a Socialist society with both high material and high cultural and ideological standards', SCC p. 17

18 June 1983, 'Luzi shi duile, zhengce bu hui bian', DXWIII pp. 29. 'The path is correct and the policies won't change', SCC p. 18

26 June 1983, 'Zhongguo dalu he Taiwan heping tongyide shexiang', DXWIII pp. 30–31. 'An idea for the peaceful reunification of the Chinese Mainland and Taiwan', SCC pp. 19–21

8 July 1983, 'Liyong waiguo zhili he guangda duiwai kaifang', DXWIII pp. 32. 'Use the intellectual resources of other countries', SCC p. 22

19 July 1983, 'Yanli daji xingshi fanzui huodong' ['Ensure severe punishment for criminal offenders'] DXWIII pp. 33–34

1 October 1983, 'Wei Jingshan xuexiao tici', DXWIII p. 35. 'Inscription for Jingshan School', SCC p. 23

12 October 1983, 'Dang zai zuzhi zhanxian he sixiang zhanxian shangde poqie

renwu', DXWIII p. 36–48. 'The Party's urgent tasks on the organizational and ideological fronts', SCC pp. 24–40

22 February 1984, 'Wending shijie jushi de xin banfa', DXWIII pp. 49–50. 'A new approach towards stabilizing the world situation', SCC pp. 41–42

24 February 1984, 'Banhao jingji tequ, zengjia duiwai kaifang chengshi', DXWIII pp. 51–52. 'Guanyu jingji tequ he zengjia duiwai kaifang chengshi wenti', JZTS pp. 36–38. 'On special economic zones and opening more cities to the outside world', SCC pp. 43–45

25 March 1984, 'Fazhan ZhongRi guanxi yao kande yuan xie' ['Develop relations between China and Japan'] DXWIII pp. 53–55

29 May 1984, 'Weihu shijie heping, gaohao guonei jianshe', DXWIII pp. 56–57. 'Safeguard world peace and ensure domestic development', SCC pp. 46–47

22–23 June 1984, 'Yige guojia, liangzhong zhidu', DXWIII pp. 58–61. 'One Country, Two Systems', SCC pp. 48–52

30 June 1984, 'Jianshe you zhongguo tese de shehui zhuyi', DXWIII pp. 62–66. 'Build Socialism with Chinese characteristics', SCC pp. 53–58

31 July 1984, 'Women feichang guanzhu Xiang Gang de guodu shiqi' ['We must pay close attention to Hong Kong's transition'] DXWIII pp. 67–68. 'Yiguo liangzhi de gouxiang shinenggou xingdei tongde' JZTS pp. 50–51. 'The "One Country, Two Systems" Concept will work', SCC pp. 59–60

29 August 1984, 'Deng Xiaoping tongzhi gei Zhonggong Guanxi Zhuangzu zizhiqu weiyuanhui dangshi ziliao zhengji weiyuanhui de fuxin' ['Comrade Deng Xiaoping replies to the Committee for the Collection of Materials on Party History of Guangxi Zhuang Autonomous Region'] in *Dangshi tongxun* [*Bulletin of Party History*] No. 2, 1985, p. 1

1 October 1984, 'Zai Zhonghua renmin gongheguo chengli sanshiwu zhou nianqing zhu dianli shangde jianghua', DXWIII pp. 69–71. 'Speech at the ceremony celebrating the 35th Anniversary of the Founding of the People's Republic of China', SCC pp. 61–63

2 October 1984, 'Xiwang haiwai qinren he pengyou tigong gengduo de zhishi he laodong' ['It is to be hoped that overseas relatives and friends provide even more knowledge and labour'] LTZ p. 172

3 October 1984, 'Baoshi Xiang Gang de fanrong he wending', DXWIII pp. 72–76. 'Maintain prosperity and stability in Hong Kong', SCC pp. 64–66

6 October 1984, 'Women de hongwei mubiao he geben zhengce', DXWIII pp. 77–80. 'The magnificent goal of our Four Modernizations, and our basic policies', SCC pp. 67–71

10 October 1984, 'Women ba gaige dangzuo yi zhong geming' ['Our reform is a kind of revolution'] DXWIII pp. 81–82

11 October 1984, 'Duiwai kaifang zhengcexia ge shiji ye bubian liushiwuniannei jiejin fada guojia shuiping (Huijian Riben gongmingdang weiyuanchang shide tanhua)' ['The policy of openness will not change for a century: in sixty-five years the state will be flourishing (Discussions when meeting the president of the Japanese Komeito)'] in *Renmin ribao* [*People's Daily*] 12 October 1984

22 October 1984, 'Zai zhongyang guwen weiyuanhui disanci quanti huiyishangde

jianghua', DXWIII pp. 83–93. 'Speech at the 3rd plenary session of the Central Advisory Commission of the Communist Party of China', SCC pp. 72–82

26 October 1984, 'Geming he jianshe dou yao zou ziji de lu', DXWIII pp. 94–95. 'We should follow our own road both in revolution and in economic development', SCC pp. 83–85

31 October 1984, 'Heping gongchu yuanze ju youqiang dasheng mingli', DXWIII pp. 96–97. 'The Principles of Peaceful Coexistence have a potentially wide application', SCC pp. 86–88

1 November 1984, 'Jundui yao fu cong zheng ge guojia jianshe daju', DXWIII pp. 98–100. 'The Army should subordinate itself to the general interest, which is to develop the country', SCC pp. 89–92

19 December 1984, 'Zhongguo shi xinshou nuoyande' ['China will keep its word'] DXWIII pp. 101–103. 'Yiguo liangzhi shi genju shiji qingkuang tichude gouxiang', JZTS pp. 80–83. 'The Concept of "One Country, Two Systems" is based on China's Realities', SCC pp. 93–96

4 January 1985, 'Guanyu yanhai kaifang chengshi he diqu rencai jianshe de bufen zhishi' ['Part of a directive on opening up the coastal cities and developing regional talent'] in *Shiyiju sanzhong quanhui yilai dangde zuzhi gongzuo wenxian xuanbian* [*Collection of organizational work documents since the 3rd plenum of the 11th Central Committee*] p. 97

19 January 1985, 'Kaifang zhengce buhui daozhi ziben zhuyi: shehuizhuyi bi zhongjiang shizhong zhan youshi (Huijian Xiang Gang haidian touzi youxian gongsi daibiaotuan shide tanhua)' ['The policy of openness will not lead to capitalism: socialism is always superior (Discussions when meeting representatives from a Hong Kong investment company)'] in *Renmin ribao* [*People's Daily*] 20 January 1985

4 March 1985, 'Heping he fazhan shi dangdai shijie de liangda wenti', DXWIII pp. 104–106. 'Peace and Development are the two outstanding issues in the world today', SCC pp. 97–100

7 March 1985, 'Gaige keji tizhi shi weile jiefang shengchanli' ['Reform of the system of science and technology can release productive forces'] DXWIII pp. 107–109

7 March 1985, 'Yikao lixiang erkao jilu caineng tuanjie qilai', DXWIII pp. 110–112. 'Unity depends on ideals and discipline', SCC pp. 101–104

28 March 1985, 'Gaige shi Zhongguo de dierci geming' ['Reform is China's Second Revolution'] DXWIII pp. 113–114

15 April 1985, 'Zhengzhishang fazhan minzhu, jingjishang shixing gaige', DXWIII pp. 115–118. 'Expand political democracy and carry out economic reform', SCC pp. 105–110

18 April 1985, 'Jiaqiang tong Ouzhoude jingji lianxi', DXWIII p. 119. 'Increase economic ties with Europe', SCC pp. 111–112

19 May 1985, 'Ba jiaoyu gongzuo renzhen zhuaqilai' ['Seriously take hold of education work'] DXWIII pp. 120–122

May/June 1985 (20 May, 6 June), 'Gao zichan jieji ziyouhua jiushi zou ziben zhuyi daolu', DXWIII pp. 123–125. 'Bourgeois liberalization means taking the capitalist road', SCC pp. 113–115

4 June 1985, 'Zai junwei guangda huiyi shangde jianghua' ['Speech at enlarged meeting of the Military Affairs Commission'] DXWIII pp. 126–129. 'Weihu shijie heping de shiji xingdong', JZTS p. 100. 'Concrete actions for the maintenance of world peace', SCC pp. 116–117

29 June 1985, 'Gaige kaifang shi hendade shiyan' ['Reform and the open policy are great experiments'] DXWIII p. 130

11 July 1985, 'Zhuazhu shiji, tuijin gaige' ['Seize the opportunity, advance reform'] DXWIII pp. 131–132

1 August 1985, 'Tequ jingji yao cong neixiang zhuandao waixiang', DXWIII p. 133. 'The special economic zones should shift their economy from a domestic orientation to an external orientation', SCC pp. 118–119

21 August 1985, 'Dui Zhongguo gaige de liangzhong pingjia' ['Two evaluations of China's reform'] DXWIII pp. 134–135

28 August 1985, 'Gaige shi Zhongguo fazhan shengchanli de biyou zhilu', DXWIII pp. 136–140. 'Reform is the only way for China to develop its productive forces', SCC pp. 120–125

23 September 1985, 'Zai Zhongguo gongchandang quanguo daibiao huiyi shangde jianghua', DXWIII pp. 141–147. 'Speech at the National Conference of the Communist Party of China', SCC pp. 126–135

23 October 1985, 'Shehui zhuyi he shichang jingji bu cunzai genben maodun' ['There is no fundamental contradiction between socialism and market economics'] DXWIII pp. 148–151

17 January 1986, 'Zai zhongyang zhengzhiju changweihui shangde jianghua', DXWIII pp. 152–154. 'Talk at a meeting of the Standing Committee of the Political Bureau of the Central Committee', SCC pp. 136–140

28 March 1986, 'Na shishilai shuohua' ['Talking about reality'] DXWIII pp. 155–156

4 April 1986, 'Jianchi shehui zhuyi, jianchi heping zhengce' ['Hold fast to socialism, hold fast to a policy of peace'] DXWIII pp. 157–158

10 June 1986, 'Zai tingqu jingji qingkuang huibao shi de tanhua', DXWIII pp. 159–160. 'Remarks on the domestic economic situation', SCC pp. 141–144

18 June 1986, 'Zhengqu zhengge Zhonghua minzu de datuanjie' ['Strive for the great unity of all China's nationalities'] DXWIII pp. 161–162

28 June 1986, 'Zai quanti renminzhong shuli fazhi guannian', DXWIII pp. 163–164. 'Gaige zhengzhi tizhi, zengqiang fazhi guannian', JZTS pp. 121–123. 'Reform the political structure and strengthen the people's sense of legality', SCC pp. 145–148

19–21 August 1986, 'Shicha Tianjin shide tanhua' ['Discussions on an inspection tour of Tianjin'] DXWIII pp. 165–166

2 September 1986, 'Da Meiguo jizhe Maike. Huajiashi wen' ['In reply to the questions of US journalist'] DXWIII pp. 167–175

September–November 1986, 'Guanyu zhengzhi tizhi gaige wenti' ['On questions of reform of the political system'] DXWIII pp. 176–180

3 September 1986, 'Bu gaige zhengzhi tizhi hui zu'ai shengchanli fazhan', JZTS pp. 124–125. 'To ensure development of the productive forces we must reform the political structure', SCC pp. 149–151

13 September 1986, 'Zhengzhi tizhi gaige yaoyouyi ge jiantu', JZTS pp. 126–127. 'We must have a plan for the reform of the political structure', SCC pp. 152–153

28 September 1986, 'Zai dangde shierju liuzhong quanhui shangde jianghua', DXWIII pp. 181–182. 'Remarks at the 6th plenary session of the Party's 12th Central Committee', SCC pp. 154–155

29 September 1986, 'Genju benguo qingkuang jinxing zhengzhi tizhi gaige', JZTS pp. 130–131. 'Reform the political structure in the light of domestic conditions', SCC pp. 156–157

18 October 1986, 'Zhongguo yao fazhan, libukai kexue' ['China's future development will not be unscientific'] DXWIII pp. 183–184

21 October 1986, 'Dao Bocheng' ['To the memory of Liu Bocheng'] DXWIII pp. 185–189

9 November 1986, 'Yong jianding de xinnian ba renmin tuanjie qilai' ['Use strong faith to unite the people'] DXWIII pp. 190–191

9 November 1986, 'Zhengzhi tizhi gaige de yixie shexiang', JZTS pp. 132–133. 'Some ideas on the reform of the political structure', SCC pp. 158–160

19 December 1986, 'Qiye gaige he jinrong gaige' ['Enterprise and finance reforms'] DXWIII pp. 192–193

30 December 1986, 'Qizhi xiangming di fandui zichan jieji ziyouhua', DXWIII pp. 194–197. 'Take a clear-cut stand against bourgeois liberalization', SCC pp. 161–166

13 January 1987, 'Paichu ganrao, jixu qianjin' ['Clear away obstacles and continue to advance'] DXWIII pp. 198–200. 'Paichu ganrao, jainding di shixing gaige kaifang zhengce', JZTS pp. 138–140. 'Clear away obstacles and adhere to the policies of reform and of opening to the outside world', SCC pp. 167–170

20 January 1987, 'Jiaqiang sixiang jiben jiance jiaoyu, jianchi gaige kaifang zhengce', DXWIII pp. 201–202. 'Promote education in the Four Cardinal Principles and adhere to the policies of reform and of opening to the outside world', SCC pp. 171–173

6 February 1987, 'Jihua he shichang dou shi fazhan shengchanli de fangfa' ['Plan and market are both ways to develop productive forces'] DXWIII p. 203

18 February 1987, 'Yong Zhongguo de lishi jiaoyu qingnian' ['Use China's history to educate youth'] DXWIII pp. 204–206

3 March 1987, 'Zhongguo zhineng zou shehui zhuyi daolu' ['China can only travel the socialist road'] DXWIII pp. 207–209

8 March 1987 'You lingdao you zhixu di jinxing shehui zhuyi jianshe' ['With leadership there is order for the promotion of socialist development'] DXWIII pp. 210–212

27 March 1987, 'Zenyang pingjia yige guojia de zhengzhi tizhi' ['How to

more thought is liberated, the faster the pace of reform'] DXWIII pp. 264–265

3 June 1988, 'Yao xishou guoji de jingyan' ['The need to absorb international experiences'] DXWIII pp. 266–267

7 June 1988, 'Zai gaigezhong baochi shengchan de jiaohao fazhan' ['Ensure production develops well during reform'] DXWIII p. 268

22 June 1988, 'Xingshi poshi women jinyibu gaige kaifang' ['Conditions force us to advance through reform and openness'] DXWIII pp. 269–270

5 September 1988, 'Zonjie lishi shiweile kaipi weilai' ['Summarize history in order to open up the future'] DXWIII pp. 271–273

5 and 12 September 1988, 'Kexue jishu shi diyi shengchanli' ['Science and technology are the first productive force'] DXWIII pp. 274–276

12 September 1988, 'Zhongyang yao you quanwei' ['The Central Committee must have authority'] DXWIII pp. 277–278

24 October 1988, 'Zhongguo bixu zai shijie gao keji lingyu zhanyou yixi zhidi' ['China must make its science and technology among the best in the world'] DXWIII pp. 279–280

21 December 1988, 'Yi heping gongchu wugong yuance wei zhunce jianli guoji xinzhixu' ['Use the five principles of peaceful co-existence to prepare for the establishment of a new international order'] DXWIII pp. 281–283

2 January 1989, 'Guanyu zhiding minzhu dangpai chengyuan canzheng he luxing jiandu zhize fangan de pishi' ['Instruction on plans to regulate the participation of democratic party members in government and the supervision of their duties'] LTZ p. 250

26 February 1989, 'Yadao yiqiede shi wending' ['Stability is everything'] DXWIII pp. 284–285

4 March 1989, 'Zhongguo buchong xuli' ['China fails to appreciate disorder'] DXWIII pp. 286–287

23 March 1989, 'Baochi jianku douzheng de chuantong' ['Preserve the tradition of tough struggle'] DXWIII pp. 288–290

23 March 1989, 'Shinian zuida de shiwu shi zai jiaoyu fangmian' ['The biggest errors of the past ten years have been in education'] in Mao Zedong and Deng Xiaoping, *Lun Zhongguo guoqing* [*On the state of the nation*] Beijing, Zhonggong zhongyang dangxiao chubanshe, 1992, p. 872

25 April 1989, 'Talks with Li Peng and Yang Shangkun' in *South China Morning Post*, 31 May 1989, p. 12

16 May 1989, 'Jieshu guoqu, kaipi weilai' ['The past is done, the future opens up'] DXWIII pp. 291–295

31 May 1989, 'Zucheng yige shixing gaige de you xiwang de lingdao jiben' ['Organize a reforming and hopeful leadership'] DXWIII pp. 296–301. 'Tong Li Peng, Yao Yilin tongzhi tanhua yaodian' ['Main points of discussions with Comrades Li Peng and Yao Yilin'] in *Zugong tongxun 1989* [*Bulletin of the Organization Department of the CCP*] pp. 159–169

9 June 1989, 'Zai jiejian shoudu jieyan buduijun yishang ganbu shi de jianghua' ['Speech on meeting cadres from Beijing's martial law troops'] DXWIII pp. 302–308. 'Deng's Talks on Quelling Rebellion in Beijing', *Beijing Review*

Vol. 32, No. 28, 10 July 1989, pp. 14–17

16 June 1989, 'Disandai lingdao jiben de dangwu zhiji' ['The pressing need for a third generation of leadership'] DXWIII pp. 309–314. 'Tong zhongyang lingdao tongzhi de tanhua' ['Discussions with leading comrades of the CCP Central Committee'] in *Zugong tongxun 1989* [*Bulletin of the Organization Department of the CCP*] pp. 160–169

4 September 1989, 'Gaige kaifang zhengce wending, Zhongguo dayou xiwang' ['The stability of the policy of reform and openness is China's greatest hope'] DXWIII pp. 315–321

4 September 1989, 'Zhi Zhonggong zhogyang zhengzhiju de xin' ['Letter to the Political Bureau of the CCP Central Committee'] DXWIII pp. 322–323

16 September 1989, 'Women you xinxin ba Zhongguo de shiqing zuode genghao' ['We have the confidence to make the project of China still better'] DXWIII pp. 324–327

19 September 1989, 'Qiangdiao yong heping gongchu wuxiang yuanze jiejue guoji zhengzhi jingji wenti' ['Emphasize the use of the five principles of peaceful co-existence to resolve questions of international politics and economics'] in *Renmin ribao* [*People's Daily*] 20 September 1989

26 October 1989, 'Shehui zhuyi de Zhongguo shei ye dongyao buliao' ['Socialist China will not waver'] DXWIII pp. 328–329

31 October 1989, 'Jieshu yanjunde ZhongMei guanxi yao you Meiguo caiqu zhudong' ['To resolve the grim relations between China and the USA, it will have to be the USA that takes the initiative'] DXWIII pp. 330–333

12 November 1989, 'Huijian canjia zhongyang junwei kuangda huiyi quanti tongzhi shi de jianghua' ['Speech on meeting comrades attending enlarged plenum of the Central Military Commission'] DXWIII pp. 334–335

20 November 1989, 'Dui erye lishi de huigu' ['Reviewing the history of the Second Field Army'] DXWIII pp. 336–343

23 November 1989, 'Jianchi shehui zhuyi, fangzhi heping yanbian' ['Hold fast to socialism, defend peaceful evolution'] DXWIII pp. 344–346

1 December 1989, 'Guojiade zhuquan he anquan yao shizhong zai diyiwei' ['The state's sovereignty and security must be uppermost from beginning to end'] DXWIII pp. 347–349

10 December 1989, 'ZhongMei guanxi zhonggui yao hao qilai caixing' ['China–US relations will eventually improve'] DXWIII pp. 350–351

17 February 1990, 'Xiang Gang jibenfa juyou lishi yiyi he guoji yiyi' ['The Hong Kong Basic Law has both historical and international significance'] DXWIII p. 352

3 March 1990, 'Guoji xingshi he jingji wenti' ['The international situation and economic matters'] DXWIII pp. 353–356

7 April 1990, 'Zhenxing Zhonghua minzu' ['Promote China's nationalities'] DXWIII pp. 357–358

11 July 1990, 'Zhongguo yongyuan buchong xu bieguo ganbu neizheng' ['China will never permit other countries to interfere in internal politics'] DXWIII pp. 359–361

15 September 1990, 'Gongtong nuli, shixian zuguo tongyi' ['Join together to ensure China's unity'] DXWIII p. 362

December 1990, 'Tong zhongyang lingdao tongzhi de tanhua' ['Talks with leading comrades of the Central Committee'] *Banyuetan* [*Fortnightly Forum*] No. 15, 1992, p. 37

24 December 1990, 'Shanyu liyong shiji jiejue fazhan wenti' ['Be good at using the opportunity to resolve the question of development'] DXWIII pp. 363–365

28 January–18 February 1991, 'Shicha Shanghai shi de tanhua' ['Discussions on an inspection tour of Shanghai'] DXWIII pp. 366–367

20 August 1991, 'Zongjie jingyan, shiyong rencai' ['Sum up experience, make use of talented people'] DXWIII pp. 368–369

18 January–21 February 1992, 'Zai Wuchang, Shenzhen, Zhuhai, Shanghai dengdi de tanhua yaodian' ['Important parts of talks in Wuhan, Shenzhen, Zhuhai, Shanghai and other places'] DXWIII pp. 370–383. 'Summary of Remarks made by Comrade Deng Xiaoping in Wuchang, Shenzhen, Zhuhai and Shanghai', BBC *Summary of World Broadcasts* FE/1346/B2/1–7, 3 April 1992

Notes

PREFACE

1 F. C. Teiwes, 'Interviews on Party History' in *CCP Research Newsletter* Nos 10 & 11, 1992, p. 1 is an invaluable guide to this topic. In the text the practice of referring to information from sources who do not wish to be identified as 'an unattributable source' has been followed.
2 'Emancipate the Mind, Seek Truth from Facts, and Unite as One in Looking to the Future' in SWII, p. 152 and p. 160.
3 'Talks with some leading comrades of the Central Committee', 25 October 1980, in SWII, p. 287.
4 See, for example, the introduction by Bo Yibo to Taihang geming genjudi shi zongbian weihui (ed.) *Taihang geming genjudi shigao* [*Outline History of the Taihang Revolutionary Base Area*] Taiyuan, Shanxi renmin chubanshe, 1987.

1 DENG XIAOPING, COMMUNISM AND REVOLUTION

1 Deng's designation as 'paramount leader' is somewhat obscured in both timing and operational function. Deng was offered the Chairmanship of the CCP in 1980 but declined. Hu Yaobang in retrospect claimed that everyone in the leadership thereafter regarded him as 'the primary architect' of policy. In talks with Gorbachev in May 1989 Zhao Ziyang is reported to have indicated that Deng's designation as paramount leader dates more formally from the 12th Congress of the CCP in 1982, and that this title was not just decorative but also carried the function of final approval in policy.
2 He was also nominated for the same honour in 1986, though, as Pye points out, on both occasions the accompanying editorials failed to link the achievements they were praising in China with Deng himself. See, L. Pye 'An Introductory Profile: Deng Xiaoping and China's Political Culture' in *The China Quarterly* No. 135, September 1993, p. 416.
3 'Deng's Talks on Quelling Rebellion in Beijing', *Beijing Review* Vol. 32, No. 28, 10 July 1989, p. 14.
4 Deng met his first wife Zhang Xiyuan in Moscow and married her when they both worked under Zhou Enlai's aegis in Shanghai in 1928. She died in childbirth in 1930. At the time Deng Xiaoping was working in Guangxi for the CCP Central Committee, but whether by chance or by design had returned to Shanghai to report on the situation in Guangxi at precisely the time when Zhang died. In 1931, when the CCP Central Committee decamped to Ruijin, Deng was accompanied on the boat out of Shanghai by Jin Weiying, whom he married within a few months. When Deng was criticized in 1933 by Li Weihan, Jin divorced him and married Li. This has given rise to speculation that some deal was struck between the two men: a lighter sentence perhaps in return for a wife-swap (Jiang Zhifeng, *Wangpai chujing de Zhongnanhai*

qiaoju [The Last Card of the Game of Zhongnanhai] San Francisco, Minzhu Zhongguo Shulin, 1990, p. 43). Though not impossible, a more reasonable explanation would be that Jin's divorce was to protect herself against any further fall-out from Deng's disgrace, and if the experience of others during the Cultural Revolution is any guide it might even have been Deng who took the initiative to suggest divorce precisely in order to protect his wife. Deng was clearly introduced to his third wife, whom he has been married to for over fifty years, by colleagues. According to one source (Yang Zhongmei, *Hu Yaobang: A Chinese Biography*, New York, M. E. Sharpe, 1988, p. 113), Hu Yaobang may have introduced Deng to Zhuo Lin. His daughter gives Teng Fa a leading role, and mentions the part played by other CCP leaders in bringing them together. For such a role to be played by older or more senior party members would certainly not be unusual. Deng Rong, *Wode Fuqin Deng Xiaoping* [My Father Deng Xiaoping] Part I, Beijing, Zhongyang wenxian chubanshe, 1993, pp. 217, 277, 288, 417, and 431ff.

5   For example, in June 1991 Deng sponsored a new edition of the four-volume *Selected Works of Mao Zedong* with his calligraphy for the title; and though Mao himself does not play a central role in his daughter's biography, there are frequent quotes from and references to Mao Zedong Thought.

6   'The "Two Whatevers" do not accord with Marxism', 24 May 1977, in SWII p. 51; and 'Mao Zedong Thought must be correctly understood as an integral whole', 21 July 1977, in SWII p. 55.

7   Qian Tingtao, 'Deng Xiaoping guanyu "Huangmao, heimao" biyude chuchu ji jiduixing' ['Deng Xiaoping on the genesis of the phrase "Black cat, white cat"'] in *Zhonggong dangshi tongxun* [*Bulletin of CCP History*] No. 12, 1990, p. 6.

8   This is largely the view articulated, though rather more elegantly, by Lucien Pye in 'Deng Xiaoping and China's Political Culture', in *The China Quarterly* No. 135, September 1993, especially pp. 428ff. It is also the view more cynically and forcefully expressed by many in China.

9   L. Pye, 'An Introductory Profile: Deng Xiaoping and China's Political Culture', pp. 415ff.

10 Yan Zhixin, 'Li Dazhao, Deng Xiaoping yu Feng Yuxiang' ['Li Dazhao, Deng Xiaoping and Feng Yuxiang'] in *Dangshi tongxun* [*Bulletin of Party History*] No. 4, 1985.

11 An account of Deng's underground activities, unremarkable though they are for all their obvious danger, may be found in Deng Rong, *Wode Fuqin Deng Xiaoping* p. 189.

12 Edgar Snow, *Red Star Over China* (2nd edition), London, Gollancz, 1968, p. 90. Easily the best account in English, and an exceptionally good read, is Harrison E. Salisbury, *The Long March: the untold story*, New York, Harper & Row, 1985.

13 The importance of the debate on agricultural co-operativization in 1955 is often overlooked, not least because of the CCP's own judgement – enshrined in the 'Resolution on Certain Questions in the History of the Party since the Establishment of the CCP' of June 1981 – that Mao only started to stray from the straight and narrow of CCP leadership discipline in 1959. See F. C. Teiwes and Warren Sun (eds) 'Mao, Deng Zihui, and the Politics of Agricultural Cooperativisation' in *Chinese Law and Government* Vol. 26, No. 3–4, 1993.

14 Roderick MacFarquhar, *The Origins of the Cultural Revolution* Vol. 1, London, Oxford University Press, 1974, pp. 26ff.

15 F. C. Teiwes, 'Mao and his lieutenants' in *The Australian Journal of Chinese Affairs* No. 19/20, 1988.

16 During the 1980s and into the 1990s a variety of 'true' stories or re-examination of these events has occurred. The most recent is Peter Hannam and Susan V. Lawrence, 'Solving a Chinese Puzzle: Lin Biao's Final Days and Death' in *US News and World Report*, 31 January 1994.

17 R. Bedeski, 'The Political Vision of Deng Xiaoping' in *Asian Thought and Society* Vol. 13, No. 37, January 1988, p. 3.

18 The obvious authority on purges in China is F. C. Teiwes, *Politics and Purges in China* (2nd edition), New York, M. E. Sharpe, 1994.

19 Details of this recycling at the provincial level may be found in David S. G. Goodman, *China's Provincial Leaders, 1949–1985*, Cardiff University Press, 1986.

20 A study of this and associated characteristics at provincial level may be found in David S. G. Goodman, 'The Provincial First Party Secretary in the People's Republic of China, 1949–1978: A Profile' in *The British Journal of Political Science* Vol. 10, No. 1, January 1980, p. 39.

21 The literature on factions and 'special relationships' [*guanxi*] in China's politics is particularly rich. The most important sources are probably Lucian Pye, *The Dynamics of Chinese Politics*, Cambridge, Mass., Oelgeschlager, Gunn & Hain, 1981; Andrew Nathan, 'A Factionalism Model for CCP Politics' in *The China Quarterly* No. 53, p. 34; and W. Whitson, 'The Field Army in Chinese Communist Military Politics' in *The China Quarterly* No. 37, p. 1.

22 K. Lieberthal and M. Oksenberg, *Policy Making in China: Leaders, Structures and Processes*, Princeton University Press, 1988; David S. G. Goodman, 'Political Change in China: Power, Policy and Process' in the *British Journal of Political Science* Vol. 19, July 1989, p. 425; and T. Tsou, 'Prolegomenon to the Study of Informal Groups in CCP Politics' in *The China Quarterly* No. 65, p. 98.

23 The CCP Central Committee's decision of 14 May 1931 may be found in *Zuo You jiang geming genjudi ziliao xuanji* [*Selected Materials on the Right and Left Rivers Revolutionary Base Areas*] Beijing, Renmin chubanshe, 1984, p. 278.

24 For example: Benjamin Yang, 'The Making of a Pragmatic Communist: The Early Life of Deng Xiaoping, 1904–1949' in *The China Quarterly* No. 135, September 1993, p. 449; Han Shanbi, *Deng Xiaoping pingzhuan* (3 vols) [*Biography of Deng Xiaoping*] Hong Kong, East West and Culture Publishers, 1988, p. 108.

25 'Answers to the Italian Journalist Oriana Fallaci' in SWII, p. 329.

26 Deng Rong, *Wode Fuqin Deng Xiaoping*, p. 193.

27 Xu Zufan, 'Deng Xiaoping 1931nian xunguan Anhui dangwu' ['Deng Xiaoping's Tour of Party Work in Anhui in 1931'] in *Zhonggong dangshi yanjiu* [*Research on CCP History*] No. 2, 1993, p. 90.

28 Luo Fu, 'Luo Ming luxian zai Jiangxi', 15 April 1933 ['The Luo Ming Line in Jiangxi']; and Luo Mai, 'Wei dangde luxian er douzheng', 6 May 1933 ['Struggle for the party line'], both in Zhonggong zhongyang shujichu (ed.) *Liu Da yilai: dangnei mimi wenjian* [*After the 6th Party Congress: Secret Internal Party Documents*] Beijing, Renmin chubanshe, 1980, pp. 351–355 and pp. 362–367, respectively.

29 Benjamin Yang, *From Revolution to Politics: Chinese Communists on the Long March*, Boulder, Colorado, Westview Press, 1990, p. 107.

30 According to party historian Hu Hua, as reported by Harrison Salisbury, Mao had recorded his concerns about Deng well before the Cultural Revolution. Harrison Salisbury, *The New Emperors: Mao and Deng, a dual biography*, London, HarperCollins, 1992, p. 290.

31 Deng's comments in 1980 may be found in SWII, p. 279. The 23 September 1957 report is 'Guanyu zhengfeng yundong de baogao' ['Report on the rectification movement'] in *Renmin ribao* [*People's Daily*] 19 October 1957.

32 Deng Rong, *Wode Fuqin Deng Xiaoping*, p. 318.

33 Chen Xilian, Ji Dengkui, Li Desheng, Liu Bocheng, Su Zhenhua, Xu Shiyou.

2 CHILDHOOD, YOUTH AND TRAVEL, 1904–1937

1   The prime source for information on Deng Xiaoping's family, native place and early life in China before he left for France is Deng Rong, *Wode Fuqin Deng Xiaoping*, chapters 2–6, 9–13.

2   Details of Deng's alien registration in France are provided in Nora Wang, 'Deng Xiaoping: The Years in France' in *The China Quarterly* No. 92, p. 699.

3   Deng Rong, *Wode Fuqin Deng Xiaoping*, pp. 32ff.

4   Mary S. Erbaugh, 'The Secret History of the Hakkas: the Chinese Revolution as a Hakka Enterprise' in *The China Quarterly* No. 132, p. 937.

5   Perhaps more interestingly, he also appears not to speak much if any French, despite his five years there.

6   Details are from Deng Rong, *Wode Fuqin Deng Xiaoping*, pp. 50ff. Uli Franz lists more children in *Deng Xiaoping: China's erneurer*, Stuttgart, DVA, 1987, p. 340.

7   The historical record is a little unclear here. According to Deng Rong, and others, Deng went to Chongqing in 1918 and enrolled in the preparatory school for France. However, the school did not actually open until 1919. It may well be that Deng attended some other school first.

8   The historical record is somewhat unclear. According to Deng Rong, and many other biographers, Deng arrived in France on 20 October 1920 on board the *Andre Lebon*. However, according to French immigration records he arrived on 13 December with the *Porthos*. The explanation may rest with immigration requirements, if indeed Deng arrived on the earlier date but failed, for whatever reason, to register at that time. The French records are examined in Nora Wang, 'Deng Xiaoping: The Years in France' in *The China Quarterly* No. 92 and this article is available to party historians in China in *Dangshi tongxun* [*Bulletin of Party History*] No. 22, 1983, pp. 20–22.

9   David Bonavia, *Deng*, Hong Kong, Longman, 1989, p. 7.

10 Benjamin Yang, 'The Making of a Pragmatic Communist: The Early Life of Deng Xiaoping, 1904–1949' in *The China Quarterly* No. 135, September 1993, p. 444.

11 Harrison Salisbury, *The Long March: the untold story*, p. 137.

12 Nora Wang, 'Deng Xiaoping: The Years in France', p. 704.

13 Uli Franz, *Deng Xiaoping: China's erneurer*, p. 47.

14 Edgar Snow, *Red Star Over China*, p. 499.

15 David Bonavia, *Deng*, p. 7.

16 Deng Rong, *Wode Fuqin Deng Xiaoping*, p. 121.

17 As even Deng Rong indicates through her use of its findings, the most reliable source on Deng Xiaoping's time in France is Nora Wang, 'Deng Xiaoping: The Years in France', p. 704.

18 Yan Zhixin, 'Li Dazhao, Deng Xiaoping yu Feng Yuxiang' ['Li Dazhao, Deng Xiaoping and Feng Yuxiang'] in *Dangshi tongxun* [*Bulletin of Party History*] No. 4, 1985; and Feng Hongda, 'Deng Xiaoping tongzhi huainian Feng Yuxiang jiangjun' ['Comrade Deng Xiaoping Commemorates General Feng Yuxiang'] in *Dangshi tongxun* [*Bulletin of Party History*] No. 7, 1983, p. 26.

19 Deng Rong, *Wode Fuqin Deng Xiaoping*, p. 193.

20 Deng Rong, *Wode Fuqin Deng Xiaoping* pp. 183ff.

21 Harrison Salisbury, *The Long March*, p. 138, reporting interview with Hu Hua. Deng Rong, *Wode Fuqin Deng Xiaoping*, pp. 204ff.

22 Sources on the Guangxi uprisings and aftermath include *Zuo You jiang geming genjudi ziliao xuanji* [*Selected Materials on the Right and Left Rivers Revolutionary Base Areas*] Beijing, Renmin chubanshe, 1984; Benjamin Yang, 'The Making of a Pragmatic Communist: The Early Life of Deng Xioping, 1904–1949'; 'The Bose Uprising' in *Beijing Review* No. 6, 1979, 9 February 1979; Diana Lary, 'The Chuang Peasant Movement and Soviet] in her *Region and Nation: The Kwangsi Clique in Chinese Politics 1925–1937*, Cambridge University Press, 1974, pp. 102–108; Yuan

Renyuan, 'Guangxi Youjiang de hongse fengbao' ['The Red Storm on Guanxi's Right River'] in *Renmin ribao* [*People's Daily*] 9 December 1978; and Chen Xinde, 'Zuo You Jiang geming genjudi shi yanjiu zongshu' ['Summary of Research on the History of the Left and Right River Revolutionary Base Areas'] in *Dangshi tongxun* [*Bulletin of Party History*] No. 1, 1986, pp. 25–30.

23 'Poor areas receive assistance from Centre' in *China Daily*, 29 December 1989.

24 Diana Lary, *Region and Nation: The Kwangsi Clique in Chinese Politics 1925–1937*, p. 106.

25 There is some historical dispute here: Benjamin Yang in 'The Making of a Pragmatic Communist: The Early Life of Deng Xioping, 1904–1949', p. 449, dates Deng's appointment as political commissar of the 7th Red Army to September 1930; Deng Rong, in *Wode Fuqin Deng Xiaoping*, p. 217, to December 1929 (but presumably in his absence).

26 For example: Benjamin Yang, 'The Making of a Pragmatic Communist: The Early Life of Deng Xiaoping, 1904–1949', p. 444.

27 This is essentially the position taken by Deng Rong in *Wode Fuqin Deng Xiaoping*, p. 267.

28 Nine out of sixty-five chapters in the Beijing edition, compared to two chapters on Deng and the construction of communist power in South-west China during 1949–52.

29 *Zuo You jiang geming genjudi ziliao xuanji* provides the CCP Central Committee's report of 14 May 1931, p. 278.

30 An unattributable source.

31 Yuan Renyuan, 'Guangxi Youjiang de hongse fengbao' ['The Red Storm on Guanxi's Right River'] in *Renmin ribao* [*People's Daily*] 9 December 1978.

32 Xu Zufan, 'Deng Xiaoping 1931nian xunguan Anhui dangwu' ['Deng Xiaoping's Tour of Party Work in Anhui in 1931'] in *Zhonggong dangshi yanjiu* [*Research on CCP History*] No. 2, 1993, p. 90.

33 Roger R. Thompson, 'The "Discovery" of Mao Zedong's *Report from Xunwu*: Deng Xiaoping Writes a New Chapter in Early Party History' in *CCP Research Newsletter* No. 3 (1989).

34 Harrison Salisbury, *The Long March*, p. 139.

35 An account of Deng Xiaoping's time in Huichang may be found in Zhong Yaqing, 'Gen Deng Xiaoping tongzhi zai Huichang gongzuo de shihou' ['Alongside Comrade Deng Xiaoping When he Worked in Huichang'] in Yang Guoyu *et al.* (eds) *Ershiba nian jian: cong shizhengwei dao zongshuji* [*In Twenty-eight Years: From Political Commissar to General Secretary*] Shanghai wenyi chubanshe, 1989, p. 256.

36 The documentation concerning the attack on the 'Luo Ming line' and the defence of those criticized may be found in Zhonggong zhongyang shujichu (ed.) *Liu Da yilai: dangnei mimi wenjian* [*After the 6th Party Congress: Secret Internal Party Documents*] Beijing, Renmin chubanshe, 1980: Luo Fu, 'Luo Ming luxian zai Jiangxi', 15 April 1933 ['The Luo Ming Line in Jiangxi'] Vol. I, pp. 351–355; Luo Man, 'Wei dangde luxian er douzheng', 6 May 1933 ['Struggle for the party line'] Vol. I, pp. 362–367; and 'Jiangxi shengwei dui Deng Xiaoping, Mao Zetan, Xie Weijun, and Gu Bo sige tongzhi erci shenmingshu de jueyi', 5 May 1933 ['Resolution of the Jiangxi Party Committee on the Second Self-criticisms of the Four Comrades Deng Xiaoping, Mao Zetan, Xie Weijun and Gu Bo'] in Vol. II, p. 51.

37 For example: Jiang Zhifeng, *Wangpai chujing de Zhongnanhai qiaoju* [*The Last Card of the Game of Zhongnanhai*] San Francisco, Minzhu Zhongguo Shulin, 1990, p. 43.

38 Deng Rong, *Wode Fuqin Deng Xiaoping*, p. 353 and p. 357.

39 Harrison Salisbury, *The Long March*, pp. 136ff.

40 Benjamin Yang, *From Revolution to Politics: Chinese Communists on the Long March*, Boulder, Westview Press, 1990, p. 107.

41 T. Kampen, 'The Zunyi Conference and Further Steps in Mao's Rise to Power' in *The China Quarterly* No. 117.

3 MILITARY SERVICE, 1937–1952

1   The forces of the 129th Division commanded by Liu and Deng also included the 344th and part of the 343rd Brigades of the 115th Division, most of whom later became part of the 2nd Field Army. These troops entered the Taihang Region alongside the 129th Division and though organizational links were maintained operated mainly in the Hebei–Shandong–Henan part of the border region and Shandong after about the start of 1940. Their most famous officers in later CCP politics included Su Zhenhua, Yang Dezhi and Yang Yong.

2   Many have recorded their memoirs of their association with Deng Xiaoping during these years. See, notably, the four volumes edited by Yang Guoyu and Chen Feiqin: *Deng Xiaoping ershibanian jian* [*Deng Xiaoping over Twenty-eight Years*] Beijing, Zhongguo zhuoyue chuban gongsi, 1989; *Ershiba nian jian: cong shizhengwei dao zongshuji* [*In Twenty-eight Years: From Political Commissar to General Secretary*] Shanghai wenyi chubanshe, 1989; *Ershiba nian jian: cong shizhengwei dao zongshuji (xubian)* [*In Twenty-eight Years: From Political Commissar to General Secretary (The Sequel)*] Shanghai wenyi chubanshe, 1990; *Ershiba nian jian: cong shizhengwei dao zongshuji (Volume III)* [*In Twenty-eight Years: From Political Commissar to General Secretary (Volume III)*] Shanghai wenyi chubanshe, 1992.

3   Liang Zheng, 'Deng Xiaoping tongzhi zai zhandong zonghui' ['Comrade Deng Xiaoping and the General Committee for Military Mobilization'] in *Shanxi dangshi tongxun* [*Bulletin of Shanxi Party History*] No. 2, 1992, p. 30.

4   Lu Jiaosong, 'Deng Xiaoping zai Fenlao' ['Deng Xiaoping in Fenlao'] in *Shanxi dangshi tongxun* [*Bulletin of Shanxi Party History*] No. 2, 1986, p. 19.

5   Agnes Smedley, *China Fights Back*, London, Gollancz, 1938, p. 85. They met on 23 October 1937.

6   'Dao Bocheng' ['To the Memory of Liu Bocheng'] 21 October 1986 in SWIII, p. 185.

7   Zhongguo gongnong hongjun disi fangmianjun zhanshi bianji weiyuanhui (ed.) *Zhongguo gongnong hongjun disi fangmianjun zhanshi* [*History of the Fourth Front Army of the China Workers and Peasants Red Army*] Beijing, Jiefangjun chubanshe, 1989.

8   Interview with Li Rui, 29 March 1993.

9   According to Benjamin Yang, 'The Making of a Pragmatic Communist: The Early Life of Deng Xiaoping, 1904–1949', p. 453, 'He was called back to Yan'an more frequently than other leaders, and would spend long nights in Mao's cave . . .' Though the first part seems unlikely, if they did spend much time chatting together it must have been during August–December 1938.

10   Li Da, *KangRi zhanzhengzhongde Balujun Yierjiushi* [*The 129th Division of the Eighth Route Army in the War Against Japan*] Beijing, Renmin chubanshe, 1985, p. 17.

11   Liu Bocheng and Deng Xiaoping, 'Jinian women de zhanyou Zuo Quan tongzhi' ['Remember our Comrade-in-arms Comrade Zuo Quan'] in *Jiefang ribao* [*Liberation Daily*] 4 July 1942.

12   Bo Yibo, 'Taiyue genjudi shi zenyang jianchi kangzhande' ['How the Taiyue base area was secured for resistance'] in *Jiefang ribao* [*Liberation Daily*] 3 July 1943.

13   Peng Dehuai, *Memoirs of a Chinese Marshal*, Beijing, Foreign Languages Press, 1984, p. 432.

14   Deng Xiaoping, 'Taihangqu guomindang wenti', 23 August 1942 ['The Nationalist Party in the Taihang Area'] in Taihangdang liunianlai wenjian xuanji bubian bianzhe, *Taihangdang liunianlai wenjian xuanji bubian* [*Supplement to Collection of Documents on the Taihang Party during the last Six Years*] 1944, p. 93.

15   Peng Dehuai, *Memoirs of a Chinese Marshal*, p. 439.

16   For example: Benjamin Yang, 'The Making of a Pragmatic Communist: The Early

Life of Deng Xioping, 1904–1949', p. 453.

17 An unattributable source.

18 For a review of the arguments, see Kathleen Hartford and Steven M. Goldstein, 'Introduction: Perspectives on the Chinese Communist Revolution' in Kathleen Hartford and Steven M. Goldstein (eds) *Single Sparks: China's Rural Revolutions*, New York, M. E. Sharpe, 1989, p. 3.

19 For example: Zhao Xiushan, 'Sanxiang zhongdade mingzhi juece' ['Three important points about a sensible strategy'] in Yang Guoyu and Chen Feiqin (eds) *Ershiba nian jian: cong shizhengwei dao zongshuji (Volume III)* 1992, p. 114.

20 Recent and informative sources include: Taihang geming genjudi shi zongbian weihui (ed.) *Taihang geming genjudi shigao* [*Outline History of the Taihang Revolutionary Base Area*] Taiyuan, Shanxi renmin chubanshe, 1987; Taihang geming genjudi shi zongbian weihui, *Taihang geming genjudi shiliao congshu, Vol. 2: Dang de jianshe* [*Historical Materials on the Taihang Revolutionary Base Area, Vol. 2: Construction of the Party*] Taiyuan, Shanxi renmin chubanshe, 1989; and Taihang geming genjudi shi zongbian weihui, *Taihang geming genjudi shiliao congshu, Vol. 4: Zhengquan jianshe* [*Historical Materials on the Taihang Revolutionary Base Area, Vol. 4: Construction of Political Power*] Taiyuan, Shanxi renmin chubanshe, 1990; and Zhonggong Shanxishengwei dangshi yanjiushi (ed.) *Taiyue geming genjudi jianshi* [*Brief History of the Taiyue Revolutionary Base Area*] Beijing, Renmin chubanshe, 1993. A somewhat briefer overview may be found in Yang Diankui, 'Liu, Deng shouzhang lingdao women you yanzhong kunnan zouxiang xinde shengli' ['The leadership of Liu and Deng led us through serious difficulties to new victories'] in *Shanxi dangshi tongxun* [*Shanxi Party History Bulletin*] No. 3, 1989, pp. 37–39.

21 Deng Xiaoping, 'Jianku fendou zhongde Jinan', 25 March 1939 ['South Hebei in Harsh Struggle'] in Zhongguo renmin daxue Zhonggong dangshixi ziliaoshi [China People's University, Department of Party History, Materials Section] (ed.) *Zhonggong dangshi jiaoxue cankao ziliao* [*Teaching and Reference Materials on CCP History*] KangRi zhanzheng shiqi [*Period of the Sino-Japanese War*] Vol. II, Beijing, Renmindaxue, 1979, pp. 303–322; and 'Shiju he jige zhengce wenti: zai beiju taolun Jinan gongzuo shi de fayan', March 1941 ['The current situation and questions of policy: talks at the symposium organized by the North China Bureau (of the CCP Central Committee) to discuss work in South Hebei'] JJLYGS 1941–1942, Vol. I, p. 13.

22 Deng Xiaoping, 'The Establishment of Base Areas and the Mass Movement', 20 February 1943 in SWI pp. 74ff; Qi Wu, *Yige geming genjudi de chengzheng: KangRi zhenzheng he jiefang zhenzheng shiqi de JinJiLuYu Bianqu gaikuang* [*The Evolution of a Revolutionary Base Area: An Outline of the JinJiLuYu Border Region of the War Against Japan and the War of Liberation*] Beijing, Renmin chubanshe, 1957, p. 7.

23 Deng Xiaoping, 'Summary Report of Political and Military Work in South Hebei', January 1943, in JJLYGS 1941–2, p. 451; Qi Wu, *Yige geming genjudi de chengzheng*, p. 84.

24 Deng Xiaoping, 'Taihangqu guomindang wenti', 23 August 1942.

25 'Deng zhengwei weihu qunzhong liyi' ['Political Commissar Deng Protected the Masses's Interests'] in *Zhibu jianshe* [*Party Branch Construction*] No. 3, 1986, p. 59; Cao Qinwen and Jiang Yanyu, 'Deng Xiaoping tongzhi guanyu dihou KangRi genjudi de jingji jianshe sixiang qiantan' ['Preliminary discussion of Comrade Deng Xiaoping's thought on economic development behind enemy lines in the base areas of the Sino-Japanese War'] in *Weiwei Taihang* [*The Towering Taihang Mountains*] No. 1, 1987, p. 4.

26 Chen Dong, 'Deng Xiaoping tongzhi yu JinJiLuYu bianqu jianshe' ['Comrade Deng Xiaoping and the Establishment of the JinJiLuYu Border Region'] in Yang Guoyu and Chen Feiqin (eds) *Ershiba nian jian: cong shizhengwei dao zongshuji (xubian)* 1990, p. 19.

27 Deng Xiaoping, 'Proposal to Establish the Shanxi–Hebei–Henan Border Region Provisional Assembly', 16 March 1941, in *Xinhua ribao* (North China Edition) 21 March 1941.

28 'Wunianlai duidi douzheng de gailue zongjie yu jinhou duidi douzheng de fangzhen: Deng Xiaoping tongzhi zai Taihang fenju gaogan huiyishang de baogao', 26 January 1943 ['Summary of conflict with the enemy during the last five-years and the consequent policy for struggle: Comrade Deng Xiaoping's report at Taihang Sub-bureau meeting of senior cadres'] *Zhandou* [*Combat*] No. 15, 15 March 1943, p. 17.

29 'Deng Xiaoping tongzhi zai Taihang fenju gaogan huiyishang de jielun diyierbufen' ['Parts 1 and 2 of the conclusions by Comrade Deng Xiaoping at the Taihang Sub-bureau meeting of senior cadres'] 20 February 1943 in Taihang dang de wenjian xuanji bianzhe, *Yijiusisannian Taihang dangde wenjian xuanji* [*Collection of Documents on the Taihang Party in 1943*] 1944, p. 107.

30 'Deng Xiaoping tongzhi eryue ershierri zai Taihang fenju gaogan huiyishang de jielun' ['Conclusions given by Comrade Deng Xiaoping at Taihang Sub-bureau meeting of senior cadres on 22 February'] 22 February 1943 in *Kangzhan yilai xuanji* Vol. I, Part 2 [*Selected Documents in the War of Resistance*] 1944, p. 103.

31 'Economic development in the Taihang Area' in SWI p. 89. The earlier and slightly different version of this speech in English may be found as 'Economic reconstruction in the Tai-hang region' in S. Gelder, *The Chinese Communists*, London, Gollancz, 1946, p. 200.

32 Bo Yibo, *Ruogan zhongda jueci yu shijian de huigu* (2 vols) [*Recollections of certain important decisions and events*] Beijing, Zhonggong zhongyang dangxiao chubanshe, 1991 and 1993.

33 Zhao Wei, *The Biography of Zhao Ziyang*, Hong Kong, Educational and Cultural Press, 1989, p. 29.

34 Yang Zhongmei, *Hu Yaobang: A Chinese Biography*, New York, M. E. Sharpe, 1988, especially p. 113.

35 'Deng zhengwei jieda shiju yu renwu zhong ji ge wenti de baogao (xi jilu gao wei jing benren shencha)', 21 June 1947 ['Political Commissar Deng Xiaoping's report provides some answers to questions about situations and tasks (unchecked by the reporter)'] JJLYGS 1945–1947, p. 132.

36 'Liu Deng guanyu yuanlai jianchi Dabieshan douzheng youjidui de qingkuang xiang junwei de baogao', 11 June 1947 ['Report from Liu and Deng to the Central Military Committee on the condition of the original guerrilla troops in the Dabie Mountains'] DZS p. 62.

37 Du Yide, 'Duhe fangong qianhou' ['Counter-attack at the crossing'] in Yang Guoyu and Chen Feiqin (eds) *Ershiba nian jian: cong shizhengwei dao zongshuji (xubian)* 1990, p. 150.

38 Hu Yaocai, 'Deng Xiaoping wei shuji de wuren zongqianwei' ['Deng Xiaoping as secretary of the five-man General Front Committee'] in Yang Guoyu and Chen Feiqin (eds) *Ershiba nian jian: cong shizhengwei dao zongshuji (xubian)* 1990, p. 242.

39 Zhong Jing (ed.) *Deng Xiaoping de lilun yu shijian zonglan (1938–1965)* [An overview of Deng Xiaoping's theory and practice (1938–1965)] Shenyang, Liaoning renmin chubanshe, 1991, p. 224. On 24 January 1947 Liu and Deng led separate arms of a pincer movement against Nationalist troops.

40 Harrison E. Salisbury, *The New Emperors – Mao & Deng: A dual biography*, London, HarperCollins, 1992, especially pp. 124ff.

41 Barry Naughton, 'The Third Front: Defence Industrialization in the Chinese Interior' in *The China Quarterly* No. 115, p. 351.

42 'Guanyu Xinan gongzuo qingkuang de baogao', 11 April 1950 ['Report on work conditions in the South-west'] in *Zhengfu gongzuo baogao huibian 1950* [*Collection of Government Work Reports for 1950*] p. 989.

43 'Overcome the current unhealthy tendencies in the party organizations of South-west

China', 6 June 1950 in SWI p. 152; Chen Biqiao, 'Jiaqiang dangde lingdao, yingjie xinde zhandou' ['Strengthen party leadership, meet the new battle'] in Yang Guoyu and Chen Feiqin (eds) *Ershiba nian jian: cong shizhengwei dao zongshuji (Volume III)* 1992, p. 265.

44 'The question of minority nationalities in the South-west', 21 July 1950 in SWI p. 162.

4 PARTY AFFAIRS AND LEADERSHIP, 1952–1960

1   Gao Lu, 'Cong Mao Zedong dao Deng Xiaoping: Gong Jiaozhi jiaoshou dawenlu' ['From Mao Zedong to Deng Xiaoping: Professor Gong Jiaozhi responds to questions'] in *Jingji ribao* [*Economics Daily*] 24 December 1993, p. 1 and p. 7.

2   Ji Dengkui later compared his own obsequious behaviour (in his view) towards Mao with that of Deng Xiaoping who was, according to Ji, both prepared to speak his mind and to stand up to Mao. Ji Dengkui, 'Wo shi Zhongguo lishishang de yiwei beiju renwu...' ['I am a tragic figure on the stage of China's history'] in *Zhongguo dabeiju de renwu* [*People in China's Great Tragedy*] Beijing, Zhongguo renmin daxue chubanshe, 1989, p. 3.

3   For the discussion at the 8th Congress of the CCP, see *Xinhua yuekan* [*New China Monthly*] Nos. 20 and 21, 1956. *New China Monthly* was a digest of articles from the press.

4   F. C. Teiwes, *Politics at Mao's Court: Gao Gang and Party Factionalism in the early 1950s*, New York, M. E. Sharpe, 1990.

5   Deng Xiaoping, 'Guanyu "Zhonghuo renmin gongheguo quanguo renmin daibiao dahui ji difang geji renmin daibiao dahui xuanjufa" caoan de shuoming', 11 February 1953 ['Explanation of the Draft Electoral Law for the PRC National People's Congress and Local People's Congress'] in *Renmin ribao* [*People's Daily*] 3 March 1953.

6   Deng Xiaoping, 'Quanguo jiceng xuanju shengli wancheng', 19 June 1954 ['The whole country victoriously completes elections'] in *Renmin ribao* [*People's Daily*] 20 June 1954.

7   Barry Naughton, 'Deng Xiaoping: The Economist' in *The China Quarterly* No. 135, September 1993, p. 491.

8   Deng Xiaoping, 'Remarks on successive drafts of the "Resolution on certain questions in the history of our Party since the founding of the People's Republic of China"' in SWII p. 279.

9   F. C. Teiwes, *Politics at Mao's Court*, p. 109.

10 Bo Yibo, '1953nian xialide quanguo caijing gongzuo huiyi' ['The National Economic and Finance Work Conference of the Summer of 1953'] in *Ruogan zhongda juece yu shijian de huigu* 1991, p. 231.

11 Rong Zihe, 'Deng Xiaoping tongzhi zai Caizhengbu' ['Comrade Deng Xiaoping in the Ministry of Finance'] in Yang Guoyu, Chen Feiqin and Wang Chuanhong (eds) *Deng Xiaoping ershibanian jian* [*Deng Xiaoping over Twenty-eight Years*] Beijing, Zhongguo zhuoyue chuban gongsi, 1989, p. 100.

12 Deng Xiaoping, 'Guanyu Yijiuwusinian guojia yusuan caoan de baogao', 17 June 1954 ['Report on Draft National Budget for 1954'] in *Xinhua yuebao* [*New China Monthly*] No. 6, 1954, p. 117.

13 Deng Xiaoping, 'Guanyu Gao Gang, Rao Shushi fandang lianmeng de baogao', 21 March 1955 in *Zhonggong dangshi jiaoxue cankao ziliao* [*Reference Materials for Teaching the History of the CCP*] Vol. 20, p. 512; translated as 'Report on the Gao Gang, Rao Shushi Anti-party Alliance' in Frederick C. Teiwes, *Politics at Mao's Court*, p. 254.

14 An unattributable source.

15 N. Khrushchev, *Khrushchev Remembers* (2 vols), Harmondsworth, Middlesex,

Penguin, 1977, Vol. I, p. 301.

16 Deng Xiaoping, 'Report on the revision of the constitution of the Communist Party of China', 16 September 1956 in SWI p. 200.

17 In SWI p. 15. Commentary on the historical linkages may be found in Rong Zihe, 'Zhongdu "Dang yu KangRi minzhu zhengquan" houde jidian huiyi' ['Emphasizing several points about "The Party and the Anti-Japanese Democratic Government"'] in Yang Guoyu, Chen Feiqin and Wang Chuanhong (eds) *Deng Xiaoping ershibanian jian* 1989, p. 20.

18 See, for example, the selection appearing in Chi Hsin, *Teng Hsiao-ping*, Hong Kong, Cosmos, 1978, pp. 44ff.

19 Liao Yilu, 'Deng Xiaoping he Suliangong ershida' ['Deng Xiaoping and the 20th Congress of the CPSU'] in Yang Guoyu and Chen Feiqin (eds) *Ershiba nian jian: cong shizhengwei dao zongshuji (Volume III)* 1992, p. 106.

20 D. Bonavia, *Deng*, Hong Kong, Longman, 1989, p. 76; D. W. Chang, *Zhou Enlai and Deng Xiaoping in the Chinese Leadership Succession Crisis*, London, University Press of America, 1984, p. 126.

21 See, for example, his activities propagandizing Mao Zedong Thought in January 1946 in Zhong Jing (ed.) *Deng Xiaoping de lilun yu shijian zonglan (1938–1965)* [*An overview of Deng Xiaoping's theory and practice (1938–1965)*] Shenyang, Liaoning renmin chubanshe, 1991, p. 216. There is even some suggestion of Deng's early involvement in the development of a cult of personality around Mao for political purposes. In 1939 Mao Zedong's personal authority had been invoked in political study campaigns in the Taihang Region. See: JinJiYu CCP area committee 'Guanyu muqian gongzuo renwude jueding' (January 1939) ['Resolution of Current Work and Tasks'] in Taihang geming genjudi shi zongbian weihui (ed.) *Dang de jianshe*, p. 135.

22 Deng Xiaoping, 'Report on the revision of the constitution of the Communist Party of China', 16 September 1956 in SWI p. 219.

23 F. C. Teiwes and Warren Sun (eds) 'Mao, Deng Zihui, and the Politics of Agricultural Cooperativisation' in *Chinese Law and Government* Vol. 26, Nos 3–4, 1993.

24 Roderick MacFarquhar, *The Origins of the Cultural Revolution* Vol. I, London, Oxford University Press, 1974, p. 26.

25 An unattributable source.

26 Liao Yilu, 'Deng Xiaoping he Suliangong ershida', p. 106.

27 Deng Xiaoping, 'Report on the revision of the constitution of the Communist Party of China', 16 September 1956 in SWI p. 230.

28 Deng Xiaoping, 'The Communist Party must accept supervision' in SWI p. 250.

29 Mao's speech 'On the Correct Handling of Contradictions Amongst the People' as delivered appears in Roderick MacFarquhar, Timothy Cheek, and Eugene Wu, *The Secret Speeches of Chairman Mao: From the Hundred Flowers to the Great Leap Forward*, Harvard University Press, 1989, p. 131; the later officially authorized and edited version may be found in *Selected Readings from the Works of Mao Zedong*, Beijing, Foreign Languages Press, 1971, p. 432.

30 In SWII p. 250.

31 Roderick MacFarquhar, *The Origins of the Cultural Revolution* Vol. I, pp. 218ff.

32 See, for example, his comments in 'The present situation and the tasks before us', 16 January 1980 in SWII p. 228; and 'Remarks on successive drafts of the "Resolution on certain questions in the history of our Party since the founding of the People's Republic of China"' in SWII p. 279.

33 'Report on the rectification campaign by Teng Hsiao-p'ing, General Secretary of the Party's Central Committee, September 23, 1957, to the Third Plenary Session (enlarged) of the Eighth Central Committee' in R. R. Bowie and J. K. Fairbank (eds) *Communist China, 1955–1959: Policy documents with analysis*, Harvard University Press, 1965, p. 341.

34 Roderick MacFarquhar, *The Origins of the Cultural Revolution* Vol. II, London, Oxford University Press, 1983.

35 See, for example, Jia Qiyun's speech on appointment as Director of the State Statistical Bureau in *Xinhua banyuekan* No. 13, 1959, p. 37.

36 'Xiaoping tongzhi zai Zunyi' ['Comrade Deng Xiaoping in Zunyi'] in *Guizhou ribao* [*The Guizhou Daily*] 13 November 1958. The newspaper story actually comments that when Deng made his suggestion the local CCP secretary 'could only smile, as he himself had not been able to make such a thorough analysis of the situation'.

37 Editorial Team of *Pedagogical Criticism*, Peking University *Guodeng jiaoyu lingyu liangtiao luxian douzheng dashiji* [*Chronology of the Two-line Struggle in Higher Education*] 20 April 1967, translated in *Survey of China Mainland Magazines* (Supplement) No. 18, 26 February 1968.

38 'Wu Lengxi tan baishu' ['Wu Lengxi confesses'] in *Qingdao ribao* [*Qingdao Daily*] 9 July 1968.

39 F. C. Teiwes, 'Peng Dehuai and Mao Zedong' in *The Australian Journal of Chinese Affairs* No. 16, 1986.

40 Fan Shuo and Ding Jiaqi, 'Ye Jianying' in Hu Hua (ed.) *Zhonggong dangshi renwuzhuan*, Xi'an, Shaanxi renmin chubanshe, 1989, No. 40, p. 87, citing *Ye Jianying zhuanlue* [*Biographical Outline of Ye Jianying*].

41 Li Rui, *Lushan huiyi shilu* [Record of the Lushan Meeting] Zhengzhou, Henan jiaoyu chubanshe, 1988.

42 In Union Research Institute, *The Case of Peng Teh-huai*, Hong Kong, 1968, p. 7.

43 Roderick MacFarquhar, *The Origins of the Cultural Revolution* Vol. II, pp. 217ff.

44 'Self-criticism at Work Conference of the Central Committee', 23 October 1966 in *Chinese Law and Government* Vol. 3, No. 4, p. 278.

45 Interview with Li Rui, 29 March 1993.

46 In *Origins of the Cultural Revolution* Vol. II, p. 229, and footnote 209 on p. 407. MacFarquhar also suggests it was broken playing table-tennis.

5 RECONSTRUCTION AND MAO, 1960–1966

1 Hong Yung Lee, *A Research Guide to Red Guard Publications 1966–1969*, New York, M. E. Sharpe, 1990.

2 For such criticism of Deng reported by Red Guards during the Cultural Revolution see, for example: Peking Red Guards, 19 January 1967, *Zhanbao* No. 3, translated in 'Documents Criticizing Teng Hsiao-p'ing's Views and Practices' in *Classified Chinese Communist Documents: A selection*, Institute of International Relations, National Chengchi University, Republic of China, Taipei, 1978, p. 249.

3 'Self-criticism at Work Conference of the Central Committee' in *Chinese Law and Government* Vol. 3, No. 4, p. 287.

4 This has been confirmed by a number of sources in China, including Li Rui in an interview on 2 June 1993.

5 F. C. Teiwes, 'Mao and his lieutenants' in *The Australian Journal of Chinese Affairs* No. 19/20, 1988.

6 The phrases 'Number one' and 'Number two' are a peculiar form of 'Chinglish' which are retained here because of common usage. However, a more accurate translation might well be 'first' and 'second'.

7 Li Rui, *Mao Zedongde zaonian yu wannian* [*Mao's Early and Late Years*] Guiyang, Guizhou renmin chubanshe, 1992, p. 87; Harrison E. Salisbury, *The New Emperors – Mao & Deng: A dual biography*, p. 324.

8 In SWII p. 329.

9 'The present situation and the tasks before us', 16 January 1980, in SWII p. 253; and 'Fayang dangde youliang chuantong he zuofeng', 18 August 1977 ['Develop the party's excellent traditions and workstyle'] in Zhonggong zhongyang dangxiao

dangjian jiaoyanshi (ed.) *Dangfeng wenti* [*Questions of Party Work-style*] Beijing, Zhonggong zhongyang dangxiao chubanshe, 1981, p. 3.

10   The extent of the problem may be seen in the revisionist official histories from the CCP's own propaganda arms, as for example: Liu Suinian and Wu Qungan (eds) *China's Socialist Economy: An outline history (1949–1984)* Beijing, *Beijing Review*, 1986, pp. 260ff.

11   The Revolutionary Liaison Station of the Red Guard GHQ for the Capital's Universities and Colleges, *Dongfanghong* [*The East is Red*] 18 February 1967, p. 20.

12   Kenneth G. Lieberthal, 'The Great Leap Forward and the Split in the Yenan Leadership' in Roderick MacFarquhar and John King Fairbank, *The Cambridge History of China, Vol. 14 The People's Republic, Part I: The Emergence of Revolutionary China 1949–1965*, Cambridge University Press, 1987, pp. 322ff.

13   On the historical linkages see D. J. Solinger, 'Economic Reform via Reformulation: Where Do Rightist Ideas Come From?' in *Asian Survey* Vol. 21, No. 9, p. 947.

14   See, for example: 'Events surrounding the Ch'ang-kuan-lou' in *East is Red*, 20 April 1967, translated in *Supplement to the Summary of China Mainland Press* No. 187, 15 June 1967, p. 23.

15   The official version of Deng's speech of 6 February is to be found in SWII p. 269. A discussion of an alternative version is to be found in Michael Schoenhals, 'Edited Records: Comparing Two Versions of Deng Xiaoping's 7000 Cadres Speech' in *CCP Research Newsletter* No. 1 (Fall 1988), p. 5. Deng's earlier speech on 'Party Building and Inner-Party Life' is abstracted in *Guanyu jianguo yilai dangde ruogan lishi wenti de jueyi zhushiben* [*Annotations on the 'Resolution on some questions in the history of the party since the founding of the country'*] Beijing, Renmin chubanshe, 1983, pp. 346ff. Deng's comments on Peng Dehuai are reported in Beijing Normal University Revolutionary Committee and the Red Guard Congress of the University Jinggangshan Commune, *Jinggangshan*, 1 August 1967.

16   Speech of 21 February 1962, on the merits of Anhui's 'individual responsibility system' in agriculture, reported in Qinghua University, *Jinggangshan*, 8 March 1967.

17   'Restore agricultural production', 7 July 1962 in SWI p. 293. In Chinese, and in the authorized translation, the cats are actually yellow and black. However, given that Deng's 'black and white cats' have now passed into contemporary legend it seems more appropriate to maintain this more usual formula. On the origins of the phrase in two of Deng's 1962 speeches, see Qian Tingtao, 'Deng Xiaoping guanyu "Huangmao, heimao" biyude chuchu ji jiduixing' ['Deng Xiaoping on the genesis of the phrase "Black cat, white cat"'] in *Zhonggong dangshi tongxun* [*Bulletin of CCP History*] No. 12, 1990, p. 6.

18   Yang Zhongmei, *Hu Yaobang*, p. 115.

19   'The establishment of base areas and the mass movement', 20 February 1943 in SWI p. 69.

20   Richard Baum, *Prelude to Revolution*, Columbia University Press, 1975, p. 15.

21   *Renmin ribao* [*People's Daily*] 23 November 1967

22   'Answers to the Italian journalist Oriana Fallaci' in SWII p. 328.

23   'Remarks on successive drafts of the "Resolution on certain questions in the history of our Party since the founding of the People's Republic of China"' in SWII p. 283 and p. 285.

24   Qiu Zhizhuo, 'Deng Xiaoping zai 1969–1972' ['Deng Xiaoping during 1969–1972'] in *Huaren shijie* [*Chinese World*] No. 1, 1988, p. 142.

25   Roxane Witke, *Comrade Chiang Ch'ing*, London, Weidenfeld & Nicolson, 1977.

26   Other examples of Deng's antipathy to Jiang Qing, which also comes through strongly in his post-Mao comments on the 'Resolution on party history', are recorded in Dick Wilson, *Mao: The People's Emperor*, London, Hutchinson, 1979, p. 379.

27   Harrison Salisbury, *The New Emperors*, p. 154.

28   'Remarks on successive drafts of the "Resolution on certain questions in the history

of our Party since the founding of the People's Republic of China"' in SWII p. 291.

29 Li Xiannian and Hu Hua, for example, reported in Harrison Salisbury, *The Long March*, p. 345.

30 See, for example, the unauthorized version of the speech of 6 February 1962 to the CCP at its so-called Seven Thousand Cadres in Michael Schoenhals, 'Edited Records: Comparing Two Versions of Deng Xiaoping's 7000 Cadres Speech' p. 5; and his speech to the 3rd plenum of the 10th Central Committee of the CCP on 20 July 1977 in *Issues and Studies*, July 1978, p. 103.

31 'Zhongguo gongchandang dibaju quanguo daibiao dahui dierci huiyi guanyu zai Moscow juxingde geguo gongchandang he gongrendang daibiao huiyi de jueyi', 23 May 1958 ['Resolution of the 2nd session of the 8th Congress of the CCP on the Moscow Meeting of Representatives of Communist and Workers' Parties'] in *Xinhua banyuekan* [*New China Semi-monthly*] No. 23, 1958, p. 11.

32 M. Schoenhals, 'Unofficial and official histories of the Cultural Revolution' in *Journal of Asian Studies* Vol. 48, No. 3, p. 564.

33 Harrison Salisbury, *The New Emperors*, pp. 154–159.

34 Liao Yilu, 'Deng Xiaoping he Suliangong ershida' ['Deng Xiaoping and the 20th Congress of the CPSU'] in Yang Guoyn and Chen Feiqin (eds) *Ershiba man jian: cong shizhengwei dao zongshuji (Volume III)* 1992, p. 106.

35 *Peking Review*, 27 July 1963.

36 'Remarks on successive drafts of the "Resolution on certain questions in the history of our Party since the founding of the People's Republic of China"' in SWII p. 286.

37 Michael Schoenhals, 'Edited Records: Comparing Two Versions of Deng Xiaoping's 7000 Cadres Speech' in *CCP Research Newsletter* No. 1 (Fall 1988), p. 5.

38 The 6th of July 1964 in *Renmin ribao* [*People's Daily*] 7 July 1964. Little was published contemporaneously and little has been made available since. This may reflect either a political control of publication or availability, or simply Deng's involvement in other activities which reduced his public profile on policy issues. See Teiwes, 'Mao and his lieutenants', p. 69.

39 Teiwes, 'Mao and his lieutenants', p. 33.

40 See, for example: 'Zai Beijing da hongweibing huiyi shangde ziwo jianshi', 2 August 1966 ['Self-examination at Large Red Guard Meeting'] DXS p. 72.

41 Hao Mengbi and Duan Haoran (eds) *Zhongguo gongchandang liushinian* (2 vols) [*Sixty years of the CCP*] Beijing, Jiefangjun chubanshe, 1984, Vol. II, p. 587.

42 Many versions, mostly similar, of Deng's 23 October 1966 self-criticism exist. In English an easily available text is to be found in 'Self-criticism at Work Conference of the Central Committee' in *Chinese Law and Government* Vol. 3, No. 4, p. 278.

43 Zhai Taifeng, Lu Ping and Zhang Weiqing, *Deng Xiaoping zhuzuo sixiang shengping dashidian Dictionary of Deng Xiaoping's works, thought, and life*] Taiyuan, Shanxi Renmin chubanshe,1993, p. 1212.

44 'Remarks on successive drafts of the "Resolution on certain questions in the history of our Party since the founding of the People's Republic of China"' in SWII p. 288; and 'Answers to the Italian journalist Oriana Fallaci' in SWII p. 326.

45 See, for example: Capital Forestry Revolutionaries, *Yuanlin geming* [*Forest Revolution*] Beijing Forestry Institute, 1967, No. 4, p. 4; and Harrison Salisbury, *The Long March*, p. 343.

46 'Answers to the Italian journalist Oriana Fallaci' in SWII p. 329.

6 MODERNIZATION AND CONFLICT, 1969–1978

1 Liu Pingping, Liu Yuanyuan, Liu Tingting, *Shengli de xianhua xian gei nin: huainian women de fuqin Liu Shaoqi* [*Flowers of Victory For You: In memoriam our father, Liu Shaoqi*] Beijing, Renmin chubanshe, 1986, p. 21.

2 Wolfgang Bartke, *Biographical Dictionary and Analysis of China's Party Leadership*

1922–1988, München, K. G. Sauer, 1990, especially p. 429.

3   Lin Qingshan, *Fengyun shinian yu Deng Xiaoping* [*Ten Years of 'Stuerm und Drang' and Deng Xiaoping*] Beijing, Jiefangjun chubanshe, 1989, p. 208.

4   Information on this period is derived largely from three sources. His daughter Deng Rong (Maomao) has written 'Zai Jiangxi de rizili' ['Jiangxi Days'] in *Renmin ribao* [*People's Daily*] 22 August 1984, p. 3, translated as 'My father's days in Jiangxi' in *Beijing Review* No. 36, 1984. This account also appears in Zhou Ming (ed.) *Lishi zai zheli chensi* [*History is drowning here*] Beijing, Huaxia chubanshe, 1986, Vol. I, p. 91. The second source is Qiu Zhizhuo, 'Deng Xiaoping zai 1969–1972' ['Deng Xiaoping during 1969–1972'] in *Huaren shijie* [*Chinese World*] No. 1, 1988. The third is Lin Qingshan, *Fengyun shinian yu Deng Xiaoping*.

5   Gao Wenqian, 'Arduous but brilliant last years of Zhou Enlai in the "Great Cultural Revolution" period' in *Renmin ribao* [*People's Daily*] 5 January 1986, translated in BBC *Summary of World Broadcasts*, 21 January 1986.

6   Deng Rong, *Wode Fuqin Deng Xiaoping*, p. 143.

7   David S. G. Goodman, 'The Provincial First Party Secretary in the People's Republic of China, 1949–1978: A Profile' in *The British Journal of Political Science* Vol. 10, No. 1, January 1980, p. 39.

8   'Remarks on successive drafts of the "Resolution on certain questions in the history of our Party since the founding of the People's Republic of China"' in SWII p. 287.

9   W. Whitson, 'The Field Army in Chinese Communist Military Politics' in *The China Quarterly* No. 37, p. 1; and W. Parish, 'Factions in Chinese Military Politics' in *The China Quarterly* No. 56, p. 667.

10 'Radical' in this context refers to political association rather than necessarily an ideological stance. Ji Dengkui, as he later accepted, was obsessively loyal to Mao during the Cultural Revolution, even when the latter was inconsistent. Li Xuefeng was implicated with Chen Boda and Lin Biao, and removed from power in 1970. Xie Fuzhi was implicated with the Gang of Four but had died in March 1972. Of these three, only Xie Fuzhi was indicted (though posthumously) for his crimes during the Cultural Revolution. Li Xuefeng was neither indicted nor listed as a victim when Lin Biao, the Gang of Four and their followers were tried at the end of 1980 and the beginning of 1981. See: Ji Dengkui 'Wo shi Zhongguo lishishang de yiwei beiju renwu...' p. 3; *Chinese Law and Government* Vol. V, No. 3–4, p. 31; and the indictments in *A Great Trial in Chinese History*, Beijing, New World Press, 1981.

11 'Senior cadres should take the lead in maintaining and enriching the Party's fine traditions', 2 November 1979 in SWII p. 218.

12 'False Charges Against Premier Zhou Enlai' in *A Great Trial in Chinese History*, p. 46. Deng's speech at the United Nations (10 April 1974) may be found in *Zhonggong dangshi jiaoxue cankao ziliao* [*Reference Materials for Teaching the History of the CCP*] Vol. 27, p. 135; and is translated in Chi Hsin, *Teng Hsiao-ping*, Hong Kong, Cosmos Books, 1978, p. 163.

13 'Zhongguo jingji wenti', 2 October 1974 ['China's Economic Problems'] DXS p. 96.

14 'Report on the Work of the Government', 13 January 1975 in *Documents of the First Session of the Fourth National People's Congress of the People's Republic of China*, Peking, Foreign Languages Press, 1975, p. 45.

15 Contemporary versions of the three specific documents are translated in Chi Hsin, *The Case of the Gang of Four*, Hong Kong, Cosmos Publishers, 1977. See also John Gittings, 'New material on Teng Hsiao-p'ing' in *The China Quarterly* No. 67, p. 489.

16 Later authorized versions may be found in 'The whole Party should take the overall interest into account and push the economy forward', 5 March 1975 in SWII p. 14; 'Some problems outstanding in the iron and steel industry', 29 May 1975 in SWII p. 18; 'Strengthen party leadership and rectify the party's style of work', 4 July 1975 in SWII p. 23; 'The task of consolidating the Army', 14 July 1975 in SWII p. 27; 'On consolidating national defence enterprises' in SWII p. 39; and 'Some comments on

industrial development', 18 August 1975 in SWII p. 43. Specific quotations are from p. 27 and p. 32.

17   'Things must be put in order in all fields', 27 September/4 October 1975 in SWII p. 49.

18   Zhonggong zhongyang dangshi yanjiushi (ed.) *Zhongguo gongchandang lishi dashiji (1919–1990)* [Chronology of Major Events in the History of the CCP] Beijing, Renmin chubanshe, 1991, p. 317.

19   The most famous statements of the so-called principle of 'bourgeois right', which they were criticizing, are to be found in Yao Wen-yuan (Yao Wenyuan), *On the Social Basis of the Lin Piao Anti-Party Clique*, Peking, Foreign Languages Press, 1975, originally published in *Hongqi* [*Red Flag*] No. 3, 1975; and Chang Chun-chiao (Zhang Chunqiao), *On Exercising All-Round Dictatorship over the Bourgeoisie*, Peking, Foreign Languages Press, 1975, originally published in *Hongqi* [*Red Flag*] No. 4, 1975.

20   'Zai Zhou zongli zhuidaohui shangde daoci' ['Speech at Memorial Meeting for Premier Zhou'] 15 January 1976 in DXS p. 102.

21   'Deng Xiaoping Zibaishu' ['Deng Xiaoping's Self-Criticism'] in Guofangbu zongz-hengzhi zuozhanwei (ed.) *Gongfei yuanshi ziliao huibian: Pipan Deng Xiaoping ziliao* [*Collection of CCP Materials: Materials Criticizing Deng Xiaoping*] Taipei, Guofangbu, 1983, p. 163.

22   Hao Mengbi and Duan Haoran (eds) *Zhongguo gongchandang liushinian* [*Sixty years of the CCP*] Beijing, Jiefangjun chubanshe, Vol. II, 1984, p. 413.

23   Hua Guofeng, 'Guanyu fanji youxiang fananfeng he pipan Deng Xiaoping wenti de jianghua', 25 February 1976 ['Speech on launching a counter-attack against those who want to reverse earlier correct verdicts and on the question of criticism of Deng Xiaoping'] in Guoli Zhengzhi Daxue Dongya yanjiu bian, *Deng Xiaoping* [*Deng Xiaoping*] Taipei, Guoli Zhengzhi Daxue, 1978, p. 304.

24   Genny Louie and Kam Louie, 'The Role of Nanjing University in the Nanjing Incident' in *The China Quarterly* No. 86, p. 332.

25   Hao Mengbi and Duan Haoran (eds) *Zhongguo gongchandang liushinian* Vol. II, p. 652.

26   Fan Shuo and Ding Jiaqi, 'Ye Jianying' in Hu Hua (ed.) *Zhonggong dangshi renwuzhuan* No. 40, p. 107; also see Fan Shuo, *Ye Jianying zai 1976* [*Ye Jianying in 1976*] Beijing, Zhonggong zhongyang dangxiao chubanshe, 1990. Ye is also a Hakka, and the events of 1976 are one source of the rumours about Deng's Hakka background.

27   Hao Mengbi and Duan Haoran (eds) *Zhongguo gongchandang liushinian* Vol. II, pp. 654ff.

28   Frederick C. Teiwes, 'Normative and prudential rules under and after Mao' in *Leadership, Legitimacy and Conflict in China*, London, Macmillan Press, 1984, p. 122.

29   See footnote 14 to SWII p. 400.

30   'Gei Wang Dongxing tongzhi chuan Hua Guofeng tongzhi de xin' ['A letter for Comrade Wang Dongxing to pass on to Comrade Hua Guofeng'] DXS p. 108.

31   Frederick C. Teiwes, 'The legitimacy of the leader' in *Leadership, Legitimacy and Conflict in China*, p. 82.

32   Hao Mengbi and Duan Haoran (eds) *Zhongguo gongchandang liushinian* Vol. II, p. 670.

33   'Gei Hua Guofeng tongzhi Ye Jianying tongzhi de xin', 10 April 1977 ['A letter to Comrade Hua Guofeng and Comrade Ye Jianying'] DXS p. 109.

34   'Mao Zedong Thought must be correctly understood as an integral whole', 21 July 1977 in SWII p. 58.

35   Both speeches may be found in *The Eleventh National Congress of the Communist Party of China (Documents)*, Peking, Foreign Languages Press, 1977. Hua's specific

comments appear on pp. 32ff; Deng's speech on p. 189.

36 David S. G. Goodman, 'Changes in Leadership Personnel after September 1976' in Juergen Domes (ed.) *Chinese Politics after Mao*, University College Cardiff Press, 1979, p. 64.

37 Yang Zhongmei, *Hu Yaobang: A Chinese Biography*, New York, M. E. Sharpe, 1988, p. 130.

38 In *Renmin ribao* [*People's Daily*] 12 May 1978.

39 Hao Mengbi and Duan Haoran (eds) *Zhongguo gongchandang liushinian* Vol. II, pp. 682ff.

40 Hao Mengbi and Duan Haoran (eds) *Zhongguo gongchandang liushinian* Vol. II, pp. 686ff; and 'Communiqué of the Third Plenum of the Eleventh Central Committee of the CPC' in *Peking Review*, 29 December 1978, p. 6.

41 *Beijing ribao* [*Beijing Daily*] and *Renmin ribao* [*People's Daily*] 16 November 1978.

7 THE FOUNDATIONS OF REFORM, 1979–1984

1 For a similar view from outside the PRC see, for example: Tang Tsou, 'Marxism, the Leninist Party, the Masses, and the Citizens in the Rebuilding of the Chinese State' in Stuart R. Schram, *Foundations and Limits of State Power in China*, The Chinese University Press, Hong Kong, 1987, p. 257.

2 Statistics are taken from *Zhongguo tongji nianjian* [*China Statistical Annual*] Beijing, Zhongguo tongji chubanshe.

3 'Central Bank Further Departs from the State', Agence France Presse, English Wire, 1 March 1994, citing *China Daily* article of 28 February 1994.

4 Most notably there is the twenty-volume collection, *Deng Xiaoping de shengping, sixiang yanjiucongshu* [*Republication of Research on Deng Xiaoping's Life and Work*] chief editor Jin Xi, published by Liaoning People's Press. A similar treatment of the relationship between Deng Xiaoping and reform was even noticeable in the most establishment parts of the press during 1983 when the first volume of *Selected Writings of Deng Xiaoping* was published. Cadres, officials and theorists of all kinds – including senior leaders Yang Shangkun and Li Desheng, as well as the well-known economist Liu Guoguang – contributed large numbers of articles on learning from the *Selected Writings of Deng Xiaoping*. See, for example: Yang Shangkun, 'Geming danlue he qiushi jingshen tongyide dianfan' ['A Model for the Unity of Revolutionary Strategy and Practical Application'] in *Jiefangjun bao* [*Liberation Army Daily*] 12 July 1983; Li Desheng, 'Deng Xiaoping tongzhi zai wodang disanci lishixing zhuanbianzhongde juece zuoyong he zhuoyue gongxian' ['The Outstanding Contribution and Strategic Function of Comrade Deng Xiaoping in The Party's Third Historical Transformation'] in *Renmin ribao* [*People's Daily*] 4 July 1983; and Liu Guoguang, 'Deng Xiaoping tongzhi zai shixian quandang gongzuo zhongdian zhuanyi douzhengzhongde zhongda gongxian' ['Comrade Deng Xiaoping's Major Contribution in the Struggle to Transform the Focus of Party Work'] in *Renmin ribao* [*People's Daily*] 12 August 1983.

5 Lucien W. Pye, 'An Introductory Profile: Deng Xiaoping and China's Political Culture', in *The China Quarterly* No. 135, September 1993, p. 415.

6 Barry Naughton, 'Deng Xiaoping: The Economist' in *The China Quarterly* No. 135, September 1993, p. 491.

7 David S. G. Goodman and Gerald Segal (eds) *China Deconstructs: Regionalism and Internationalisation*, London, Routledge, 1994.

8 Hu Yaobang, 'Lilun gongzuo wuxu hui yinyan' ['Introduction to Meeting on theory, work and ideological guidelines'] in Zhonggong zhongyang wenxian yanjiushi (ed.) *Sanzhong quanhui yilai*, Beijing, Renmin chubanshe, 1982, Vol. I, p. 48

9 'Zai Wuchang, Shenzhen, Zhuhai, Shanghai dengdi de tanhua yaodian', 18 January– 21 February 1992 ['Important parts of talks in Wuhang, Shenzhen, Zhuhai, Shanghai

and other places'] DXWIII p. 377; and 'Summary of Remarks made by Comrade Deng Xiaoping in Wuchang, Shenzhen, Zhuhai and Shanghai', BBC *Summary of World Broadcasts* FE/1346/B2/4, 3 April 1992.

10 Chen Yun, 'Jianchi anbili yuance tiaozheng guomin jingji' ['Hold fast to the principle of proportionate development to readjust the national economy'] 21 March 1979 in *Chen Yun wenxuan 1956–1985* [*Selected Writings of Chen Yun*] Beijing, Renmin chubanshe, 1986, pp. 226.

11 Hao Mengbi and Duan Haoran (eds) *Zhongguo gongchandang liushinian* Vol. II, pp. 699ff.

12 Chi Fulin and Huang Hai, *Deng Xiaoping zhengzhi tizhi gaige sixiang yanjiu*, Beijing, Chunqiu chubanshe, 1988, p. 55 ascribe this initiative to Deng personally. However, no further corroborating evidence is provided.

13 'Restore agricultural production', 7 July 1962 in SWI p. 292.

14 'Wunianlai duidi douzheng de gailue zongjie yu jinhou duidi douzheng de fangzhen: Deng Xiaoping tongzhi zai Taihang fenju gaogan huiyishang de baogao', 26 January 1943 ['Summary of conflict with the enemy during the last five years and the consequent policy for struggle: Comrade Deng Xiaoping's report at Taihang Sub-bureau meeting of senior cadres'] *Zhandou* [*Combat*] No. 15, 15 March 1943, p. 17.

15 For details, see the speech of the then First CCP Secretary of the province, Li Jingquan, to the 8th CCP Congress, in *Xinhua banyuekan* [*New China Semi-monthly*] No. 20, 1956, p. 52.

16 David Shambaugh, *The Making of a Premier: Zhao Ziyang's Provincial Career*, Boulder, Colorado, Westview Press, 1984, especially Chapter 6 'The "Sichan Experience": Blueprint for a Nation, 1976–1979', pp. 75ff.

17 *Nanfang ribao* [*Southern Daily*] 11 June 1984.

18 'Zai Wuchang, Shenzhen, Zhuhai, Shanghai dengdi de tanhua yaodian', Third part, DXWIII p. 377.

19 See, for example, Deng Xiaoping, 'Taiwan guihui zuguo tishang juti richeng', 1 January 1979 ['Let's put forward a specific programme for the return of Taiwan to the homeland'] LTZ p. 92.

20 David Shambaugh, 'Deng Xiaoping: The politician' in *The China Quarterly* No. 135, p. 482.

21 Shi Xiaochong, 'Jianquan guojia zhengzhi zhidu wenti chuyi' ['Proposals on the issue of perfecting the state's political system'] in *Minzhu yu fazhi* [*Democracy and the legal system*] No. 10, 1981, p. 6.

22 'Tiananmen shijian zhenxiang' ['The truth about the Tiananmen Incident'] in *Renmin ribao*, 21 and 22 November 1978, translation from *Peking Review* No. 48, 1978, p. 17.

23 In SWII pp. 155–156.

24 'Uphold the four cardinal principles', 30 March 1979 in SWII p. 166.

25 See, for example: 'Emancipate the mind, seek truth from facts and unite as one in looking to the future' 13 December 1978 in SWII p. 151; and 'Adhere to the Party line and improve methods of work' 29 February 1980 in SWII p. 259.

26 *Guanyu jianguo yilai dangde ruogan lishi wenti de jueyi zhushiben*, p. 7.

27 An account of the trial and its results may be found in *A Great Trial in Chinese History*, Beijing, New World Press, 1981 (no author given).

28 'Zhonnggong zhongyang zhengzhiju huiyi tongbao', 5 December 1980 ['Communi-qué of the Political Bureau of the CCP Central Committee'] in *Sanzhong quanhui yilai* [*Since the Third Plenum*] Beijing, Renmin chubanshe, 1982, p. 596; 'Comrade Hu Yao-pang's Speech to the Closing Session of the Plenum', 29 June 1981 in *Issues and Studies*, December 1981, p. 75. Presumably Deng agreed to become Chairman of the Central Military Commission to allay any concerns his former military colleagues might still harbour about the current direction of politics. According to Hu Yaobang this was the occasion on which his colleagues all agreed that Deng was the 'primary

architect' whatever his formal position in the hierarchy.

29 'The present situation and the tasks before us', 16 January 1980 in SWII pp. 241–242. 'Big character posters' is the official translation for what is more usually referred to in English as 'wall posters'.

30 Jerome Silbergeld and Gong Jisui, *Contradictions: Artistic Life, the Socialist State, and the Chinese Painter Li Huasheng*, Seattle, University of Washington Press, 1993, pp. 98ff.

31 Adopted by the 6th plenum of the 11th Central Committee of the CCP, 27 June 1981. English text in *Resolution on CPC History (1949–81)*, Beijing, Foreign Languages Press, 1981.

32 In SWII p. 302.

33 See, for example, the case of the debate on political reform during the first half of 1987 discussed in David S. G. Goodman, 'China: the Transition to the Post-revolutionary Era' in *Third World Quarterly* Vol. 10, No. 1, January 1988, p. 120.

34 'The Party and the Anti-Japanese Democratic Government', 15 April 1941 in SWI p. 15.

35 David S. G. Goodman, 'The Chinese Political Order after Mao: "Socialist Democracy" and the Exercise of state power' in *Political Studies* Vol. 33, No. 2, June 1985, p. 218.

36 As articulated in contemporary statements such as, for example, 'Senior cadres should take the lead in maintaining and enriching the Party's fine traditions', 2 November 1979 in SWII p. 208.

37 'Zai Wuchang, Shenzhen, Zhuhai, Shanghai dengdi de tanhua yaodian', second part, DXWIII p. 374 (the lack of controversy) and p. 372 (on errors).

38 *Beijing Review*, 7 April 1980, p. 11.

39 *New China News Agency*, Daily Report, 6 April 1984; and *Nanfang ribao [Southern Daily]* 11 June 1984.

40 Lucien W. Pye, 'An Introductory Profile: Deng Xiaoping and China's Political Culture', p. 417.

41 'Fazhan ZhongMei guanxi de yuance lichang', 4 January 1981 ['Develop a principled relationship between China and America'] in Zhonggong zhongyang wenxian yanjiushi (ed.) *San zhong quanhui yilai: zhongyao wenxian xuanbian [Since the Third Plenum: collection of important documents]* Beijing, Renmin chubanshe, 1982, Vol. 2, p. 649.

42 'Jieshu guoqu, kaipi weilai', 16 May 1989 ['The past is done, the future opens up'] DXWIII p. 291.

43 'Speech at 3rd plenum of 10th Central Committee', 20 July 1977 in *Issues and Studies*, July 1978, p. 103.

44 *Ming Bao* (Hong Kong) 3 March 1979.

45 Chen Yun, 'Speech to Work Conference, April 1979' in *Inside China Mainland*, September 1979, p. 3.

46 'Communiqué of the 3rd plenum of the 12th Central Committee of the CPC' in *New China News Agency*, Daily Report, 20 October 1984.

47 Chen Yun, 'Zai dangde shierju sanzhong quanhui shangde shumian fayan', 20 October 1984 ['Written report to the 3rd plenum of the 12th Central Committee'] in *Chen Yun wenxuan 1956–1985*, p. 297.

48 'Gaige de buzi yao jiakuai', 12 June 1987 in DXWIII p. 240; 'We shall speed up reform' in SCC p. 192.

49 'Xiqu lishi jingyan, fangzhi cuowu qinxiang', 30 April 1987 in DXWIII p. 229; 'We shall draw on historical experiences and guard against erroneous tendencies' in SCC p. 184.

50 *New China News Agency*, Daily Report, 29 January 1986.

8 REACTION, READJUSTMENT AND RETIREMENT, 1985 AND AFTER

1 'Zai Wuchang, Shenzhen, Zhuhai, Shanghai dengdi de tanhua yaodian', DXWIII p. 380.

2 These views were reflected in Deng's speeches of the 1970s. See, for example: 'The Army needs to be consolidated', 25 January 1975 in SWII p. 11; 'The task of consolidating the Army', 14 July 1975 in SWII p. 27; 'On consolidating national defence enterprises', 3 August 1975 in SWII p. 39; 'Yao zhibu shixian zhihui xitong de xiandaihua', 13 May 1978 ['Phase in the modernization of the command structure'] in LGJJ p. 149; 'Gao renmin zhanzheng bushi buyao jundui xiandaihua', 17 July 1978 ['People's War does not exclude military modernization'] in LGJJ p. 263; 'Xiandai zhanzheng yao qude zhikongquan', 18 January 1979 ['Modern warfare has domination in the air'] in LGJJ p. 263; and 'Haijun jianshe yao jiang zhenzhengde zhandouli', 29 July 1979 ['The development of the navy must address its real combat effectiveness'] in LGJJ p. 264.

3 'Streamline the Army and raise its combat effectiveness', 12 March 1980 in SWII p. 269.

4 'The Army should subordinate itself to the general interest, which is to develop the country', 1 November 1984, speech to the Military Affairs Commission of the CCP, in SCC p. 89.

5 Fan Shuo, *Ye Jianying zai 1976* [*Ye Jianying in 1976*] Beijing, Zhonggong zhongycang dangxiao chubanshe, 1990, p. 315.

6 *Jiefangjun bao* [*Liberation Army Daily*] 13 June 1985 editorial; and Deng Xiaoping, 'Zai junwei guangda huiyi shangde jianghua', 4 June 1985 ['Speech at Enlarged Meeting of the Military Affairs Commission'] DXWIII p. 126.

7 You Ji and Ian Wilson, 'Leadership politics in the Chinese party-army state: the fall of Zhao Ziyang', *Working Paper 195, The Strategic and Defence Studies Centre, ANU*, 1989, in particular Table 3, which lists the senior military figures and their backgrounds.

8 The five were Xu Xiangqian, Yang Shangkun, Zhang Aiping, Hong Xuezhi and Yang Dezhi. The three others were Ye Jianying, Nie Rongzhen and Yu Qiuli.

9 Documents from the National Party Conference may be found in *Beijing Review*, 30 September 1985 and 7 October 1985.

10 Chen Yun, 'Zai Zhongguo gongchandang quanguo daibiao huiyishangde jianghua' ['Speech at National Party Conference of the CCP'] 23 September 1985 in *Chen Yun wenxuan 1956–1985* [*Selected Writings of Chen Yun, 1956–1985*] Beijing, Renmin chubanshe, 1986, p. 303.

11 'Zai Zhongguo gongchandang quanguo daibiao huiyi shangde jianghua', 23 September 1985 in DXWIII p. 141; 'Speech at the National Conference of the Communist Party of China' in SCC p. 126.

12 David S. G. Goodman, 'The National CCP Conference of September 1985 and China's Leadership Changes' in *The China Quarterly* No. 105, March 1986, p. 123.

13 'Answers to the Italian Journalist Oriana Fallaci', p. 332.

14 Lowell Dittmer, 'China in 1988: the continuing dilemma of socialist reform' in *Asian Survey* Vol. 29, No. 1, p. 20.

15 Qian Chaoying, 'I am for the retirement of Deng Xiaoping: a discussion with Comrade Wei Yin' in *Shenzhen qingnian bao* [*Shenzhen Youth Daily*] 21 September 1986. This article responded to Wei Yin, 'Deng Xiaoping, please postpone your retirement for a while!' in *Yangcheng wanbao* [*Guangzhou Evening News*] 15 September 1986.

16 'Zai dangde shierju liuzhong quanhui shangde jianghua', 28 September 1986 in DXWIII p. 181.

17 Report of November 1986 meeting of the CCP Secretariat in *Zheng Ming*, 1 February 1987, translated in *Foreign Broadcast Information Services*, 29 January 1987, K2.

18 'Paichu ganrao, jixu qianjin', 13 January 1987 in DXWIII p. 198; and 'Clear away obstacles and adhere to the policies of reform and of opening to the outside world' in SCC p. 167. The interview originally appeared in *Renmin ribao* [*People's Daily*] 14 January 1987.

19 Ruan Ming, *Deng Xiaoping diguo* [*The Empire of Deng Xiaoping*] Taipei, Shibao chuban qiye gongsi, 1992, pp. 166ff.

20 Zhao Ziyang, 'Advance along the road of socialism with Chinese characteristics' in *Documents of the Thirteenth National Congress of the Communist Party of China*, Beijing, Foreign Languages Press, 1987, p. 3.

21 At least this is what Zhao Ziyang is reported to have told Gorbachev in Beijing during May 1989.

22 Lowell Dittmer, 'China in 1989: the crisis of incomplete reform' in *Asian Survey* Vol. 30, No. 1, p. 25; and Jürgen Domes, 'The Rulers: China's Last Communist Leadership?' in G. Hicks (ed.) *The Broken Mirror: China after Tiananmen*, London, Longman, 1990, pp. 121ff.

23 Jonathan D. Spence, *The Gate of Heavenly Peace*, London, Faber & Faber, 1982.

24 Amongst the many accounts of the Beijing demonstrations, those by Tony Saich and Geremie Barme are exceptional. See Tony Saich, 'The Rise and Fall of the Beijing People's Movement', and Geremie Barme, 'Beijing Days, Beijing Nights', both in Jonathan Unger (ed.) *The Pro-Democracy Protests in China*, Sydney, Allen & Unwin, 1991.

25 It will undoubtedly be some time before adequate sources of information on the decision-making process in the lead-up to military intervention in Tiananmen Square in the early morning of 4 June 1989 are made available.

26 'Talks with Li Peng and Yang Shangkun', 25 April 1989 in *South China Morning Post*, 31 May 1989, p. 12.

27 This was certainly the view taken by Marlowe Hood, the Hong Kong *South China Morning Post* correspondent in Beijing, even before the use of military force in the early morning of 4 June: see, Marlowe Hood, 'Deng overtaken by own reforms' in *South China Morning Post*, 31 May 1989, p. 12.

28 Lowell Dittmer, 'The Tiananmen Massacre' in *Problems of Communism*, September–October 1989, pp. 2ff.

29 As reported in *Far Eastern Economic Review*, 14 December 1989, p. 27.

30 Marlowe Hood, 'Deng overtaken by own reforms' in *South China Morning Post*, 31 May 1989, p. 12.

31 See, for example, Jürgen Domes, 'The Rulers', pp. 122ff.

32 Willy Wo-Lap Lam, 'Throwing new light on June 4' in *South China Morning Post*, 19 September 1980, p. 19, reporting reference materials circulating in China.

33 'Zai jiejian shoudu jieyan buduijun yishang ganbu shi de jianghua' ['Speech on meeting cadres from Beijing's martial law troops'] DXWIII pp. 302–308; 'Deng's Talks on Quelling Rebellion in Beijing' in *Beijing Review* Vol. 32, No. 28, 10 July 1989, p. 14.

34 'Women you xinxin ba Zhongguo de shiqing zuode genghao', 16 September 1989 ['We have the confidence to make the project of China still better'] DXWIII p. 324; and Geoffrey Crothall, 'Deng key to June 4 massacre' in *South China Morning Post*, p. 1.

35 Russell Skelton, 'Deng lays Tienanmen blame on leaders' in *The Australian*, 24 May 1990, p. 1.

36 Willy Wo-Lap Lam, 'Throwing new light on June 4', p. 19.

37 'Zai Wuchang, Shenzhen, Zhuhai, Shanghai dengdi de tanhua yaodian' in DXWIII p. 377.

38 Excerpts in *Beijing Review*, 12 February 1990, p. 19.

39 Asia Research Centre, *Southern China in Transition*, Canberra, Australian Government Publishing Service, 1992.

40   'Korean leader pays unofficial visit here' in *China Daily*, 13 November 1989, p. 1.

41   Huang Lianjiang, 'Films on historic theme succeed' in *China Daily*, 15 September 1989, p. 5.

42   Deng Rong, *Wode Fuqin Deng Xiaoping*, pp. 2-3.

43   'Deng meets last guest in official capacity' in *China Daily*, 14 November 1989, p. 1.

44   Zhang Ping, 'Jiang and Deng have talks with Nyerere' in *China Daily*, p. 1.

45   See, for example: Ling Hsueh-chun, 'Inside story of struggle over drafting government's NPC work report' in *Zheng Ming*, 1 April 1992; translated in BBC *Summary of World Broadcasts*, 3 April 1992, FE/1346, B2/7.

46   Michael D. Swaine, *The Military and Political Succession in China*, Santa Monica, California, Rand Corporation, 1993, p. 123.

47   Zheng Yi, *Zhu Rongyi pingzhuan* 1992, pp. 179–180.

48   'Zai Wuchang, Shenzhen, Zhuhai, Shanghai dengdi de tanhua yaodian', 18 January–21 February 1992 ['Important parts of talks in Wuhang, Shenzhen, Zhuhai, Shanghai and other places'] in DXWIII p. 370; translated in 'Summary of Remarks made by Comrade Deng Xiaoping in Wuchang, Shenzhen, Zhuhai and Shanghai', BBC *Summary of World Broadcasts*, 3 April 1992, FE/1346/B2/1.

49   David S. G. Goodman, 'The politics of regionalism: economic development, conflict and negotiation' in David S. G. Goodman and Gerald Segal, *China Deconstructs*, London, Routledge, 1994, p. 17.

50   Deng's Journey South has rapidly developed its own mythology and a sizeable literature. See, for example: Leng Rong and Gao Yi (eds) *Xuexi Deng Xiaoping tongzhi nanxun zhongyao tanhua* [*Study Comrade Deng Xiaoping's Talks on his Southern Inspection Tour*] Taiyuan, Renmin chubanshe, 1992; Yuan Shang and Han Zhu, *Deng Xiaoping nanxun houde Zhongguo* [*China after Deng Xiaoping's Southern Inspection Tour*] Beijing, Gaige chubanshe, 1992; and *Nanfang ribao she* (ed.) *Deng Xiaoping zai Guangdong* [*Deng Xiaoping in Guangdong*] Guangdong renmin chubanshe, 1992.

51   Wen Lechung, 'Deng Xiaoping yu Zhonggong dangshi yanjiu' ['Deng Xiaoping and Research on Party History'] in *Zhonggong dangshi yanjiu* [*Research on CCP History*] No. 4, 1992, p. 63; and Cheng Zhanyi, 'Renzhen xuexi guanche Deng Xiaoping tongzhi de zhongyao tanhua jingshen: jinyibu kaichuang wosheng dangshi gongzuo de xin jumian' ['Seriously study and implement the spirit of Comrade Deng Xiaoping's important talk: advance and initiate a new phase in this province's work on party history'] in *Shanxi dangshi tongxun* [*Bulletin of Shanxi Party History*] No. 4, 1992, p. 1.

52   Zhai Taifeng, Lu Ping, Zhang Weiqing (eds) *Deng Xiaoping zhuzuo sixiang shengping dashidian*, p. 1456.

53   See, for example, Deng's remarks about the War of Liberation in his 'Report on the Revision of the CPC Constitution' (1956) in SWI p. 206; or his remarks on the Taihang Region in 'Encourage Thorough and Meticulous Work' (1961) in SWI p. 263.

54   Report in *South China Morning Post*, 4 June 1993, p. 9.

55   *Agence France Presse*, English Wire Service, 20 February 1994.

9 COMRADE DENG

1   An explanation is perhaps in order here. In Chinese the term 'comrade' would be more usually applied to either Deng's whole name or just his personal name, as in 'Comrade Deng Xiaoping' or 'Comrade Xiaoping'. The use of 'Comrade Deng' is a deliberate device to produce an English-language equivalent, with a similar meaning.

2   Deng Rong, 'My father's days in Jiangxi' in *Beijing Review* No. 36, 3 September 1984, p. 18.

3   As reported in Tanjug (Yugoslav News Agency) 23 July 1977; translated in BBC

Summary of World Broadcasts, FE/5574.

4   Harrison Salisbury, *The New Emperors*, p. 328.
5   As cited in Edgar Rice, *Mao's Way*, Berkeley, University of California Press, 1972, p. 262.
6   'Jiangxi: memorial to Mao Zetan inaugurated', *New China News Agency* (in Chinese), 27 April 1986; translated in BBC *Summary of World Broadcasts*, 2 May 1986.
7   For example: Suo Yunping, Wang Chaozhu and Liu Xing, 'The Decisive Huai-Hai Campaign' in *Jiefangjun wenyi* [*PLA Art and Literature*] No. 5, 1988, p. 78.
8   Lucian W. Pye, 'An Introductory Profile: Deng Xiaoping and China's Political Culture', p. 412.
9   'Zai Wuchang, Shenzhen, Zhuhai, Shanghai dengdi de tanhua yaodian', fourth section, DXWIII pp. 378–379.
10 People's University Three-red Grab Liu and Deng Group (First Division), Capital Red Guard Congress, *Deng Xiaoping fandang fanshehuizhuyi fanMao Zedong sixiang di yanlun zhaibian* [*A Digest of Deng Xiaoping's Remarks Against the Party, Socialism, and Mao Zedong Thought*] Beijing, April 1967.
11 'Shehui zhuyi bixu baituo pinqiong', 26 April 1987 in DXWIII p. 223; 'We must continue to build socialism and eliminate poverty' in SCC p. 178.
12 'Zai Wuchang, Shenzhen, Zhuhai, Shanghai dengdi de tanhua yaodian', second section, DXWIII p. 373.
13 'Answers to the Italian journalist Oriana Fallaci', 21/23 August 1980 in SWII p. 329.
14 'Zucheng yige shixing gaige de you xiwang de lingdao jiben', 31 May 1989 ['Organize a reforming and hopeful leadership'] DXWIII p. 301.
15 'The present situation and the tasks before us', 16 January 1980 in SWII pp. 251ff.

10 DENG XIAOPING IN HIS OWN WORDS

1   For confirmation, and a description of this process, see Rong Zihe, 'Deng Xiaoping tongzhi zai caizhengbu' ['Comrade Deng Xiaoping in the Ministry of Finance'] in Yang Guoyu *et al.* (eds) *Deng Xiaoping ershibanian jian* [*Deng Xiaoping over Twenty-eight Years*] Beijing, Zhongguo zhuoyue chuban gongsi, 1989, p. 100.
2   S. R. Schram, *The Political Thought of Mao Tse-tung*, 2nd edition, Harmondsworth, Penguin, 1969, p. 113.
3   The first reported uses of this phrase were in 1962: in February at a CCP Central Committee Secretariat meeting on rural work, and in July at the 3rd session of the 7th Congress of the China Youth League. Asked later precisely what he had meant by this comment, Deng is reported to have said on different occasions that he could not remember and that it was specific to the situation at the time. See Qian Tingtao, 'Deng Xiaoping guanyu "Huangmao, heimao" biyude chuchu ji jiduixing' ['Deng Xiaoping on the genesis of the phrase "Black cat, white cat"'] in *Zhonggong dangshi tongxun* [*Bulletin of CCP History*] No.12, 1990, p. 6.
4   Deng Rong, *Wode Fuqin Deng Xiaoping*, p. 513.
5   'The Selected Writings of Deng Xiaoping, Volume Three and the Third Plenary Session' in *Ming Pao Monthly*, Hong Kong, December 1993, pp. 56–57; and 'Deification of Deng Xiaoping Strengthens Core Around Jiang Zemin' in *The Nineties*, Hong Kong, December 1993, pp. 27–29, both translated in *Inside China Mainland*, February 1994, pp. 8–16.
6   'Resolution on certain questions in the history of our party since the founding of the People's Republic of China', 27 June 1981 in *Resolution on CPC History*, Beijing, Foreign Languages Press, 1981, p.27 says of the rectification campaign of that year: 'the scope of this struggle was made far too broad and a number of intellectuals, patriotic people and Party cadres were unjustifiably labelled "Rightists", with unfortunate consequences' .
7   'Guanyu chengli JinJiYu bianqu linshi canyihui de tiyi', 16 March 1941 ['Proposal

to Establish the Shanxi–Hebei–Henan Border Region Provisional Assembly'] was originally published in *Xinhua ribao* (Northern Edition) [*New China Daily*] 21 March 1941. The republication appeared in Zhonggong Zuo Quan xianweiyuanhui, Zuo Quan xian renmin zhengfu, *Balujun zongbu zai Matian* [*The Headquarters of the Eighth Route Army in Matian*] Taiyuan, Shanxi renmin chubanshe, p. 27.

Bibliography

Until recently there had been relatively little written – in either Chinese or English – on Deng Xiaoping's life, work or writings. This remains largely true for many aspects of Deng's career before he became China's 'paramount leader'. Until his formal retirement from official position in November 1989 there were relatively few books on Deng's life and works published even within the PRC. At least partially in consequence biographies of Deng Xiaoping published outside the PRC reflect that weak information base and the lack of reliable detail.

The lack of a literature on and about Deng Xiaoping started to change dramatically during the early 1990s. In China, particularly after his retirement, though the process was clearly under way and in preparation well beforehand,[1] accounts of his life, commentaries on his ideas – particularly during the 1980s – and the compilation of his speeches and writings[2] grew rapidly. There are many individual books of note that have been published, and two pre-eminent series. One is a twenty-volume compendium published by Liaoning People's Publishing House on *Deng Xiaoping's life and thought* under an editorial group led by Jin Xi. The other is the series of memoirs edited by Yang Guoyu and others, all with variants of the title *Deng Xiaoping over twenty-eight years*. The years in question are from 1938, when Deng was appointed political commissar of the 129th Division of the Eighth Route Army, to 1965, when he was still General Secretary of the CCP but about to be forced out of office. The first of these to be published openly appeared in 1989 and whereas a further three volumes concentrated more on Deng as soldier, and in relationship to the PLA, the first focused on his more civilian activities.

The year 1994 is likely to prove a 'boom' one for the Deng industry, and that includes the production of books and articles, as well as television programmes, films, and all kinds of memorabilia on and about Deng. Already during 1993 in excess of some sixty books on Deng Xiaoping's life, work and thought were published in the PRC. Of these probably the most significant and certainly the most publicized were the first part of a biography of Deng by his youngest daughter, Deng Rong, who publishes under the name Mao Mao – *My Father Deng Xiaoping* – and the third volume of the *Selected Writings of Deng Xiaoping*, which deals with the decade 1982–1992. The year 1993 also saw the publication of an encyclopedia prepared by Zhai Taifeng, Lu Ping and Zhang Weiqing as *Deng Xiaoping zhuzuo sixiang shengping dashidian* [*Dictionary of Deng Xiaoping's works, thought and life*] in Taiyuan.

The biography and the encyclopedia together provide a solid foundation for the study of Deng Xiaoping. However, they both, like almost all the China-based literature, have to be handled with care: one central problem is the variable and unreliable relationship between openly published and restricted circulation material. Some writers only rely on openly published materials, others will cite some levels of restricted circulation publications, and others will use restricted publications but provide no references.[3] An analyst of Deng's Thought with respect to any topic may not be able to cite (or not directly) those of Deng's speeches or writings on that topic which are not openly published, and in some cases may not even have access to them. Whilst this may be frustrating for the academic outside the PRC, it may be less so for the author in China for whom the context of production is inherently political. Detailed as such biographies, commentaries and encyclopediae may be, they thus flatter to deceive. These problems are common to both Deng Rong's biography and the latest encyclopedia, but they are also shared by most of the China-based literature.

Volume One of *My Father Deng Xiaoping* deals with the first half of Deng's life, from his birth in 1904 to 1952, and certainly makes entertaining reading. However, it is less of an authoritative biography than might appear to be the case at first sight. In approaching any biography written by Deng's daughter it would be reasonable to expect that the author would have access to new and probably personal sources of information not available to everyone else, not least of which would be access to Deng himself. There is evidence of the former – for example, on her interview with Chen Zaidao, she states quite categorically that he 'was only talking to me, and so openly, because I was Deng's daughter' (pp. 411–412). Moreover, the detail on her father's family is prodigious and clears up many previous inconsistencies and ambiguities.

However, there is less evidence of direct access to Deng in the preparation of the biography. Deng Rong's main sources of information on her father's career and work appear for the most part to be other books, articles and memoirs published during the late 1980s, outside as well as inside the PRC. There is very little evidence of first-hand research and she appears not to have checked very much at all with her father, let alone to have given him the text and then cross-questioned him.

There are occasions when Deng Rong writes that she explicitly asked her father about something. However, it is far from clear that these questions were asked in the context of preparing this biography. Certainly the replies are sometimes startling in their brevity: 'What did you do on the Long March?' – 'I went along' (p. 353); 'What was it like in 1945?' – 'The going was tough' (p. 496).

Deng Rong does frequently use devices such as 'Deng Xiaoping has said ...' or ' When my father says ...', as opposed to 'I asked father ...' which as just indicated resulted in laconic and not particularly revealing replies. However, as far as can be ascertained – references generally are not provided for all quotes, or citations of specialized information – these comments all refer to published works, either in the three volumes of his *Selected Writings*, other published speeches or writings, or the published memoirs of other participants in contemporary CCP activities. The production of memoirs was extremely fashionable during the 1980s, and the term includes not only the autobiographical memoirs of events written by famous leaders – those of Li Weihan, Chen Zaidao and Liu Bocheng are frequently quoted in the biography – but also memoirs of significant leaders by their colleagues and subordinates. Amongst the latter, the four volumes of memoirs of Deng edited by former subordinates Yang Guoyu and Chen Feiqin, and previously noted, are works freely employed by Deng Rong.

Memoirs apart, Deng Rong's biography seems to draw heavily on other published material. Whole passages appear to have been rewritten from some of the more standard – though not necessarily readily available – accounts of Deng Xiaoping's life. Some of these sources are acknowledged in the brief endnotes that accompany most chapters. Those which do not include Uli Franz's description of Deng's time in France – taken from *Deng Xiaoping: China's erneurer* (Stuttgart, DVA, 1987) – though acknowledged elsewhere for later periods; Han Shanbi's three-volume *Deng Xiaoping pingzhuan* [*The Career of Deng Xiaoping*] (Hong Kong, East West and Culture Publishers, 1988); Luo Zhengkai, Jin Xi and others, *Deng Xiaoping zaoqi geming huodong* [*Deng Xiaoping's Early Revolutionary Activities*] (Shenyang, Liaoning People's Publishing House, 1992); and 'A Brief Biography of Deng Xiaoping' in *Dangshi Tongxun* [*Bulletin of Party History*] No. 9, 1984.

My Father Deng Xiaoping is a fairly detailed introduction to Deng's life and work, if not the definitive biography. Once translated, it will undoubtedly take its place amongst the standard currently available biographies in English – those by Franz, Chang and Bonavia

– as well as Ruan Ming's more polemical *The Empire of Deng Xiaoping*. However, a most scholarly and reliable series of versions of Deng Xiaoping is to be found in *The China Quarterly* No. 135 (September 1993). This is a special edition which the editor, David Shambaugh, has put together to produce *Deng Xiaoping: An Assessment* – a collection of seven articles that after Lucien Pye's discussion of Deng and China's political culture, and Benjamin Yang's analysis of Deng between 1904 and 1949, then examines Deng as politician, economist, social reformer, soldier and statesman.

The encyclopedia edited by Zhai Taifeng, Lu Ping and Zhang Weiqing is a very useful resource despite its limitations. Its great strength is its analytical lists. It provides details of all Deng's openly published speeches and writings, including publication details and analysis of contents. It has a dictionary of words, phrases and concepts to be found in Deng's speeches and writings, with detailed references. It provides lists and analyses of books on Deng Xiaoping, his life and work, both in China and overseas. Its final section is a detailed chronology of Deng's life from 1904 to the end of 1992. Its great weakness is that it only refers to openly published material. It is not the only compendium of this sort currently available in China but it does seem to be the most detailed. Perhaps the most useful of the other collections of this sort listed in the Bibliography is the volume of the *China in Reform* encyclopedia edited by Xing Bensi on *Deng Xiaoping's reformist thought* (Dalian chubanshe, 1992). It is reported that the Shanghai Encyclopedia Publishing Company is to publish a *Dictionary of Deng Xiaoping Thought and Theory* in 1994.[4]

The Bibliography that follows is divided into two parts. Because of the inherently political context of all CCP and PRC publications, these have been placed in the first section of the bibliography. The second section lists articles and books published outside the PRC. No detailed bibliography of Deng's speeches and writings is provided here as that appears in Chapter 10, 'Deng Xiaoping in his own words'.

NOTES

1   The CCP Central Committee published its pictorial biography – which contains the first official and openly published biography, also separately produced as *Deng Xiaoping zhuanlue* [*A Brief Biography of Deng Xiaoping*] Beijing, Renmin chubanshe, 1988 – of Deng Xiaoping in January 1988. This was based on 'A Brief Biography of Deng Xiaoping' in *Dangshi yanjiu* [*Research on Party History*] No. 9, 1984.

2   Zhonggong zhongyang wenxian yanjiushi (ed.) *Deng Xiaoping tongzhi zhongyao tanhua (eryue dao qiyue 1987)* [*Comrade Deng Xiaoping's most important talks (February to July 1987)*] Beijing, Renmin chubanshe, 1987; Zhonggong zhongyang wenxian yanjiushi (ed.) *Deng Xiaoping tongzhi lun jianchi sixiang jiben yuance fandui zichan jieji ziyouhua* [*Comrade Deng Xiaoping on adherence to the Four Cardinal Principles and opposition to bourgeois liberalization*] Beijing, Renmin chubanshe, 1989; Zhonggong zhongyang wenxian yanjiushi (ed.) *Deng Xiaoping tongzhi lun gaige kaifang* [*Comrade Deng Xiaoping on reform and openness*] Beijing, Renmin chubanshe, 1989; Zhonggong zhongyang wenxian yanjiushi (ed.) *Deng Xiaoping tongzhi lun jiaqiang dang tong renmin qunzhong de guanxi* [*Comrade Deng Xiaoping on strengthening the relationship between the party and the masses*] Beijing, Zhongguo gongren chubanshe, 1990; Zhonggong zhongyang wenxian yanjiushi (ed.) *Deng Xiaoping tongzhi lun minzhu yu fazhi* [*Comrade Deng Xiaoping on democracy and the legal system*] Beijing, Falu chubanshe, 1990; Zhonggong zhongyang wenxian yanjiushi (ed.) *Deng Xiaoping tongzhi lun jiaoyu* [*Comrade Deng Xiaoping Discusses Education*] Beijing, Renmin jiaoyu chubanshe, 1990; Zhonggong zhongyang wenxian yanjiushi (ed.) *Deng Xiaoping lun tongyi zhanxian* [*Deng Xiaoping on the United Front*] Beijing, Zhongyang wenxian chubanshe, 1991; Zhonggong zhongyang xuanchuanbu and Zhonggong zhongyang wenxian yanjiushi (ed.) *Deng Xiaoping tongzhi lun zhexue* [*Comrade Deng Xiaoping on philosophy*]

Beijing, Xueyuan chubanshe, 1990; Zhonggong zhongyang xuanchuanbu wenyiju bianji, *Deng Xiaoping lun wenyi* [*Deng Xiaoping discusses art and literature*] Beijing, Renmin wenxue chubanshe, 1989; Zhonggong zhongyang zhengce yanjiushi dang jianzu (ed.) *Mao Zedong, Deng Xiaoping Lun Zhongguo guoqing* [*Mao Zedong and Deng Xiaoping on the state of the nation*] Beijing, Zhonggong zhongyang dangxiao chubanshe, 1992; Zhongguo renmin jiefangjun junshi kexuanyuan, Zhonggong zhongyang wenxian yanjiushi (ed.) *Deng Xiaoping lun guofang he jundui jianshe* [*Deng Xiaoping discusses the development of national defence and the military*] Beijing, Junshi kexue chubanshe, 1992.

3 Examination of restricted publications and documents may be found in Flemming Christiansen, 'The *Neibu* Bibliography: A Review Article' in *CCP Research Newsletter* No. 4, Fall–Winter 1989–90, p.13; and Huai Yan and Suisheng Zhao, 'Notes on China's Confidential Documents' in *The Journal of Contemporary China*' No. 4, Fall 1993, p. 75.

4 *Deng Xiaoping sixiang lilun dacidian*, to be published by Shanghai Cishu chubanshe, reported in *Beijing Wanbao* [*Beijing Evening News*] 15 February 1994, p. 13.

CCP AND PRC PUBLICATIONS

Beijing Institute of Physical Education for Workers, Peasants and Soldiers, *Dadao Deng Xiaoping* [*Down with Deng Xiaoping*] Beijing, March 1967

Beijing Railways Institute, Red Flag Commune, *He qi du ye!* [*How evil it all is!*] Beijing, April 1967, translated in *Survey of the China Mainland Press* (Supplement) No. 208, p. 1

Beijing zuzhi renshi kexue yanjiusuo (ed.) *Zhongyang lingdao tongzhi lun dangde jianshe: Shiyiju sanzhonghui dao shisida* [*Leading Comrades of the CCP Central Committee Discuss the Development of the Party: From the Third Plenum of the Eleventh Congress to the Fourteenth Congress*] Beijing, Dangjian duwu chubanshe, 1993

'The Bose Uprising', *Beijing Review* No. 6 1979, 9 February 1979

Bo Yibo, *Lingxiu, yuanshuai, zhanyou* [*Leaders, Marshals, Comrades-in-arms*] Beijing, Zhonggong zhongyang dangxiao chubanshe, 1992 (2nd revised edition)

Bo Yibo, *Ruogan zhongda juece yu shijian de huigu* (2 vols) [*Recollections of certain important decisions and events*] Beijing, Zhonggong zhongyang dangxiao chubanshe, 1991 and 1993

Bo Yibo, *Bo Yibo wenxuan (1937–1992)* [*Selected Writings of Bo Yibo*] Beijing, Renmin chubanshe, 1992

Cao Qinwen and Jiang Yanyu, 'Deng Xiaoping tongzhi guanyu dihou KangRi genjudi de jingji jianshe sixiang qiantan' ['Preliminary discussion of Comrade Deng Xiaoping's thought on economic development behind enemy lines in the base areas of the Sino-Japanese War'] in *Weiwei Taihang* [*The Towering Taihang Mountains*] No. 1, 1987, pp. 4–7

Capital Forestry Revolutionaries, *Yuanlin geming* No. 4, Beijing Forestry Institute, 1967

Capital Liaison Committee to Totally Smash the Counter-revolutionary Revisionist Line of Liu and Deng, *Cedi cuihui Liu Deng fangeming xiuzheng zhuyi luxian* [*Completely Root Out Liu and Deng's Counter-revolutionary Revisionist Line*] Beijing, 12 April 1967

Chen Feiqin *et al.* (eds) *Liu–Deng dajun zhengzhanji wenxuebian* [*Collection of Literature Recording the Battles of the Liu–Deng Army*] Beijing, Junshi fanwen chubanshe, 1987

Chen Feiqin *et al.* (eds) *Liu–Deng dajun zhengzhanji xinwenbian* [*Collection of New Stories Recording the Battles of the Liu–Deng Army*] Beijing, Xinhua chubanshe, 1987

Chen Xinde, 'Zuo You Jiang geming genjudi shi yanjiu zongshu' ['Summary of Research on the History of the Left and Right River Revolutionary Base Areas'] in *Dangshi tongxun* [*Bulletin of Party History*] No. 1, 1986, pp. 25–30

Chen Yujin, *Deng Xiaoping rencai sixiang yanjiu* [*A Study of Deng Xiaoping's Thought on Human Resources*] Beijing, Jiefangjun chubanshe, 1988

Chen Zhili (ed.) *Zhongguo gongchandang jianshe shi* [*History of the Development of the CCP*] Shanghai renmin chubanshe, 1991

Chen Zhiliang *et al*. (eds) *Deng Xiaoping yu dangdai Zhongguo* [*Deng Xiaoping and Contemporary China*] Shenyang, Liaoning renmin chubanshe, 1992

Chen Zhiliang *et al*. (eds) *Deng Xiaoping zhexue sixiang yanjiu* [*Study of Deng Xiaoping's thought on philosophy*] Shenyang, Liaoning renmin chubanshe, 1992

Cheng Linsheng (ed.) *Deng Xiaoping 'Yiguo liangzhi' sixiang yanjiu* [*Study of Deng Xiaoping's thought on 'One country, two systems'*] Shenyang, Liaoning renmin chubanshe, 1992

Cheng Zhanyi, 'Renzhen xuexi guanche Deng Xiaoping tongzhi de zhongyao tanhua jingshen: jinyibu kaichuang wosheng dangshi gongzuo de xin jumian' ['Seriously study and implement the spirit of Comrade Deng Xiaoping's important talk: advance and initiate a new phase in this province's work on party history'] in *Shanxi dangshi tongxun* [*Bulletin of Shanxi Party History*] No. 4, 1992, p. 1

Chi Fulin and Huang Hai, *Deng Xiaoping zhengzhi tizhi gaige sixiang yanjiu* [*Study of Deng Xiaoping's thought on reform of the political system*] Beijing, Chunqiu chubanshe, 1988

Chi Fulin and Zhang Zhanwu (eds) *Deng Xiaoping zhezuo xuexi dacidian* [*Dictionary for Study of Deng Xiaoping's Works*] Taiyuan, Shanxi jingji chubanshe, 1992

Chi Maohua, 'Deng Xiaoping guanhuai Taihang shanqu' ['Deng Xiaoping shows appreciation to the Taihang Mountains region'] in *Jinri Shanxi* [*Shanxi Today*] No. 1, 1993, pp. 3–7

Contemporary History Bureau, Chinese Academy of Social Sciences, Beijing, *Zhongguo gongchandang lici daibiao dahui* [*Congresses of the CCP*] CCP Central Committee Publishing House, Beijing, 1982

Editorial Committee on Party Literature, Central Committee of the Communist Party of China, *Selected Works of Deng Xiaoping 1975–1982*, Beijing, Foreign Languages Press, 1984

Department for Research on Party Literature, Central Committee of the Communist Party of China, *Fundamental Issues in Present-Day China*, Beijing, Foreign Languages Press, 1987

Editorial Committee on Party Literature, Central Committee of the Communist Party of China, *Selected Works of Deng Xiaoping 1938–1965*, Beijing, Foreign Languages Press, 1992

CCP Central Committee, Department for Research on Party Literature and NCNA, *Deng Xiaoping*, Beijing, Central Party Literature Publishing House, 1988

B. Denes, *Deng Xiaoping*, Beijing, Jiefangjun chubanshe, 1988

Deng Rong [Maomao] 'Zai Jiangxi de rizili' ['Jiangxi days'] in *Renmin ribao* [*People's Daily*] 22 August 1984, p. 3; translated as 'My father's days in Jiangxi' in *Beijing Review* No. 36, 3 September 1984. Also in Zhou Ming (ed.) *Lishi zai zheli chensi* [*History is Drowning Here*] Vol.1, Beijing, Huaxia chubanshe, 1986, p. 91.

Deng Rong [Maomao] *Wode Fuqin Deng Xiaoping* Vol. I [*My Father Deng Xiaoping*] Beijing, Zhongyang wenxian chubanshe, 1993

Fan Shuo, *Ye Jianying zai 1976* [*Ye Jianying in 1976*] Beijing, Zhonggong zhongyang dangxiao chubanshe, 1990

Feng Hongda, 'Deng Xiaoping tongzhi huainian Feng Yuxiang jiangjun' ['Comrade Deng Xiaoping Commemorates General Feng Yuxiang'] in *Dangshi tongxun* [*Bulletin of Party History*] No. 7, 1983, p. 26.

Gan Weihan, 'Duanzheng dangfengde ruili sixiang wupin' ['A Sharp Ideological Weapon Ensures an Upright Party Work-style'] in *Jiefangjun bao* [*People's Liberation Army Daily*] 12 August 1983

Gao Lu, 'Cong Mao Zedong dao Deng Xiaoping' ['From Mao Zedong to Deng Xiaoping'] in *Jingji ribao* [*Economics Daily*] 24 December 1993, p. 1 and p. 7

Gao Zhiqian and Li Yanqi (eds) *Deng Xiaoping yu dangdai Zhongguo gaige* [*Deng Xiaoping and the Reform of Modern China*] Beijing, Zhongguo renmin daxue chubanshe, 1990

Gong Jiaozhi, 'Zhongguode Makesizhuyide zhongyao wenxian' ['Important Literature of Chinese Marxism'] in *Renmin ribao* [*People's Daily*] 8 July 1983

Gong Jiaozhi, 'Duanzheng dangde zhishi fenzi zhengce de juedingxing douzheng' ['The Struggle for Determination of a Correct Party Policy on Intellectuals'] in *Hongqi* No. 19, 1989

Hao Mengbi and Duan Haoran (eds) *Zhongguo gongchandang liushinian* (2 vols) [*Sixty years of the CCP*] Beijing, Jiefangjun chubanshe, 1984

He Dong, Yang Xiancai and Wang Xunsheng, *Zhongguo geming shi renwu cidian* [*Biographical Dictionary of the Chinese Revolution*] Beijing chubanshe, 1991

He Li *et al.* (eds) *Baituan dazhan shiliao* [*Historical Materials on the Hundred Regiments Campaign*] Beijing, Renmin chubanshe, 1982

He Li *et al.* (eds) *Balujun shijian renwu lu* [*Record of Eighth Route Army People and Events*] Shanghai renmin chubanshe, 1988

Hongqi zazhishe lilun jiaoyu bianjisji (ed.) *'Deng Xiaoping wenxuan' ruogan zhongyao lundian chanshi* [*Explanation of several theoretical points in 'Selected Works of Deng Xiaoping'*] Beijing, Hongqi chubanshe, 1984

Hu Hua (ed.) *Zhonggong dangshi renwuzhuan* (50 vols) [*Biographies of People in the History of the CCP*] Xi'an, Shaanxi Renmin chubanshe, 1980–91

Hua Guofeng, 'Guanyu fanji youxiang fananfeng he pipan Deng Xiaoping wenti de jianghua', 25 February 1976 ['Speech on launching a counter-attack against those who want to reverse earlier correct verdicts and on the question of criticism of Deng Xiaoping'] in Guoli Zhengzhi Daxue Dongya yanjiu bian, *Deng Xiaoping* [*Deng Xiaoping*] Taipei, Guoli Zhengzhi Daxue, 1978, pp. 304–307

Huang Shaoqun (ed.) *Deng Xiaoping guanyu dangde jiben luxian sixiang yanjiu* [*Study of Deng Xiaoping's thought on the party's basic line*] Shenyang, Liaoning renmin chubanshe, 1992

Ji Dengkui, 'Wo shi Zhongguo lishishang de yiwei beiju renwu...' ['I am a tragic figure on the stage of China's history'] in *Zhongguo dabeiju de renwu* [*People in China's Great Tragedy*] Beijing, Zhongguo renmin daxue chubanshe, 1989, p. 3

Jiang Liu, 'Kexue shehuizhuyi xinshengli de zhinan' ['A Guide to New Victories for Scientific Socialism'] in *Dangshi tongxun* [*Bulletin of Party History*] No. 22, 1983, pp. 28–29

Jiang Zemin, 'Liu Fa, Bi qingong yingxue de huiyi' ['Reminiscences of diligent work and thrifty study in Belgium and France'] in *Pufa qingong jianxue yundong shiliao* [*Historical Materials on the Work-Study Movement in France*] Beijing, Beijing renmin chubanshe, 1981, Vol. 3

Jiang Yingguang, *Deng Xiaoping duiwai kaifang sixiang yanjiu* [*Study of Deng Xiaoping's thought on opening to the outside world*] Shenyang, Liaoning renmin chubanshe, 1992

Jiangxi Academy of Social Sciences, *Deng Xiaoping de sixiang chutan* [*Preliminary Discussion of Deng Xiaoping's Thought*] Jiangxi renmin chubanshe, 1988

Jin Xi *et al.* (eds) *Deng Xiaoping de shengping, sixiang yanjiu zongmu* [*Comprehensive table of study on Deng Xiaoping's life and thought*] Shenyang, Liaoning renmin chubanshe, 1992

Jin Xi *et al.* (eds) *Deng Xiaoping guoji zhanlue sixiang yanjiu* [*Study of Deng Xiaoping's thought on international strategy*] Shenyang, Liaoning renmin chubanshe, 1992

Jin Xi (ed.) *Deng Xiaoping shehuizhuyi xiandaihua zhanlue sixiang yanjiu* [*Study of Deng Xiaoping's thought on the strategy for socialist modernization*] Shenyang, Liaoning renmin chubanshe, 1992

Jin Xi *et al.* (eds) *Deng Xiaoping shehuizhuyi jingshen wenming jianshe sixiang yanjiu* [*Study of Deng Xiaoping's thought on the development of a socialist spiritual civilization*] Shenyang, Liaoning renmin chubanshe, 1992

Jin Yu and Chen Xiankui, *Dangdai Zhongguo dasilu* [*Contemporary China's Great Theoretical Road*] Beijing, Zhongguo renmin daxue chubanshe, 1989

Junshi kexueyuan junshi tushuguan bianzhe, *Zhongguo renmin jiefangjun zuzhi yange he geji lingdao chengyuan minglu* [*PLA Organizational Development and Name List at Each Level of Leadership*] Beijing, Junshi kexue chubanshe, 1987

Leng Rong, 'Deng Xiaoping yu xinjiefangqu nongcun gongzuo zhengcede zhuanbian' ['Deng Xiaoping and the Transformation of Policy on Rural Work in Newly Liberated Areas'] in *Zhonggong dangshi yanjiu* [*Research on CCP History*] No. 6, 1989, pp. 1–6

Leng Rong and Gao Yi (eds) *Xuexi Deng Xiaoping tongzhi nanxun zhongyao tanhua* [*Study Comrade Deng Xiaoping's Talks on his Southern Inspection Tour*] Taiyuan, Renmin chubanshe, 1992

Li Bingying (ed.) *Deng Xiaoping shehuizhuyi shichang jingji sixiang yanjiu* [*Study of Deng Xiaoping's thought on the socialist market economy*] Shenyang, Liaoning renmin chubanshe, 1992

Li Da, *KangRi zhanzhengzhongde Balujun Yierjiushi* [*The 129th Division of the Eighth Route Army in the War Against Japan*] Beijing, Renmin chubanshe, 1985

Li Desheng, 'Deng Xiaoping tongzhi zai wodang disanci lishixing zhuanbianzhongde juece zuoyong he zhuoyue gongxian' ['The Outstanding Contribution and Strategic Function of Comrade Deng Xiaoping in The Party's Third Historical Transformation'] in *Renmin ribao* [*People's Daily*] 4 July 1983

Li Jian (ed.) *Deng Xiaoping: sanjin sanchu Zhongnanhai* [*Deng Xiaoping: three times in and three times out of Zhongnanhai*] Beijing, Zhongguo dadi chubanshe, 1993

Li Mingde, 'Deng Xiaoping tongzhi zai douzheng shixianzhong yongxinde jingyan fengfu he fazhanle Mao Zedong sixiang' ['Comrade Deng Xiaoping in Line Struggle Uses Rich Experience and Develops Mao Zedong Thought'] in *Guangming ribao* [Guangming Daily] 2 July 1983

Li Qinzhi and Wang Yuezong (eds) *Weidade shixian, guanghuide sixiang: Deng Xiaoping geming huodong dashiji* [*Great practice, splendid thought: Record of events in Deng Xiaoping's revolutionary activities*] Beijing, Hualing chubanshe, 1990

Li Rui, *Lushan huiyi shilu* [*Record of the Lushan Meeting*] Zhengzhou, Henan jiaoyu chubanshe, 1988

Li Rui, *Mao Zedongde zaonian yu wannian* [*Mao's Early and Late Years*] Guiyang, Guizhou renmin chubanshe, 1992

Li Rui, *Mao Zedong de gongguo shi fei* [*Mao Zedong's Evil Achievements*] Taipei, Xinrui chubanshe, 1994

Li Shi'an *et al.*, 'Dabieshanqu de sannian youjizhan he Gao jingting tongzhi' ['Comrade Gao Jingting and Three Years of Guerrilla War in the Dabie Mountains'] in *Geming huiyilu* [*Reminiscences of the Revolution*] No. 7, 1982, pp. 55–81

Li Weihan, *Huiyi yu yanjiu* [*Reminiscences and Research*] Beijing, Zhonggong wenxian chubanshe, 1986

Li Xinzhi and Wang Yuezong, *Weidade shixian, guanghuide sixiang: Deng Xiaoping geming huodong dashiji* [*Great Achievements, Brilliant Thought: Chronology of Deng Xiaoping's Revolutionary Activities*] Beijing, Hualing chubanshe, 1990

Liang Biye, 'Sixiang jiben yuanze shi xinshiqi zhengzhi gongzuode genben lingdao yuanze' ['The Four Basic Principles are the Fundamental Leadership Principles of Political Work in the New Era'] in *Jiefangjun bao*, 18 August 1983

Liang Zheng, 'Deng Xiaoping tongzhi zai zhandong zonghui' ['Comrade Deng Xiaoping and the General Committee for Military Mobilization'] in *Shanxi dangshi tongxun* [*Bulletin of Shanxi Party History*] No. 2, 1992, p. 30

Liaowang reporter, 'Shi Deng Xiaoping de huazhuan, ye shi Zhongguo geming de shihua' ['Deng Xiaoping's life in pictures is a historical picture of China's revolution'] in *Liaowang* No. 7, 15 February 1988

Lin Qingshan, *Fengyun shinian yu Deng Xiaoping* [*Ten Years of 'Stuerm und Drang' and Deng Xiaoping*] Beijing, Jiefangjun chubanshe, 1989

Lin Yingjia *et al.*, *Deng Xiaoping xinshiqi junshi zhexue sixiang* [*Deng Xiaoping's military philosophy and thought in the new era*] Beijing, Junshi kexue chubanshe, 1991

Liu Bocheng *et al.*, *Liu Bocheng huiyilu* (3 vols) [*Reminiscences of Liu Bocheng*] Shanghai wenyi chubanshe, 1981, 1985, 1987

Liu Guoguang, 'Deng Xiaoping tongzhi zai shixian quandang gongzuo zhongdian zhuanyi douzhengzhongde zhongda gongxian' ['Comrade Deng Xiaoping's Major Contribution in the Struggle to Transform the Focus of Party Work'] in *Renmin ribao* [*People's Daily*] 12 August 1983

Liu Guoguang, *Xuexi 'Deng Xiaoping wenxuan' fazhan he fanrong shehui kexue* [*Study 'Selected Works of Deng Xiaoping' to develop a flourishing social science*] Beijing, Zhongguo shehui kexue chubanshe, 1984

Liu Jianming (ed.) *Deng Xiaoping xuanchuan sixiang yanjiu* [*Study of Deng Xiaoping's thought on propaganda*] Shenyang, Liaoning renmin chubanshe, 1990

Liu Peng, Li Qinghua and Xia Aiping (eds) *Deng Xiaoping shehuizhuyi jingji sixiang lun* [*On Deng Xiaoping's Socialist Economic Thought*] Beijing, Zhonggong zhongyang dangxiao chubanshe, 1992

Liu Xianyan (ed.) *Deng Xiaoping junshi sixiang yanjiu* [*Study of Deng Xiaoping's thought on military affairs*] Shenyang, Liaoning renmin chubanshe, 1992

Lu Jiaosung, 'Deng Xiaoping zao Fenlao' ['Deng Xiaoping in Fenlao'] in *Shanxi dangshi tongxun* [*Bulletin of Shanxi Party History*] No. 2, 1986, p. 19

Luo Fu, 'Luo Ming luxian zai Jiangxi', 15 April 1933 ['The Luo Ming Line in Jiangxi'] in Zhonggong zhongyang shujichu (ed.) *Liu Da yilai: dangnei mimi wenjian* [*After the 6th Party Congress: Secret Internal Party Documents*] Beijing, Renmin chubanshe, 1980, pp. 351–355

Luo Man, 'Wei dangde luxian er douzheng', 6 May 1933 ['Struggle for the party line'] in Zhonggong zhongyang shujichu (ed.) *Liu Da yilai: dangnei mimi wenjian* [*After the 6th Party Congress: Secret Internal Party Documents*] Beijing, Renmin chubanshe, 1980, pp. 362–367

Luo Songrong and Wei Mingsheng, 'Dangshi yanjiu yao jiaqiang dui Deng Xiaoping de jingji sixiang de yanjiu' ['Party History Must Strengthen its Research on Deng Xiaoping's Economic Thought'] in *Zhonggong dangshi yanjiu* [*Research on CCP History*] No. 5, 1992, pp. 70–73

Luo Zhengkai, Jin Xi *et al.*, *Deng Xiaoping zaoqi geming huodong* [*Deng Xiaoping's Early Revolutionary Activities*] Shenyang, Liaoning renmin chubanshe, 1992

Mao Zedong, 'Speech at the Group Leaders Forum of the Enlarged Conference of the Military Affairs Commission' (excerpts) (28 June 1958) in *Chinese Law and Government* Vol. 1, No. 4, pp. 15–21

Nanfang ribao she (ed.) *Deng Xiaoping zai Guangdong* [*Deng Xiaoping in Guangdong*] Guangdong renmin chubanshe, 1992

Pan Qi (ed.) *Deng Xiaoping kexue jishu sixiang yanjiu* [*A Study of Deng Xiaoping's Scientific and Technical Thought*] Nanning, Guangxi kexue jishu chubanshe, 1992

Pan Songting, Huang Hai *et al.*, *'Deng Xiaoping wenxuan' xuexi tiyao* [*Guide to Studying 'Selected Writings of Deng Xiaoping'*] Jiangsu renmin chubanshe, 1983

Peng Dehuai, *Memoirs of a Chinese Marshal*, Beijing, Foreign Languages Press, 1984

People's University Three-red Grab Liu and Deng Group (First Division), Capital Red Guard Congress, *Deng Xiaoping fandang fanshehuizhuyi fanMao Zedong sixiang di yanlun zhaibian* [*A Digest of Deng Xiaoping's Remarks Against the Party, Socialism, and Mao Zedong Thought*] Beijing, April 1967

Qian Tingtao, 'Deng Xiaoping guanyu "Huangmao, heimao" biyude chuchu ji jiduixing' ['Deng Xiaoping on the genesis of the phrase "Black cat, white cat"'] in *Zhonggong dangshi tongxun* [*Bulletin of CCP History*] No.12, 1990, p. 6

Qing Ye and Fang Lei, *Deng Xiaoping zai 1976* (2 vols) [*Deng Xiaoping in 1976*] Shenyang, Chunfeng wenyi chubanshe, 1993

Qiu Zhizhuo, 'Deng Xiaoping zai 1969–1972' ['Deng Xiaoping during 1969–1972'] in

Huaren shijie [*Chinese World*] No. 1, 1988

Red Sun, *Deng Xiaoping and the 'General Program'*, San Francisco, Red Sun Publishers, 1977

Sichuansheng Deng Xiaoping sixiang yanjiu xiaozu (ed.) *Deng Xiaoping dui Mao Zedong sixiangde xinfazhan* [*Deng Xiaoping's new development of Mao Zedong Thought*] Chengdu, Chengdu chubanshe, 1991

Su Ya and Jia Lusheng, *Baimao heimao: Zhongguo gaige xianzhuang toushi* [*White cats, black cats: Perspectives on China's reform and the current situation*] Changsha, Hunan renmin chubanshe, 1992

Sun Liancheng, *Deng Xiaoping: Zhongguo xinshiqi de zongshe jishi* [*Deng Xiaoping: The architect of China's new era*] Zhengzhou, Henan renmin chubanshe, 1990

Suo Yunping, Wang Chaozhu, Liu Xing, 'The Decisive Huai-Hai Campaign' in *Jiefangjun wenyi* [PLA Art and Literature] No. 5, 1988, p. 78

Taihang geming genjudi shi zongbian weihui (ed.) *Taihang geming genjudi shigao* [*Outline History of the Taihang Revolutionary Base Area*] Taiyuan, Shanxi renmin chubanshe, 1987

Taihang geming genjudi shi zongbian weihui, *Taihang geming genjudi shiliao congshu, Vol. 2: Dang de jianshe* [*Historical Materials on the Taihang Revolutionary Base Area, Vol. 2: Construction of the Party*] Taiyuan, Shanxi renmin chubanshe, 1989

Taihang geming genjudi shi zongbian weihui, *Taihang geming genjudi shiliao congshu, Vol. 4: Zhengquan jianshe* [*Historical Materials on the Taihang Revolutionary Base Area, Vol. 4: Construction of Political Power*] Taiyuan, Shanxi renmin chubanshe, 1990

Teng Dun *et al.* (eds) *Deng Xiaoping jiaoyu sixiang yanjiu* [*Study of Deng Xiaoping's thought on education*] Shenyang, Liaoning renmin chubanshe, 1992

Teng Wensheng and Jia Chunfeng, 'Jianshe you Zhongguo tesede shehui zhuyi' ['Building Socialism with Chinese Characteristics'] in *Guangming ribao* [*Guangming Daily*] 22 August 1983

Tian Fu *et al.* (eds) *Deng Xiaoping dangjian lunzhu yanjiu* [*Research into Deng Xiaoping on the development of the party*] Jinan, Shandong renmin chubanshe, 1991

Tianjin University Investigation Team, August 13 Red Guards Liaison Station for Criticizing Liu, Deng and Tao, *Ba yi san hongweibing* [*August 13 Red Guards*] 17 April 1967

Wang Shigen, *Liu Deng dajun yanjin Dabieshan* [*The Liu Deng Army Enters the Dabie Mountains*] Shanghai renmin chubanshe, 1987

Wang Zhengping *et al.* (eds) *Deng Xiaoping jianchi sixiang jiben yuanze sixiang yanjiu* [*Study of Deng Xiaoping's thought on adherence to the Four Cardinal Principles*] Shenyang, Liaoning renmin chubanshe, 1992

Wei Xinsheng, 'Deng Xiaoping yu dang zai shehuizhuyi chuji jieduande jiben luxian' ['The Basic Line of Deng Xiaoping and the Party in the Primary Stage of Socialism'] in *Zhonggong dangshi yanjiu* [Research on CCP History] No. 3, 1993, pp. 8–14

Wen Lechung, 'Deng Xiaoping yu Zhonggong dangshi yanjiu' ['Deng Xiaoping and Research on Party History'] in *Zhonggong dangshi yanjiu* [*Research on CCP History*] No. 4, 1992, p. 63

Wu Jiaxiang, *Deng Xiaoping: Sixiang yu shijian (1977–1987)* [*Deng Xiaoping: Thought and Practice*] Changsha, Hunan Renmin chubanshe, 1988

Wu Jie, *Deng Xiaoping sixiang lun* [*A Discussion of Deng Xiaoping's Thought*] Beijing, Renmin chubanshe, 1992

Wu Xin and Lin Qing, 'Hong qi ba jun zongzhihui Li Mingrui lieshi shiji' ['Memoir of Commander Li Mingrui of the Red 7th and 8th Armies'] in *Geming huiyilu* [*Reminiscences of the Revolution*] No. 7, 1982, pp. 99–115

Xiang Feng, 'Deng Xiaoping tongzhi heshi dao Balujun Yierjiushi gongzuo' ['When did Comrade Deng Xiaoping Arrive for Work at the 8th Route Army's 129 Division'] in *Dangshi tongxun* [*Bulletin of Party History*] No. 9, 1985, p. 34

Xiang Meiqing and Wang Furu (eds) *Deng Xiaoping jianshe you Zhongguo tese shehuizhuyi lilun yanjiu* [*Study of Deng Xiaoping's theory of building socialism with Chinese characteristics*] Shenyang, Liaoning renmin chubanshe, 1992

Xinhua shudian, *Dihou KangRi genjudi jieshao* [*An Introduction to Anti-Japanese Base Areas behind the Enemy Lines*] Xinhua shudian, n.d.

Xing Bensi (ed.) *Zhongguo gaige quanshu: Deng Xiaoping gaige sixiang quan* [*Encyclopedia of Reform in China: Volume on Deng Xiaoping's reformist thought*] Dalian chubanshe, 1992

Xu Fenglan and Zheng Naofei, *Chen Geng jiangjun zhuan* [*Biography of General Chen Geng*] Beijing, Jiefangjun chubanshe, 1988

Xu Mingshan, *Deng Xiaoping xinshiqi zhengzhi gongzuo lilun yanjiu* [*A study of Deng Xiaoping's political work and theory in the new era*] Beijing, Haichao chubanshe, 1992

Xu Xiangqian, *Lishi de huigu* (3 vols) [*Recalling History*] Beijing, Jiefangchun chubanshe, 1984

Xu Zufan, 'Deng Xiaoping 1931nian xunguan Anhui dangwu' ['Deng Xiaoping's Tour of Party Work in Anhui in 1931'] in *Zhonggong dangshi yanjiu* [*Research on CCP History*] No. 2, 1993, pp. 90–91

Yan Zhixin, 'Li Dazhao, Deng Xiaoping yu Feng Yuxiang' ['Li Dazhao, Deng Xiaoping and Feng Yuxiang'] in *Dangshi tongxun* [*Bulletin of Party History*] No. 4, 1985

Yang Chunchang, *Deng Xiaoping xinshiqi jianjun sixiang yanjiu* [*Study of Deng Xiaoping's Thought on the Development of the Army during the New Era*] Beijing, Jiefangjun chubanshe, 1989

Yang Diankui, 'Liu, Deng shouzhang lingdao women you yanzhong kunnan zouxiang xinde shengli' ['The leadership of Liu and Deng led us through serious difficulties to new victories'] in *Shanxi dangshi tongxun* [*Shanxi Party History Bulletin*] No. 3, 1989, pp. 37–39

Yang Guoyu, *Liu Deng mixia shisan nian* [*Thirteen Years under the Command of Liu and Deng*] Beijing, Renmin chubanshe, 1986

Yang Guoyu et al. (eds) *Zhanzhengqin liji: Liu–Deng dajun laozhanshi zuopinji* vols [*Close to the Action: Writings by Former Fighters in the Liu–Deng Army*] Tianjin, Baihua wenyi chubanshe, 1988

Yang Guoyu and Chen Feiqin, *Dierye zhanjun jishi* [*Chronology of the Second Field Army*] Shanghai wenyi chubanshe, 1988

Yang Guoyu, Chen Feiqin and Wang Chuanhong (eds) *Deng Xiaoping ershibanian jian* [Deng Xiaoping over Twenty-eight Years] Beijing, Zhongguo zhuoyue chuban gongsi, 1989

Yang Guoyu, Chen Feiqin and Wang Chuanhong (eds) *Ershiba nian jian: cong shizhengwei dao zongshuji* [*In Twenty-eight Years: From Political Commissar to General Secretary*] Shanghai wenyi chubanshe, 1989

Yang Guoyu and Chen Feiqin (eds) *Ershiba nian jian: cong shizhengwei dao zongshuji (xubian)* [*In Twenty-eight Years: From Political Commissar to General Secretary (The Sequel)*] Shanghai wenyi chubanshe, 1990

Yang Guoyu and Chen Feiqin (eds) *Ershiba nian jian: cong shizhengwei dao zongshuji (Volume III)* [*In Twenty-eight Years: From Political Commissar to General Secretary (Volume III)*] Shanghai wenyi chubanshe, 1992

Yang Guoyu, Chen Feiqin and Wan Wei (eds) *Liu–Deng jun zhanli* [*The Fighting Strength of the Liu–Deng Army*] Yunnan renmin chubanshe, 1984

Yang Pengyu, *Weidade gaigejia Deng Xiaoping* [*Deng Xiaoping the Great Reformer*] Beijing, Zhongguo xinwen chubanshe, 1989

Yang Shangkun, 'Geming danlue he qiushi jingshen tongyide dianfan' ['A Model for the Unity of Revolutionary Strategy and Practical Application'] in *Jiefangjun bao* [*Liberation Army Daily*] 12 July 1983

Yao Chuanwang et al. (eds) *Deng Xiaoping zhuzuo zhuanti yanjiu* [*Specialist Research on*

Deng Xiaoping's Writings] Beijing, Renmin chubanshe, 1988

Yao Chuanwang *et al.* (eds) *Deng Xiaoping gaige sixiang yanjiu* [*Study of Deng Xiaoping's thought on reform*] Shenyang, Liaoning renmin chubanshe, 1992

Yao Ping (ed.) *Xinshiqi Deng Xiaoping zhanlue sixiang yanjiu* [*Study of Deng Xiaoping's Strategic Thought in the New Era*] Xi'an, Shaanxi renmin chubanshe, 1989

Yuan Renyuan, 'Guangxi Youjiang de hongse fengbao' ['The Red Storm on Guangxi's Right River'] in *Renmin ribao* [*People's Daily*] 9 December 1978

Yuan Shang and Han Zhu, *Deng Xiaoping nanxun houde Zhongguo* [*China after Deng Xiaoping's Southern Inspection Tour*] Beijing, Gaige chubanshe, 1992

Yue Zong and Xin Zhi, *Deng Xiaoping shengping yu lilun yanjiu huibian* [*Collection of Research on the Life and Theory of Deng Xiaoping*] Beijing, Zhonggong dangshi ziliao chubanshe, 1988

Zang Leyuan, Wang Yongshan, Mu Xiukun (eds) *Deng Xiaoping sixiang yanjiu* [*Research on Deng Xiaoping Thought*] Guangxi renmin chubanshe, 1988

Zhai Taifeng, Lu Ping, Zhang Weiqing (eds) *Deng Xiaoping zhuzuo sixiang shengping dashidian* [*Dictionary of Deng Xiaoping's works, thought, and life*] Taiyuan, Shanxi renmin chubanshe, 1993

Zhang Chenzhong *et al.* (eds) *Deng Xiaoping guanyu zhishi fenzi wenti de sixiang yanjiu* [*Study of Deng Xiaoping's thought on intellectuals*] Shenyang, Liaoning renmin chubanshe, 1992

Zhang Shiming and Zheng Shaoguo (eds) *Deng Xiaoping zhenwenlu* [*Deng Xiaoping's Treasured Words*] Beijing, Zhishi chubanshe, 1993

Zhang Yiling *et al.* (eds) *Deng Xiaoping keji sixiang yanjiu* [*Study of Deng Xiaoping's thought on science and technology*] Shenyang, Liaoning renmin chubanshe, 1992

Zhen Xiaoying (ed.) *Deng Xiaoping jiandang sixiang yanjiu* [*Study of Deng Xiaoping's thought on strengthening the party*] Shenyang, Liaoning renmin chubanshe, 1992

Zhong Fuju, 'Deng Xiaoping "Zhongdian zhuanyi" sixiang chutan' ['Preliminary Investigation of Deng Xiaoping's "Important Transformation"'] in *Xinan shifandaxuebao* [*Journal of South-west Normal University*] No. 2, 1993, pp. 1–5

Zhong Jing (ed.) *Deng Xiaoping de lilun yu shijian zonglan (1938–1965)* [*An overview of Deng Xiaoping's theory and practice (1938–1965)*] Shenyang, Liaoning renmin chubanshe, 1991

Zhonggong Shanxishengwei dangshi yanjiushi (ed.) *Taiyue geming genjudi jianshi* [*Brief History of the Taiyue Revolutionary Base Area*] Beijing, Renmin chubanshe, 1993

Zhonggong Shenzhen shiwei xuanchuanbu (ed.) *Deng Xiaoping yu Shenzhen: Yijiujiuer chun* [*Deng Xiaoping and Shenzhen: Spring 1992*] Shenzhen, Haitian chubanshe, 1992

Zhonggong zhongyang, 'Zhongguo gongchandang dibaju quanguo daibiao dahui dierci huiyi guanyu zai Moscow juxingde geguo gongchandang he gongrendang daibiao huiyi de jueyi' (23 May 1958) ['Resolution of the 2nd session of the 8th Party Congress on the Moscow Meeting of Representatives of Communist and Workers' Parties'] in *Xinhua banyuekan* [*New China Semi-monthly*] No. 12, 1958, pp. 11–14

Zhonggong zhongyang bangongting mishuju ziliaoshi, *Deng Xiaoping lun dangde jianshe* [*Deng Xiaoping on party development*] Beijing, Renmin chubanshe, 1990

Zhonggong zhongyang dangshi yanjiushi (ed.) *Zhongguo gongchandang lishi dashiji (1919–1990)* [*Chronology of Major Events in the History of the CCP*] Beijing, Renmin chubanshe, 1991, p. 317

Zhonggong zhongyang dangshi ziliao zhengji weiyuanhui (ed.) *Huai-Hai Zhanyi* (3 vols) [*The Battle of Huai-Hai*] Beijing, Zhonggong dangshi ziliao chubanshe, 1988

Zhonggong zhongyang dangxiao dangshi jiaoyanshi (ed.) *Zhongguo gongchandang lishi dashiji* [*Chronology of Major Events in the History of the CCP*] Beijing, Renmin chubanshe, 1989

Zhonggong zhongyang dangxiao dangshi jiaoyanshi (ed.) *Zhonggong gongchandang lishi – Vol. 2: 1937–1949* [*History of the CCP*] Beijing, Renmin chubanshe, 1990

Zhonggong zhongyang dangxiao dangshi jiaoyanshi ziliaozu (ed.) *Zhongguo gongchan-*

dang lici zhongyao huiyi ji: Vol. 1 [*Important Meetings of the CCP*] Shanghai, Renmin chubanshe, 1982

Zhonggong zhongyang shujichu (ed.) *Liu Da yilai: dangnei mimi wenjian* [*After the 6th Party Congress: Secret Internal Party Documents*] Beijing, Renmin chubanshe, 1980

Zhonggong zhongyang shujichu, Zhonggong zhongyang wenxian yanjiushi, *Jianchi gaige kaifang gaohuo* [*Support Reform, Openness and Flexibility*] Beijing, Renmin chubanshe, 1987

Zhonggong zhongyang shujichu, Zhonggong zhongyang wenxian yanjiushi, *Deng Xiaoping zhuanlue* [*A Brief Biography of Deng Xiaoping*] Beijing, Renmin chubanshe, 1988

Zhonggong zhongyang wenxian bianji weiyuanhui, *Deng Xiaoping wenxuan 1938–1965* [*Selected writings of Deng Xiaoping 1938–1965*] Beijing, Renmin chubanshe, 1989

Zhonggong zhongyang wenxian bianji weiyuanhui, *Deng Xiaoping wenxuan 1975–1982* [*Selected writings of Deng Xiaoping 1975–1982*] Beijing, Renmin chubanshe, 1983

Zhonggong zhongyang wenxian bianji weiyuanhui, *Deng Xiaoping wenxuan Vol. III* [*Selected writings of Deng Xiaoping Vol. III*] Beijing, Renmin chubanshe, 1993

Zhonggong zhongyang wenxian yanjiushi (ed.) *San zhong quanhui yilai: zhongyao wenxian xuanbian* [*Since the Third Plenum: collection of important documents*] Beijing, Renmin chubanshe, 1982

Zhonggong zhongyang wenxian yanjiushi (ed.) *Jianguo yilai Mao Zedong wengao* vols [*Mao Zedong's Writings after 1949*] Beijing, Zhongyang wenxian chubanshe, 1987–

Zhonggong zhongyang wenxian yanjiushi (ed.) *Deng Xiaoping tongzhi zhongyao tanhua (eryue dao qiyue 1987)* [*Comrade Deng Xiaoping's most important talks (February to July 1987)*] Beijing, Renmin chubanshe, 1987

Zhonggong zhongyang wenxian yanjiushi (ed.) *Jianshe you Zhongguo tesede shehuizhuyi* [*Build socialism with Chinese characteristics*] Beijing, Renmin chubanshe (2nd edition) 1987

Zhonggong zhongyang wenxian yanjiushi (ed.) *Deng Xiaoping tongzhi lun jianchi sixiang jiben yuance fandui zichan jieji ziyouhua* [*Comrade Deng Xiaoping on adherence to the Four Cardinal Principles and opposition to bourgeois liberalization*] Beijing, Renmin chubanshe, 1989

Zhonggong zhongyang wenxian yanjiushi (ed.) *Deng Xiaoping tongzhi lun gaige kaifang* [*Comrade Deng Xiaoping on reform and openness*] Beijing, Renmin chubanshe, 1989

Zhonggong zhongyang wenxian yanjiushi (ed.) *Deng Xiaoping tongzhi lun jiaqiang dang tong renmin qunzhong de guanxi* [*Comrade Deng Xiaoping on strengthening the relationship between the party and the masses*] Beijing, Zhongguo gongren chubanshe, 1990

Zhonggong zhongyang wenxian yanjiushi (ed.) *Deng Xiaoping tongzhi lun minzhu yu fazhi* [*Comrade Deng Xiaoping on democracy and the legal system*] Beijing, Falu chubanshe, 1990

Zhonggong zhongyang wenxian yanjiushi (ed.) *Deng Xiaoping tongzhi lun jiaoyu* [*Comrade Deng Xiaoping Discusses Education*] Beijing, Renmin jiaoyu chubanshe, 1990

Zhonggong zhongyang wenxian yanjiushi (ed.) *Deng Xiaoping lun tongyi zhanxian* [*Deng Xiaoping on the United Front*] Beijing, Zhongyang wenxian chubanshe, 1991

Zhonggong zhongyang wenxian yanjiushi (ed.) *Shierda yilai: zhongyao wenxian xuanbian* (3 vols) [*Since the 12th Party Congress: A collection of important documents*] Beijing, Renmin chubanshe, 1986

Zhonggong zhongyang wenxian yanjiushi (ed.) *Shisanda yilai: zhongyao wenxian xuanbian* (3 vols) [*Since the 13th Party Congress: A collection of important documents*] Beijing, Renmin chubanshe, 1991

Zhonggong zhongyang xuanchuanbu and Zhonggong zhongyang wenxian yanjiushi (eds) *Deng Xiaoping tongzhi lun zhexue* [*Comrade Deng Xiaoping on philosophy*] Beijing, Xueyuan chubanshe, 1990

Zhonggong zhongyang xuanchuanbu wenyiju bianji, *Deng Xiaoping lun wenyi* [Deng

Xiaoping discusses art and literature] Beijing, Renmin wenxue chubanshe, 1989

Zhonggong zhongyang zhengce yanjiushi dang jianzu (ed.) *Mao Zedong, Deng Xiaoping Lun Zhongguo guoqing* [*Mao Zedong and Deng Xiaoping on the state of the nation*] Beijing, Zhonggong zhongyang dangxiao chubanshe, 1992

Zhongyangju, 'Jiangxi shengwei dui Deng Xiaoping, Mao Zetan, Xie Weijun, Gu Bo sige tongzhi erci shenmingshu de jueyi', 5 May 1933 ['Resolution of the Jiangxi Party Committee on the Second Self-criticisms of the Four Comrades Deng Xiaoping, Mao Zetan, Xie Weijun and Gu Bo'] in Zhongyang danganguan, *Liudayilai: Dangnei jimi wenjian*, Beijing, Renmin chubanshe, 1980, pp. 51–52

Zhongyang tongyi zhanxian gongzuobu, Dongfanghongshe, *Deng Xiaoping zai tongyi zhanxian, minzu, zongjiao gongzuo ganmian di fangeming xiuzhengzhuyi yanlun huibian* [*Collection of Deng Xiaoping's Completely Counter-revolutionary, Revisionist Comments in United Front, Nationalities and Religious Work*] Beijing, July 1967

Zhongguo gongchandang lishi dacidian bianji weiyuanhui, *Zhongguo gongchandang lishi dacidian: Xinminzhuzhuyi geming shiqi* [*Historical Encyclopedia of the CCP: Period of the New Democratic Revolution*] Beijing, Zhonggong zhongyang dangxiao chubanshe, 1991

Zhongguo gongchandang lishi dacidian (ed.) *Zhongguo gongchandang lishi dacidian: zonglun, renwu* [*Historical Encyclopedia of the CCP: Overview, People*] Beijing, Zhonggong zhongyang dangxiao chubanshe, 1991

Zhongguo Mao Zedong jingji sixiang yanjiuhui chouweihui (ed.) *Deng Xiaoping gaige kaifang yu jingji fazhan sixiang yanjiu* [*A Study of Deng Xiaoping's Thought on Reform, Openness and Economic Development*] Chengdu, Xinan caijing daxue chubanshe, 1992

Zhongguo renmin jiefangjun dier yezhanjun shiliao xuan bianzhe, *Zhongguo renmin jiefangjun dier yezhanjun shiliao xuan* [*Selected Historical Materials on the Second Field Army of the PLA*] Beijing, Renmin chubanshe, 1989

Zhongguo renmin jiefangjun dier yezhanjun zhanshi bianjishi, *Yierjiushi ji JinJiLuYu junqu KangRi zhanzheng zhanshi* [*Military History of the 129th Division and the JinJiLuYu Military Region in the War of Resistance to Japan*] Beijing, Renmin chubanshe, 1962

Zhongguo renmin jiefangjun junshi kexuanyuan, Zhonggong zhongyang wenxian yanjiushi (ed.) *Deng Xiaoping lun guofang he jundui jianshe* [*Deng Xiaoping discusses the development of national defence and the military*] Beijing, Junshi kexue chubanshe, 1992

Zhongguo shehui kexueyuan xiandaishi yanjiushi (ed.) *Zhongguo gongchandang lici daibiao dahui: Xinminzhuzhuyi geming shiqi* [*The Congresses of the CCP: Period of the New Democratic Revolution*] Beijing, Zhonggong zhongyang dangxiao chubanshe, 1982

Zhu Junfeng *et al.* (eds) *Deng Xiaoping shehuizhuyi minzhu yu fazhi sixiang yanjiu* [*Study of Deng Xiaoping's thought on democracy and the legal system*] Shenyang, Liaoning renmin chubanshe, 1992

Zong Jun, *Zong sheji shi* [*Architect of the Grand Design*] Beijing, Zhonggong zhongyang dangxiao chubanshe, 1993

BOOKS AND ARTICLES PUBLISHED OUTSIDE THE PRC

A. Doak Barnett, *The Making of Foreign Policy in China*, London, I. B. Tauris, 1985

Wolfgang Bartke, *Biographical Dictionary and Analysis of China's Party Leadership 1922–1988*, München, K. G. Sauer, 1990

Wolfgang Bartke and Peter Schier, *China's New Party Leadership*, London, Macmillan, 1985

Richard Baum, *Prelude to Revolution*, New York, Columbia University Press, 1975

R. Bedeski, 'The Political Vision of Deng Xiaoping' in *Asian Thought and Society* Vol. 13,

No. 37, January 1988, p. 3

David Bonavia, *Deng*, Hong Kong, Longman, 1989

Chang Chen-pang, 'The Dual Nature of Teng Hsiao-ping's Thought' in *Issues and Studies* Vol. 25, No. 7, p. 11

D. W. Chang, *Zhou Enlai and Deng Xiaoping in the Chinese Leadership Succession Crisis*, London, University Press of America, 1984

D. W. Chang, *China under Deng Xiaoping: Political and Economic Reform*, London, Macmillan, 1988

Jerome Ch'en, 'The Chinese Communist Movement to 1927' in John King Fairbank (ed.) *The Cambridge History of China*, Vol. 12 *Republican China 1912–1949, Part I*, Cambridge, Cambridge University Press, 1983, p. 505

Jerome Ch'en, 'The Communist Movement 1927–1937' in John King Fairbank and Albert Feuerwerker (eds) *The Cambridge History of China, Vol. 12 Republican China 1912–1949, Part 2*, Cambridge, Cambridge University Press, 1986, p. 168

Chi Hsin, *The Case of the Gang of Four*, Hong Kong, Cosmos, 1977

Chi Hsin, *Teng Hsiao-ping*, Hong Kong, Cosmos, 1978

The China Quarterly, Deng Xiaoping: An Assessment, Special Issue, No. 135, September 1993

Chung Hua Lee, *Deng Xiaoping: The Marxist Road to the Forbidden City*, Princeton, Kingston Press, 1985

Paul A. Cohen, 'The post Mao reforms in historical perspective' in *The Journal of Asian Studies* Vol. 47, No. 3, pp. 518–540

Deng Xiaoping, Hong Kong, The Lives of Famous People Publishing House, 1978

Lowell Dittmer, 'The Tiananmen Massacre' in *Problems of Communism*, September–October 1989, pp. 2ff.

Jürgen Domes, *The Internal Politics of China 1949–1972*, London, Hurst, 1973

Jürgen Domes, *China after the Cultural Revolution*, London, Hurst, 1976

Jürgen Domes, *The Government and Politics of the PRC*, Boulder, Colorado, Westview Press, 1985

Jürgen Domes, *Peng Te-huai: the man and the image*, London, Hurst, 1985

June Teufel Dreyer, 'Deng Xiaoping: The Soldier' in *The China Quarterly* No. 135, September 1993, p. 536

Mary S. Erbaugh, 'The Secret History of the Hakkas: the Chinese Revolution as a Hakka Enterprise' in *The China Quarterly* No. 132, pp. 937–968

R. Evans, *Deng Xiaoping and the Making of Modern China*, London, Hamish Hamilton, 1993

John King Fairbank, *The Cambridge History of China, Vol. 12 Republican China 1912–1949, Part 1*, Cambridge, Cambridge University Press, 1983

John King Fairbank and Albert Feuerwerker, *The Cambridge History of China, Vol. 13 Republican China 1912–1949, Part 2*, Cambridge, Cambridge University Press, 1986

Uli Franz, *Deng Xiaoping: China's erneurer* [*Deng Xiaoping: China's Reformer*] Stuttgart, DVA, 1987

John Gardner, *Chinese Politics and the Succession to Mao*, London, Macmillan, 1982

Stuart Gelder, *The Chinese Communists*, London, Victor Gollancz, 1946

John Gittings, 'New material on Teng Hsiao-p'ing' in *The China Quarterly* No. 67, p. 489

David S. G. Goodman, *China's Provincial Leaders, 1949–1985*, Cardiff, Cardiff University Press, 1986

David S. G. Goodman, *China's Coming Revolution: The dynamics of political change*, London, Research Centre for the Study of Conflict, *Conflict Study* No. 266, 1993

David S. G. Goodman, 'The political economy of change' in David S. G. Goodman and B. Hooper (eds) *China's Quiet Revolution*, Melbourne, Longman Cheshire, 1994

David S. G. Goodman and G. Segal (eds) *China in the Nineties: Crisis management and beyond*, Oxford, Oxford University Press, 1991

J. Guillermaz, *A History of the Chinese Communist Party, 1921–1949*, London, Methuen, 1972

Guofangbu zongzhengzhi zuozhanwei (ed.) *Gongfei yuanshi ziliao huibian: Deng Xiaoping yanlunji 1957–1980* [*Collection of CCP Materials: Deng Xiaoping's Speeches 1957–1980*] Taipei, Guofangbu, 1983

Guofangbu zongzhengzhi zuozhanwei (ed.) *Gongfei yuanshi ziliao huibian: Pipan Deng Xiaoping ziliao* [*Collection of CCP Materials: Materials Criticizing Deng Xiaoping*] Taipei, Guofangbu, 1983

Guoli Zhengzhi Daxue Dongya yanjiu bian, *Deng Xiaoping* [*Deng Xiaoping*] Taipei, Guoli Zhengzhi Daxue, 1978

Guoli Zhengzhi Daxue Dongya yanjiu bian, *Deng Xiaoping yu sirenbang* [*Deng Xiaoping and the Gang of Four*] Taipei, Guoli Zhengzhi Daxue, 1979

Carol Lee Hamrin, *China and the Challenge of the Future*, Boulder, Colorado, Westview Press, 1990

Han Shanbi, *Deng Xiaoping pingzhuan* (3 vols) [*Biography of Deng Xiaoping*] Hong Kong, East West and Culture Publishers, 1988

Han Shanbi *et al.*, *Deng Xiaoping: 1904–1984*, Hong Kong, East West and Culture Publishers, 1993

Han Wenfu (Han Shanbi), *Deng Xiaoping zhuan* (2 vols) [*Biography of Deng Xiaoping*] Taipei, Shibao wenhua chuban qiye youxian gongsi, 1993

Harry Harding, 'The Chinese state in crisis' in Roderick MacFarquhar and John King Fairbank, *The Cambridge History of China, Vol. 15 The People's Republic, Part 2: Revolutions within the Chinese Revolution 1966–1982*, Cambridge, Cambridge University Press, 1991, p. 107

Harry Harding, *China's Second Revolution*, Sydney, Allen & Unwin, 1989

George Hicks (ed.) *The Broken Mirror: China after Tiananmen*, London, Longman, 1990

M. Hood, 'Deng's Days of Darkness' in *The South China Morning Post*, 26 March and 2 April 1988

Jiang Zhifeng, *Wangpai chu jing de Zhongnanhai qiaoju* [*The Last Card of the Game of Zhongnanhai*] San Francisco, Minzhu Zhongguo Shulin, 1990

T. Kampen, 'The Zunyi Conference and Further Steps in Mao's Rise to Power' in *The China Quarterly* No. 117

N. Khrushchev, *Khrushchev Remembers* (2 vols), Harmondsworth, Penguin, 1977

Donald W. Klein and Anne B. Clark, *Biographic Dictionary of Chinese Communism, 1921–1965* (2 vols), Harvard University Press, 1971

Warren Kuo, *Analytical History of the Chinese Communist Party* (4 vols), Taipei, Institute of International Relations, 1970

L. Ladany, *The Communist Party of China and Marxism, 1921–1985*, London, Hurst, 1988

Willy Wo-lap Lam, *Towards a Chinese-style Socialism: an assessment of Deng Xiaoping's reforms*, Hong Kong, Oceanic Cultural Service Co., 1987

Diana Lary, *Region and Nation: The Kwangsi Clique in Chinese Politics 1925–1937*, Cambridge, Cambridge University Press, 1974

Li Tianming, *Deng Xiaoping*, Taipei, 1986

Kenneth G. Lieberthal, 'The Great Leap Forward and the Split in the Yenan Leadership' in Roderick MacFarquhar and John King Fairbank, *The Cambridge History of China, Vol. 14 The People's Republic, Part I: The Emergence of Revolutionary China 1949–1965*, Cambridge, Cambridge University Press, 1987, p. 293

Kenneth G. Lieberthal and Bruce J. Dickson, *A Research Guide to Central Party and Government Meetings in China, 1949–1986*, New York, M. E. Sharpe, 1989

Kenneth G. Lieberthal and Michael Oksenberg, *Policy Making in China: Leaders, Structures and Processes*, Princeton, Princeton University Press, 1988

Roderick MacFarquhar, *The Origins of the Cultural Revolution* (2 vols), London, Oxford

University Press, 1974 and 1983

Roderick MacFarquhar, Timothy Cheek and Eugene Wu, *The Secret Speeches of Chairman Mao: From the Hundred Flowers to the Great Leap Forward*, Cambridge, Mass., Harvard University Press, 1989

Roderick MacFarquhar and John King Fairbank, *The Cambridge History of China, Vol. 14 The People's Republic, Part 1: The Emergence of Revolutionary China 1949–1965*, Cambridge, Cambridge University Press, 1987

Roderick MacFarquhar, 'The succession to Mao and the end of Maoism' in Roderick MacFarquhar and John King Fairbank, *The Cambridge History of China, Vol. 15 The People's Republic, Part 2: Revolutions within the Chinese Revolution 1966–1982*, Cambridge, Cambridge University Press, 1991, p. 305

Roderick MacFarquhar and John King Fairbank, *The Cambridge History of China, Vol. 15 The People's Republic, Part 2: Revolutions within the Chinese Revolution 1966–1982*, Cambridge, Cambridge University Press, 1991

Barry Naughton, 'The Third Front: Defence Industrialisation in the Chinese Interior' in *The China Quarterly* No. 115, p. 351

Barry Naughton, 'Deng Xiaoping: The Economist' in *The China Quarterly* No. 135, September 1993, p. 491

Victor Nee and David Mozingo, *State and Society in Contemporary China*, Ithaca, Cornell University Press, 1983

Michel Oksenberg, 'The Deng era's uncertain political legacy' in Kenneth G. Lieberthal *et al.* (eds) *Perspectives on Modern China*, New York, M. E. Sharpe, 1991

William Parish, 'Factions in Chinese Military Politics' in *The China Quarterly* No. 56, p. 667

Suzanne Pepper, 'The KMT–CCP conflict 1945–1949' in John King Fairbank and Albert Feuerwerker (eds) *The Cambridge History of China, Vol. 12 Republican China 1912–1949, Part 2*, Cambridge, Cambridge University Press, 1986, p. 723

Elizabeth J. Perry and Christine Wong (eds) *The Political Economy of Reform in Post-Mao China*, Cambridge, Mass., Harvard University Press, 1985

Lucian W. Pye, *Mao Tse-tung: The man in the leader*, New York, Basic Books, 1976

Lucian W. Pye, *The Dynamics of Chinese Politics*, Cambridge, Mass., Oelgeschlager, Gunn & Hain, 1981

Lucian W. Pye, *The Mandarin and the Cadre: China's political cultures*, Ann Arbor, University of Michigan, 1988

Lucian W. Pye, 'An Introductory Profile: Deng Xiaoping and China's Political Culture' in *The China Quarterly* No. 135, September 1993, p. 412

E. Rice, 'The Second Rise and Fall of Teng Hsiao-p'ing' in *The China Quarterly* No. 67, p. 494

Carl Riskin, *China's Political Economy: the quest for development since 1949*, Oxford, Oxford University Press, 1987

R. S. Ross, 'From Lin Biao to Deng Xiaoping: elite instability and China's US policy' in *The China Quarterly* No. 118, p. 265

Ruan Ming, *Deng Xiaoping diguo* [*The Empire of Deng Xiaoping*] Taipei, Shibao chuban qiye gongsi, 1992

Harrison E. Salisbury, *The Long March: the untold story*, New York, Harper & Row, 1985

Harrison E. Salisbury, *The New Emperors – Mao & Deng: A dual biography*, London, HarperCollins, 1992

Michael Schoenhals, 'Edited Records: Comparing Two Versions of Deng Xiaoping's 7000 Cadres Speech' in *CCP Research Newsletter* No. 1 (Fall 1988), p. 5

Michael Schoenhals, 'Unofficial and official histories of the Cultural Revolution' in *Journal of Asian Studies* Vol. 48, No. 3, 1989, p. 563

Stuart Schram, *Mao Tse-tung*, Harmondsworth, Middlesex, Penguin, 1966

H. F. Schurmann, *Ideology and Organisation in Communist China* (2nd edition), Berkeley, University of California Press, 1968

Mark Selden, *The Yenan Way in Revolutionary China*, Cambridge, Mass., Harvard University Press, 1971

David Shambaugh, *The Making of a Premier: Zhao Ziyang's Provincial Career*, Boulder, Colorado, Westview, 1984

David Shambaugh, 'Introduction: Assessing Deng Xiaoping's Legacy' in *The China Quarterly* No. 135, September 1993, p. 409

David Shambaugh, 'Deng Xiaoping: The Politician' in *The China Quarterly* No. 135, September 1993, p. 457

Shi Chuijin, *Deng Xiaoping de jiushinian* [*Deng Xiaoping's Ninety Years*] Taipei, Zhiqing budao chuban yougongsi, 1994

Susan L. Shirk, *The Political Logic of Economic Reform in China*, Berkeley, University of California Press, 1993

Shu Yang, *Deng Xiaoping sishenghuo* [*The Private Life of Deng Xiaoping*] Hong Kong, Kehua tushu chubanshe, n.d.

Shu Yang, *Zhonggong diyi qiangren – Deng Xiaoping* [*China's Most Powerful Person – Deng Xiaoping*] Taipei, Dongcha chubanshe, 1987

K. K. Shum, *The Chinese Communists' Road to Power*, Hong Kong, Oxford University Press, 1986

Agnes Smedley, *China Fights Back*, London, Gollancz, 1938

Edgar Snow, *Random Notes on Red China, 1936–1945*, East Asia Research Center, Harvard University, 1957

Edgar Snow, *Red Star Over China* (2nd edition), London, Gollancz, 1968

Michael D. Swaine, *The Military and Political Succession in China*, Santa Monica, California, Rand Corporation, 1993

Keizo Tanagi, *To Sho-hei Sho-ten* [*Biography of Deng Xiaoping*] Tokyo, Elite Press, 1978

F. C. Teiwes, *Politics and Purges in China*, New York, M. E. Sharpe, 1979

F. C. Teiwes, *Leadership, Legitimacy and Conflict in China*, London, Macmillan Press, 1984

F. C. Teiwes, 'Peng Dehuai and Mao Zedong' in *The Australian Journal of Chinese Affairs* No. 16, 1986

F. C. Teiwes, 'Establishment and consolidation of the new regime' in Roderick MacFarquhar and John King Fairbank, *The Cambridge History of China, Vol. 14 The People's Republic, Part I: The Emergence of Revolutionary China 1949–1965*, Cambridge, Cambridge University Press, 1987, p. 51

F. C. Teiwes, 'Mao and his lieutenants' in *The Australian Journal of Chinese Affairs* No. 19/20, 1988

F. C. Teiwes, *Politics at Mao's Court: Gao Gang and Party Factionalism in the early 1950s*, New York, M. E. Sharpe, 1990

F.C. Teiwes, *Politics and Purges in China* (2nd edition), New York, M. E. Sharpe, 1994

F.C. Teiwes and Warren Sun (eds) 'Mao, Deng Zihui, and the Politics of Agricultural Cooperativisation' in *Chinese Law and Government* Vol. 26, No. 3–4, 1993.

Roger R. Thompson, 'The "Discovery" of Mao Zedong's *Report from Xunwu*: Deng Xiaoping Writes a New Chapter in Early Party History' in *CCP Research Newsletter* No. 3, 1989

Ting Wang, *Chairman Hua*, London, Hurst, 1980

Tang Tsou, *The Cultural Revolution and Post-Mao Reforms*, Chicago, University of Chicago Press, 1986

Lyman Van Slyke, 'The Chinese Communist movement during the Sino-Japanese War 1937–1945' in John King Fairbank and Albert Feuerwerker (eds) *The Cambridge History of China, Vol. 12 Republican China 1912–1949, Part 2*, Cambridge, Cambridge University Press, 1986, p. 609

Wang Hsuan, *About Teng Hsiaoping*, Taipei, 1978

Wang Jian, *Hua Guofeng yu Deng Xiaoping* [*Hua Guofeng and Deng Xiaoping*] Hong Kong, Ming Pao Publishers, n.d.

Nora Wang, 'Deng Xiaoping: The Years in France' in *The China Quarterly* No. 92, and in *Dangshi tongxun* [*Bulletin of Party History*] No. 22, 1983, pp. 20–22

W. Whitson, 'The Field Army in Chinese Communist Military Politics' in *The China Quarterly* No. 37, p. 1

Martin King Whyte, 'Deng Xiaoping: The Social Reformer' in *The China Quarterly* No. 135, September 1993, p. 515

Dick Wilson (ed.) *Mao Tse-tung in the scales of history*, Cambridge, Cambridge University Press, 1977

Wu An-chia, 'Teng Hsiao-p'ing's checkered career and its impact on mainland China's politics' in *Issues and Studies* Vol. 24, No. 12, p. 81

Xu Xing, *Deng Xiaoping kaifang shidai* [*The Open Era of Deng Xiaoping*] Hong Kong, Kaishi chubanshe, 1987

Michael Yahuda, 'Deng Xiaoping: The Statesman' in *The China Quarterly* No. 135, September 1993, p. 551

Benjamin Yang, *From Revolution to Politics: Chinese Communists on the Long March*, Boulder, Colorado, Westview Press, 1990

Benjamin Yang, 'The Making of a Pragmatic Communist: The Early Life of Deng Xioping, 1904–1949' in *The China Quarterly* No. 135, September 1993, p. 444

Yang Zhongmei, *Hu Yaobang: A Chinese Biography*, New York, M. E. Sharpe, 1988

You Ji, 'Zhao Ziyang and the Politics of Inflation' in *The Australian Journal of Chinese Affairs* No. 25

You Ji and Ian Wilson, 'Leadership politics in the Chinese party-army state: the fall of Zhao Ziyang', Working Paper 195, The Strategic and Defence Studies Centre, ANU, 1989

Zhao Wei, *The Biography of Zhao Ziyang*, Hong Kong, Educational and Cultural Press, 1989

Zhou Xun, *Deng Xiaoping*, Hong Kong, Wide Angle Publishers, 1983

Index